Middlesex County Virginia

MARRIAGE RECORDS

1853-1904

Catherine Moore Traylor

HERITAGE BOOKS
2008

HERITAGE BOOKS
AN IMPRINT OF HERITAGE BOOKS, INC.

Books, CDs, and more—Worldwide

For our listing of thousands of titles see our website
at
www.HeritageBooks.com

Published 2008 by
HERITAGE BOOKS, INC.
Publishing Division
100 Railroad Ave. #104
Westminster, Maryland 21157

Copyright © 1998 Catherine Moore Traylor

Other books by the author:
Federal Census 1880 Middlesex County, Virginia

This work was originally published as part of *Middlesex County Marriage Records, 1853-1904 and Federal Census 1880 Middlesex County, Virginia*

All rights reserved. No part of this book may be reproduced or transmitted in any form or by any means, electronic or mechanical, including photocopying, recording or by any information storage and retrieval system without written permission from the author, except for the inclusion of brief quotations in a review.

International Standard Book Numbers
Paperbound: 978-0-7884-4698-6
Clothbound: 978-0-7884-7276-3

Dedication

These compiled records are presented to honor

Mrs. Louise Eubank Gray

by former students
friends
and
family

1997

1880 FEDERAL CENSUS - MIDDLESEX COUNTY, VIRGINIA

FOREWORD

In the course of time, we meet a special person who has influenced our life and then realize that they have not only had profound influence on our life but the lives of many others. For this reason, former students, friends and family, have contibuted to the publication of this compiled record of Middlesex County, Virginia marriages 1853-1904 and the 1880 Federal Census of Middlesex County.

Louise Eubank Gray is a member of Saluda Baptist Church, where she was a Sunday School Teacher and continues to be an active member. She was an Educator in the Middlesex County Schools, and on retirement, an advocate for the preservation of History, not only in Middlesex County, but King and Queen County as well.

Her verbal contributions to the history of both Middlesex County and King and Queen County is documented in several books. She has given a legacy of wit, humor, history, and personal committment to anyone who has known her. It is in appreciation of these many gifts that her former students, friends, and family wish to honor her with another publication to preserve the rich history of Middlesex County.

From Mrs. Gray's Book, "**Reflections: Windows on the Past**" page 153, "Virginians have been credited with a kind of snobbishness. One quote goes: 'To be a Virginia either by birth, marriage, adoption, or even on one's mother's side is an introduction to any state in the union, a passport to any foreign country, and a benediction from above.'" It is the desire of this editor that anyone finding a relative named on these pages will find a sense of belonging to Virginia, and more specifically, Middlesex County, Virginia.

Catherine Moore Traylor

ACKNOWLEDGEMENT

The author wishes to acknowledge the support and generosity of the following persons who have made possible the publication of these historic records.

Helen Nichols Battleson
Mary S. Marshall
Allen & Frances Krowe
Myra Clements
Alex Wiatt
Beth Thompson
Vickie C. Weymouth
Pat Royal Perkinson
Connie Frazer
George Hendrickson
Joan B. Madsen
Ada Foster Powell
Ruth & Vaughan Noble
June (Pruitt)Tyler Crockett
Dorothy Soles Moore
Paul & Sarah Davis
Caroline Gwaltney Jones
J. Hubert & Josephine Major
Elvin Miller
Ruth T. Horton
Ronnie, Cathy & Shannon Russell
Betty H. Sandman
Frances Hundley Frost
Mary Wyatt Lloyd
Bettie J. Simmons
Carolyn Green Grinels
Laura Green Reca
Louise Thrift Owen

Corinne Daniel
Marie Major Anton
Sharon Topping
Charles & Lillian D. Oliver
Doris Davis Hunt
Clarence E. Major
Glenn O. Traylor
Jeanne Porter Barton
Jeanne M. Luttrell
William J. & Peggy Davis
Roberta Bland Bennett
Anonymous
Ann Davis
O.A. & Ruth Turner Norton
Ethel Marie Burton Lee
Evelyn Byrd Selby
Susie E. & Preston F. Shelton, Jr.
Mary Elizabeth Elmore
Charlotte S. Clark
Helen H. King
Louise Davis Oliver
Clinton & Jean Oliver
Fred Helsabeck, Sr.
Elizabeth D. H. Jones
The Association for The Preservation of Virginia
    Antiquities - Ralph Wormley Branch
Cynthia K. Barlowe
Mary E. Redden
A. Bennett Wilson, Jr.
Douglas & Velma Gray
Mary O. Smith
Dorothy Marler
Elizabeth A. Leaf
Richard & Alice Armstrong
Middle Peninsula Club-Westhampton College
    Alumni Association
Mary Edna Glenn
Anita S. Wilson
Jean W. Clark

Kay Amory-Moshier
Beth Pettus Maxwell
Martha Lena Walden
Mary Steed Ewell
Earl and Edith Collier
Ric Davila, D.D.S.
Joan Miller Hines
Joe D. Parker, Sr.
Ben and Dorothy Daniel
Charlotte Albright Izzo
Joyce Milby Green

This list would not be complete with out adding the name of Tom Hardin, Editor, Southside Sentinel, Urbanna, Virginia, who has given the public a running account of activity each month. Pat Perkinson and Virginia Hutchinson for directing me to Carolyn Jett and the patience of the clerks in the Court House who have made the records available whenever needed. The encouragement given by the Middlesex County Museum Board and the notes from many of the contibutors has made this a rewarding project.

Middlesex County, Virginia
Marriage Records
1853-1904

Contents

Dedication iii

Foreword v

Acknowledgement vii

Contents xi

Middlesex County Marriage Records abstracted by **Carolyn H. Jett** from the files at Middlesex County Court House, Saluda, Virginia

Marriage Records..1853-1876 1-76

    Index of Grooms 77-85

    Index of Brides 86-94

Marriage Records..1876-1890 1-72

    Index of Grooms 73-81

    Index of Brides 82-90

Marriage Records..1890-1904 1-77

    Index of Grooms 78-87

    Index of Brides 88-97

Middlesex County, Virginia
Marriage Records
1853-1904

Transcribed by
Carolyn H. Jett

Includes
**Register of Marriages, 1853-1876
Marriage Register 2, 1876-1890
Marriage Register 3, 1890-1904**

Introduction

Appreciation is expressed to Peggy W. Walton, Middlesex County Clerk of Court, and her Deputy Clerks, Janet T. Marshall and Lynn L. Dunlevy. Their courteous assistance made the gathering of these records a pleasant task.

Marriage records of Middlesex County include not only the registers, but also the original marriage licenses. These are loose papers, folded and filed in a cabinet in the Clerk's Office.

It often is helpful for the researcher to look at the license as well as the registers to be certain of having all the available information. Many abbreviations of given names were used, particularly in Register of Marriages, 1853-1876. But in the licenses, the names often are spelled out, and additional information is given in some, including the race of the couple.

The marriage registers are kept on open shelves in the Clerk's Office, Middlesex County Court House, Saluda, Virginia. One may examine the early records after signing a guest book. To look at the marriage licenses, one should always ask permission from the Clerk or staff.

Remember that spelling was not as standardized in the 1800s as it is today. (For example, Clayville is also shown as Claybill, Clavel and Clayvell.) A name might be spelled a variety of ways, often in the same record. Therefore, it is wise to check the index for every possible variation.

Though every effort has been made to make this transcript accurate, no doubt the reader will find errors, some made, perhaps, by the clerk on the original record, others made by the clerks who copied them into the registers, and others made by this transcriber, either in copying or in typing them. The names, if misspelled in the registers, also are misspelled here.

These marriage records are presented with the hope that the reader will discover an ancestor within these pages.

Carolyn H. Jett

Register of Marriages, 1853-1876
Transcribed by
Carolyn H. Jett

The records for this period have been entered into two books. Register of Marriages, 1853-1876, which is the book used for this transcript, lists each marriage on a numbered line across two pages of the register. Marriage Register 1 also lists the marriages for this period, but in a different format. The first record in Register of Marriages, 1853-1876 is shown here, with an explanation of the information it contains.

1:01 - 26 Jul. 1853 - **Wm. W. Stone**, 30, single, tailor, b. King & Queen, residing Essex, son of Wm. Stone, married **Isabella F. McKan**, 21, single, b. & residing Mid., dau. of Robert McKan. Minister-Rich'd A. Christian.

- 1:01 - Page 1, line 01, is where the marriage is recorded in the register.
- 26 Jul. 1853 - The date of the marriage.
- **Wm. W. Stone** - Name of the groom.
- 30, single, tailor - The groom's age, his marital status, and his occupation.
- b. King & Queen - Groom's county of birth - (Virginia county, unless specifically stated otherwise).
- residing Essex - Groom's county of residence.
- son of Wm. Stone - Groom's parent or parents. In most records both parents' names were given, but in others, only one parent was given. Other records have a blank space for the given name of one parent, such as
 "John and   Jones," or
 "   and Nancy Brown."
Rather than put the blank spaces in this transcript, for the first example above, the parent will be shown as "John Jones," and for the second example, the parent will be shown as "Nancy Brown."
- married **Isabella F. McKan** - The bride's name.
- 21, single - The bride's age and marital status.
- b. & residing Mid. - The bride was born and resides in Middlesex County.
- dau. of Robert McKan - The bride is the daughter of Robert McKan.
- Minister-Rich'd A. Christian - The minister who married the couple.

1:01 - 26 Jul. 1853 - **Wm. W. Stone**, 30, single, tailor, b. King & Queen, residing Essex, son of Wm. Stone, married **Isabella F. McKan**, 21, single, b. & residing Mid., dau. of Robert McKan. Minister-Rich'd A. Christian.
1:02 - 27 Sep. 1853 - **Obedia W. Lee**, 34, widower, farmer, b. & residing Mid., son of Lewis Lee, married **Euzalia Gardner**, 16, single, b. & residing Mid., dau. of Larkin Gardner. Minister-Rich'd A. Christian.
1:03 - 23 Aug. 1853 - **Warner T. Cook**, 32, single, farmer, b. & residing Gloucester, son of Jno. Cook & Eliza Burkner, married **Ellen Cath. Booth**, 25, single, b. & residing Mid., dau. of Mord. Cook Booth & Eliza. Minister-Thomas B. Evans.
1:04 - 3 Oct. 1853 - **Cam. H. Gatewood**, 25, single, farmer, b. & residing King & Queen, son of Joseph & Hannah G., married **Eusabia N. Montague**, 24, single, b. & residing Mid., dau. of P. T. & Martha Montague. Minister-Thomas B. Evans.
1:05 - 6 Oct. 1853 - **R'd C. Burton** married **Margaret E. Walker**. [No other info given.]
1:06 - 10 Oct. 1853 - **Jas. H. Jackson**, 30, widower, merchant, b. Accomack, residing Mid., son of Jno. M. & Rebecca Jackson, married **Anna H. Boss**, 23, single, b. & residing Mid., dau. of Jno. J. & Ann Boss. Minister-Holland Walker.
1:07 - 2 Nov. 1853 - **Alfred Muse**, 45, widower, painter, b. Essex, residing Mid., married **E. P. Crittenden**, 23, widow, b. Essex, residing Mid. Minister-Richard A. Christian. [No other info given.]
1:08 - 15 Dec. 1853 - **Jno. D. Palmer**, 25, single, merchant, b. & residing Mid., son of Thos. J. & Polly Palmer, married **Mary F. Davis**, 21, single, b. & residing Mid., dau. of Ric'd A. & Eliz. B. Davis. Minister-Holland Walker.
1:09 - 22 Dec. 1853 - **Ro. M. Blake**, 24, single, farmer, b. & residing Mid., son of Jno. B. Blake & Nancy Miller, married **Sarah E. Neale**, 18, single, b. King William, residing Mid., dau. of Jno. C. Neale & Susan F. Slaughter. Minister-Holland Walker.
1:10 - 16 Feb. 1854 - **Lewis Mickelborough**, 23, single, huckster, b. Mid., residing Baltimore, Maryland, son of Lewis & Henrietta, married **Elizabeth Clare**, 27, widow, b. & residing Mid., dau. of Thomas Good & Elizabeth. Minister-Zack Street.
1:11 - 15 Feb. 1854 - **Wm. Jas. Sibley**, 25, single, sailor, b. & residing Mid., son of Daniel & Julia Sibley, married **Martha E. Groom**, 21, single, b. & residing Mid., dau. of Thos. Groom & Elizab. Long. Minister-Holland Walker.

1:12 - 23 Feb. 1854 - **Sam'l R. Jackson**, 28, widower, physician, b. Accomack, residing Mid., son of Jno. M. Jackson & Rebecca, married **Mary E. A. Towill**, 17, single, b. & residing Mid., dau. of M. W. Towill. & M. E. Pace. Minister-Holland Walker.

1:13 - 18 May 1854 - **Andrew S. South**, 30, single, b. & residing Mid., son of Jno. South & Mary, married **Ann E. Waddle**, 22, single, b. & residing Mid., dau. of Jno. & Ann Waddle. Minister-Archer Bland.

1:14 - 10 Aug. 1854 - **Lewis W. Shaw**, 25, single, sailor, b. New Jersey, son of H. &. S. Shaw, married **Isabella Garder**, 22, single, b. & residing Mid., dau. of James & Jeanett Garder. Minister-Zack Street.

1:15 - 27 Mar. 1854 - **John W. Daniel**, 40, widower, merchant, b. & residing. Mid., son of Jno. & Lucy Daniel, married **Mira A. Bristow**, 24, single, b. & residing Mid., dau. of Larkin E.[or S.] & Catharine Bristow. Minister-Holland Walker.

1:16 - 21 Sep. 1854 - **Jno. W. Clements**, 31, widower, coach maker, b. Richmond Co., residing Mid., son of Jas. T. Clements & Olivia Mitchell, married **Hester A. Clarke**, 20, single, b. & residing Mid., dau. of Braxton Clarke & Mary Wood. Minister-Holland Walker.

1:17 - 3 Oct. 1854 - **Thos. R. Burton**, 30, widower, farmer, b. & residing King & Queen, son of Jno. Y. Burton & Ann Davis, married **Frances E. Bray**, 28, single, b. & residing Mid., dau. of Jno. Bray & Eliz. B. Bristow. Minister-Thomas B. Evans.

1:18 - 21 Nov. 1854 - **Ed. T. Purkins**, 25, single, merchant, b. & residing Mid., son of Caster & Mary A. Purkins, married **Betty H. Jones**, 22, single, b. & residing Mid., dau. of Lewis & Sarah Jones. Minister-Rob. Michaels.

1:19 - 30 Nov. 1854 - **Jno. H. Fitzhugh**, 31, single, merchant, b. King & Queen, residing Kentucky, son of Phil. & Mary Fitzhugh, married **Harriet Bullitt**, 18, single, b. Shelby Co., Kentucky, residing Kentucky, dau. of C. & Har. Bullitt. Minister-A. F. Scott., married in Gloucester Co.

1:20 - 13 Dec. 1854 - **R. T. Thrift**, 44, widower, carpenter, b. Georgia, residing Mid., son of W. & Cath. Thrift, married **Nancy Gardner**, 43, single, b. & residing Mid., dau. of Geo. & Cath. Garder. Minister-Zack Street.

1:21 - 26 Dec. 1854 - **Jos. Haile**, 42, widower, farmer, b. Essex, son of W. & Mary Haile, married **Rebecca Walden**, 40, widow, b. King & Queen, dau. of Jno. & Mary Oliver. Minister-Zack Street.

1:22 - 30 Nov. 1854 - **John H. Bowden**, 24, single, farmer, b. Gloucester, son of Jno. Bowden & Sarah Roane, married **Julia A. Roane**, 26, single, b. Gloucester, residing Mid., dau. of Chas. Roane & Polly Dutton. Minister-Archer Bland.

1:23 - 21 Dec. 1854 - **W. M. Major**, 25, single, farmer, b. & residing Mid., son of Jno. A. Major & Julia Umphries, married **Eliz. C. Taylor**, 26, single, b. Gloucester, residing Mid., dau. of Wm. Taylor & Cath. Minister-Archer Bland.

1:24 - 21 Nov. 1854 - **Alfred Palmer**, 34, widower, b. & residing Mid., son of Opie & Nancy Palmer, married **Sophronia Sadler**, 34, single, b. Essex, residing Mid., dau. of Wm. & Victoria Sadler. Minister-Ric'd A. Christian, married in Urbanna.

1:25 - Dec. 1854 - **James W. Thrift**, 31 yrs./3 mo./10 days, single, sailor, b. Richmond Co., residing Mid., son of Wm. H. Thrift & Jane Northan, married **Mary M. Clements**, 24 yrs./3 mo./9 days, single, b. Richmond Co., residing Mid., dau. of Jas. T. Clements & Mary Mitchell. Minister-M. W. Towill.

1:26 - 9 Jan. 1855 - **Thos. M. Wiatt**, 31 yrs./9 mo./3 days, single, farmer, b. Gloucester, residing Lancaster, son of Peter & Cordelia, married **Sarah C. Segar**, 24 yrs./27 days, single, b. & residing Mid., dau. of Ric'd M. & Polly. Minister-Ric'd A. Christian, married in Urbanna.

1:27 - 18 Jan. 1855 - **B. Trevillian** [Given name in index: **Boscoe**], 36, widower, farmer, b. Gloucester, son of Christopher & Elizab'h Masy, married **Orinda Clements**, 22, single, b. Richmond Co., dau. of J. T. Clements & Mary Mitchell. Minister-Holland Walker.

1:28 - 15 Jan. 1855 - **Robert Alvis**, 36, single, trader, b. Louisa Co., residing Richmond, Virginia, son of Henry & Agnes, married **Sarah Alvace** [**Sarah Ware** in index], 20, single, b. King & Queen, dau. of Wm. S. & Mary Ann. Minister-Ric'd A. Christian, married at Woodville.

1:29 - 25 Jan. 1855 - **Edward A. Pippin**, 27, single, tailor, b. & residing Gloucester, son of E. H. & Ann E., married **M. E. Vaughn** [**Martha E. Vaughan** in index], 23, single, b. Gloucester, residing Mid., dau. of Jos. L. & M. F. Vaughn. Minister-A. F. Scott.

1:30 - 12 Feb. 1855 - **Joseph Worril**, 21, single, farmer, b. King & Queen, residing Gloucester, son of Corbin & Elizabeth, married **M. C. Lewis**, 20, single, b. Middlesex, residing Gloucester, dau. of Jno. Lewis & L. M. Hall. Minister-Archer Bland.

1:31 - 13 Mar. 1855 - **William Oberg**, 23 yrs./2 mo./3 days, single, b. Hanover, Germany, occup.- "none particular," residing Mid., married **Rachel Croswell**, 22, single, b. Northumberland, residing Mid., dau. of Thos. Croswell & Jane. Minister-H. Walker.

1:32 - 14 Mar. 1855 - **John Gabor**, 34, widower, fire engineer, b. Birne, Germany, residing Mid., son of Geo. Gabor & Ellen Nor, married **Elizabeth Barrick**, 32 supposed, widow, b. Gloucester, residing Mid., dau. of W. Blossinger & Fran. Minister-H. Walker.

1:33 - 14 Mar. 1855 - **Sa. P. Fitchett** [**Salathiel** in index], 21 yrs./5 mo./11 days, single, b. Mathews, residing Mid., son of R. Fitchett & A. Parrish, married **Cath. Murcer**, 23 yrs./4 mo./23 days, single, b. & residing Mid., dau. of Jas. Murser & Mary Dunlevy. Minister-H. Walker.

1:34 - 16 Apr. 1855 - **Walter Bristow**, 30, widower, wheelwright, b. & residing Mid., son of Ed Bristow & Polly Buchner, married **Adeline Wiatt**, 18, single, b. & residing Mid., dau. of Thos. Wiatt & Pegg. Brooker [or Brookes]. Minister-Thomas B. Evans.

1:35 - 10 May 1855 - **John E. Segar**, 31, single, merchant, b. & residing Mid., son of R. M. Segar & Polly Roane, married **Mary E. Eubank**, 19, single, b. & residing Mid., dau. of Jas A. Eubank & Cornelia Roane. Minister-R. A. Christian.

1:36 - 8 May 1855 - **Jas. Chowning**, 38, widower, farmer, b. Gloucester, residing Mid., son of Baley Chowning & Sara Garland, married **Mary E. Spencer**, 18, single, b. King & Queen, residing Mid., dau. of M. D. Spencer & R. F. P. Clayton. Minister-R. A. Christian.

1:37 - 6 Sep. 1855 - **T. C. Parker**, 47, widower, painter, b. Charleston, South Carolina, residing Mid., son of C. C. Parker & E. Dinkney [or Dinknett], married **Eliz. C. Kidd**, 22, single, b. & residing Mid., dau. of J. Kidd & H. Sibley. Minister-T. B. Evans.

1:38 - 24 Oct. 1855 - **A. J. South**, 26, single, farmer, b. Gloucester, residing Mid., son of Andrew & Mary H. South, married **M. S. Kenningham**, 18, single, b. Gloucester, residing Mid., dau. of Claiborn & Margaret. Minister-R. A. Christian.

1:39 - 14 Sep. 1855 - **John F. McGeorge**, 44, widower, b. & residing King William, son of Wm. McGeorge & Elizabeth Rowe, married **Maria L. Lee**, 22, single, b. & residing Mid., dau. of Curry Lee & Mildred Hutchings. Minister-Holland Walker.

1:40 - 4 Dec. 1855 - **A. B. Sadler** [**Arthur B.** in index], 26, single, occup.- "none particular," b. Mathews, residing Mid., son of Henry B. Sadler & Susan Fitchett, married **Mary Jane New**, 21, single, b. & residing Mid., dau. of John C. New & Mary A. Barrick. Minister-Holland Walker.

1:41 - 15 Jan. 1856 - **Robert Groom**, 23, single, farmer, b. & residing Mid., son of Thos. Groom & Elizabeth Redd, married **Betty Long**, 21, single, b. &

residing Mid., dau. of Ro. Long & Eliza Robinson.
Minister-Holland Walker.
1:42 - 24 Jan. 1856 - **Sam'l B. Cary**, 50, widower,
doctor, b. & residing Gloucester, son of Jno. R. Cary &
Maryann [or Haryann] Pryor, married **Winifred E. McCarty**,
34, single, b. Richmond Co., residing Mid., dau. of Ro.
W. McCarty & Winifred McCarty. Minister-G. S. Carraway.
1:43 - 26 Mar. 1856 - **Everest Horn**, 23, single,
baker, b. Germany, residing Mid., son of Awbroy [or
Ambroy] Horn & Barbara Nutter, married **Joanna Blake**, 22,
single, b. & residing Mid., dau. of John Blake & Joanna
Long. Minister-Holland Walker.
1:44 - 22 Apr. 1856 - **Sam'l R. Jackson**, 30, widower,
physician, b. Accomack, residing Mid., son of John &
Rebecca Jackson, married **Saphronia Walker**, single, b. &
residing Mid., dau. of Hiram Walker & Eliza L. Barrick.
Minister-Holland Walker.
1:45 - 25 Apr. 1856 - **Wm. G. Wathen** [**Wortham** in
index], 26, single, merchant, b. & residing Mid., son of
Wm. Wathen & Anna F. Montague, married **Louisa Garland**,
22, single, b. & residing Mid., dau. of Ro. C. Garland &
Sarah Barrick. Minister-Holland Walker.
1:46 - 20 Mar. 1856 - **Ransom Greenwood**, 22, single,
b. & residing Mid., son of Ransom Greenwood & Elizabeth
Greenwood, married **Elizabeth Davis**, 21, single, b. &
residing Mid., dau. of Bartlett & Nancy Davis.
Minister-R. H. Crittenden.
1:47 - 10 Apr. 1856 - **James Ingram**, 22, single, b.
Lancaster, residing Mid., son of James & Lecia Ingram,
married **Elizabeth Shrieves**, 19, single, b. Accomack,
residing Mid., dau. of Wm. & Louisa Shrieves. Minister-
R. H. Crittenden.
1:48 - 5 Jun. 1856 - **Thomas Deliever**, 25, single,
shoemaker, b. & residing Essex, son of Wm. Deliever &
Betsy Lorkley [or Lockley], married **Amelia Morris**, 18,
single, b. & residing Mid., dau. of Squire Morris &
Betsy Key. "Free people of color." Minister-T. B.
Evans.

2:01 - 5 Jun. 1856 - **Hiram Deagle**, 21, single, b. &
residing Mid., son of James & Nancy Deagle, married
Elizabeth Roberts, 18, single, b. Fredericksburg,
residing Mid., dau. of Lorenzo & Mary Ann Roberts.
Minister-R. H. Crittenden.
2:02 - 8 July 1856 - **Wm. F. Barrick**, 26, widower,
minister, b. Richmond Co., residing Mid., parents not
given, married **Mary E. Boss**, 21, single, b. & residing
Mid., dau. of John J. Boss & Ann W. Berry. Minister-
Thomas B. Evans.
2:03 - 17 Jul. 1856 - **John A. Hundley**, 29, single,

farmer, b. Essex, residing Mid., son of Lewis Hundley & Frances Dunn, married **Frances Carlton** [**Martha F. Carlton** in index], 20, single, b. & residing Mid., dau. of John A. Carlton & Sarah A. Mackan. Minister-Thomas B. Evans.

2:04 - 31 July 1856 - **Andrew L. Bristow**, 27, single, mechanic, b. & residing Mid., son of Lewis L. & Francis Bristow, married **Elizabeth W. Davis**, 26, single, b. & residing Mid., dau. of Rich'd A. & Elizabeth Davis. Minister-Holland Walker.

2:05 - 13 Aug. 1856 - **Jacob S. Blake**, 32, widower, farmer, b. & residing Mid., son of Jacob S. & Julia Sibley, married **Frances S. Blake**, 26, single, b. & residing Mid., dau. of Geo. & Jane Benns. Minister-Holland Walker.

2:06 - 24 Sep. 1856 - **Wm. W. Pitman**, 26, single, farmer, b. & residing Caroline, son of John H. & Dorotha S. Pittman, married **Henrietta A. Beazley**, 22, single, b. Essex, residing Mid., dau. of Jno. H. & Laura Beazley. Minister-R. A. Christian.

2:07 - 16 Oct. 1856 - **Addison Hall**, 30, single, physician, b. Lancaster, residing Northumberland, son of Ad. & Susan C. Hall, married **Ann M. Walker**, 17, single, b. & residing Mid., dau. of Holland & Ann M. Walker. Minister-R. A. Christian., married at "Greenbranch Neck."

2:08 - 6 Nov. 1856 - **Julius E. Healy**, 21, single, farmer, b. & residing Mid., son of Enos & Elizabeth Healy, married **Henrietta A. Muse**, 20, single, b. & residing Mid., dau. of Henry & Ann Muse. Minister-R. A. Christian.

2:09 - 8 Oct. 1856 - **Thomas G. Trader**, 22, single, oysterman, b. & residing Mid., son of Wm. & Priscilla Trader, married **Mary Walden**, 21, single, b. & residing Mid., dau. of Ro. & Mary E. Bray. Minister-Holland Walker.

2:10 - 6 Nov. 1856 - **Richard H. Hundley**, 21, single, farmer, b. Richmond Co., residing Mid., son of John & Elizabeth Hundley, married **Amanda Bray**, 18, single, b. & residing Mid., dau. of Ro. & Mary E. Bray. Minister-Thomas B. Evans.

2:11 - 13 Nov. 1856 - **Edmund C. Done** [**Doane** in index], 28, single, teacher, b. Maine, residing Mid., son of Ed. C. & Margret W. Done, married **Frances E. Carter**, 18, single, b. Alabama, residing Mid., dau. of Wm. H. & Harriett Ball. Minister-Holland Walker.

2:12 - 11 Dec. 1856 - **Wm. F. Newcomb**, 35, widower, farmer, b. & residing Mid., son of Frank & Elizabeth Newcomb, married **Mary J. Johnson** [**Mary Jane** in index], 20, single, b. Essex, residing Mid., dau. of Wm. & Bethell Johnson. Minister-Thomas B. Evans.

2:13 - 16 Dec. 1856 - **Rich'd C. Hart**, 22, single, farmer, b. King & Queen, residing Mid., son of Jacob & Elizabeth Hart, married **Mary E. Blackley**, 21, single, b. Essex, residing Mid., dau. of Ro. & Amie [or Annie] Blackley. Minister-Thomas B. Evans.
2:14 - 16 Dec. 1856 - **Wm. Johnson**, 48, widower, farmer, b. Essex, residing Mid., son of Rich'd & Elizabeth Johnson, married **Martha A. Bristow**, 28, single, b. & residing Mid., dau. of Z. W. & Maria Bristow. Minister-Thomas B. Evans.
2:15 - 23 Dec. 1856 - **Rich'd T. Wood**, 24, single, farmer, b. & residing Mid., son of Thos. & Sarah Wood, married **Elizabeth Thurston**, 19, single, b. & residing Mid., dau. of Thacker & Ann K. Thurston. Minister-Thomas B. Evans.
2:16 - 10 Feb. 1857 - **Thos. Henry Parrow** [**Parrin** in index], 23, single, farmer, b. & residing Mid., son of John Parren & Lilly Ann Clarke, married **Hannah Cath. Taylor**, 25, single, b. & residing Mid., dau. of Richard Taylor & Maria Parren. Minister-Thomas B. Evans.
2:17 - 18 Nov. 1856 - **James Micham Smith**, 28, widower, farmer, b. & residing Mid., son of John R. Smith & Frances M. Stiff, married **Mary Susan Fitchett**, 18, single, b. Mathews, residing Mid., dau. of Ro. Fitchett & Melivonie Parish. Minister-Holland Walker.
2:18 - 24 Feb. 1857 - **Walter M. Major**, 28, widower, farmer, b. & residing Mid., son of Jno. Major & Julia Humprice, married **Mary Elizabeth Seaward**, 17, single, b. & residing Mid., dau. of Robert Seaward & Ann Catharine Healy. Minister-Holland Walker.
2:19 - 3 Feb. 1857 - **John C. Whitheuse**, 24, single, shoemaker, b. Germany, residing Mid., son of Henry C. & Margrett Whitheuse, married **Miriam** [**Mirianna** in index] **Greenwood**, 24, single, b. & residing Mid., dau. of Wm. G. & Eliza Greenwood. Minister-Holland Walker.
2:20 - 19 Feb. 1857 - **Lewis M. Gardner**, 42, widower, farmer, b. & residing Mid., son of Geo. & Cath. Gardner, married **Elizabeth H. Fisher** [**Foster** penciled in, but **Fisher** in index], 22, single, b. Essex, residing Mid., dau. of Jas. W. & Eliza'h Fisher. Minister-Thomas B. Evans.
2:21 - 19 Feb. 1857 - **Thos. F. Royster**, 19, single, farmer, b. Gloucester, residing Mid., son of Jos. K. Royster & Elizab., married **Mary Wheely**, 21, single, b. & residing Mid., dau. of Carter & Va. Wheely. Minister-Thomas B. Evans.
2:22 - 19 Mar. 1857 - **Rich'd L. Fleet** [**Rob't** penciled in & **Ro.** in index], 23, single, carpenter, b. King & Queen, residing Mid., son of Wm. B. & Eliza'h Fleet, married **Mary J. Montague**, 22, single, b. Essex, residing

Mid., dau. of L. B. & Cath. Montague. Minister-Thomas B. Evans.

2:23 - 4 Apr. 1857 - **N. C. Sibley**, 37, widower, overseer, b. & residing Mid., son of Dan'l B. & Eliz. Sibley, married **Lucy E. New**, 17, single, b. & residing Mid., dau. of J. C. & Louisa M. New. Minister-Holland Walker.

2:24 - 23 Apr. 1857 - **Jos. A. Muse**, 27, single, carpenter, b. & residing Mid., son of N. Muse & M. Major, married **Leonora E. Clare**, 23, single, b. & residing Mid., dau. of R. Clare & E. Humphes. Minister-M. W. Towill.

2:25 - 24 Feb. 1857 - **J. E. Summers**, 31, single, waterman, b. Somerset, Maryland, residing Mathews, son of J. Summers & M. Muse, married **Ann H. Chesley**, 23, single, b. Mathews, residing Mid., dau. of J. Chesley. Minister-M. W. Towill.

2:26 - 24 Jan. 1857 - **Albert Hearn**, 23, single, farmer, b. & residing Mid., son of John & Elizabeth Hearn, married **Sarah Callis**, 17, single, b. Mathews, residing Mid., dau. of George & Sarah Callis. Minister-R. H. Crittenden.

2:27 - 6 May 1857 - **John W. Marchant**, 22, single, farmer, b. & residing Mathews, son of Jno. & Lucy Marchant, married **Lucy C. Jackson**, 19, single, b. & residing Mid., dau. of Jno. L. & Lucy Jackson. Minister-R. H. Crittenden.

2:28 - 19 Aug. 1857 - **Jacob W. Abrech**, 24, single, brickmaker, b. Prussia, Germina[sic], residing Mid., son of Jacob & Mary Abrech, married **Sarah B. Lewis**, 24, single, b. & residing Mid., dau. of Wm. & Elizabeth Lewis. Minister-Holland Walker.

2:29 - 10 Sep. 1857 - **Rich'd Broach**, 23, single, overseer, b. & residing Mid., son of Rich'd & Frances Broach, married **Va. A. Watts**, 24, single, b. & residing Mid., dau. of Cas. L. & Frances Watts. Minister-B. W. Nash.

2:30 - 3 Nov. 1857 - **J. B. Greenwood**, 20, single, dentist, b. & residing Mid., son of Ev. & Mary A. Greenwood, married **M. L. Purkins**, 17, single, born & residing Mid., dau. of Cart. & Mary A. Purkins. Minister-R. A. Christian.

2:31 - 1857 - **Jas. Sterling**, 26, single, waterman, b. & residing Maryland, son of Isaac & Hester Sterling, married **Sarah B. Moore**, 23, single, b. Maryland, residing Mid., dau. of Ro. & L. P. Moore. Minister-Jno. J. Boss.

2:32 - 6 Dec. 1857 - **Benj. Groom**, 31, widower, b. King & Queen, residing Mid., [parents not given], married **Ann E. Boss**, 33, single, b. & residing Mid.,

dau. of Meacham & Mary Boss. Minister-R. A. Christian.
2:33 - 20 Jan. 1858 - **Adolphus Rock**, 24, single,
labourer, b. Northumberland, residing Mid., son of
Francis & Eliza. Rocke, married **Mary F. Hudgins**, 23,
single, b. Mathews, residing Mid., dau. of Thos. L.
Hudgins & Mary. Minister-Holland Walker.
2:34 - 20 Jan. 1858 - **Jas. S. Crafton**, 22, single,
sailor, b. & residing Mid., son of John J. Crafton,
married **Mary B. South**, 14, single, b. & residing Mid.,
dau. of Andrew & Mary H. South. Minister-Holland
Walker.
2:35 - 10 Jun. 1857 - **Ro. T. Gardner**, 36, single,
farmer, b. & residing Mid., son of Geo. & Caty Gardner,
married **Mary W. Fisher**, 21, single, b. Essex, residing
Mid., dau. of Jas. W. & Elizabeth Fisher. Minister-
Thomas B. Evans.
2:36 - 17 Sep. 1857 - **Thos. D. Weston**, 40, widower,
farmer, b. Mathews, residing Mid., son of Ro. & Dorothy
Weston, married **Mary A. Jenkins**, 18, single, b.
Fredericksburg, Virginia, dau. of Tasco & Almira
Jenkins. Minister-R. H. Crittenden.
2:37 - 1 Dec. 1857 - **M. A. Seward**, 24, single,
farmer, b. Gloucester, residing Mid., son of W. F. &
Elvira Seward, married **S. A. Seward**, 15, single, b. &
residing Mid., dau. of Leroy & Ann Seward. Minister-
Thomas B. Evans.
2:38 - 3 Dec. 1857 - **Jas. R. Foster**, 23, single,
sailor, b. Mathews, residing Mid., son of Wm. & Sarah
Foster, married **Irena Harrow**, 16, single, b. & residing
Mid., dau. of A. J. & Emily Harrow. Minister-R. H.
Crittenden.
2:39 - 28 Jan. 1858 - **R. M. Taylor**, 21, single,
farmer, b. & residing Mid., son of Rich'd & Maria
Taylor, married **S. C. Daniel**, 18, single, b. & residing
Mid., dau. of Meck. & Elizabeth Daniel. Minister-Thomas
B. Evans.
2:40 - 4 Feb. 1858 - **Wm. H. Norton**, 23, single,
pilot, b. & residing Mid., son of Wm. L. & Eliza'h
Norton, married **E. D. H. Harrow**, 21, single, b. &
residing Mid., dau. of Wm. M. & Al. Harrow. Minister-R.
H. Crittenden.
2:41 - 18 Mar. 1858 - **Enos Walden**, 32, widower,
farmer, b. & residing Mid., son of John & Maria Walden,
married **Louisa Mercer**, 22, single, b. & residing Mid.,
dau. of Jas. & Mary Mercer. Minister-Holland Walker.
2:42 - 20 Mar. 1858 - **Ro. H. Walker.**, 31, single,
farmer, b. & residing Mid., son of Hiram & Eliza.
Walker, married **Julia F. Walker**, 19, single, b. &
residing Mid., dau. of Geo. & Julia Walker. Minister-
Holland Walker.

2:43 - 25 Mar. 1858 - **J. H. Thurston**, 40, widower, farmer, b. & residing Mid., son of Henry & Patsy Thurston, married **D. M. Milby**, 32, widow, b. & residing Mid., dau. of Ro. & Eliza'h Trice. Minister-Thomas B. Evans.

2:44 - 4 Apr. 1858 - **L. L. Fogg**, 35, widower, farmer, b. King William, residing Mid., son of Jos. & S. M. Fogg, married **L. A. Powers**, 20, single, b. Gloucester, residing Mid., dau. of Jas. & Polly Powers. Minister-Thos. B. Evans.

2:45 - 13 Apr. 1858 - **Ro. Daniel**, 24, single, farmer, b. & residing Mid., son of J. C. & Jane Daniel, married **Lucy B. Daniel**, 17, single, b. & residing Mid., dau. of Wm. H. & Martha Daniel. Minister-Thomas B. Evans.

2:46 - 4 May 1858 - **Ro. Pines**, 29, single, farmer, b. King & Queen, residing Mid., son of Wm. & Eliza'h Pines, married **Va. Bryant**, 20, single, b. & residing Mid., dau. of Ro. & Susanna Bryant. Minister-Holland Walker.

2:47 - 14 May 1858 - **Jos. H. Walden**, 30, single, farmer, b. & residing Mid., son of J. & Maria Walden, married **Otera Dugan**, 21, single, b. King William, residing Mid., dau. of B. F. & Elvira Dugan. Minister-Thomas B. Evans.

2:48 - 3 June 1858 - **Jos. Stewart**, 22, single, mariner, b. Somerset Co., Maryland, residing Mid., son of Wm. & S. Stewart, married **Rebecca Sadler**, 21, single, b. Mathews, residing Mid., dau. of O. S. & Mary Sadler. Minister-R. H. Crittenden.

3:01 - 7 Jul. 1858 - **Jas. Dudley**, 52, widower, farmer, b. & residing Mid., son of Ro. & Alice Dudley, married **S. J. Bennett**, 17, single, b. & residing Mid., dau. of Esrua R. H. & M. A. Bennett. Minister-Rich'd H. Crittenden.

3:02 - 7 Jul. 1858 - **Ed. Greenwood**, 48, widower, farmer, b. Essex, residing Mid., son of Jas. & Ann Greenwood, married **Lucy C. Prince**, 18, single, b. Gloucester, residing Mid., dau. of R. J. & A. D. Prince. Minister-J. C. Hummer.

3:03 - 7 Jul. 1858 - **Jos. D. Ailworth**, 48, widower, farmer, b. & residing Mid., son of Wm. & Ann Ailworth, married **A. F. Dudley**, 20, single, b. & residing Mid., dau. of Jas. & J. Dudley. Minister-Rich'd H. Crittenden.

3:04 - 13 Jul. 1858 - **Ro. R. Ball**, 27, single, farmer, b. King & Queen, residing Mid., son of Killis & Judy Ball, married **F. A. E. Dudley**, 32, single, b. & residing Mid., dau. of Chas. & Jane Dudley. Minister-Thomas B. Evans.

3:05 - 7 Aug. 1858 - **John Gouldman**, 22, single,

farmer, b. Gloucester, residing Mid., son of Sarah
Meggs, married **E. Bird**, 20, single, b. & residing Mid.,
dau. of Arthur Bird & Chrissey Cook. "Col'd persons."
Minister-Holland Walker.

3:06 - 12 Aug. 1858 - **J. R. Lumpkin**, 22, single,
merchant, b. Mathews, residing Mid., son of J. R. &
Cath. Lumpkin, married **L. C. Palmer**, 17, single, b. &
residing Mid., dau. of J. W. & E. C. Palmer. Minister-
J. C. Hummer.

3:07 - 1 Sep. 1858 - **M. W. Towill**, 46, widower,
farmer, b. Lancaster, residing Mid., son of Sarah
Towill, married **A. M. Pace**, 30, widow, b. & residing
Mid., dau. of Ro. & S. C. Barrick. Minister-Holland
Walker.

3:08 - 14 Sep. 1858 - **E. J. Robinson**, 25, single,
mariner, b. & residing Mid., son of B. F. & E. Robinson,
married **M. M. Daniel**, 16, single, b. & residing Mid.,
dau. of J. C. & Jane Daniel. Minister-J. C. Hummer.

3:09 - 23 Sep. 1858 - **Jas. Hart**, 21, single, mariner,
b. & residing Mid., son of R. H. Hart, married **M. E.
Weston**, 21, single, b. Mathews, residing Mid., dau. of
Thos. D. Weston. Minister-Jno. J. Boss.

3:10 - 25 Sep. 1858 - **Sam. S. Buckan**, 26, single,
farmer, b. & residing Lancaster, married **M. J. Hardy**,
20, single, b. & residing Mid., dau. of John & Mary
Hardy. Minister-M. W. Towill.

3:11 - 13 Oct. 1858 - **Thos. S. Cook**, 40, widower,
coachmaker, b. & residing Gloucester, son of Wm. & Ann
Cooke, married **Mary F. Gwyn**, 28, single, b. & residing
Mid., dau. of H. & E. Gwyn. Minister-J. C. Hummer.

3:12 - 22 Oct. 1858 - **John Edwards**, single,
shoemaker, b. Gloucester, residing Mid., son of Jos. &
F. Edwards, married **M. A. Oakes**, 20, single, b. &
residing Mid., dau. of Major & Sarah Oakes. Minister-
Holland Walker.

3:13 - 27 Oct. 1858 - **S. P. Fitchett**, 25, widower,
carpenter, b. Mathews, residing Mid., son of Rob. & M.
Fitchett, married **S. D. E. Blackburn**, 22, single, b. &
residing Mid., dau. of F. & J. Blackburn. Minister-
Holland Walker.

3:14 - 28 Oct. 1858 - **E. B. Montague**, 25, single,
attorney, b. Mid., residing King & Queen, son of L. B. &
C. S. Montague, married **S. V. Eubank**, 21, single, b.
Essex, residing Mid., dau. of Jas. C. & Ed. Eubank.
Minister-[not given].

3:15 - 28 Oct. 1858 - **H. W. Deagle**, 25, widower,
sailor, b. & residing Mid., son of Jas. & Nancy Deagle,
married **F. E. Hearne**, 21, widow, b. Mathews, residing
Mid., dau. of Callis. Minister-Jno. J. Boss.

3:16 - 11 Nov. 1858 - **John Deagle**, 25, widower,

labourer, b. & residing Mid., son of Jas. Deagle, married **M. S. Walden**, 21, single, b. Mathews, residing Mid., dau. of Walden. Minister-Jno. J. Boss.

3:17 - 25 Nov. 1858 - **Gideon Hall**, 43, widower, farmer, b. Cecil Co., Maryland, residing Mid., son of Wm. A. & F. Hall, married **Leti'a A. Revere**, 30, widow, b. Mathews, residing Mid., dau. of J. B. & Nancy Blake. Minister-Holland Walker.

3:18 - 1 Dec. 1858 - **N. J. Revere**, 25, single, carpenter, b. Baltimore, Maryland, residing Mid., son of J. B. & Ad. Revere, married **H. P. Buckner**, 30, widow, b. King & Queen, residing Mid., dau. of H. P. & Cath. Crittenden. Minister-Holland Walker.

3:19 - 4 Dec. 1858 - **Ed. Ailworth**, 40, widower, farmer, b. Accomack, residing Mid., son of Wm. & May Ailworth, married **M. A. Johnson**, 28, widow, b. & residing Mid., dau. of Z. & Maria Bristow. Minister-R. A. Christian.

3:20 - 23 Dec. 1858 - **Ro. Yates**, 21, single, farmer, b. Mathews, residing Mid., son of Ro. & Eliza Yates, married **Mary A. Ailworth**, 18, single, b. & residing Mid., dau. of J. D. & Ro. Ailworth. Minister-R. H. Crittenden.

3:21 - 24 Dec. 1858 - **An. McTyre**, 30, single, farmer, b. & residing Mid., son of Wm. & Caty Mctyre, married **Co. Dugan**, 18, single, b. King William, dau. of B. F. & El. Dugan. Minister-Thomas B. Evans.

3:22 - 28 Dec. 1858 - **James R. Cox**, 24, widower, blacksmith, b. & residing Essex, son of Geo. & Agnes Cox, married **R. H. Dunn**, 18, single, b. Essex, residing Mid., dau. of Lewis & Letty Dunn. Minister-Thomas B. Evans.

4:01 - 5 Jan. 1859 - **Wm. C. Bristow**, 34, single, mail contractor, b. & residing Mid., son of J. P. & M. A. Bristow, married **Maria A. Bristow**, 25, single, b. & residing Mid., dau. of Z. W. & Maria Bristow. Minister-J. C. Hummer.

4:02 - 12 Jan. 1859 - **James D. Yates**, 35, single, b. Mathews, residing Mid., son of B. H. & N. Yates, married **Ann R. Parks**, 30, widow, b. & residing Mid., dau. of Geo. & Martha Trader. Minister-Holland Walker.

4:03 - 19 Jan. 1859 - **James Chewning**, 42, widower, b. & residing Mid., son of B. & S. Chewning, married **Anne[?] E. Smith**, 20, single, b. & residing Mid., dau. of G. W. & H. J. Smith. Minister-R. A. Christian.

4:04 - 27 Jan. 1859 - **James Deagle**, 18, single, oysterman, b. & residing Mid., son of E. E. & S. Deagle, married **Emily Christopher**, 22, single, b. & residing Mid., dau. of Thos. & S. Christopher. Minister-R. H. Crittenden.

4:05 - 1 Feb. 1859 - **Andrew J. Palmer**, 24, single, merchant, b. Mid., residing Baltimore, Maryland, son of T. J. & P. A. Palmer, married **Emily A. Davis**, 22, single, b. & residing Mid., dau. of R. A. & E. B. Davis. Minister-Holland Walker.

4:06 - 24 Apr. 1859 - **John Newbill**, 45, widower, farmer, b. King & Queen, residing Mid., son of J. & Ann Newbill, married **Elizabeth Broach**, 26, single, b. & residing Mid., dau. of R. & M. F. Broach. Minister-Edward S. Seward.

4:07 - 29 Mar. 1859, **N. C. Bird**, 23, single, mariner, b. & residing Mid., son of Major & Lucy Bird, married **Rosanna Jackson**, 20, single, b. & residing Mid., dau. of J. B. & A. Jackson. Minister-R. H. Crittenden.

4:08 - 19 May 1859 - **Ro. E. Dudley**, 26, single, mariner, b. & residing Gloucester, son of Jas. & Judith Dudley, married **S. A. Carter**, 20, single, b. & residing Mid., dau. of H. & E. P. S. P. Carter. Minister-R. H. Crittenden.

4:09 - 31 May 1859 - **Jas. Kidd**, 50, widower, farmer, b. & residing Mid., son of Jas. & Frances Kidd, married **Eliza Royster**, 46, widow, b. Gloucester, residing Mid., dau. of Chas. & Franky Lawson. Minister-Edward S. Seward.

4:10 - 5 May 1859 - **Wm. R. Didlake**, 27, single, farmer, b. Gloucester, residing Mid., son of H. &. Cath. Didlake, married **S. F. South**, 15, single, b. & residing Mid., dau. of Andrew & Mary South. Minister-Holland Walker.

4:11 - 15 Jun. 1859 - **J. S. Blake**, 34, widower, farmer, b. & residing Mid., son of Jacob & Julia Blake, married **D. E. Wood**, 32, widow, b. Mathews, residing Mid., dau. of Thos. & Coatney Blake. Minister-Holland Walker.

4:12 - 18 Aug. 1859 - **Geo. W. Montague**, 29, single, clerk in store, b. & residing Mid., son of Phillip & Frances Montague, married **Sarah F. Shackleford**, 28, single, b. King & Queen, residing Mid., dau. of P. T. & J. M. Shackleford. Minister-Edward S. Seward.

4:13 - 24 Aug. 1859 - **Wm. S. Trymyer**, 22, single, farmer, b. King & Queen, residing Essex, son of John F. & Eliza'h Trimyer, married **Frances A. Jackson**, 24, single, b. & residing Mid., dau. of Jas. R. & Jiny D. Jackson. Minister-R. H. Crittenden.

4:14 - 24 Aug. 1859 - **Thos. E. Ingram**, 24, single, mariner, b. & residing Lancaster, son of Thos. H. & S. F. Ingram, married **Mary Ingram**, 18, single, b. Lancaster, residing Mid., dau. of Jas. & Sarah L. Ingram. Minister-R. H. Crittenden.

4:15 - 2 Aug. 1859 - **Thomas Christopher**, 18, single,

farmer, b. & residing Mid., son of Thos. & Susan Christopher, married **Ann E. Hart**, 19, single, b. & residing Mid., dau. of R. H. & Sarah Hart. Minister-R. H. Crittenden.

4:16 - 6 Oct. 1859 - **Ro. R. Carter**, 30, single, mariner, b. & residing Mid., parents not given, married **Mary A. Bull**, 30, widow, b. & residing Mid., dau. of Thos. & Mary Miles. Minister-R. H. Crittenden.

4:17 - 8 Mar. 1859 - **M. D. Cooke**, 24, single, farmer, b. & residing King & Queen, son of Dawson & Ann L. Cook, married **Emily F. Roane**, 20, single, b. King & Queen, residing Mid., dau. of Thos. N. & Mary N. Roane. Minister-Thomas B. Evans

4:18 - 23 Mar. 1859 - **Geo. T. Bristow**, 32, single, farmer, b. & residing Mid., son of Z. W. & Marie Bristow, married **M. A. Ailworth**, 17, single, b. Mathews, residing Mid., dau. of Ed. & Augusta E. Ailworth. Minister-Thomas B. Evans.

4:19 - 27 Apr. 1859 - **Geo. Key**, 27, single, farmer, b. & residing Mid., son of Thos. & Caty Key, married **Mary A. Key**, 25, single, b. & residing Mid., dau. of Jas. & Eliza Key. "Colored." Minister-Thomas B. Evans.

4:20 - 8 Sep. 1859 - **J. D. Crittenden**, 55, widower, farmer, b. King & Queen, residing Mid., married **Joicy Banks**, 22, single, b. Mathews, residing Mid., dau. of Wm. & S. A. Banks. Minister-Holland Walker.

4:21 - 8 Dec. 1859 - **Henry Kinner**, 22, single, mariner, born Northumberland, residing Lancaster, son of Winder & Frances Kenner, married **Sarah C. Ailworth**, 16, single, b. & residing Mid., dau. of Josiah D. & Roberta Ailworth. Minister-R. H. Crittenden.

4:22 - 18 Dec. 1859 - **Geo. W. Broach**, 23, single, carpenter, b. & residing Mid., son of Rich'd & Mary F. Broach, married **Mary A. Brinm**, 21, single, b. & residing Mid., dau. of Jno. H. & Eliza Brinm. Minister-John H. Payne.

4:23 - 22 Dec. 1859 - **Geo. Bohanon**, 23, single, farmer, b. & residing Essex, son of A. G. & Mary E. Bohanon, married **Anna F. Mason**, 19, single, b. & residing Mid., dau. of Miles F. & Frances Mason. Minister-John H. Payne.

4:24 - 22 Dec. 1859 - **J. Lee Rilee**, 20 single, mechanic, b. Gloucester, residing Mid., son of Thos. R. & Susan U. Rilee, married **Mira C. Seward**, 18, single, b. & residing Mid., dau. of Lewis B. & Sarah Seward. Minister-Edward S. Seward.

4:25 - 27 Dec. 1859 - **Chas. Birch**, 21, single, mechanic, b. King & Queen, residing Mid., son of S. & Frances Birch, married **Frances A. Wood**, 20, single, b. & residing Mid., dau. of Thos. & Alice Wood. Minister-

Edward S. Seward.
4:26 - 26 Oct. 1859 - **Jas. W. Howlet**, 24, single, b. Gloucester, residing Mid., son of Isaac & Ann Kemp Howlet, married **Eliz. F. Mossey**, 19, single, b. Gloucester, residing Mid., dau. of Ro. Mossey & Frances Key. Minister-Holland Walker.
4:27 - 29 Nov. 1859 - **Wm. Jas. Sibley**, 30, widower, b. & residing Mid., son of Daniel & Julia Sibley, married **Mary C. Taper**, 21, single, b. Mathews, residing Mid., dau. of Jos. Taper & Sarah Forest. Minister-not given.
4:28 - 16 June 1859 - **Wm. C. Fleet**, 23, single, farmer, b. King & Queen, residing Mid., son of J. R. & M. J. Fleet, married **Lucy D. Roane**, 20, single, b. King William, residing Mid., dau. of Sam'l & A. F. Roane. Minister-Thomas B. Evans.
4:29 - 18 Dec. 1859 - **J. R. Butler**, 21, single, farmer, b. King & Queen, residing Mid., son of J. & M. Butler, married **F. H. Evans**, 20, single, b. & residing Mid., dau. of T. B. & E. M. Evans. Minister-Thomas B. Evans.
5:01 - 1 Feb. 1860 - **Richard H. Clements**, 25, single, mechanic & farmer, b. Richmond Co., residing Mid., son of Jas. T. & Orinda Clements, married **Ophelia V. Seward**, 24, single, b. & residing Mid., dau. of Edw'd L. & Lucy Seward. Minister-Edward S. Seward.
5:02 - 16 Feb. 1860 - **William T. French**, 35, widower, farmer, b. & residing Mid., son of Jas. French & Lucinda Clare, married **Edna E. Watkins**, 20, single, b. King & Queen, residing Mid., dau. of Ed. T. Watkins & Nancy Griph. Minister-Holland Walker.
5:03 - 1 Mar. 1860 - **Bezabeel P. Cornelius**, 23, single, mariner, b. & residing Lancaster, son of Bailey & Milsey Cornelius, married **Sarah E. Deagle**, 16, single, b. & residing Mid., dau. of Wm. H. & Nancy Deagle. Minister-R. H. Crittenden.
5:04 - 8 Mar. 1860 - **Joseph H. Ware**, 24, single, carpenter, b. & residing Mid., son of Reuben Ware & Sarah Hardy, married **Melvina Fitchett**, 23, single, b. Mathews, residing Mid., dau. of Ro. R. Fitchett & Melissa [or Melinor] Parish. Minister-Holland Walker.
5:05 - 26 Apr. 1860 - **K. R. S. Daniel**, 27, single, farmer, b. & residing Mid., son of Geo. B. & Sarah Daniel, married **Mary L. Buckner**, 18, single, b. Gloucester, residing Mid., dau. of Payton G. & M. R. Buckner. Minister-John H. Payne.
5:06 - 3 May 1860 - **Wm. A. Muse**, 28, single, clerk, b. Spotsylvania, residing Baltimore, Maryland, son of A. A. & Cath. Muse, married **Mary A. Mathews**, 18, single, b.

Mathews, residing Mid., dau. of J. & Lucy B. D. Mathews. Minister-John H. Payne.

5:07 - 24 May 1860 - **L. C. Brushwood**, 29, single, b. King & Queen, residing Gloucester, son of J. & S. Brushwood, married **E. B. Garland**, 18, single, b. & residing Mid., dau. of R. C. & S. Garland. Minister-[not given].

5:08 - 5 Apr. 1860 - **J. A. Blakey**, 32, widower, farmer, b. & residing Mid., son of R. &. F. Blakey, married **L. E. Eubank**, 20, single, b. & residing Mid., dau. of J. A. & C. Eubank. Minister-Holland Walker.

5:09 - 7 Aug. 1860 - **Thos. Winder**, 25, single, oysterman, b. Mathews, residing Mid., son of G. & D. Winder, married **E. P. Wilson**, 21, single, b. & residing Mid., dau. of D. & E. Wilson. Minister-R. H. Crittenden.

5:10 - 2 May 1860 - **L. M. Bristow**, 27, single, farmer, b. & residing Mid., son of Z. W. & M. Bristow, married **M. E. Williams**, 16, single, b. Essex, residing Mid., dau. of Thos. & E. Williams. Minister-Edward S. Seward.

5:11 - 25 Oct. 1860 - **G. H. Heath**, 24, single, oysterman, b. Gloucester, residing Mid., son of Jos. & F. Heath, married **Ann E. Gale**, 38, widow, b. Mathews, residing Mid., dau. of Jno. & Ann Fitchett. Minister-John H. Payne.

5:12 - 20 Sep. 1860 - **Apheus L. Blake**, 22, single, carpenter, b. & residing Mid., son of Wm. S. & Cord. Blake, married **Ann L. Smither**, 18, single, b. Gloucester, residing Mid., dau. of Lewis & Ann Smither. Minister-John H. Payne.

5:13 - 28 Oct. 1860 - **Rich'd Cooper**, 45, widower, farmer, b. & residing Mid., son of Wm. & Polly Cooper, married **Juliza Goode**, 37, widow, b. King & Queen, residing Mid., dau. of Rich'd & F. Broach. Minister-Thomas B. Evans.

5:14 - 24 Oct. 1860 - **Rich'd H. Blake**, 20, single, farmer, b. & residing Mid., son of Ro. Blake, married (in Henrico Co.) **Judith E. Berry**, 18, single, b. & residing Mid., dau. of Jno. D. & Eliza Berry. Minister-Ed. J. Willis.

5:15 - 27 Jan. 1859 - **Geo. W. Mickleborough**, 24, single, farmer, b. & residing Mid., son of L. T. & H. Mickelborough, married **A. Thornton**, 20, single, b. Gloucester, residing Mid., dau. of No. & Cath. Thornton. Minister-A. F. Scott.

5:16 - 20 Nov. 1860 - **Thomas H. Northam**, 41, single, farmer, b. & residing Richmond Co., son of Ed. & Mary Northam, married **Jane Daniel**, 25, single, b. & residing Mid., dau. of M. & E. Daniel. Minister-Ed. S. Seward.

5:17 - 16 Dec. 1860 - **F. S. Trimyer**, 25, widower,

mechanic, b. K. William, residing Mid., son of F. S. &
H. Trimyer, married **Sally B. Hundley,** 21, single, b.
Essex, residing Mid., dau. of Thos. & Ann Hundley.
Minister-Ed. S. Seward.
    5:18 - 20 Dec. 1860 - **Wm. R. Eastwood,** 25, single,
plasterer, b. Norfolk, residing Portsmouth, son of W. &
Lydia Eastwood, married **Mary Taylor,** 21, single, b. &
residing Mid., dau. of Evan & Betsy Taylor. Minister-
Thos. B. Evans.
    5:19 - 28 Dec. 1860 - **Ed. W. Beazley,** 24, single,
farmer, b. Essex, residing Mid., son of J. H. & Laura
Beazley, married **Cath. Kinningham,** 26, single, b. &
residing Mid., dau. of T. Q. & Cath. Kinningham.
Minister-Thos. B. Evans.
    5:20 - 11 Dec. 1860 - **Wm. F. Parish,** 25, single,
mechanic, b. New Kent, residing Mid., son of John & T.
A. Parish, married **Cor. T. Layton,** 19, single, b.
Richmond Co., residing Mid., dau. of H. L. & V. Layton.
Minister-Holland Walker, married at Brandon.
    5:21 - 20 Dec. 1860 - **R. A. Davis,** 26, single,
attorney, b. Northumberland, residing Mid., son of R. A.
& E. B. Davis, married **Julia Broocke,** 18, single, b.
King & Queen, residing Mid., dau. of P. & H. Broocke.
Minister-Holland Walker, married at Harmony Church.
    5:22 - 25 Dec. 1860 - **Joseph D. Mathews,** 27, single,
merchant, b. Mathews, residing Mid., son of John &
Elizabeth Mathews, married **Mary E. Barrack,** 25, widow,
b. & residing Mid., dau. of John J. & Ann W. Boss.
Minister-R. H. Crittenden.

    6:01 - 11 Jan. 1861 - **Ro. O'Brien,** 34, single,
tailor, b. Ireland, residing Mid., son of Pat & Mary
O'Brien, married **E. J. Thornton,** 30, single, b.
Gloucester, residing Mid., dau. of Cath. V. Thornton.
Minister-C. R. Hains.
    6:02 - 22 Jan. 1861 - **Geo. H. Broocke,** 21, single,
farmer, b. Gloucester, residing Mid., son of Peter &
Harriet Broocke, married **Virginia Gressett,** 16, single,
b. & residing Mid., dau. of M. B. & Mary S. Gressett.
Minister-John G. Rowe, married at Saluda.
    6:03 - 31 Jan. 1861 - **Robert Smith,** 23, single, b. &
residing Mid., son of William & Delinda South, married
Cath. Blake, 35, widow, b. King & Queen, residing Mid.,
dau. of C. C. & E. Edwards. Minister-Holland Walker.
    6:04 - 27 Feb. 1861 - **Geo. T. Shrieves,** 21, single,
oysterman, b. & residing Mid., son of Wm. & Louisa
Shrieves, married **Mary C. Gipson,** 21, single, b. &
residing Mid., dau. of John & Nancy Gipson. Minister-
R. H. Crittenden.
    6:05 - 25 Apr. 1861 - **Ed. Richards,** 58, widower,

farmer, b. Essex, residing Mid., son of Major Brooke &
Diana Richards, married **Polly Key**, 34, single, b. &
residing Mid., dau. of Thos. & Caty Key. Minister-
Thos. B. Evans.
    6:06 - 28 Mar. 1861 - **Jas. E. Ingram**, 23, widower, b.
Lancaster, residing Mid., son of Jas. & Lucy Ingram,
married **Leonora Gipson**, 15, single, b. & residing Mid.,
dau. of John & Nancy Gipson. Minister-R. H. Crittenden.
    6:07 - 24 May 1861 - **Jas. H. Orell**, 23, single, b.
King & Queen, residing Mid., son of Ro. & Frances Orell,
married **Loui'a Pritchett**, 16, single, b. & residing
Mid., dau. of Jas. & Susan Pritchett. Minister-R. H.
Crittenden.
    6:08 - 29 Sep. 1861 - **Fred'k A. Kain**, 46, widower,
tailor, b. Prussia, residing Mid., son of John & Bar.
Kain, married **Lucy A. Kidd**, 21, single, b. & residing
Mid., dau. of Chowning and Kidd. Minister-John G. Rowe.
    6:09 - 25 Dec. 1861 - **Isaiah Forest**, 27, single,
farmer, b. Mathews, residing Mid., son of Ed. & Luc.
Forest, married **Roxanah Camey**, 32, widow, b. King
William, residing Mid., dau. of John & Frances Orell.
Minister-R. H. Crittenden.
    6:10 - 1 June 1862 - **Thos. Y. Lawson**, 40, widower,
merchant, b. Gloucester, residing Mid., son of Rich'd B.
& Eliz. B. Lawson, married **Sallie A. Fleet**, 20, single,
b. Mathews, residing Mid., dau. of Wm. H. & Eliz. Fleet.
Minister-Holland Walker.
    6:11 - 8 Jan. 1862 - **Rich'd H. Kellum**, 46, widower,
farmer, b. & residing Mid., son of Abel & Nancy Kellum,
married **Martha Wake**, 30, widow, b. King & Queen,
residing Mid., dau. of Jno. & Harriett Pitts. Minister-
M. W. Towill.

    7:01 - Repeat of # 6:11, above.
    7:02 - 26 Feb. 1862 - **Archibald Taylor**, 33, single,
physician, b. Norfolk, residing Chas. City, son of Ar. &
Frances F. Taylor, married **Martha Fauntleroy**, 25,
single, b. & residing Mid., dau. of Thos. W. & Ju. M.
Fauntleroy. Minister-John Pollard, Jr.
    7:03 - 28 May 1861 - **Jas. T. Yerby**, 47, widower,
farmer, b. Lancaster, residing Richmond Co., son of Wm.
T. & Maria Yerby, married **Dorothy A. Daniel**, 19, single,
b. & residing Mid., dau. of Mack. & Eliz. Daniel.
Minister-Thos. B. Evans.
    7:04 - 5 Dec. 1861 - **Sam'l H. Roane**, 24, single,
farmer, b. King William, residing Mid., son of Sam'l &
Ann F. Roane, married **Lucy F. Bagby**, 23, single, b. King
& Queen, residing Mid., dau. of Rich'd & Dor. A. Bagby.
Minister-Thos. B. Evans, married King & Queen.
    7:05 - 21 Jan. 1862 - **Geo. Norris**, 25, single,

farmer, b. & residing Mid., son of Squire & B. Norris, married **Camelia [or Amelia] Key**, 26, single, b. & residing Mid., dau. of Thos. & Cath. Key. Minister-Thos. B. Evans.

7:06 - 8 June 1862 - **John A. Deagle**, 33, widower, farmer, b. & residing Mid., son of Ephrian E. & Ailcy Deagle, married **Mary M. Callis**, 22, single, b. Mathews, residing Mid., dau. of Ro. & Martha Callis. Minister-R. H. Crittenden.

7:07 - 4 Aug. 1862 - **Chas. C. Abbott**, 35, widower, seaman, b. West Indies, residing King & Queen, son of Wm. H. & Malvien Abbott, married **Lucetta E. McTyre**, 29, single, b. & residing Mid., dau. of Geo. & Pris. McTyre. Minister-Thos. B. Evans.

7:08 - 24 Apr. 1862 - **Jas. Wm. Norris**, 18, single, farmer, b. & residing Mid., son of Jas. & Vir. Norris, married **Sarah E. Barford**, 22, single, b. Maryland, residing Mid., dau. of Wm. & Eliz. Barford. Minister-R. H. Crittenden.

7:09 - 9 Oct. 1862 - **Jos. G. Covington**, 24, single, farmer, b. Essex, residing Mid., son of W. G. & Al. A. Covington, married **Sarah E. Seward**, 22, single, b. & residing Mid., dau. of L. B. & S. Seward. Minister-John Pollard, Jr.

7:10 - 22 Oct. 1862 - **Thos. Lewis**, 40, widower, farmer, b. Accomack, residing Lancaster, son of Thos. & Sarah Lewis, married **Ann E. Heath**, 18, single, b. Gloucester, residing Mid., dau. of Jos. & Francis Heath. Minister-Thos. B. Evans.

7:11 - 16 Sep. 1862 - **Jacob W. Abrisch**, 30, widower, miller, b. Prussia, residing Lancaster, son of Jacob & Eliz. Abrisch, married **Mary A. South**, 32, single, b. & residing Mid., dau. of Wm. & Sarah E. South. Minister-R. H. Crittenden.

8:01 - 5 Jan. 1863 - **John Norton**, 50, widower, farmer, b. Gloucester, residing Mid., son of Thos. & Peggy Norton, married **Lucinda Clements**, 26, single, b. Richmond Co., residing Mid., dau. of Jas. & Orin. Clements. Minister-Holland Walker.

8:02 - 13 Mar. 1863 - **Wm. H. Blake**, 22, single, farmer, b. & residing Mid., son of Wm. S. & Cor. Blake, married **Sarah F. Cauthen**, 22, single, b. & residing, Mid., dau. of [not given]. Minister-Holland Walker.

8:03 - 1 Apr. 1863 - **Jos. Daniel**, 17, single, farmer, b. & residing Mid., son of J. C. & Jane Daniel, married **Eliz. A. Robinson**, 21, single, b. & residing Mid., dau. of B. F. & Eli. Robinson. Minister-John Pollard, Jr.

8:04 - 9 Apr. 1863 - **J. H. Boss**, 19, single, sailor, b. & residing Mid., son of Geo. & Eliza A. Boss, married

Margiana Patterson, 24, widow, b. & residing Mid., dau. of John & Milly Paterson. Minister-R. H. Crittenden.
 8:05 - 16 Apr. 1863 - **John W. Wister [or Wiston]**, 51, widower, farmer, b. Mathews, residing Mid., son of Geo. & Polly Wister [Wiston], married **Rebecca Haile**, 53, widow, b. King & Queen, residing Mid., dau. of Geo. & Ann Weston. Minister-R. H. Crittenden.
 8:06 - 15 Sep. 1863 - **Rich'd Trader**, 20, single, sailor, b. & residing Mid., son of Geo. & Parmelia Trader, married **Sarah E. Hart**, 18, single, b. & residing Mid., dau. of R. H. & Sarah Hart. Minister-R. H. Crittenden.
 8:07 - 18 Nov. 1863 - **Booker Garnett**, 23, single, merchant, b. & residing Essex, son of Muscoe & S. H. Garnett, married **Ann E. Gatewood**, 20, single, b. & residing Mid., dau. of Wm. L. & Lucy A. Gatewood. Minister-G. A. Conaway.
 8:08 - 9 Dec. 1863 - **Jos. D. Ailworth**, 53, widower, farmer, b. Accomack, residing Mid., son of Wm. & Nancy Ailworth, married **Sallie E. Crittenden**, 23, widow, b. Mathews, residing Mid., dau. of Boyd & Mary Walker. Minister-R. H. Crittenden.
 8:09 - 20 Dec. 1863 - **Elisha Claybell**, 26, single, sailor, b. Accomack, residing Mid., son of Thos. H. Claybell, married **Mary J. Bruce**, 28, widow, b. & residing Mid., dau. of Rich'd & Sally Hart. Minister-R. H. Crittenden. [See Clayvell or Clayville in subsequent registers.]
 8:10 - 20 Dec. 1863 - **Zadock Claybell**, 27, single, sailor, b. Accomack, residing Mid., son of Thos. H. Claybell, married **Sarah A. Hudgins**, 27, widow, b. & residing Mid., dau. of [not given]. Minister-R. H. Crittenden. [See Clayvell or Clayville in subsequent registers.]
 8:11 - 9 Dec. 1863 - **John Hardy**, 55, widower, farmer, b. & residing Mid., son of Jos. & Jane Hardy, married **Eli'th Saunders**, 45, widow, b. Mathews, residing Mid., dau. of [not given]. Minister-Holland Walker.
 8:12 - 24 Dec. 1863 - **Thos. S. Browne**, 51, widower, farmer, b. & residing Mid., son of Jno. & Mary Browne, married **Mary L. Blake**, 36, widow, b. & residing Mid., dau. of Bart & Sarah Blake. Minister-Holland Walker.

 9:01 - 21 Feb. 1864 - **Job Moore**, 66, widower, farmer, b. Somerset, Maryland, residing Mid., son of Job. & Sally Moore, married **Julia A. Williams**, 30, widow, b. & residing Mid., dau. of Wm. & Eliz. Christopher. Minister-R. H. Crittenden.
 9:02 - 23 Feb. 1864 - **Jas. M. Jeffries**, 24, single, lawyer, b. & residing King & Queen, son of Jos. M. & Neal M. Jeffries, married **Lucie B. Gatewood**, 20, single,

Neal M. Jeffries, married **Lucie B. Gatewood**, 20, single, b. & residing Mid., dau. of Wm. S. & Lucy A. Gatewood. Minister-G. A. Conaway.

9:03 - 4 May 1864 - **Joel Revere**, 39, widower, farmer, b. & residing Mid., son of Bush. & Nancy Revere, married **Eliz. Parkes**, 28, widow, b. & residing Mid., dau. of Ann Deagle. Minister-M. W. Towill.

9:04 - 22 May 1864 - **Griffin Cundiff**, 28, widower, farmer, b. & residing Mid., son of Grif. & Mary Cundiff, married **Ann Hundley**, 18, single, b. & residing Mid., dau. of Thos. & E. Hundley. Minister-R. H. Crittenden.

9:05 - 16 Nov. 1864 - **Lewis L. Fogg**, 42, widower, farmer, b. King William, residing Mid., son of Jos. & Sarah Fogg, married **D. M. Thurston**, 38, widow, b. & residing Mid., dau. of Ro. & Eliz. Trice. Minister-J. Pollard.

9:06 - 3 Nov. 1864 - **Bev. W. Jinkins**, 25, widower, farmer, b. & residing King George, son of Thos. & Car. Jinkins, married **Sary Kenningham**, 20, single, b. & residing Mid., dau. of Wm. & Eliz. Kenningham. Minister-Thos. B. Evans.

10:01 - 5 Jan. 1865 - **Wm. H. Daniel**, 47, widower, farmer, b. & residing Mid., son of Robt. Daniel, married **Arabella Corr**, 24, single, b. & residing Mid., dau. of Braxton & Polly Corr. Minister-John Pollard, Jr.

10:02 - 23 Feb. 1865 - **R. H. Hilyard**, 26, single, mechanic, b. King & Queen, residing Mid., son of Westly & Polly Hilyard, married **Frances A. Seward**, 28, single, b. & residing Mid., dau. of Lewis B. & S. J. Seward, Minister-John Pollard, Jr.

10:03 - 20 July 1865 - **H. W. Garrett**, 20, single, farmer, b. & residing Mid., son of Ed. & L. E. Garrett, married **J. F. Dickinson**, 22, single, b. Richmond City, residing Mid., dau. of R. H. & V. S. Dickinson. Minister-Holland Walker.

10:04 - 1 Aug. 1865 - **Hiram Carter**, 41, single, mariner, b. & residing Mid., son of H. & E. P. S. P. Carter, married **Ann E. Berry**, 21, single, b. & residing Mid., dau. of J. A. & M. A. Berry. Minister-R. H. Crittenden.

10:05 - 3 Aug. 1865 - **J. A. Stringer**, 21, single, teacher, b. Ash Co., North Carolina, residing Mid., son of W. & E. Stringer, married **Mary E. Watts**, 22, single, b. & residing Mid., dau. of J. & F. Watts. Minister-Thos. B. Evans.

10:06 - 12 Sep. 1865 - **Sam'l Richeson**, 27, single, b. Rockingham, residing St. Mary's, Maryland, son of J. & M. Richeson, married **L. B. Northam**, 25, single, b. & residing Mid., dau. of Wm. & A. Northam. Minister-[not given].

10:07 - 31 Oct. 1865 - **Z. W. Bristow**, 62, widower, b. & residing Mid., son of B. & E. Bristow, married **V. Broach**, 35, widow, b. & residing Mid., dau. of Ch. & F. Watts. Minister-[not given].

10:08 - 12 Nov. 1865 - **Seldon F. Crask**, 36, single, farmer, b. & residing Westmoreland, son of John & Sharly Crask, married **Maria Beale**, 21, single, b. St. Mary's Co., Maryland, dau. of Jas. & Eliz. Beale. Minister-A. J. Huntington.

10:09 - 14 Nov. 1865 - **R. W. Wyatt**, 32, single, merchant, b. Caroline, residing Richmond City, son of Wm. R. B. & Martha Wyatt, married **Mary E. Eubank**, 24, single, b. Essex, residing Mid., dau. of Joseph C. & Edmonia Eubank. Minister-Jas. D. Coulling.

10:10 - 30 Nov. 1865 - **H. H. Walker**, 33, single, physician, b. & residing Mid., son of H. & Eliz. Walker, married **J. E. Blake**, 23, widow, b. & residing Mid., dau. of J. D. & E. S. Berry. Minister-John Pollard, Jr.

10:11 - 7 Dec. 1865 - **N. Mason**, 45, widower, farmer, b. & residing Mid., son of J. & S. Mason, married **M. Christopher**, 33, widow, b. Mathews, residing Mid., dau. of L. & D. Peade. Minister-R. H. Crittenden.

10:12 - 19 Dec. 1865 - **G. H. Smith**, 28, single, farmer, b. & residing Mid., son of J. R. & S. S. Smith, married **N. E. Bennett**, 19, single, b. & residing Mid., dau. of Wm. J. & A. Bennett. Minister-Holland Walker.

10:13 - 21 Dec. 1865 - **H. Walden**, 22, single, farmer, b. & residing Mid., son of Ed. & R. Walden, married **M. J. Kellum**, 21, single, b. & residing Mid., dau. of R. & E. Kellum. Minister-R. H. Crittenden.

10:14 - 27 Dec. 1865 - **R. Ridgwell**, 24, single, farmer, b. St. Mary's, Maryland, residing Mid., son of U. & P. Ridgwell, married **M. E. Trader**, 15, single, b. & residing Mid., dau. of J. H. & S. Trader. Minister-R. H. Crittenden.

10:15 - 27 Dec. 1865 - **R. M. Tod**, 23, single, farmer, b. & residing Mid., son of B. & E. W. Tod, married **A. H. Foster**, 23, single, b. & residing Mid., dau. of Wm. & S. B. Foster. Minister-R. H. Crittenden.

10:16 - 25 Nov. 1865 - **Ric'd Taylor**, 62, widower, b. Essex, residing Mid., son of Wm. & Nanny Taylor, married **Ann E. Johnson**, 26, single, b. Essex, residing Mid., dau. of Hen. & Mag't Johnson. Minister-Thos. B. Evans.

10:A - 30 Nov. 1865 - **Elijah Dungee** married **Mrs. Nancy Cook**, "at res. of Elijah Dungee." Minister-J. Pollard, Jr. [This record is not recorded in the register, but was found in loose papers.]

11:01 - 2 Jan. 1866 - **Jas. D. Trader**, 26, single, farmer, b. & residing Mid., son of Wm. & Priscilla

Trader, married **Eliz. Ann Blake**, 18, single, b. &
residing Mid., dau. of Wm. J. & Lear Blake. Minister-
Holland Walker.

11:02 - 4 Jan. 1866 - **Wm. H. Clare**, 23, single,
farmer, b. & residing Mid., son of Ro. & Eliza Clare,
married **Almade C. Seward**, 22, single, b. & residing
Mid., dau. of Ro. S. & Ann C. Seward. Minister-John
Pollard, Jr.

11:03 - 9 Jan. 1866 - **Jno C. Clarke**, 29, single,
sailor, b. Essex, residing Mid., son of Jas. E. & Emily
Clarke, married **Eliz. A. Topping**, 24, single, b.
Accomack, residing Mid., dau. of Ed. & Keziah Topping.
Minister-Holland Walker.

11:04 - 16 Jan. 1866 - **Jas. W. Thrift**, 45, widower,
sailor, b. Richmond Co., residing Mid., son of Wm. &
Jane Thrift, married **Frances A. Blake**, 27, single, b. &
residing Mid., dau. of B. R. & S. Blake. Minister-
Holland Walker.

11:05 - 18 Jan. 1866 - **L. O. B. Major**, 23, single,
farmer, b. & residing Mid., son of Ro. S. & Lucy B.
Major, married **Mary O. Beazley**, 21, single, b. &
residing Mid., dau. of J. H. & Laura Beazley. Minister-
John Pollard, Jr.

11:06 - 18 Jan. 1866 - **Jos. S. Heath**, 24, single,
oysterman, b. Gloucester, resides Mid., son of Jos &
Fanny Heath, married **Malvina J. Ware**, 25, widow, b.
Mathews, residing Mid., dau. of Ro. B. & Malvina
Fitchett. Minister-Holland Walker.

11:07 - 24 Jan. 1866 - **Jos. A. Bristow**, 27, single,
farmer, b. & residing Mid., son of L. S. & C. B.
Bristow, married **Mary M. Roane**, 25, single, b.
Gloucester, residing Mid., dau. of Chas. & Mary Roane.
Minister-A. J. Huntington.

11:08 - 8 Mar. 1866 - **Hollis M. Rose**, 25, single,
confectioner, b. Waldo Co., Maine, residing Connecticut,
son of Daniel & Mary Rose, married **Ellen Didlake**, 17,
single b. & residing Mid., dau. of Ammon & M. U.
Didlake. Minister-[not given].

11:09 - 6 Feb. 1866 - **Jno. W. Hart**, 26, single,
blacksmith, b. Mathews, residing Mid., son of Wm. A. &
Va. F. Hart, married **Mary W. Watkins**, 25, single, b.
King & Queen, residing Mid., dau. of Ed. T. & Nancy
Watkins. Minister-Holland Walker.

11:10 - 7 Feb. 1866 - **Hiram A. Seward**, 34, single,
farmer, b. & residing Mid., son of Ed. S. & Lucy A.
Seward, married **Rosarelia Burch**, 15, single, b. King &
Queen, residing Mid., dau. of Henry & Fenton Burch.

Minister-Ed. S. Seward.

11:11 - 15 Feb. 1866 - **A. N. Croften**, 23, single, farmer, b. & residing Mid., son of J. J. & Permelia Crofton, married **M. E. Roane**, 23, single, b. King & Queen, residing Mid., dau. of Thos. N. & Mary Roane. Minister-A. J. Huntington.

11:12 - 20 Feb. 1866 - **T. H. Montague**, 46, single, farmer, b. & residing Mid., son of Phillip & Frances Montague, married **C. B. Mickelborough**, 23, single, b. & residing Mid., dau. of Jas. & Ann Mickelborough. Minister-John Pollard, Jr.

11:13 - 20 Feb. 1866 - **Ro. F. Crofton**, 21, single, b. & residing Mid., son of J. J. & Permelia Crofton, married **Ozela A. Roane**, 19, single, b. King & Queen, residing Mid., dau. of Thos. N. & Mary Roane. Minister-Geo. E. Booker.

11:14 - 22 Feb. 1866 - **R. Braxton Bristow**, 26, single, attorney-at-law, b. & residing Mid., son of J. S. & Lenora Bristow, married **Lucinda E. Jones**, 32, widow, b. Essex, residing Mid., dau. of Amos Cauthorn. Minister-John Pollard, Jr.

11:15 - 28 Feb. 1866 - **Charles Roane**, 65, widower, farmer, b. Gloucester, residing Mid., son of Wm. & Mary Roane, married **Harriet J. Dutton**, 34, single, b. Gloucester, residing Mid., dau. of Jas. & Nancy Dutton. Minister-Geo. E. Booker.

11:16 - 15 Mar. 1866 - **Albrecht Nieman**, 23, single, farmer, b. Sippo, Denmark, residing Mid., son of Wm. & Julia Nieman, married **Sarah F. Montague**, 29, widow, b. & residing Mid., dau. of Philip & M. Shackelford. Minister-Ed. S. Seward.

11:17 - 23 Mar. 1866 - **Rich'd H. Hart**, 23, single, farmer, b. & residing Mid., son of R. H. & Sarah Hart, married **Amanda Jackson**, 22, single, b. & residing Mid., dau. of Jer. & Amanda Jackson. Minister-Morris Montgomery.

11:18 - 22 Mar. 1866 - **Joel Reveer**, 42, widower, farmer, b. & residing Mid., son of Bushrod & Nancy Reveer, married **Mary Trader**, 28, widow, b. & residing Mid., dau. of John & Maria Walden. Minister-Holland Walker.

11:19 - 3 Apr. 1866 - **Jas. Moore**, 25, single, mariner, b. Somerset, Maryland, residing Mid., son of Job & Leah Moore, married **Cornelia Norris**, 16, single, b. & residing Mid., dau. of Jas. & Va. Norris. Minister-R. H. Crittenden.

11:20 - 3 Apr. 1866 - **A. N. Hodges**, 35, widower,

farmer, b. Mathews, residing Mid., son of M. S. & Martha
Hodges, married **Laura Kelly**, 17, single, b. Baltimore,
Maryland, residing Mid., dau. of W. H. & Nancy Kelly.
Minister-Geo. E. Booker.

11:21 - 3 Apr. 1866 - **Geo. W. Mercer**, 26, single, b.
& residing Mid., son of Jas. & Mary Mercer, married **Lucy
Walden**, 17, single, b. & residing Mid., dau. of Enos &
Eliz. Walden. Minister-[not given].

11:22 - 29 Apr. 1866 - **Geo. H. Dunn**, 25, single,
farmer, b. & residing Essex, son of J. P. & P. A. Dunn,
married **Lucy A. Hundley**, 22, single, b. Essex, residing
Mid., dau. of Thos. & L. A. Hundley. Minister-J. H.
Hundley.

11:23 - 6 May 1866 - **Wm. J. Daniel**, 49, single,
farmer, b. & residing Mid., son of Chris. & Eliz.
Daniel, married **Eliz. P. Winder**, 28, widow, b. &
residing Mid., dau. of D. & Eliz. Wilson. Minister-R.
H. Crittenden.

11:24 - Feb. 1866 - **Ferrol Winstead**, 22, single, b. &
residing Northumberland, son of & Agnes Winstead,
married **Betty Daniel**, 22, single, b. & residing Mid.,
dau. of Mickleboro & Elizabeth Daniel. Minister-Thos.
B. Evans.

11:25 - 7 Jan. 1866 - **Wm. A. Bird**, 24, single,
farmer, b. & residing Mid., son of Wm. A. & Christy
Bird, married **Farsulie Green**, 21, single, b. King &
Queen, residing Mid., dau. of Larken & Mary Green.
Minister-Thos. B. Evans.

11:26 - 12 Jul. 1866 - **W. H. Ingram**, 21, single,
merchant, b. Northumberland, residing Mid., son of
Griffin & Frances H. Ingram, married **Maria E. Bourne**,
21, single, b. Calvert Co., Maryland, residing Mid.,
dau. of Jas. T. & Ann W. Bourne. Minister-Geo. E.
Booker.

11:27 - 21 Jul. 1866 - **Phillip Smith**, 48, single,
farmer, b. & residing Mid., son of Jacob & Dianna Smith,
married **Kittie Wake**, 23, single, b. & residing Mid.,
dau. of Anderson & Patsy Wake. Minister-Holland Walker.

11:28 - 24 Jul. 1866 - **Jno. W. Ryland**, 29, single,
minister, b. & residing King & Queen, son of Jos. &
Priscilla Ryland, married **Lucy F. Roane**, 27, widow, b.
King & Queen, residing Mid., dau. of Rich'd & Dorothy
Bagby. John Pollard, Jr.

11:29 - 28 Aug. 1866 - **Rich'd H. Street**, 25, single,
farmer, b. & residing Mid., son of John & Mary Street,
married **Virg'a H. Taylor**, 22, single, b. & residing
Mid., dau. of Rich'd & Maria Taylor. Minister-Thos. B.

Evans.

11:30 - 9 Sep. 1866 - **James Smith**, 55, widower, farmer, b. Caroline, residing Mid., son of Henry & Nancy Smith, married **Ann Epps**, 40, widow, b. & residing Mid., dau. of Davy Burrell & Caroline. Minister-Thos. B. Evans.

11:31 - 11 Sep. 1866 - **R. A. Thurston**, 20, single, farmer, b. & residing King & Queen, son of Benj. & Juliet Thurston, married **Lucy E. Dudley**, 21, single, b. & residing Mid., dau. of Chas. & Jane Dudley. Minister-Thos. B. Evans.

11:32 - 13 Sep. 1866 - **Rich'd H. Parron**, 24, single, farmer, b. & residing Mid., son of John & Lilly Parron, married **Emma G. Williams**, 21, single, b. & residing Mid., dau. of Lewis & Eliz. Williams. Minister-Thos. B. Evans.

11:33 - 23 Sep. 1866 - **Frank Johnson**, widower, farmer, residing Mid., married **Harriet Smith**, 38, residing Mid. Minister-Thos. B. Evans.

11:34 - 18 Aug. 1866 - **Wm. Chapman**, 37, widower, farmer, b. Westmoreland, residing Mid., son of David & Chaney Chapman, married **Amanda Petersen**, 21, single, b. & residing Mid., dau. of Thos. & Charlotte Petersen. Minister-M. W. Towill.

11:35 - 30 Aug. 1866 - **Ro. Nelson**, 25, single, b. & residing Mid., son of Warner & Franky Nelson, married **Mary A. Foster**, 24, widow, b. & residing Mid., dau. of Caesar Tuckson. Minister-H. Walker. Married at Water View, Mid. Co.

11:36 - 3 Oct. 1866 - **Thos. Calhoun**, 30, single, sailor, b. Sussex, Delaware, son of Levin & Rachel Calhoun, married **Em. Hundley**, 16, single, b. & residing Mid., dau. of Thos. & Eliz. Hundley. Minister-M. W. Towill.

11:37 - 14 Oct. 1866 - **Sol. Ward**, 21, single, farmer, b. & residing King & Queen, son of Nelson & Franky Ward, married **Alice Hill**, 18, single, b. & residing Mid., dau. of Har. & Eliz. Hill. Minister-L. Harvey Hundley.

11:38 - 20 Oct. 1866 - **Wm. Wood**, 55, widower, farmer, b. & residing Mid., son of Sprig & Sally Wood, married **Milly Daniel**, 25, widow, b. Hanover, residing Mid., dau. of Thos. & Sally Coleman. Minister-Holland Walker.

11:39 - 22 Nov. 1866 - **Ro. H. Barrick**, 19, single, farmer, b. & residing Mid., son of H. D. & Vir. Barrick, married **Nancy W. Berry**, 18, single, b. & residing Mid., dau. of John D. & Disa Berry. Minister-Holland Walker.

11:40 - 28 Nov. 1866 - **John R. French**, 26, single,

farmer, b. & residing Mid., son of Jas. & Lucy French, married **E. J. French** [sic - however, original minister's return shows **Emily Josephine Prince**], 16, single, b. Gloucester, residing Mid., dau. of Rich'd & Cath. Prince. Minister-Holland Walker.

11:41 - 29 Nov. 1866 - **Jas. C. Keinningham**, 36, widower, sailor, b. Gloucester, residing Mid., son of Cl. & Marg. Keinningham, married **Lucy L. Sutton**, 24, single, b. & residing Mid., dau. of Thos. R. Sutton. Minister-Holland Walker.

11:42 - 12 Dec. 1866 - **Ro. N. Ailworth**, 19, single, farmer, b. & residing Mid., son of J. D. & Roberta Ailworth, married **Mary E. Cundiff**, 17, single, b. & residing Mid., dau. of John & Jane Cundiff. Minister-R. H. Crittenden.

11:43 - 15 Dec. 1866 - **Wm. Carter**, 27, single, farmer, b. & residing Mid., son of John & Haney Carter, married **Mary Smith**, 21, single, b. & residing Mid., dau. of Thos. and Marg. Smith. Minister-John Pollard.

11:44 - 19 Dec. 1866 - **Jerry Miles**, 22, single, farmer, b. & residing Mid., son of Lewis & Lucy Miles, married **Lucy Coleman**, 23, widow, b. & residing Mid., dau. of Sam'l & Jinny Coleman. Minister-John Pollard.

11:45 - 20 Dec. 1866 - **Jas. J. Williamson**, 25, single, mechanic, b. & residing Gloucester, son of Jas. H. & Martha Williamson, married **Maria F. Gale**, 26, single, b. Gloucester, residing Mid., dau. of Math. & Ann E. Gale. Minister-John Pollard.

12:01 - 22 Dec. 1866 - **Moses Johnson**, 47, widower, farmer, b. & residing Mid., son of Ben & Hannah Johnson, married **Char. Taliaferro**, 37, widow, b. & residing Mid., daughter of Murry & Delzie Robinson. Minister-R. H. Crittenden.

12:02 - 25 Dec. 1866 - **Ro. H. Thornton**, 19, single, farmer, b. & residing Mid., son of Chaney Williams, married **Madlund Wake**, 17, single, b. & residing Mid., dau. of Sarah A. Townley. "Colored people." Minister-Holland Walker.

12:03 - 25 Dec. 1866 - **Jos. Webb**, 24, single, farmer, b. & residing Mid., son of John & Harriett Webb, married **Julia Morris**, 18, single, b. & residing Mid., dau. of Geo. & Ester Morris. Minister-John Pollard.

12:04 - 26 Dec. 1866 - **Geo. W. Milby**, 25, single, b. & residing Mid., son of Wm. & Jane Milby, married **Missouri E. Major**, 21, single, b. Gloucester, residing Mid., dau. of Benj. & Frances Major. Minister-Holland

Walker.

12:05 - 27 Dec. 1866 - **Zadock Clavel**, 30, widower, farmer, b. Accomack, residing Mid., son of Thos. & Comfort Clavel, married **Sarah Johnson**, 30, single, residing Mid., dau. of Lewis & Mar. A. Johnson. Minister-R. H. Crittenden. [See Claybill, Clayville]

12:06 - 27 Dec. 1866 - **John M. Revere**, 24, single, farmer, b. & residing Mid., son of Isaac N. & Martha A. Revere, married **Sarah Smith**, 22, single, b. & residing Mid., dau. of John & Sarah Smith. Minister-Holland Walker.

12:07 - 31 Dec. 1866 - **Ro. White**, 21, widower, farmer, b. & residing Mid., son of Samuel & Patsy White, married **Clara Webb**, 16, single, b. & residing Mid., dau. of John & Harriett Webb. Minister-John Pollard.

12:08 - 1 Aug. 1866 - **Na. S. Wood**, 27, single, brick mason, b. & residing Mid., son of Thos. & Alice Wood, married **Cora A. Williams**, 21, single, b. & residing Mid., dau. of Starke & Ann Williams. Minister-Thos. B. Evans.

12:09 - 4 Oct. 1866 - **Ro. H. McKan**, 36, single, farmer, b. & residing Mid., son of Henry & Kitty McKan, married **Ann Thurston**, 22, single, b. & residing Mid., dau. of Thacker & Ann Thurston. Minister-Thos. B. Evans.

12:10 - 11 Dec. 1866 - **F. S. Chowning**, 21, single, b. & residing Fredericksburg, son of Frank & Eliz. Chowning, married **Ann C. Woodward**, 20, single, b. & residing Mid., dau. of Wm. P. & Mary Woodward. Minister-Thos. B. Evans.

12:11 - 24 Dec. 1866 - **Lewis Brim**, 24, single, farmer, b. & residing Mid., son of John & Eliza Brim, married **Lucie A. Broach**, 21, single, b. & residing Mid., dau. of Rich'd & Fanny Broach. Minister-Thos. B. Evans.

12:12 - 29 Dec. 1866 - **Henry Curtis**, 21, single, farmer, b. Gloucester, residing Mid., son of John & Pinkey Curtis, married **Lucy A. Carter**, 17, single, b. & residing Mid., dau. of Stephen & Judy Carter. Minister-Thos. B. Evans.

12:13 - 28 Apr. 1866 - **James Dudley**, 31, single, farmer, b. Gloucester, residing Mid., son of Henry & Eliza Dudley, married **Anna Bundy**, 23, single, b. & residing Mid., dau. of Sam'l & Jane Bundy. "Free colored." Minister-Holland Walker.

12:A - 2 Feb. 1866 - **Mr. Jos. Davis** married **Miss Emma Holmes**. "Colored." Minister-John Pollard, Jr. [This record, which is unindexed in the marriage register, was found in loose papers.]

12:B - 15 Mar. 1866 - **Mr. Samuel Howard** married **Miss Sally Gaines**. [This record was found in loose papers. The date shown is the date of the marriage license. No minister's return was found.]

13:01 - 2 Jan. 1867 - **Ro. V. Revere**, 27, single, farmer, b. & residing Mid., son of George B. & Lucy A. Revere, married **Ann E. Palmer**, 27, single, b. & residing Mid., dau. of John & Eliza Palmer. Minister-Holland Walker.

13:02 - 3 Jan. 1867 - **Adolphus Rock**, 32, widower, oysterman, b. Lancaster, residing Mid., son of Francis & Eliz. Rocke, married **Eu. F. Hudgins**, 20, single, b. & residing Mid., dau. of Wm. H. & Ellen W. Hudgins. Minister-Holland Walker.

13:03 - 6 Jan. 1867 - **Rich. Burrell**, 20, single, farmer, b. & residing Mid., son of Robert & Any Burrell, married **Sarah V. Taylor**, 17, single, b. Richmond Co., residing Mid., dau. of Charlotte Taylor. Minister-Holland Walker.

13:04 - 24 Jan. 1867 - **Wm. Kellum**, 21, single, farmer, b. & residing Mid., son of Abel & Frances Kellum, married **Alice Wilson**, 17, single, b. & residing Mid., dau. of Lafayette & Caroline Wilson. Minister-Morris Montgomery.

13:05 - 27 Jan. 1867 - **John R. Bennett**, 38, widower, farmer, b. Somerset Co., Maryland, residing Mid., son of John & Mary Bennett, married **Mary V. Berry**, 20, single, b. & residing Mid., dau. of James & Mary Ann Berry. Minister-R. H. Crittenden.

13:06 - 12 Jan. 1867 - **Phillip Banks**, 25, single, farmer, b. Mid., son of Henry & Beckey Banks, married **Eliza Webstead**, 21, single, b. Lancaster. [From minister's return - "Married in a log cabin in the woods."] Minister-John Pollard, Jr.

13:07 - 20 Jan. 1867 - **Calvin Bristow**, 25, single, farmer, b. Mid., son of Lewis L. & Frances Bristow, married **Mary E. Hackney**, 21, single, b. Mid., dau. of Jos. H. & Mary A. Hackney. Minister-H. P. Mitchell.

13:08 - 24 Jan. 1867 - **Wm. Hern**, 21, single, farmer, b. & residing Mid., son of Wm & Betty Hern, married **Sarah Jackson**, 23, single, b. & residing Mid., dau. of Jerry & Amanda Jackson. Minister-Morris Montgomery.

13:09 - 30 Jan. 1867 - **Rich'd T. Humphreys**, 25, single, farmer, b. & residing Mid., son of John & Margaret S. Humphreys, married **Lucie A. Major**, 26, single, b. & residing Mid., dau. of John A. & Julia A. Major. Minister-M. W. Towill.

13:10 - 16 Feb. 1867 - **John Holmes**, 23, single, farmer, b. King & Queen, residing Mid., son of Hubbard &

Letty Holmes, married **Martha Wormley**, 23, single, b. & residing Mid., dau. of [not given]. Minister-Holland Walker.

13:11 - 7 Mar. 1867 - **Geo. W. Smith**, 58, widower, farmer, b. King William, residing Mid., son of James Smith & Elizabeth Pannell, married **Mary Chapman**, 43, widow, b. Charleston Dist., South Carolina, residing Mid., dau. of John Turner & Emily Miles. Minister-Jas. H. Crown.

13:12 - 13 Mar. 1867 - **Geo. Robinson**, 24, single, farmer, b. & residing Mid., son of Christopher & Maria Robinson, married **Amanda Johnson**, 22, single, b. Lancaster, residing Mid., dau. of Chas. & Louisa Johnson. Minister-R. H. Crittenden.

13:13 - 7 Mar. 1867 - **Jas. Wilson**, 54, widower, farmer, b. & residing Mid., son of Jas. & Silvey Wilson, married **Eliza Griffin**, 35, widow, b. & residing Mid., dau. of Henry & Lucy Hall. Minister-Holland Walker.

13:14 - 26 Mar. 1867 - **Jas. Smith**, 21, single, farmer, b. Essex, residing Mid., son of Lewis & Elisa Smith, married **Maria Montague**, 21, widow, b. King & Queen, residing Mid., dau. of Jinney Dangerfield. Minister-Holland Walker.

13:15 - 23 Mar. 1867 - **Ro. Johnson**, 21, single, farmer, b. Mid., son of Doctor & Jane Johnson, married **Susan Carter**, 21, single, b. Mid., dau. of John & Haney Carter. Minister-John Pollard, Jr.

13:16 - 2 Apr. 1867 - **J. W. Clements**, 46, widower, mechanic, b. Richmond Co., residing Mid., son of Jas. & Orinda Clements, married **Mary E. Sibley**, 22, single, b. & residing Mid., dau. of Norma & Mary Sibley. Minister-R. H. Crittenden.

13:17 - 2 Apr. 1867 - **James Fitchett**, 51, widower, farmer, b. & residing Mid., son of Daniel & Jana Fitchett, married **Cath. Montague**, 40, widow, b. & residing Mid., dau. of Frank Rust. Minister-Holland Walker.

13:18 - 4 Apr. 1867 - **John Parker**, 48, widower, mechanic, b. Essex, residing Mid., son of Levi & Nancy Parker, married **Mary E. Browne**, 21, single, b. & residing Mid., dau. of Thos. S. & Eliz. Browne. Minister-John Pollard, Jr.

13:19 - 4 Apr. 1867 - **Jos. A. Stiff**, 23, single, farmer, b. & residing Mid., son of Lewis L. & Mary Jane Stiff, married **A. E. Bull**, 21, single, b. & residing Mid., dau. of Thos. R. & Mary A. Bull. Minister-Jas. H. Crown.

13:20 - 6 Apr. 1867 - **Dinx Lewis**, 24, single, farmer, b. Hanover, residing Mid., son of Richard & Ellen Lewis, married **Eliza Johnson**, 20, single, b. & residing Mid., dau. of George & Cornelia Johnson. Minister-John Pollard, Jr.

13:21 - 27 Apr. 1867 - **John H. Nelson**, 27, single, farmer, b. Mid., son of Cary & Eliza Nelson, married **Milly Holmes**, 26, single, b. Mid., dau. of Billy & Cloa Holmes. Minister-John Pollard, Jr.

13:22 - 30 Apr. 1867 - **Rob. D. Walker**, 31, single, farmer, b. & residing Mid., son of Holland & Debora Walker, married **Lucie H. Robinson**, 22, single, b. & residing Mid., dau. of John S. & Alice Robinson. Minister-John Pollard, Jr.

[Transcriber's note: Following is a continuation of the 1867 records. Although the page number changed, the line number continues from p. 13.]

14:23 - 10 Jun. 1867 - **Henry Burrell**, 30, single, sailor, b. & residing Mid., son of Nelson & Pru. Nelson, married **Netta Taylor**, 21, single, b. & residing Mid., dau. of Nancy Diggs. Minister-Jas. H. Crown.

14:24 - 25 Jun. 1867 - **Thos. S. Browne**, 54, widower, farmer, b. & residing Mid., son of John & Mary Browne, married **Eliz. Blake**, 21, single, b. & residing Mid., dau. of Wm. S. & Cordelia Blake. Minister-Holland Walker.

14:25 - 27 Jun. 1867 - **Geo. W. Thomas**, 28, single, sailor, b. & residing Talbot Co., Maryland, son of Geo. & Mary A. Thomas, married **Mary A. New**, 18, single, b. & residing Mid., dau. of James & Lucy A. New. Minister-Holland Walker.

14:26 - 27 Jun. 1867 - **Doctor Johnson**, 25, single, farmer, b. & residing Mid., son of Doctor & Jane Johnson, married **Aman. Thomas**, 18, single, b. & residing Mid., dau. of Corey Linsey. Minister-M. W. Towill.

14:27 - 29 May 1867 - **Ro. M. Taylor**, 28, widower, farmer, b. & residing Mid., son of Richard & Maria Taylor, married **Levinia Corr**, 21, single, b. & residing Mid., dau. of Thos. & Catharine Corr. Minister-J. Henry Hundley.

14:28 - 13 Jul. 1867 - **Noah Young**, 22, single, oysterman, b. & residing Mid., son of Harry & Peggy Young, married **Sena Burrell**, 23, single, b. & residing Mid., dau. of Harry & Mary Johnson. Minister-M. W. Towill.

14:29 - 14 Jul. 1867 - **Ro. Browne**, 60, widower, miller, b. Lancaster, residing Mid., son of George & Susan Browne, married **Mary Lockley**, 30, widow, b. & residing Mid., dau. of John & Lucy Burrell. Minister-John Pollard, Jr.

14:30 - 8 Aug. 1867 - **Wm. P. Farmer**, 21, single, farmer, b. Caroline, residing Essex, son of Phillip S. &

Martha Farmer, married **Sallie E. Smith**, 18, single, b. & residing Mid., dau. of Cath. Cooper. Minister-J. Henry Hundley.

14:31 - 22 Aug. 1867 - **Wm. Dameral**, 39, single, farmer, b. & residing Lancaster, son of Dennis & Betsy Dameral, married **Sarah E. Christopher**, 28, widow, b. Dorchester, Maryland, residing Mid., dau. of Thos. & Eliz'h Claybell. Minister-R. H. Crittenden.

14:32 - 31 Aug. 1867 - **Wash. Smith**, 21, single, farmer, b. Gloucester, residing Mid., son of John & Jane Smith, married **Julia A. Lee**, 24, single, b. King & Queen, residing Mid., dau. of Ned & Ann M. Hill. Minister-John Pollard, Jr.

14:33 - 4 Aug. 1867 - **Wm. B. Chowning**, 26, single, farmer, b. & residing Mid., son of James & Ann C. Chowning, married **Betsy A. Garrett**, 20, single, b. & residing Mid., dau. of Henry & Mary Garrett. Minister-John Pollard, Jr.

14:34 - 25 Aug. 1867 - **Henry Lockley**, 21, single, farmer, b. & residing Mid., son of Wm. & Winney Lockley, married **Amanda Roy**, 22, single, b. & residing Mathews, dau. of Garrett & Susan Roy. Minister-Holland Walker.

14:35 - 8 Sep. 1867 - **Jas. King**, 21, single, farmer, b. King & Queen, residing Mid., son of J. Williams & Sarah King, married **Mar. A. Lewis**, 22, single, b. & residing Mid., dau. of Tuscoe & Clara Lewis. Minister-Holland Walker.

14:36 - 20 Sep. 1867 - **John M. Wood**, 22, single, farmer, b. & residing Mid., son of Thos. & Alsy Wood, married **Ann E. Lewis**, 23, widow, b. Gloucester, residing Mid., dau. of Jos. & Frances Heath. Minister-Thos. B. Evans.

14:37 - 27 Oct. 1867 - **Thos. R. Watlington**, 40, single, "planting oysters," b. & residing Gloucester, son of Paul & Frances Watlington, married **Mary F. Seward**, 27, single, b. Essex, residing Mid., dau. of Wm. B. B. & Mary E. Seward. Minister-Thos. B. Evans.

14:38 - 13 Nov. 1867 - **J. R. Ferneyhough**, 23, single, farmer, b. Essex, residing Spotsylvania, son of Ro. W. & Frances P. Ferneyhough, married **In. C. Segar**, 22, single, b. & residing Mid., dau. of Wm. R. & Lucy M. Segar. Minister-John Pollard, Jr.

14:39 - 14 Nov. 1867 - **Thos. C. Seward**, 22, single, farmer, b. & residing King & Queen, son of Jas. & Catharine Seward, married **Ann S. Bristow**, 17, single, b. & residing Mid., dau. of Henry & Eliz. Bristow. Minister-Thos. B. Evans.

14:40 - 17 Nov. 1867 - **Lewis Gaines**, 20, single, farmer, b. & residing Mid., son of Benj'n & Mary Gaines, married **Rosa Coleman**, 25, single, b. & residing

Mid., dau. of Sam'l & Jinny Coleman. Minister-John Pollard, Jr.

14:41 - 17 Oct. 1867 - **Jacob Robinson**, 22, single, farmer, b. & residing Mid., son of Christopher & Mary Robinson, married **Lucy Johnson**, 16, single, b. & residing Mid., dau. of Lewis & Julia Johnson. Minister-Holland Walker.

14:42 - 20 Nov. 1867 - **B. H. Morgan**, 27, single, merchant, b. St. Mary's, Maryland, residing Mid., son of Charles Morgan, married **Mary A. Gressitt**, 17, single, b. & residing Mid., dau. of M. B. & Mary Gressitt. Minister-John Pollard, Jr.

14:43 - 23 Nov. 1867 - **Ro. Taylor**, 21, single, farmer, b. & residing Mid., son of Ed. & Nancy Taylor, married **Marg. Fauntleroy**, 18, single, b. & residing Mid., dau. of Sarah Fauntleroy. Minister-John Pollard, Jr.

14:44 - 4 Dec. 1867 - **L. S. Bristow, Sr.**, 66, widower, farmer, b. & residing Mid., son of Leonard & Lucy B. Bristow, married **Ann C. Seward**, 46, widow, b. & residing Mid., dau. of Edmund & Elizabeth Healy. Minister-John Pollard, Jr.

14:45 - 27 Sep. 1867 - **Geo. Revel**, 48, widower, sailor, b. Dorchester, Maryland, residing Mid., son of Wm. & Polly Revel, married **Harriet Kellum**, 30, widow, b. & residing Mid., dau. of Eliza Hern. Minister-R. H. Crittenden.

14:46 - 21 Mar. 1867 - **Jas. Campbell**, 23, single, farmer, b. & residing Mid., son of Lee & Louisa Campbell, married **Espe Key**, 24, single, b. & residing Mid., dau. of Thos. & Cath. Key. Minister-Thos. B. Evans.

[Transcriber's note: Page 15 is a continuation of 1867 records. Although the page number changes, the line numbers continue on from p. 14.]

15:47 - 27 Oct. 1867 - **Charles Laws**, 21, single, farmer, b. & residing Mid., son of John & Anna Laws, married **Vio. Washington**, 21, single, b. & residing Mid., dau. of Geo. & Lucy Anne Washington. Minister-Holland Walker.

15:48 - 18 Dec. 1867 - **Richard L. Milbey**, 24, single, farmer, b. & residing Mid., son of Wm. & Jane R. Milbey, married **C. W. Miller**, 19, single, b. & residing Mid., dau. of Chris. & Ellen E. Miller. Minister-Holland Walker.

15:49 - 19 Dec. 1867 - **John A. Owen**, 36, widower, farmer, b. & residing Mid., son of John & Sarah E.R. Owen, married **Anna M. Bird**, 36, single, b. King & Queen, residing Mid., dau. of Parmenus Bird. Minister-Thos. B. Evans.

15:50 - 25 Dec. 1867 - **Lewis E. Ashburn**, 24, single, oysterman, b. & residing Lancaster, son of Wm. G. & Sarah P. Ashburn, married **Martha E. Deagle**, 17, single, b. & residing Mid., dau. of Wm. H. & Nancy Deagle. Minister-R. H. Crittenden.

15:51 - 26 Dec. 1867 - **Lewis Lee**, 20, single, farmer, b. & residing Mid., son of Kendal & Mahany Lee, married **Lucy A. Madison**, 19, single, b. King & Queen, residing Mid., dau. of John & Lucy Madison. Minister-Holland Walker.

15:52 - 26 Dec. 1867 - **Ed. Griffin**, 36, single, brick mason, b. & residing Mid., son of Lewis & Barbara Griffin, married **Maria Lomax**, 22, single, b. & residing Mid., dau. of Geo. Lomax. Minister-Holland Walker.

15:53 - 28 Dec. 1867 - **Jessee Burrell**, 27, widower, farmer, b. & residing Mid., son of Ellick & Isabella Burrell, married **Hester Peterson**, 24, widow, b. & residing Mid., dau. of John & Harriet Webb. Minister-R. B. Beadles.

15:54 - 29 Dec. 1867 - **Cyrus Charles**, 40, single, farmer, b. & residing Mid., son of Iverson & Martha E. Charles, married **Mary E. Daniel**, 21, single, b. & residing Mid., dau. of N. C. & Ellen Daniel. Minister-R. B. Beadles.

15:55 - 31 Dec. 1867 - **Thomas F. Taff**, 56, widower, farmer, b. Mid., residing Essex, son of Peter & Mary Taff, married **Mary F. Carlton**, 40, widow, b. Essex, residing Mid., dau. of Michael & Maria Dyke. Minister-Thos. B. Evans.

16:01 - 11 Feb. 1868 - **John Tyson**, 35, single, wood cutter, residing Baltimore Co., Maryland, son of [not given], married **Hester Rilie**, 30, widow, b. Gloucester, residing Mid., dau. of [not given]. Minister-John Pollard, Jr.

16:02 - 22 Jan. 1868 - **John J. Wake**, 45, single, farmer, b. & residing Mid., son of Leroy & Elizabeth Wake, married **Sarah J. Clarke**, 30, single, b. & residing Mid., dau. of Braxton & Mary Clarke. Minister-Holland Walker.

16:03 - 27 Jan. 1868 - **Wm. H. Scott**, 49, single, farmer, b. & residing Mid., son of Anderson & Cordey Scott, married **Eliza Johnson**, 30, single, b. & residing Mid., dau. of Phil. & Maria Johnson. Minister-Holland Walker.

16:04 - 6 Feb. 1868 - **Jas. C. Mercer**, 40, widower, farmer, b. & residing Mid., son of Jas. & Mary Mercer, married **Eliza B. Bushwood**, 26, widow, b. & residing Mid., dau. of Ro. C. & Sarah Garland. Minister-Holland Walker.

16:05 - 8 Feb. 1868 - **Geo. W. Thurston,** 22, single, farmer, b. & residing Mid., son of Sam'l & Harriet Thurston, married **Frances A. Lockley,** 21, single, b. & residing Mid., dau. of Wm. & Winney Lockley. Minister-Holland Walker.

16:06 - 7 Jan. 1868 - **Thos. H. Northern,** 48, widowed, b. & residing Richmond Co., son of Edmund & Mary Northern, married **Lucy E. Parron,** 24, single, b. & residing Mid., dau. of Thos. & Lucy Parron. Minister-Thos. B. Evans.

16:07 - 4 Feb. 1868 - **Ro. M. Trice,** 33, single, b. & residing Mid., son of Thos. & Mary A. Trice, married **Lucy F. Newcomb,** 23, single, b. Gloucester, residing Mid., dau. of Wm. F. & Louisa Newcomb. Minister-R. B. Beadles.

16:08 - 13 Feb. 1868 - **A. R. Miles,** 22, single, merchant, b. & residing Mid., son of John A. & Mary V. Miles, married **O. A. Stiff,** 18, single, b. & residing Mid., dau. of Andrew & Eliz. Stiff. Minister-M. W. Towill.

16:09 - 20 Feb. 1868 - **Henry Turner,** 25, single, oysterman, b. King William, residing Mid., son of Reubin & Isabella Turner, married **Mary E. Fleet,** 21, single, b. Mathews, residing Mid., dau. of [not given]. Minister-Holland Walker.

16:10 - 22 Feb. 1868 - **James Wilson,** 49, widower, farmer, b. Gloucester, residing Mid., son of Robert & Rutha Wilson, married **Betsy Dawson,** 25, single, b. & residing Mid., dau. of Isaac & Julia Dawson. Minister-Thos. B. Evans.

16:11 - 23 Feb. 1868 - **Wm. H. Gaines,** 23, single, oysterman, b. & residing Mid., son of Jas. W. & Louisiana Gaines, married **E. Vir. Cundiff,** 21, single, b. & residing Mid., dau. of John & Mary June Cundiff. Minister-R. H. Crittenden.

16:12 - 14 Jan. 1868 - **Wm. T. Thrift,** 25, single, farmer, b. & residing Mid., son of Robert T. & Eliz. Thrift, married **Lu. A. Haile,** 18, single b. & residing Mid., dau. of Wm. H. & Anna Haile. Minister-Thos. B. Evans.

16:13 - 7 Mar. 1868 - **Carter Moody,** 40, widower, farmer, b. Essex, residing Mid., son of Sam'l & Lucy Moody, married **Pre. Anderson,** 22, widow, b. King & Queen, residing Mid., dau. of Churchill & Matilda Anderson. Minister-Washington Holmes.

16:14 - 7 Mar. 1868 - **F. Holland,** 28, single, farmer, b. Franklin Co., residing Mid., son of Lewis & Nelly Holland, married **Lou. Beverly,** 20, single, b. & residing Mid., dau. of Ellick & Easter Beverly. Minister-Thos. B. Evans.

16:15 - 12 Mar. 1868 - **Jas. H. Sale**, 30, single, farmer, b. Essex, residing Mid., son of Henry & Polly Sale, married **M. J. M. Johnson**, 26, single, b. Essex, residing Mid., dau. of Henry & Margaret M. Johnson. Minister-Thos. B. Evans.

16:16 - 26 Mar. 1868 - **A. M. Sadler**, 35, single, farmer, b. & residing Mid., son of Henry & Eliza Sadler, married **Ma. J. Blake**, 29, single, b. & residing Mid., dau. of Geo. & Caroline Blake. Minister-Holland Walker.

16:17 - 9 Apr. 1868 - **Jno. W. Scott**, 37, widower, farmer, b. Gloucester, residing Lancaster, son of Robert & Clara Scott, married **Har. Smith**, 19, single, b. Essex, residing Mid., dau. of Harriet Smith. Minister-Holland Walker.

16:18 - 16 Apr. 1868 - **N. Forrest**, 55, widower, farmer, b. Mathews, residing Mid., son of Ed. & Sally Forrest, married **Eliz. Wilson**, 50, widow, b. Accomack, residing Mid., dau. of Wm & Lea Christopher. Minister-R. H. Crittenden.

16:19 - 16 Apr. 1868 - **Jas. W. Carter**, 30, single, mariner, b. & residing Mid., son of Hiram & Emily P. Carter, married **Vic. A. Cole**, single, b. & residing Mid., dau. of Sam'l R. Cole. Minister-M. W. Towill.

16:20 - 17 Apr. 1868 - **D. Harris**, 26, single, oysterman, b. & residing Mid., son of David & Sally Harris, married **K. A. Healy**, 22, single, b. & residing Mid., dau. of Mary Ann Burrell. Minister-M. W. Towill.

16:21 - 23 Apr. 1868 - **Aug. Johnson**, 22, widower, farmer, b. & residing Mid., son of Peter & Ann Johnson, married **E. M. Jones**, 21, single, b. & residing Mid., dau. of Nell & Eliza Jones. Minister-Holland Walker.

16:22 - 1 May 1868 - **Thos. L. Healy**, 35, single, farmer, b. & residing Mid., son of Thos. L. & Ann J. Healy, married **Mary F. Healy**, 46, widow, b. King William, residing Mid., dau. of Jos. & Sarah Fogg. Minister-J. Pollard.

16:23 - 2 June 1868 - **Aron Young**, 67, widower, farmer, b. & residing Mid., son of Jas. & Diana Young, married **Louisa Wood**, 50, widow, b. & residing Mid., dau. of Spencer & Hannah Banks. Minister-Holland Walker.

17:01 - 11 June 1868 - **Alpheus Greenwood**, 25, single, oysterman, b. & residing Mid., son of Ben & Delajah Greenwood, married **Mary J. Revere**, 23, single, b. & residing Mid., dau. of Jos. B. & Adaline Revere. Minister-Holland Walker.

17:02 - 21 June 1868 - **Green Griffin**, 22, single, laborer, b. Sumpter Co., South Carolina, residing Mid., son of Hiram & Judy Griffin, married **Judith Yerby**, 17, single, b. & residing Mid., dau. of John & Lucinda

Yerby. Minister-John Pollard, Jr.

17:03 - 23 June 1868 - **J. R. Ross**, 42, single, merchant, b. Norfolk, residing Gloucester, son of Jonathan F. & Matilda Ross, married **Ed. C. Palmer**, 21, single, b. & residing Mid., dau. of Alfred & Matilda Palmer. Minister-John Pollard, Jr.

17:04 - 12 Jul. 1868 - **Wm. Johnson**, 28, single, farmer, b. Chatham Co., North Carolina, residing Mid., son of Andy Thompson & Hannah Johnson, married **Susan Hoskins**, 24, single, b. King & Queen, residing Mid., dau. of Rachel Hoskins. Minister-John Pollard, Jr.

17:05 - 26 Jul. 1868 - **Alfred Lewis**, 21, single, farmer, b. & residing Mid., son of Albert & Grace Lewis, married **Winney Carter**, 20, single, b. Lancaster, residing Mid., dau. of Dinah Carter. Minister-John Pollard, Jr.

17:06 - 6 Aug. 1868 - **Wm. L. Wilson**, 25, single, teacher, b. Jefferson Co., residing Columbia College, District of Columbia, son of Benjamin & Mary A. Wilson, married **Nannie Huntington**, 23, single, b. & residing Mid., dau. of A. J. & Bettie G. Huntington. Minister-John Pollard, Jr.

17:07 - 3 Sep. 1868 - **Wm. Davis**, 21, single, farmer, b. Richmond City, residing Mid., son of Wm. & Eliza Davis, married **Fanny Holmes**, 22, single, b. & residing Mid., dau. of Wm. & Clara Holmes. Minister-John Pollard, Jr.

17:08 - 27 Sep. 1868 - **Deaton Carter**, 23, single, farmer, b. & residing Mid., son of Chas. & Nancy Carter, married **Eliz. Cook**, 24, single, b. & residing Mid., dau. of James & Betsy Cook. Minister-John Pollard, Jr.

17:09 - 6 Oct. 1868 - **F. A. Bristow**, 26, single, merchant, b. & residing Mid., son of Jas. & Leonora Bristow, married **Vir. E. Brook**, 24, widow, b. & residing Mid., dau. of Mordecai B. & Mary Gressitt. Minister-John Pollard, Jr.

17:10 - 13 Oct. 1868 - **Wm. L. Trimyer**, 32, widower, farmer, b. King & Queen, residing Mid., son of John F. & Elizabeth Trimyer, married **Sarah S. Hundley**, 18, single, b. & residing Mid., dau. of Jas. & Elizabeth Hundley. Minister-R. H. Crittenden.

17:11 - 22 Oct. 1868 - **Henry Bates**, 23, single, farmer, b. Prince William, residing Mid., son of Ro. & Celia Bates, married **Elnora Thomas**, 18, single, b. & residing Mid., dau. of Ro. & Letty Thomas. Minister-Holland Walker.

17:12 - 9 Nov. 1868 - **Ro. Davis**, 28, single, oysterman, b. & residing Mid., son of Bartlett & Nancy Davis, married **Mary A. Montgomery**, 23, single, b. & residing Mid., dau. of Seth & Hester A. Montgomery. Minister-R. H. Crittenden.

17:13 - 28 Nov. 1868 - **Julius Lewis**, 22, single, farmer, b. & residing Mid., son of Albert & Grace Lewis, married **Alice Morris**, 16, single, b. & residing Mid., dau. of Maria Morris. Minister-John Pollard, Jr.

17:14 - 3 Dec. 1868 - **Moses Lomax**, 23, single, farmer, b. & residing Mid., son of Geo. & Peggy Lomax, married **Anna Waites**, 30, widow, b. & residing Mid., dau. of Peter & Sally Waites. Minister-John Pollard, Jr.

17:15 - 29 Dec. 1868 - **Wm. B. Thurston**, 21, single, farmer, b. & residing Mid., son of Jas. & Martha Thurston, married **Lucy Ellen Major**, 22, single, b. & residing Mid., dau. of Robert D. & Lucy Major. Minister-John Pollard, Jr.

17:16 - 24 Dec. 1868 - **Daniel Hodges**, 24, single, farmer, b. Nansemond, residing Mid., son of Anthony & Venus Hodges, married **Mary Holloway**, 21, single, b. King & Queen, residing Mid., dau. of Harrison & Catharine Holloway. Minister-John Pollard, Jr.

17:17 - 30 Dec. 1868 - **Geo. H. Muire**, 25, single, oysterman, b. & residing Mid., son of Geo. & Precilla Muire, married **Matilda S. Weston**, 15, single, b. & residing Mid., dau. of Thomas & Nancy Weston. Minister-R. H. Crittenden.

17:18 - 17 Dec. 1868 - **Sam'l H. Hurley**, 24, widower, farmer, b. Kent, Maryland, residing Mid., son of Sam'l & Rachel Hurley, married **Lucia H. Garland**, 22, single, b. & residing Mid., dau. of Ro. C. & Sarah Garland. Minister-M. W. Towill.

17:19 - 2 Aug. 1868 - **Geo. Sample**, 26, single, farmer, b. Accomack, residing Mid., son of James & Lila Sample, married **Grace Taliaferro**, 21, single, b. & residing Mid., dau. of Baylor & Kesiah Taliaferro. Minister-Thos. B. Evans.

17:20 - 29 Aug. 1868 - **John Bell**, 38, widower, farmer, b. Essex, residing Mid., son of Sam'l & Suckey Baylor, married **Hannah Foster**, 37, widow, b. & residing Mid., dau. of Harry & Martha Lomax. Minister-Thos. B. Evans.

17:21 - 19 Nov. 1868 - **Henry Easter**, 29, single, farmer, b. Gates Co., North Carolina, residing Mid., son of Miles & Catharine Easter, married **Lucy A. Bluefoot**, 28, single, b. & residing Mid., dau. of Wm. & Eliza Bluefoot. Minister-Thos. B. Evans.

17:22 - 31 Dec. 1868 - **Jay Evans**, 26, single, farmer, b. Connecticut, residing Mid., son of Alanson & Annis Evans, married **Sarah E. Wheeler**, 20, single, b. & residing Mid., dau. of Carter & Virginia Wheeler. Minister-Thos. B. Evans.

17:23 - 15 Mar. 1868 - **Ed Laurence**, 32, widower, farmer, b. Nansemond, residing Mid., son of Chas. &

Emeline Green, married **Sarah Dudley**, 35, widow, b. & residing Mid., dau. of Douglas. Minister-R. B. Beadles.

17:24 - 18 Mar. 1868 - **Allen Brooking**, 22, single, farmer, b. & residing Mid., son of Isaac & Nancy Brooking, married **Betsy Daniel**, 32, widow, b. & residing Mid., dau. of Henry & Lucy Dawson. Minister-R. B. Beadles.

17:25 - June 1868 - **Daniel Barner** [or **Barmer**], 51, widower, farmer, b. James City, residing Mid., son of Sam'l & Mary Barmer, married **Jane Bird**, 34, widow, b. & residing Mid., dau. of Lewis & Fanny Weeks. Minister-R. B. Beadles.

17:26 - 19 Jul. 1868 - **Wm. Pratt**, 40, widower, farmer, b. Essex, residing Mid., son of Phillis Harris, married **Jane Dean**, 25, single, b. & residing Mid., dau. of Peter & Lucy Dean. Minister-R. B. Beadles.

18:01 - 4 Jan. 1869 - **Phil Johnson**, 26, single, oysterman, b. Mathews, residing Mid., son of Nicolas & Sarah Johnson, married **Jane Thurston**, 20, single, b. & residing Mid., dau. of Beverly & Lucy Thurston. Minister-R. H. Crittenden.

18:02 - 3 Jan. 1869 - **Baldron Heany**, 22, single, laborer, b. Northumberland, residing Mid., son of Walter & Eliz. Heany, married **M. A. Campbell**, 17, single, b. & residing Mid., dau. of Warner & Easter Campbell. Minister-M. W. Towill.

18:03 - 8 Jan. 1869 - **Wm. H. Cooke**, 49, single, clerk, b. Dorchester Co., Maryland, residing Mid., son of Thomas & Mary Cooke, married **Sarah Wilson**, 50, widow, b. & residing Mid., dau. of George & Martha Trader. Minister-R. H. Crittenden.

18:04 - 17 Jan. 1869 - **Rich'd Reddick**, 49, widower, laborer, b. Nansemond, residing Mid., son of Thomas & Charlotte Reddick, married **Ellen Young**, widow, b. King William, residing Mid. [Other information not given.] Minister-John Pollard, Jr.

18:05 - 1 Jan. 1869 - **Steven Jones**, 21, single, farmer, b. & residing Mid., son of Willia A. Jones, married **Mary E. Dunnaway**, 21, single, b. & residing Mid., dau. of Jas. & Martha Dunnaway. Minister-Thos. B. Evans.

18:06 - 12 Jan. 1869 - **Ro. Daniel**, 35, widower, merchant, b. & residing Mid., son of John C. & Jane Daniel, married **Mary J. Fleet**, 33, widow, b. & residing Mid., dau. of Lewis B. & Catharine Montague. Minister-Thos. B. Evans.

18:07 - 14 Jan. 1869 - **Ed. W. Moffitt**, 21, single, sailor, b. Delaware Co., Pennsylvania, residing Baltimore, Maryland, son of Jos. & Susan Moffitt, married **Evaline Norton**, 21, widow, b. & residing Mid., dau. of Wm. M. & Almedia Harrow. Minister-R. H. Crittenden.

18:08 - 17 Jan. 1869 - **Silas Morris**, 36, single, farmer, b. & residing Mid., son of Squire & Betsy Morris, married **Sarah A. Corbin**, 25, single, b. & residing Mid., dau. of Wm. & Jackson. Minister-Washington Holmes.

18:09 - 10 Jan. 1869 - **Geo. W. Crittenden**, 22, single, sailor, b. Mid., residing New York City, son of Rich'd H. & Mary Crittenden, married **Columbia F. Cole**, 21, single, b. & residing Mid., dau. of Sam'l & Maria Cole. Minister-John J. Boss.

18:10 - 14 Jan. 1869 - **Jas. R. Graham**, 23, single, sailor, b. Philadelphia, residing Mid., son of Isaac & Jane Graham, married **Cor. F. Deagle**, 15, single, b. & residing Mid., dau. of Wm. H. & Nancy Deagle. Minister-John J. Boss.

18:11 - 25 Nov. 1868 - **Wm. Powers**, 34, single, farmer, b. & residing Mid., son of Robert & Charity Powers, married **Anna Bird**, 18, single, b. & residing Mid., dau. of Pine Bird. Minister-Holland Walker.

18:12 - 16 Dec. 1868 - **Geo. H. Harris**, 30, single, farmer, b. & residing Mid., son of Jacob & Anna Harris, married **Eliza Jones**, 30, widow, b. & residing Mid., dau. of Patrick & Louisa Henry. Minister-Holland Walker.

18:13 - 28 Dec. 1869 - **Thos. D. Adams**, 30, single, carpenter, b. Armstrong Co., Pennsylvania, residing Mid., son of Andrew & Mary Adams, married **Rosie E. Richardson**, 18, single, b. King William, residing Mid., dau. of John & Sarah Richardson. Minister-R. B. Beadles.

18:14 - 21 Jan. 1869 - **John Goldman**, 31, widower, farmer, b. Gloucester, residing Mid., son of Robin Wilson & Sally Meiggs, married **Frances Meigs**, 28, widow, b. King & Queen, residing Mid., dau. of Patsy Davenport. Minister-R. B. Beadles.

18:15 - 30 Jan. 1869 - **Wm. H. Groom**, 49, widower, farmer, b. & residing Mid., son of Thomas & Sarah Groom, married **Julia Fleet**, 32, single, b. King & Queen, residing Mid., dau. of Wm. & Elizabeth Fleet. Minister-Thos. B. Evans.

18:16 - 31 Jan. 1869 - **Noah Easton**, 27, widower, farmer, b. North Carolina, residing Mid., son of Miles & Carter Easton, married **Julia Ricks**, 21, single, b. & residing Mid., dau. of John & Caty Ricks. Minister-Thos. B. Evans.

18:17 - 3 Mar. 1869 - **Jos. B. McKenny**, 32, widower, farmer, b. Westmoreland, residing Lancaster, son of Wm. & Cath. McKenny, married **Sarah A. Dudley**, 26, widow, b.

& residing Mid., dau. of Hiram & Emily P. Carter. Minister-M. W. Towill.

18:18 - 13 Mar. 1869 - **John Banks**, 26, single, farmer, b. & residing Mid., son of Henry & Beckey Banks, married **Laura Davis**, 22, single, b. & residing Mid., dau. of Jack & Laura Davis. Minister-Thos. B. Evans.

18:19 - 14 Mar. 1869 - **John Boyd**, 25, single, farmer, b. & residing Mid., son of Phil & Sally Boyd, married **Julia Ward**, 26, single, b. & residing Mid., dau. of [not given]. Minister-Thos. B. Evans.

18:20 - 10 Feb. 1869 - **John A. Hall**, 26, single, farmer, b. & residing Mid., son of Gid. G. W. & Anna Hall, married **Lucy H. Revere**, 27, single, b. & residing Mid., dau. of George B. & Lucy A. Revere. Minister-Holland Walker.

18:21 - 27 Feb. 1869 - **W. W. Taylor**, 18, single, farmer, b. King & Queen, residing Mid., son of Robert & Mary Taylor, married **Mira A. Gaines**, 17, single, b. & residing Mid., , dau. of Benjamin & Mary Gaines. Minister-John Pollard.

18:22 - 10 Mar. 1869 - **Ad. H. Ward**, 26, single, farmer, b. Somerset, Maryland, residing Mid., son of Geo. T. Ward, married **Eudora Roane**, 26, single, b. & residing Mid., dau. of Thomas N. & Mary N. Roane. Minister-John Pollard.

18:23 - 18 Mar. 1869 - **Joshua Dudley**, 35, widower, oysterman, b. Gloucester, residing Mid., son of [not given], married **Sally Henry**, 18, single, b. & residing Mid., dau. of Richard & Mildred Henry. Minister-Holland Walker.

18:24 - 27 Mar. 1869 - **Wash. Boyd**, 26, single, b. & residing Mid., son of Phil & Sally Boyd, married **Chris. Webb**, 21, single, b. & residing Mid., dau. of John & Harriet Webb. Minister-John Pollard, Jr.

19:25 - 22 Apr. 1869 - **Jas. R. Prince**, 22, single, farmer, b. James City, residing Mid., son of Richard & Nancy Prince, married **Eliz. Sibley**, 23, single, b. Fredericksburg, residing Mid., dau. of James & Susan Sibley. Minister-John Pollard, Jr.

19:26 - 29 Apr. 1869 - **Ro. C. Garland**, 29, single, farmer, b. & residing Mid., son of Robert C. & Sarah A. Garland, married **Am. E. Topping**, 20, single, b. & residing Mid., dau. of Edward & Kesiah Topping. Minister-Holland Walker.

19:27 - 5 May 1869 - **Jos. Taper**, 21, single, oysterman, b. Mathews, residing Mid., son of Joseph & Sarah Taper, married **Eliz. Harrow**, 21, single, b. & residing Mid., dau. of Wm. N. & Mary F. Harrow. Minister-R. H. Crittenden.

19:28 - 19 May 1869 - **J. W. Foster**, 21, single, farmer, b. Mathews, residing Mid., son of Wm. R. & Sarah B. Foster, married **Cath. Sparrow**, 22, single, b. Accomack, residing Mid., dau. of David & Saly Sparrow. Minister-R. H. Crittenden.
19:29 - 8 May 1869 - **J. H. Rust**, 22, single, farmer, b. & residing Mid., son of Archibald & Winny Rust, married **Peggy Armstrong**, 22, widow, b. King & Queen, residing Mid., dau. of Henry & Harriet Muse. Minister-John Pollard, Jr.
19:30 - 29 May 1869 - **Thos. Hoskins**, 21, single, farmer, b. King & Queen, residing Mid., son of Washington & Rachel Hoskins, married **Lucy Muse**, 18, single, b. King & Queen, residing Mid., dau. of Henry & Harriet Muse. Minister-John Pollard, Jr.
19:31 - 11 Jul 1869 - **Chas. Pall**, 29, single, sailor, b. Europe, residing Mid., son of [not given], married **Fran. C. Schrieves**, 20, single, b. & residing Mid., dau. of Wm. & Louiza Schrieves. Minister-R. H. Crittenden.
19:32 - 27 Jul. 1869 - **Ro. Carr**, 21, single, farmer, b. & residing Mid., son of Thos. & Ellen Carr, married **Oney Johnson**, 23, widow, b. & residing Mid., dau. of Sydnor & Ellen Ellis. Minister-R. B. Beadles.
19:33 - 29 Jul. 1869 - **Chas. Walker**, 27, single, farmer, b. & residing Mid., son of Lee & Maria Walker, married **Haz. Griffin**, 17, single, b. Lancaster, residing Mid., dau. of Charels Griffin. "Colored." Minister-R. H. Crittenden.
19:34 - 2 Sep. 1869 - **Loyd H. Ingram**, 22, single, farmer, b. Lancaster, residing Mid., son of James & Sally Ingram, married **Sarah Sparrow**, 18, single, b. Accomack, dau. of David & Sarah Sparrow. Minister-R. H. Crittenden.
19:35 - 16 Sep. 1869 - **Jno. W. Barrick**, 20, single, farmer, b. & residing Mid., son of Henry & Virginia Barrick, married **Frances B. Ransome**, 17, single, b. Fredericksburg, residing Mid., dau. of Robert & Bettie Ransome. Minister-Holland Walker.
19:36 - 28 Sep. 1869 - **Wm. C. Robinson**, 36, single, sailor, b. & residing Mid., son of John & Alice Robinson, married **Ar. N. Walker**, 22, single, b. & residing Mid., dau. of Joel & Mary C. Walker. Minister-Holland Walker.
19:37 - 4 Nov. 1869 - **Jas. A. Wood**, 22, single, oysterman, b. & residing Mid., son of John T. & Alice Wood, married **Har. C. Parks**, 22, single, b. & residing Mid., dau. of Abel & Rebecca Parks. Minister-Holland Walker.
19:38 - 27 May 1869 - **Abram Key**, 30, single, farmer, b. & residing Mid., son of Thos. & Catharine Key,

married **Lea Ann Bird,** 26, single, b. & residing Mid., dau. of Author & Chrissey Bird. Minister-Thos. B. Evans.

19:39 - 18 Aug. 1869 - **Henry C. Penrod,** 26, single, farmer, b. Bedford Co., Pennsylvania, residing Mid., son of John & Hannah Penrod, married **Ro. Ann Seward,** 21, single, b. & residing Mid., dau. of Edward S. & Lucy A. Seward. Minister-Thos. B. Evans.

19:40 - 14 Nov. 1869 - **David Strother,** 58, widower, farmer, b. & residing Mid., son of Sam'l & Polly Strother, married **Betsy Corbin,** 54, widow, b. Caroline, residing Mid., dau. of Berket & Nancy Gray. Minister-Thos. B. Evans.

19:41 - 2 Dec. 1869 - **Walter H. Key,** 28, single, farmer, b. & residing Mid., son of Thos. & Catey Key, married **Mary Armstead,** 22, single, b. King William, residing Mid. Minister-Thos. B. Evans.

19:42 - 23 Dec. - **Wm. D. Shrieves,** 19, single, sailor, b. & residing Mid., son of Wm. & Louisa Shrieves, married **Va. S. Gibson,** 19, single, b. & residing Mid., dau. of Wm. & Louisa Gibson. Minister-R. H. Crittenden.

19:43 - 24 Dec. 1869 - **Sam'l Mayo,** 25, single, farmer, b. North Carolina, residing Mid., son of Ned & Agy Mayo, married **Eliz. Johnson,** 27, widow, b. King & Queen, residing Mid., dau. of [not given]. Minister-John Pollard, Jr.

19:44 - 26 Dec. 1869 - **Phil Foster,** 35, widower, farmer, b. & residing Mid., son of Cornelius & Susan Foster, married **Ellen Lee,** 30, widow, b. & residing Mid., dau. of [not given]. Minister-Thos. B. Evans.

19:45 - 26 Dec. 1869 - **H. W. F. Walker,** 45, single, farmer, b. & residing Mid., son of Holland & Debrah Walker, married **Vir. Edmunds,** 31, single, b. Lancaster, residing Mid., dau. of Robert Edmunds. Minister-John Pollard, Jr.

19:46 - 28 Dec. 1869 - **El. B. Daniel,** 21, single, farmer, b. & residing Mid., son of Ellison & Mary Daniel, married **Mary E. Haile,** single, b. & residing Mid., dau. of W. H. & Anna Haile. Minister-John Pollard, Jr.

19:47 - 28 Dec. 1869 - **Lewis Brimm,** 29, widower, farmer, b. & residing Mid., son of John & Elisa Brimm, married **Rosa B. Newbill,** 21, single, b. King & Queen, residing Mid., dau. of John Newbill. Minister-John Pollard, Jr.

19:48 - 29 Dec. 1869 - **J. H. Nelson,** 29, widower, farmer, b. & residing Mid., son of Cary & Eliz. Nelson, married **Frances Lewis,** 21, single, b. Essex, married Mid., dau. of Sam'l Lewis. Minister-John Pollard, Jr.

19:49 - 25 Nov. 1869 - **J. H. Robinson**, 27, single, farmer, b. & residing Mid., son of John D. & Sarah Robinson, married **Marg. F. Sibley**, 21, single, b. & residing Mid., dau. of Daniel & Sarah Sibley. Minister-John Pollard, Jr.

20:01 - 3 Jan. 1870 - **Oscar Jones**, 21, single, laborer, b. King & Queen, residing Mid., son of Stephen & Lydia Jones, married **Lucy B. Lee**, 22, single, b. & residing Mid., dau. of Jeff & Caroline Lee. Minister-Thos. B. Evans.

20:02 - 5 Jan. 1870 - **Sam'l Thurston**, 28, single, farmer, b. & residing Mid., son of Sam'l & Harriet Thurston, married **Lucy Robinson**, 23, single, b. & residing Mid., dau. of Robert & Nancy Robinson. Minister-M. W. Towill.

20:03 - 28 Dec. 1869 - **Jos. Stewart**, 26, single, laborer, b. Mecklinburg, residing Mid., son of Frank & Mary Stewart, married **Cath. Grimes**, 22, single, b. Caroline, residing Mid., dau. of [not given]. Minister-Thos. H. Boggs.

20:04 - 13 Jan. 1870 - **John V. Nagle**, 28, single, farmer, b. York Co., Pennsylvania, residing Mid., son of Michael & Rebecca Nagle, married **Mary J. Didlake**, 19, single, b. & residing Mid., dau. of Ammon Didlake. Minister-R. H. Crittenden.

20:05 - 20 Jan. 1870 - **Ro. H. Lewis**, 35, single, laborer, b. Mid., residing Gloucester, son of John & Lucy Lewis, married **Eliza C. Gibbs**, 25, single, b. Gloucester, residing Mid., dau. of Frances Gibbs. Minister-John Pollard, Jr.

20:06 - 25 Jan. 1870 - **Jas. M. Williams**, 57, widower, farmer, b. King & Queen, residing Essex, son of John & Elizabeth Williams, married **Louisa E. Healy**, 51, widow, b. Essex, residing Mid., dau. of Amos Cauthorn. Minister-John Pollard, Jr.

20:07 - 25 Jan. 1870 - **Oscar T. Harris**, 22, single, farmer, b. Essex, residing Mid., son of Wm. & Lucinda Harris, married **Martha E. Curtis**, 19, single, b. & residing Mid., dau. of Alex & Charlotte Curtis. Minister-Thos. B. Evans.

20:08 - 17 Mar. 1870 - **Jas. Davis**, 24, single, sailor, b. Delaware, residing Virginia, son of Jos. & Rebecca Davis, married **Mil. G. Fitchett**, 18, single, b. & residing Mid., dau. of Ro. & Melvina Fitchett. Minister-John Pollard.

20:09 - 7 Dec. 1869 - **Judge Jackson**, 49, widower, farmer, b. & residing Mid., son of Wm. & Frances Jackson, married **Betsy Tabb**, 20, single, b. & residing Mid., dau. of Isaac & Rachel Tabb. Minister-Holland Walker.

20:10 - 28 Dec. 1869 - **Miles C. Laws**, 22, single, farmer, b. & residing Mid., son of Linsey & Coley Laws, married **Frances Upshaw**, 24, single, b. & residing Mid., dau. of Daniel & Frances Upshaw. Minister-Holland Walker.

20:11 - 30 Dec. 1869 - **Moses Burke**, 19, single, farmer, b. & residing Mid., son of Ned & Polly Burke, married **Lidia A. Hundley**, 20, single, b. & residing Mid., dau. of Chas. & Eliz. Hundley. Minister-Holland Walker.

20:12 - 3 Feb. 1870 - **John M. Major**, 27, single, farmer, b. & residing Mid., son of John & Juliet Major, married **Ellen F. Palmer**, 21, single, b. & residing Mid., dau. of John W. & Eliz. Palmer. Minister-Holland Walker.

20:13 - 3 Feb. 1870 - **Jas. T. Lewis**, 22, single, waterman, b. & residing Mid., son of Thos. & Frances Lewis, married **Louisa Blake**, 23, single, b. & residing Mid., dau. of George & Caroline Blake. Minister-Holland Walker.

20:14 - 9 Feb. 1870 - **David Burrell**, 70, widower, farmer, b. & residing Mid., son of Nathaniel & Aggy Burrell, married **Tamer Jackson**, widow, b. & residing Mid., dau. of Winney. Minister-John Pollard, Jr.

20:15 - 14 Feb. 1870 - **Jas. H. Scott**, 23, single, oysterman, b. Gloucester, residing Mid., son of Robert & Clara Scott, married **Lucy B. Griffin**, 17, single, b. & residing Mid., dau. of Richard & Anna Griffin. Minister-Holland Walker.

20:16 - 3 May 1870 - **Jas. B. Allen**, 52, widower, farmer, b. Delaware, residing Mid., son of [not given], married **Rosa M. Thompson**, 46, widow, b. Baltimore, residing Mid., dau. of [not given]. Minister-Thos. H. Boggs.

20:17 - 28 Apr. 1870 - **Curtis Johnson**, 21, single, farmer, b. & residing Mid., son of Lewis & Letty Johnson, married **Cordelia Gresham**, 21, single, b. & residing Mid., dau. of [not given]. Minister-Holland Walker.

20:18 - 5 May 1870 - **Lewis Banks**, 21, single, oysterman, b. & residing Mid., son of York & Lusinda Banks, married **Eudora Jackson**, 21, single, b. & residing Mid., dau. of John & Mary Jackson. Minister-Holland Walker.

20:19 - 18 May 1870 - **Wm. Watson**, 21, single, oysterman, b. Mathews, residing Mid., son of John Watson, married **Geo. Anna Parry**, 16, single, b. & residing Mid., dau. of Elisha & Mary Parry. Minister-R. H. Crittenden.

20:20 - 2 Jun. 1870 - **Peter Grigry**, 22, single,

farmer, b. Mathews, residing Mid., son of Jas. & Mary Ann Grigry, married **Mary A. Jackson**, 20, single, b. & residing Mid., dau. of Joseph & Jane Jackson. Minister-Holland Walker.

20:21 - 9 Jun. 1870 - **Lewis Banks**, 21, single, farmer, b. & residing Mid., son of Washington & Judy Banks, married **Nancy Lomax**, 20, single, b. & residing Mid., dau. of Henry & Judy Lomax. Minister-John Pollard, Jr.

20:22 - 3 Jul. 1870 - **Benjamin Johnson**, 43, widower, farmer, b. & residing Mid., son of Henry & Maria Johnson, married **Tamar Risby**, 22, single, b. Mathews, residing Mid., dau. of Reubin & Fanny Risby. Minister-R. H. Crittenden.

20:23 - 8 Jul. 1870 - **Henry Davis**, 26, single, farmer, b. & residing Mid., son of Henry & Edy Davis, married **Virginia Reade**, 22, widow, b. Norfolk, Virginia, residing Mid., dau. of Brister & Sarah Foreman. Minister-John Pollard, Jr.

20:24 - 26 Jul. 1870 - **Ric'd Barrell**, 25, single, farmer, b. & residing Mid., son of Alexander & Isabella Barrell, married **F. A. Banks**, 23, single, b. Gloucester, residing Mid., dau. of Louisa Banks. Minister-James Kenner.

21:01 - 28 Jun. 1870 - **Ro. R. Woodward**, 24, single, farmer, b. & residing Mid., son of Thos. H. & Eliz. Woodward, married **Car. F. Smith**, 24, single, b. Gloucester, residing Mid., dau. of Geo. W. & Ann F. Smith. Minister-Thos. B. Evans.

21:02 - 11 Aug. 1870 - **Ben. Johnson**, 68, widower, farmer, b. & residing Mid., son of Benj. & Hannah Johnson, married **Julia A. Wood**, 56, widow, b. & residing Mid., dau. of Lewis & Henny Peyton. Minister-Holland Walker.

21:03 - 8 Sep. 1870 - **Phillip Peyton**, 34, widower, farmer, b. & residing Mid., son of Lewis & Henny Peyton, married **Lucy Carr**, 18, single, b. & residing Mid., dau. of Thomas Carr. Minister-James Kenner.

21:04 - 28 May 1870 - **Edmond Wake**, 54, widower, farmer, b. & residing Mid., son of Ransome & Molly Wake, married **Eliza Rust**, 30, single, b. & residing Mid., dau. of Robert & Betsy Rust. Minister-M. W. Towill.

21:05 - 16 Sep. 1870 - **Scipio Winkfield**, 52, single, farmer, b. & residing Mid., son of Bluff & Verma Winkfield, married **M. Winkfield**, 25, single, b. & residing Mid., dau. of Edmond & Milly Thomas. Minister-James Kenner.

21:06 - 27 Sep. 1870 - **Robert Thomas**, 21, single, farmer, b. & residing Mid., son of Robert & Judy Thomas, married **Frances Cary**, 20, single, b. & residing Mid., dau. of Lucy Cary. Minister-Holland Walker.

21:07 - 27 Oct. 1870 - **James Kembril**, 27, single, farmer, b. & residing Mid., son of Zeik & Minerva Kembrill, married **Sallie King**, 22, single, b. & residing Mid., dau. of Lewis & Jane King. Minister-James Kenner.

21:08 - 13 Oct. 1870 - **John W. Daniel**, 55, widower, merchant, b. & residing Mid., son of John & Lucy Daniel, married **M. E. Bristow**, 30, single, b. & residing Mid., dau. of L. S. & Cath. Bristow. Minister-John Pollard, Jr.

21:09 - 15 Nov. 1870 - **Henry C. Lewis**, 22, single, farmer, b. & residing Mid., son of Charles & Betsy Lewis, married **M. J. Williams**, 25, single, b. & residing Mid., dau. of Thos. & Edy Williams. Minister-James Kenner.

21:10 - 8 Nov. 1870 - **Charles Grimes**, 32, widower, farmer, b. & residing Mid., son of Jack & Fannie Grimes, married **Elvina Moton**, 22, single, b. & residing Mid., dau. of Benj. & Mary Moton. Minister-James Kenner.

21:11 - 27 Sep. 1870 - **George Jones**, 21, single, farmer, b. & residing Mid., son of A. & Gilly Jones, married **Maria King**, 18, single, b. & residing Mid., dau. of Sally King. Minister-James Kenner.

21:12 - 26 Nov. 1870 - **Ammon Didlake**, 50, widower, farmer, b. & residing Mid., son of Robert & Fannie Didlake, married **A. E. Daniel**, 30, widow, b. & residing Mid., dau. of David & Elizabeth Willon. Minister-R. H. Crittenden.

21:13 - 3 Oct. 1869 - **Chas. Bush**, 23, single, farmer, b. Charles Co., Maryland, residing Mid., son of Norbird Sweetring & Milly, married **Hannah E. Lee**, 18, single, b. & residing Mid., dau. of Maria Dunaway. Minister-John Pollard.

21:14 - 26 Jun. 1870 - **Chas. Green**, 28, single, farmer, b. Gloucester, residing Mid., son of Mary Green, married **Mary Aytes** [or **Ayles**], 23, single, b. Essex, residing Mid., dau. of Iveson Aytes. Minister-Thos. B. Evans.

21:15 - 10 Oct. 1870 - **William Wright**, 60, widower, farmer, b. Essex, residing Mid., son of Isaac & Fanny Wright, married **Robinet Daniel**, 40 single, b. & residing Mid., dau. of Robert Daniel. Minister-Thos. B. Evans.

21:16 - 19 Oct. 1870 - **Amus Nelson**, 21, single, farmer, b. & residing Mid., son of James & Liza Ann Nelson, married **Dianna Wood**, 16, single, b. & residing Mid., dau. of Dick & July Ann Wood. Minister-Holland Walker.

21:17 - 17 Nov. 1870 - **Alfred H. N. Thomas**, 22, single, boatman, b. & residing York, son of George &

Nancy Thomas, married **Mariah R. Deagle**, 14, single, b. & residing Mid., dau. of Henry & Nancy Deagle. Minister-John J. Boss.

21:18 - 1 Dec. 1870 - **Henry Johnson**, 23, single, oysterman, b. & residing Mid., son of Menser & Diana Johnson, married **Betty Young**, 21, single, b. & residing Mid., dau. of Harry & Peggy Young. Minister-Holland Walker.

21:19 - 1 Dec. 1870 - **Henry Mathews**, 23, single, farmer, b. & residing Mid., son of Lausen & Martha Mathews, married **Liney Henry**, 21, single, b. & residing Mid., dau. of Patrick & Lizie Henry. Minister-Holland Walker.

21:20 - 30 Nov. 1870 - **Thomas Gore**, 21, single, farmer, b. Kent Co., Maryland, residing Mid., son of Jas. Gore, married **Ann E. Wiggins**, 21, single, b. Queen Anne Co., Maryland, residing Mid., dau. of Wiggins. Minister-R. H. Crittenden.

21:21 - 20 Dec. 1870 - **Joseph R. Parker**, 23, single, farmer, b. Westchester, NY, residing King & Queen, son of Joseph & Eliz. Parker, married **Willie A. Callis**, 17, single, b. & residing Mid., dau. of John W. & V. A. Callis. Minister-Thos. B. Evans.

21:22 - 25 Dec. 1870 - **Robert Fields**, 22, single, farmer, b. & residing Mid., son of Fielding & Cath. Fields, married **Melinda Harris**, single, b. & residing Mid., dau. of John & Betsy Harris. Minister-Thos. B. Evans.

21:23 - 28 Dec. 1870 - **Frank Everett**, 22, single, farmer, b. South Hampton, [probably Southampton Co.], residing Mid., son of Thomas & Celia Wells, married **Mildred Noel**, 19, single, b. & residing Mid., dau. of James Noel & Char. Morris. Minister-James Kenner.

21:24 - 29 Dec. 1870 - **Richard T. Bristow**, 25, single, farmer, b. & residing Mid., son of Larkin S. & Cath. S. Bristow, married **Lucy E. Saunders**, 25, single, b. & residing Mid., dau. of George & Lucy Saunders. Minister-Thos. B. Evans.

22:01 - 22 Dec. 1870 - **Americus W. Slaughter**, 25, single, farmer, b. Gloucester, residing Mid., son of Geo. B. & Sarah A. Slaughter, married **Emma J. Slaughter**, 25, single, b. & residing Mid., dau. of P. R. & Ann F. Slaughter. Minister-Holland Walker.

22:02 - 22 Dec. 1870 - **J. Burrell**, 33, widower, b. & residing Mid., son of Nelson & Lena Burrell, married **Betty Robinson**, 25, widow, b. & residing Mid., dau. of Patrick & Louisa Henry. Minister-Holland Walker.

23:01 - 19 Jan. 1871 - **W. T. Thornton**, 30, single, mechanic, b. Gloucester, residing Mid., son of John S. & Math. N. Thornton, married **Martha E. Thurston**, single,

b. & residing Mid., dau. of James H. & Martha Thurston. Minister-Thos B. Evans.

23:02 - 19 Jan. 1871 - **Clay Banks**, 21, single, farmer, b. & residing Mid., son of Ming. & Emily Banks, married **Grace Davis**, 22, single, b. & residing Mid., dau. of John & Mary Davis. Minister-James Kenner.

23:03 - 26 Jan. 1871 - **Patric Henry**, 26, widower, farmer, b. & residing Mid., son of Patric & Louisa Henry, married **Betty Ann Bundy**, 17, single, dau. of Sam'l & Jane Bunday. Minister-M. W. Towill.

23:04 - 7 Feb. 1871 - **Stuart Harrington**, 42, widower, merchant, b. Dorchester, Maryland, residing Mid., son of John & Elizabeth Harrington, married **Mary Ann Daniel**, 40, single, b. & residing Mid., dau. of Geo. W. & Mary Daniel. Minister-R. H. Crittenden.

23:05 - 16 Feb. 1871 - **C. Chamberlain**, single, woodcutter, b. King & Queen, residing Mid., son of Washington, married **Matilda Reade**, 18, single, b. Essex, residing Mid., dau. of Reade. Minister-Thos B. Evans.

23:06 - 19 Feb. 1871 - **J. B. Jackson**, 20, single, farmer, b. & residing Mid., son of J. B. & Amanda Jackson, married **Eliz. J. Bruce**, 16, single, b. & residing Mid., dau. of Maria J. Bruce. Minister-John J. Boss.

23:07 - 19 Feb. 1871 - **C. H. Trader**, 22, single, oysterman, b. & residing Mid., son of James & Susan Trader, married **Matilda Muse**, 16, widow, b. & residing Mid., dau. of Thos. D. & Sally Weston. Minister-John J. Boss.

23:08 - 22 Feb. 1871 - **Asey Cook**, 26, single, farmer, b. & residing Mid., son of James & Mary Cook, married **Rusey Key**, 21, single, b. & residing Mid., dau. of Polley Key. Minister-James Kenner.

23:09 - 23 Mar. 1871 - **Allen Becket**, 22, single, farmer, b. & residing Mid., son of W. & Roberta Becket, married **M. Jackson**, 19, single, b. & residing Mid., dau. of John & Mary Jackson. Minister-Holland Walker.

23:10 - 30 Mar. 1871 - **D. H. Harris**, 27, widower, oysterman, b. & residing Mid., son of D. & Salliaris Harris, married **Mary Henry**, 24, single, b. & residing Mid., dau. of Richard & M. Henry. Minister-Holland Walker.

23:11 - 6 Apr. 1871 - **Titus Bagby**, 58, widower, farmer, b. King & Queen, residing Mid., son of Bagby, married **Cath. Laws**, widow, b. & residing Mid., dau. of Laws. Minister-John McClelland.

23:12 - 18 Apr. 1871 - **W. G. New**, 25, single, mechanic, b. & residing Mid., dau. of John C. & Louisa New, married **Sarah E. Boss**, 21, single, b. & residing Mid., dau. of J. B. & N. A. Boss. Minister-John

McClelland.
23:13 - 20 Apr. 1871 - **M. F. Towill**, 23, single, farmer, b. & residing Mid., son of Mark W. & J. F. Towill, married **Sarah E. Blake**, 21, single, b. & residing Mid., dau. of J. L. & Elizabeth Blake. Minister-M. W. Towill.
23:14 - 25 Apr. 1871 - **H. E. Pace**, 19, single, farmer, b. & residing Mid., son of John R. & A. Pace, married **Fannie E. Martin**, 18, single, b. & residing Mid., dau. of H. C. & E. P. Martin. Minister-M. W. Towill.
23:15 - 27 Apr. 1871 - **B. Foreman**, 46, widower, "lumber getting," b. & residing Mid., son of Bristow & Abby Foreman, married **Maria Dunaway**, 40, widow, b. Essex, residing Mid., dau. of Jack Ramsey & Hannah Covington. Minister-James Kenner.
23:16 - 21 June 1871 - **J. W. Walden**, 29, single, farmer, b. & residing Mid., son of Louis & Patsey Walden, married **H. F. Sibley**, 22, single, b. & residing Mid., dau. of Sibley. Minister-R. H. Crittenden.
23:17 - 3 Aug. 1871 - **J. W. Wilson**, 25, single, farmer, b. Mid., residing Gloucester, son of John & Susan Wilson, married **C. E. Blake**, 21, single, b. & residing Mid., dau. of Berkley & Susan Blake. Minister-Holland Walker.
23:18 - 10 Aug. 1871 - **Chas. Wood**, 35, widower, farmer, b. & residing Mid., son of C. & Nancy Wood, married **Ada Williams**, 35, widow, b. & residing Mid., dau. of John & Aggy. Minister-Holland Walker.
23:19 - 22 Aug. 1871 - **J. Abrisch**, 37, widower, miller, b. Prussia, residing Mid., son of Jacob & Mary Abrisch, married **M. Norton**, 23, single, b. & residing Mid., dau. of John & Sarah Nortin. Minister-Holland Walker.
23:20 - 1871 - **J. Rister**, 27, single, professor, b. Baltimore, Maryland, residing Mid., son of Elias & E. Rister, married **Anna Gordy**, 42, widow, b. & residing Mid., dau. of John L. & C. Jackson. Minister-R. H. Crittenden.
23:21 - 31 Aug. 1871 - **W. H. Hart**, single, farmer, b. King & Queen, residing Mid., son of Benj. & Holland Hart, married **M. E. Sutton**, 21, single, b. & residing Mid., dau. of T. R. & Martha Sutton. Minister-Holland Walker.
23:22 - 31 Aug. 1871 - **Jas. Roy**, 21, single, oysterman, b. & residing Mid., son of Susan Roy, married **D. Burke**, 19, single, b. & residing Mid., dau. of W. & Susan Burke. Minister-Holland Walker.
23:23 - Sep. 1871 - **F. Lomax**, 24, single, farmer, b. & residing Mid., son of George & Peggy Lomax, married

Milly Ward, 24, single, b. & residing Mid., dau. of Zack & Martha Ward. Minister-Holland Walker.
23:24 - Sep. 1871 - **Jas. Morris**, 29, single, farmer, b. & residing Mid., son of Zack & Cath. Morris, married **M. E. Lewis**, 35, widow, b. King & Queen, residing Mid., dau. of [not given]. Minister-[not given].
24:25 - 15 Oct. 1871 - **Peter Waites, Jr.**, 21, single, farmer, b. & residing Mid., son of Peter & Anna Waites, married **Virginia Burrell**, 16, single, b. & residing Mid., dau. of Lewis & Betsy Burrell. Minister-Thos B. Evans.
24:26 - 3 Dec. 1871 - **Jos. Robinson**, 23, single, laborer, b. & residing Mid., son of Polida & Racheal Robinson, married **Agnes Burrell**, 16, single, b. & residing Mid., dau. of Richard & Patsy Burrell. Minister-Thos B. Evans.
24:27 - 5 Dec. 1871 - **Daniel Fisher**, 21, single, laborer, b. Dinwiddie, residing Mid., son of Daniel & Jane Fisher, married **Mary Smith**, 17, single, b. & residing Mid., dau. of Cordelia Smith. Minister-James Kenner.
24:28 - 12 Dec. 1871 - **Weston Bristow**, 23, single, merchant, b. & residing Mid., son of Lewis S. & Jane Bristow, married **Ida M. Northan**, 17, single, b. & residing Mid., dau. of Zororabell & Eliz. Northan. Minister-W. W. Wood.
24:29 - 19 Dec. 1871 - **R. B. Spencer**, 23, single, farmer, b. & residing King & Queen, son of Gideon & Mary Spencer, married **India Callis**, 21, single, b. & residing Mid., dau. of James H. & Mary Callis. Minister-Thos B. Evans.
24:30 - 17 Dec. 1871 - **Henry Harris**, 23, single, "laborer in sugar refinery," b. Mid., residing Baltimore, Maryland, son of Robert & Francis Harris, married **Virginia Scott**, 23, single, b. Lancaster, residing Mid., dau. of Robert Scott. Minister-James Kenner.
24:31 - 21 Dec. 1871 - **John W. Barnes**, 21, single, sailor, b. & residing St. Marys, Maryland, son of Jack & Jane Barnes, married **Louisa Thornton**, 16, single, b. & residing Mid., dau. of Ben & Mary Thornton. Minister-James Kenner.
24:32 - 26 Dec. 1871 - **Andrew Groom**, 23, single, farmer, b. & residing Gloucester, son of Richard & Matilda Groom, married **Martha Hall**, 22, single, b. Gloucester, residing Mid., dau. of Wm. & Patsy Hall. Minister-John McClelland.
24:33 - 27 Dec. 1871 - **Augustus Taliaferro**, 22, single, farmer, b. & residing Mid., son of Baylor & Kesiah Taliaferro, married **Fanny Webb**, 20, single, b. &

residing Mid., dau. of John & Hannah Webb. Minister-James Kenner.

24:34 - 27 Dec. 1871 - **James H. Thrift**, 24, single, farmer, b. & residing Mid., son of Roy & Eliz. Thift, married **Emma J. Newbill**, 21, single, b. King & Queen, residing Mid., dau. of John & Eliza Newbill. Minister-J. H. Newbill.

24:35 - 28 Dec. 1871 - **John M. Major**, 29, widower, farmer, b. & residing Mid., son of John & Julia Major, married **Fanny A. Seward**, 20, single, b. & residing Mid., dau. of Ro. & Ann C. Seward. Minister-W. W. Wood.

24:36 - 29 Dec. 1871 - **Henry L. Harris**, 21, single, farmer, b. Essex, residing Mid., son of Wm. & Lucinda Harris, married **Cath. Jackson**, 21, single, b. Essex, residing Mid., dau. of Gowen & Eliza Jackson. Minister-Thos B. Evans.

24:37 - 28 Dec. 1871 - **Robert Burrell**, 21, single, farmer, b. & residing Mid., son of Cordelia Burrell, married **Milly Miles**, 22, single, b. & residing Mid., dau. of Milly Miles. Minister-James Kenner.

24:38 - 28 Dec. 1871 - **Elijah Peterson**, 26, single, farmer, b. & residing Mid., son of Harvey & Violet Peterson, married **Nancy Griffin**, 18, single, b. & residing Mid., dau. of Robt. & Jane Griffin. Minister-James Kenner.

25:01 - 6 Jan. 1872 - **Braxton Gardner**, 38, widower, farmer, b. King & Queen, residing Mid., son of Moses & Winney Gardner, married **Adelia Washington**, 30, widow, b. & residing Mid., dau. of Geo. & Francis Washington. Minister-Thos. B. Evans.

25:02 - 8 Jan. 1872 - **Sam Hacket**, 21, single, farmer, b. Kent Co., Maryland, son of Phil & Charlotte Hacket, married **Lucinda Patterson**, 24, single, b. & residing Mid., dau. of [not given]. Minister-W. W. Wood.

25:03 - 18 Jan. 1872 - **O. D. Marston**, 28, single, farmer, b. Charles City Co., residing Mid., son of Thos. H. & Rebecca Marston, married **Lucy C. Campbell**, 20, single, b. & residing Mid., dau. of Alex & Betty M. Campbell. Minister-Thos. B. Evans.

25:04 - 16 Jan. 1872 - **James Dillin**, 22, single, farmer, b. Kent Co., Maryland, son of [not given], married **Virginia F. Hart**, 21, single, b. & residing Mid., dau. of Wm. & Virginia Hart. Minister-Holland Walker.

25:05 - 8 Jan. 1872 - **Robert Taylor**, 22, single, farmer, b. Caroline, residing Mid., son of John & Grace Taylor, married **Alice Sales**, 20, single, b. Essex, residing Mid., dau. of Robet & Eliza. Sales. Minister-Thos. B. Evans.

25:06 - 25 Jan. 1872 - **Joel C. Wilson**, 21, single, farmer, b. & residing Gloucester, son of John T. & Susan Wilson, married **Emily S. Blake**, 23, single, b. & residing Mid., dau. of Berkly R. & Susanna Blake. Minister-John McClelland.

25:07 - 28 Jan. 1872 - **R. R. Henry**, 25, single, sailor, b. Baltimore, Maryland, residing Mid., son of Robert R. & Mary C. Henry, married **Lucy A. Deagle**, 20, single, b. & residing Mid., dau. of Deale. Minister-R. H. Crittenden.

25:08 - 1 Feb. 1872 - **Taswell Ball**, 43, widower, mechanic, b. King & Queen, residing Mid., son of Jas. & Nancy Ball, married **Mary Broach**, 32, widow, b. & residing Mid., dau. of John & Eliza. Brim. Minister-R. A. Fox.

25:09 - 18 Feb. 1872 - **John R. Marchant**, 35, single, merchant, b. Mathews, residing Mid., son of Thos. & Mary Marchant, married **J. E. Blackburn**, 25, single, b. & residing Mid., dau. of Paulin A. & Nancy S. Blackburn. Minister-J. Harvey Hundley.

25:10 - Feb. 1872 - **Sandy J. Parker**, 30, single, farmer, b. Essex, residing Mid., son of John & Emily Parker, married **Emily S. New**, 22, single, b. & residing Mid., dau. of John C. & Louisa New. Minister-Holland Walker.

25:11 - 25 Feb. 1872 - **Wm. Moore**, 21, single, farmer, b. & residing Mid., son of Job. & Nancy Moore, married **Mary A. Morris**, 22, single, b. & residing Mid., dau. of James & Virginia Morris. Minister-John J. Boss.

25:12 - 27 Feb. 1872 - **Rich'd P. Armstrong**, 23, single, farmer, b. & residing Mid., son of Wm. H. & Martha Armstrong, married **Sarah E. Bristow**, 22, single, b. & residing Mid., dau. of Zack W. & Maria Bristow. Minister-Thos. B. Evans.

25:13 - 29 Feb. 1872 - **John Cundiff**, 59, widower, carpenter, b. & residing Mid., son of Griffin & Mary Cundiff, married **Julia Ann Moore**, widow, b. & residing Mid., dau. of Wm. & Eliza. Christopher. Minister-John McClelland.

25:14 - 7 Mar. 1872 - **J. F. Groom**, 23, single, farmer, b. Gloucester, residing Mid., son of Wm. & Eliza. Groom, married **Paulina Blake**, 18, single, b. & residing Mid., dau. of Wm. J. & Leah Blake. Minister-Holland Walker.

25:15 - 20 Mar. 1872 - **Stephen Page**, 20, single, farmer, b. King & Queen, residing Mid., son of Stephen & Elenor Page, married **Mary Burrell**, 21, single, b. & residing Mid., dau. of Archy & Alsy Burrell. Minister-Thos. B. Evans.

25:16 - 4 Apr. 1872 - **Hen. Williams**, 22, single,

laborer, b. St. Marys, Maryland, residing Mid., son of Mingo & Clara Williams, married **Cath. Lewis**, 18, single, b. & residing Mid., dau. of Albert & Grace Lewis. Minister-James Kenner.

25:17 - 11 Apr. 1872 - **Jesse Davis**, 22, single, farmer, b. Essex, residing Mid., son of Peter & Matilda Davis, married **F. B. Haise**, 21, single, b. & residing Mid., dau. of Jesse & Judy Haise. Minister-L. D. Robinson.

25:18 - 18 Apr. 1872 - **D. A. Taylor**, 22, single, sailor, b. Accomack, residing Mid., son of Savage & Nancy Taylor, married **A. E. Saunders**, 17, single, b. & residing Mid., dau. of John H. & Sarah A. Saunders. Minister-R. H. Crittenden.

25:19 - 25 Apr. 1872 - **Sam'l L. Sparrow**, 27, single, farmer, b. Accomack, residing Mid., son of David & Sarah Sparrow, married **M. F. Long**, 27, single, b. & residing Mid., dau. of David & Susan Long. Minister-John McClelland.

25:20 - 2 May 1872 - **Thos. H. Jefferson**, 23, single, farmer, b. & residing Mid., son of Robert & Anna Jefferson, married **Violet Washington**, 22, widow, b. & residing Mid., dau. of George & Lucy Ann Washington. Minister-James Kenner.

25:21 - 23 May 1872 - **S. Jackson**, 21, single, oysterman, b. & residing Mid., son of John & Nancy Jackson, married **Fanny Jones**, 20, single, b. & residing Mid., dau. of Edward & Eliza Jones. Minister-Holland Walker.

25:22 - 1 Jun. 1872 - **Isaih** [sic] **Harris**, 28, single, farmer, b. & residing Mid., son of Sam'l & Virginia Harris, married **Julia Williams**, 22, single, b. Spotsylvania, residing Mid., dau. of Thos. & Susan Williams. Minister-James Kenner.

25:23 - 1 June 1872 - **Wm. Burwell**, 21, single, sailor, b. & residing Mid., son of Jacob & Racheal Burwell, married **Fanny Davis**, 21, single, b. & residing Mid., dau. of [not given]. Minister-James Kenner.

25:24 - Jun. 1872 - **B. Sears**, 54, widower, farmer, b. & residing Gloucester, son of John & Caroline Sears, married **L. A. Horsley**, 44, widow, b. Gloucester, residing Mid., dau. of Andrew & Mary South. Minister-John McClelland.

26:25 - 9 Jun. 1872 - **Thos. Bratten**, 26, single, sailor, b. Delaware, residing Pennsylvania, son of Thos. & Anna Bratten, married **Rosetta Harrow**, 21, single, b. & residing Mid., dau. of Wm. M. & Almeda Harrow. Minister-John J. Boss.

26:26 - 11 Jun. 1872 - **J. H. Archibald**, 30, single, mechanic, b. Nova Scotia, residing Mid., son of Ephraim

& Marga. Archibald, married **M. F. Bristow**, 16, single, b. & residing Mid., dau. of Rd. H. & F. A. Bristow. Minister-John McClelland.

26:27 - 27 Jun. 1872 - **J. T. C. Hundley**, 31, widower, mechanic, b. King & Queen, residing Mid., son of Lambeth & Mary E. Hundley, married **Mary E. Ingram**, 24, single, b. King & Queen, residing Mid., dau. of George & Ann Ingram. Minister-John McClelland.

26:28 - 18 Jul. 1872 - **Wm. Ewell**, 24, single, laborer, b. Accomack, residing Mid., son of Henry & Nancy Ewell, married **Mary Smith**, 24, single, b. & residing Mid., dau. of James & Susan Smith. Minister-John J. Boss.

26:29 - 24 Jul. 1872 - **Allen Brooker**, 25, widower, farmer, b. & residing Mid., son of Isaac & Nancy Brooker, married **Polly Robinson**, 26, widow, b. & residing Mid., dau. of Robinson. Minister-James Kenner.

26:30 - 8 Aug. 1872 - **Wm. J. Kennard**, 32, widower, farmer, b. Kent Co., Maryland, residing Mid., son of James & Rebecca Kennard, married **Martha J. Hundley**, 19, single, b. & residing Mid., dau. of Hundley. Minister-M. W. Towill.

26:31 - 19 Sep. 1872 - **Rich'd Cooper**, 58, widower, farmer, b. & residing Mid., son of Wm. & Polly Cooper, married **Ann E. Wood**, 28, widow, b. Gloucester, residing Mid., daughter of Heath. Minister-Thos. B. Evans.

26:32 - Sep. 1872 - **Moses Lee**, 37, single, farmer, b. District of Columbia, residing Mid., son of Wm. & Milly Lee, married **N. Taliaferro**, 23, single, b. & residing Mid., dau. of Simon & Minerva Taliaferro. Minister-M. W. Towill.

26:33 - 10 Oct. 1872 - **W. Fitchett**, 26, single, laborer, b. & residing Mid., son of James & Molly Fitchett, married **Cath. Richeson**, 17, single, b. Gloucester, residing Mid., dau. of Joseph & Mary Richeson. Minister-Holland Walker.

26:34 - 10 Oct. 1872 - **F. Montague**, 36, single, farmer, b. & residing Mid., son of Alfred & Cath. Montague, married **Maria Upton**, 36, widow, b. & residing Mid., dau. of [not given]. Minister-Holland Walker.

26:35 - 27 Oct. 1872 - **Wm. Burke, Jr.**, 19, single, oysterman, b. & residing Mid., son of Wm. & Susan Burke, married **Ellen Wood**, 23, single, b. & residing Mid., dau. of [not given]. Minister-James Kenner.

26:36 - 13 Nov. 1872 - **Wm. L. Street**, 25, single, farmer, b. & residing Mid., son of John & Mary Street, married **V. E. Sadler**, 17, single, b. & residing Mid., dau. of G. W. & Puss Sadler. Minister-Thos. B. Evans.

26:37 - 23 Nov. 1872 - **John Castor**, 17, single, laborer, b. & residing Mid., son of Stephen & Judy

Castor, married **Maria Thornton**, 22, single, b. Gloucester, residing Mid., dau. of Riban & Rosa Thornton. Minister-Thos. B. Evans.

26:38 - 23 Nov. 1872 - **Marcus Epps**, 22, single, farmer, b. & residing Mid., son of Yates & Gates, married **M. A. Foster**, 28, single, b. & residing Mid., dau. of Geo. & Hannah Foster. Minister-Thos. B. Evans.

26:39 - 28 Nov. 1872 - **James M. Cole**, 22, single, laborer, b. Chesterfield, residing Mid., son of George & Susan Cole, married **M. C. Rilie**, 26, widow, b. & residing Mid., dau. of Lewis B. & Sarah Seward. Minister-J. W. Ryland.

26:40 - 27 Nov. 1872 - **S. Jackson**, 24, single, farmer, b. & residing Mid., son of Wm. & Martha Jackson, married **S. E. Tousley**, 22, single, b. & residing Mid., dau. of George & Sarah A. Tousley. Minister-M. W. Towill.

26:41 - 28 Nov. 1872 - **C. H. Anderton**, 22, single, mechanic, b. Mathews, residing Mid., son of John G. & Anna W. Anderton, married **Mary L. Trice**, 19, single, b. King & Queen, residing Mid., dau. of James C. Trice. Minister-W. W. Wood.

26:42 - 4 Dec. 1872 - **Leo S. Blake**, 24, single, farmer, b. & residing Mid., son of Jacob & Lucy Blake, married **Susan Hart**, 22, single, b. & residing Mid., dau. of Wm. & Virginia Hart. Minister-Holland Walker.

26:43 - 19 Dec. 1872 - **E. Daniel, Jr.**, 23, widower, farmer, b. & residing Mid., son of Ellyson & Mary E. Daniel, married **F. B. Haile**, 20, single, b. & residing Mid., dau. of Robert & Saphor. Haile. Minister-Thos. B. Evans.

26:44 - 24 Dec. 1872 - **John Miller**, 22, single, farmer, b. Essex, residing Mid., son of Sam. & Valinda Miller, married **Susan A. Bagby**, 20, single, b. & residing Mid., dau. of Armstead & Maria A. Bagby. Minister-Thos. B. Evans.

26:45 - 24 Dec. 1872 - **E. S. Smither**, 25, single, mechanic, b. Essex, residing Mid., son of Ribon M. & Cath. W. Smither, married **B. E. Smither**, 22, single, b. & residing Mid., dau. of Joseph & Lucy E. Smither. Minister-J. W. Ryland.

26:46 - 24 Dec. 1872 - **Wm. E. Payne**, 22, single, farmer, b. Lancaster, residing Mid., son of Thos. & Cath. E. Payne, married **Mary Prince**, 18, single, b. & residing Mid., dau. of Rich'd J. & Cath. H. Prince. Minister-Holland Walker.

26:47 - 26 Dec. 1872 - **G. W. Timons**, 23, single, farmer, b. & residing Mid., son of Robert & Letty Ann Timons, married **Lucy Page**, 22, single, b. King William, residing Mid., dau. of [not given]. Minister-Holland Walker.

26:48 - 31 Dec. 1872 - **Charles Roy**, 26, widower, farmer, b. Mathews, residing Mid., son of Garrett & Susan Roy, married **Betty Dabney**, 20, single, b. King & Queen, residing Mid., dau. of Peter & Malinda Dabney. Minister-Thos. B. Evans.
26:49 - Repeat of line 44, above.
26:50 - Repeat of line 43, above.

27:01 - 23 Jan. 1873 - **William Wilson**, 23, single, laborer, b. & residing Mid., son of Wm. & Jane Wilson, married **M. V. Allen**, 18, single, b. & residing Mid., dau. of Thos. & Mary Allen. Minister-R. H. Crittenden.

27:02 - 15 Jan. 1873 - **C. C. Cornwell**, 35, single, sailor, b. Maryland, residing Mid., son of Joel & Susan M. Cornwell, married **B. E. Layton**, 24, single, b. & residing Mid., dau. of H. L. & S. V. Layton. Minister-W. W. Wood.

27:03 - 27 Jan. 1873 - **J. R. Butler**, 35, widower, merchant, b. King & Queen, residing Baltimore, son of James & M. A. Butler, married **L. R. Evans**, 26, single, b. & residing Mid., dau. of Thos. B. & Eliz. M. Evans. Minister-Thos. B. Evans.

27:04 - 5 Feb. 1873 - **S. D. Sibley**, 45, widower, farmer, b. & residing Mid., son of D. B. & Eliz. Sibley, married **Mary L. Daniel**, 32, widow, b. Gloucester, residing Mid., dau. of P. G. & M. R. Buckner. Minister-John McClelland.

27:05 - 8 Feb. 1873 - **Roy Fauntleroy**, 50, widower, farmer, b. & residing Mid., son of Duke & Letty Fauntleroy, married **Sarah Thurston**, 21, single, b. & residing Mid., dau. of Beverly & Lucy Thurston. Minister-R. H. Crittenden.

27:06 - 9 Feb. 1873 - **Thos. Gaines**, 22, single, farmer, b. King & Queen, residing Mid., son of J. W. & Louisiana Gaines, married **S. J. Cundiff**, 21, single, b. & residing Mid., dau. of Jno. & Jane T. Cundiff. Minister-John J. Boss.

27:07 - 13 Feb. 1873 - **Thos. J. Stiff**, 27, single, farmer, b. & residing Mid., son of Wm. & Nancy C. Stiff, married **Fannie A. Eubank**, 21, single, b. & residing Mid., dau. of Jas. A. & Cornelia Eubank. Minister-Holland Walker.

27:08 - 27 Feb. 1873 - **B. S. Blake**, 24, single, farmer, b. & residing Mid., son of Wm. S. & Cordelia Blake, married **C. A. Miller**, 22, single, b. & residing Mid., dau. of C. A. & Eleanor Miller. Minister-Holland Walker.

27:09 - 4 Mar. 1873 - **Jno. Chowning**, 29, single, mechanic, b. & residing Mid., son of Jas. & Ann C. Chowning, married **F. H. Montague**, 29, single, b.

Gloucester, residing Mid., dau. of Thos. H. Montague. Minister-J. W. Ryland.

27:10 - 13 Mar. 1873 - **Ed. S. Dillard,** 43, widower, mechanic, b. & residing Mid., son of Edmund & Cath. Dillard, married **Alice Street,** 21, single, b. & residing Mid., dau. of John & Mary F. Street. Minister-Thos. B. Evans.

27:11 - 22 Mar. 1873 - **Cornwell Thurston,** 65, widower, farmer, b. & residing Mid., son of [not given], married **Christiana Wood,** 30, single, b. & residing Mid., dau. of Wm. Wood. Minister-M. W. Towill.

27:12 - 1 Apr. 1873 - **J. W. Bristow,** 43, widower, farmer, b. & residing Mid., son of Z. W. & Maria A. Bristow, married **Manda J. Hundley,** 38, widow, b. & residing Mid., dau. of Robert & Mary E. Bray. Minister-J. W. Ryland.

27:13 - 17 Apr. 1873 - **J. H. Thomas,** 24, single, mechanic, b. & residing York Co., son of Wm. & Sarah Thomas, married **A. A. Nichols,** 18, single, b. & residing Mid., dau. of Edgar & Lucy Nichols. Minister-M. W. Towill.

27:14 - 27 Apr. 1873 - **Wm. H. Vaughan,** 40, single, merchant, b. Gloucester, residing Mid., son of Wm. P. & Harriet Vaughan, married **Nancy W. Barrick,** 24, widow, b. & residing Mid., dau. of Jno. D. & Nancy Berry. Minister-J. W. Ryland.

27:15 - 11 May 1873 - **Jno. M. Hughes,** 25, single, merchant, b. Mathews, residing Mid., son of Wm. & Virginia Hughes, married **Ida A. Kelly,** 17, single, b. Baltimore, residing Mid., dau. of Wm. & Nancy Kelly. Minister-John J. Boss.

27:16 - 25 May 1873 - **Ves. Vaughan,** 36, single, merchant, b. Gloucester, residing Mid., son of Wm. P. & Harriet Vaughan, married **Julia M. Boss,** 24, single, b. & residing Mid., dau. of John J. & Amanda Boss. Minister-John McClelland.

27:17 - 18 May 1873 - **R. P. Fones,** 26, single, farmer, b. Westmoreland, residing Richmond Co., son of Jas. B. & M. A. Fones, married **M. S. Pittman,** 21, single, b. Caroline, residing Mid., dau. of J. F. & C. F. Pittman. Minister-John McClelland.

27:18 - 28 May 1873 - **Al. H. Parker,** 29, single, oysterman, b. Essex, residing Mid., son of John & Emily Parker, married **Hen. Major,** 27, single, b. & residing Mid., dau. of Jno. & Julia A. Major. Minister-Holland Walker.

27:19 - 16 May 1873 - **Wilson Green,** 22, single, farmer, b. South Carolina, residing Mid., son of Albert & Adaline Green, married **Louisa Jackson,** 21, single, b. & residing Mid., dau. of Wm. & Adaline Jackson. Minister-R. H. Crittenden.

27:20 - 8 Jun. 1873 - **Jas. A. Croxton**, 38, widower, farmer, b. & residing Essex, son of Fielding & Juliet Croxton, married **Alice R. Dunn**, 24, single, b. Essex, residing Mid., dau. of Lewis & Letty Dunn. Minister-Thos. B. Evans.

27:21 - 11 Jun. 1873 - **Hardy Thompson**, 23, single, farmer, b. Portsmouth, residing Mid., son of Henry & Maria Thompson, married **Julia Robinson**, 21, single, b. & residing Mid., dau. of Isaac & Polly Robinson. Minister-[not given].

27:22 - 26 Jun. 1873 - **R. Milbay**, 33, widower, farmer, b. & residing Mid., son of [not given], married **Sallie Robinson**, 33, single, b. & residing Mid., dau. of Jno. S. & Alsy Robinson. Minister-W. W. Wood.

27:23 - 13 Jul. 1873 - **J. H. Jackson**, 50, widower, merchant, b. Accomack, residing Mid., son of Jno. M. & Rebecca Jackson, married **E. P. Kelly**, 20, single, b. Baltimore, residing Mid., dau. of W. H. & Nancy Kelly. Minister-J. W. Ryland.

27:24 - 4 Jul. 1873 - **A. B. Gardner**, 42, single, farmer, b. & residing Mid., son of Elliot & Lucy Gardner, married **Vir. F. Fisher**, 23, single, b. Essex, residing Mid., dau. of Jas. W. & Eliz. Fisher. Minister-Thos. B. Evans.

28:01 - 22 Sep. 1873 - **John F. Cundiff**, 25, single, mariner, b. & residing Mid., son of John & Jane Cundiff, married **J. Kelley**, 23, single, b. Baltimore, residing Mid., dau. of W. H. & Mary Kelley. Minister-R. H. Crittenden.

28:02 - 30 Oct. 1873 - **J. H. Braxton**, 42, widower, farmer, b. King & Queen, residing Mid., son of Jerry & Polly Braxton, married **Maria Norris**, 30, widow, b. King & Queen, residing Mid., dau. of [not given]. Minister-[not given].

28:03 - 8 Oct. 1873 - **Mathew Glenn**, 44, widower, farmer, b. & residing Mid., son of Mathew & Frances E. Glenn, married **M. A. Harrington**, 21, widow, b. Gloucester, residing Mid., dau. of Geo. W. & Mary Daniel. Minister-John J. Boss.

28:04 - 11 Oct. 1873 - **Tho. C. Hammonds**, 26, single, sailor, b. Gloucester, residing Mid., son of Joseph & Mary Hammonds, married **Martha J. Boss**, 18, single, b. & residing Mid., dau. of Jos. & Cath. Boss. Minister-John McClelland.

28:05 - 12 Nov. 1873 - **Julius G. Keinningham**, 22, single, merchant, b. & residing Mid., son of John C. Keinningham, married **Mollie H. Hudgins**, 21, single, b. & residing Mid., dau. of W. H. & Mildred C. Hudgins. Minister-Holland Walker.

28:06 - 14 Oct. 1873 - **Jas. Amey**, 19, single, farmer, b. Tennessee, residing Mid., son of Henry & Eliza Amey, married **Amanda Peterson**, single, b. & residing Mid., dau. of Joseph & Fanny Peterson. Minister-J. W. Ryland.
28:07 - 18 Oct. 1873 - **G. S. Healy**, 21, single, farmer, b. & residing Mid., son of Ro. & Betty Healy, married **S. C. Gatewood**, 19, single, b. & residing Mid., dau. of W. L. & Lucy Gatewood. Minister-Hervey Hundly.
28:08 - 21 Oct. 1873 - **Jas. Oliver**, 22, single, oysterman, b. & residing Mid., son of Jesse & Mary Oliver, married **F. A. Christopher**, 30, widow, b. & residing Mid., dau. of Jas. & Nancy Stunt. Minister-R. H. Crittenden.
28:09 - 21 Oct. 1873 - **Geo. Cottingham**, 32, single, merchant, b. Worcester, Maryland, residing Lancaster, son of Levin & Mary A. Cottingham, married **V. S. Palmer**, 20, single, b. & residing Mid., dau. of Tho. J. & Emily Palmer. Minister-A. B. Dunaway.
28:10 - 22 Oct. 1873 - **Wilson Littlepage**, 44, single, farmer, b. King William, residing Mid., son of Wilson & Dorothy Littlepage, married **Catharine Jones**, 22, widow, b. & residing Mid., dau. of Sam. & Maria Jones, Minister-Holland Walker.
28:11 - 29 Oct. 1873 - **Geo. W. Daniel**, 47, single, merchant, b. & residing Mid., son of William & Eliz. Daniel, married **Mary E. Spillman**, 30, widow, b. Lancaster, residing Mid., dau. of Jas. & Frances Ingrahm. Minister-R. H. Crittenden.
28:12 - 31 Oct. 1873 - **Griffin Ruffin**, 20, single, farmer & oysterman, b. Essex, residing Mid., son of Jesse & Adeline Ruffin, married **Susan A. Bird**, 21, single, b. & residing Essex, dau. of Alex & Martha Bird. Minister-J. W. Ryland.
28:13 - 11 Nov. 1873 - **W. H. Stiff**, 30, single, merchant, b. & residing Mid.; son of Wm. & Mary C. Stiff, married **Mary L. Chowning**, 23, single, b. & residing Mid., dau. of W. N. & C. A. Chowning. Minister-J. W. Williams.
28:14 - 19 Nov. 1873 - **N. G. Wilson**, 20, single, farmer, b. & residing Mid., son of Geo. W. & Sarah Wilson, married **S. E. Trader**, 28, widow, b. & residing Mid., dau. of Richard W. & Sally Hart. Minister-R. H. Crittenden.
28:15 - 1 Dec. 1873 - **Geo. Jordan**, 22, single, oysterman, b. Portsmouth, Virginia, residing Mid., son of Nancy J. Jorden, married **Anna Boyd**, 21, single, b. & residing Mid., dau. of Henry & Henryetta Boyd. Minister-James Kenner.
28:16 - 6 Dec. 1873 - **Robt. N. Trice**, 38, widower, farmer, b. & residing Mid., son of Thos. & Mary A.

Trice, married **Ann C. Newcomb**, single, b. Gloucester, residing Mid., dau. of W. T. & Louisa Newcomb. Minister-J. W. Ryland.

28:17 - 11 Dec. 1873 - **Ro. E. Wilkins**, 65, widower, tailor, b. Charles City, residing Mid., son of Ro. & Ann H. Wilkins, married **E. A. Blake**, 55, widow, b. King William, residing Mid., dau. of Geo. B. & E. A. Slaughter. Minister-J. W. Ryland.

28:18 - 16 Dec. 1873 - **M. T. Kemp**, 33, single, merchant, b. Gloucester, residing Baltimore, Maryland, son of John J. & Sarah Kemp, married **S. V. Towill**, 31, single, b. & residing Mid., dau. of Mark W. & E. Towill. Minister-M. W. Towill.

28:19 - 19 Nov. 1873 - **Geo. H. Harris**, 42, widower, merchant, b. & residing Mid., son of Jacob & Anna Harris, married **C. Braxton**, 25, single, b. Gloucester, residing Mid., dau. of [not given]. Minister-Geo. H. Harris [sic].

28:20 - 20 Dec. 1873 - **Harry Smith**, 23, single, laborer, b. & residing Mid., son of A. & Nancy Smith, married **Margaret Washington**, 20, single, b. & residing Mid., dau. of Geo. & Matilda Washington. Minister-James Kenner.

28:21 - 22 Dec. 1873 - **Aron Gaines**, 25, single, farmer, b. & residing Essex, son of Thos. & Nancy Gaines, married **Laura Williams**, 25, single, b. & residing Mid., dau. of [not given]. Minister-J. W. Ryland.

28:22 - 23 Dec. 1873 - **J. T. Lewis**, 23, single, farmer, b. & residing Mid., son of S. & Jane Lewis, married **L. Bourrel**, 18, single, b. & residing Mid., dau. of Thos. & Nancy J. Bourrel. Minister-James Kenner.

28:23 - 24 Dec. 1873 - **J. J. Dunlavy**, 21, single, waterman, b. & residing Mid., son of W. B. & M. E. Dunlavy, married **S. F. Ingram**, 21, single, b. Westmoreland, residing Mid., dau. of M. L. & W. Ingram. Minister-Holland Walker.

28:24 - 25 Dec. 1873 - **S. W. Robins**, 22, single, oysterman, b. & residing Lancaster, son of J. M. & S. A. Robins, married **R. B. B. Ingram**, 18, single, b. & residing Mid., dau. of C. W. & M. R. Ingram. Minister-R. H. Crittenden.

29:01 - Repeat of 26:48.

29:02 - 6 Jan. 1874 - **J. H. Beale**, 25, single, oysterman, b. Fauquier, residing Mid., son of Ro. & H. Beale, married **Sally Billups**, 24, single, b. Mathews, residing Mid., dau. of John & Maria Billups. Minister-R. H. Crittenden.

29:03 - 21 Jan. 1874 - **L. S. Bristow**, 26, physician,

b. & residing Mid., son of L. S. & C. S. Bristow, married **M. A. Gaines**, 21, single, b. & residing Mid., dau. of John T. & M. F. Gaines. Minister-W. W. Wood.
  29:04 - 22 Jan. 1874 - **George Lee**, 21, single, farmer, b. & residing Mid., son of Jefferson & C. Lee, married **L. Lewis**, 20, single, b. Essex, residing Mid., dau. of Betsy Lewis. Minister-Thos. B. Evans.
  29:05 - 24 Jan. 1874 - **Geo. Davis**, 22, single, laborer, b. Gloucester, residing Mid., son of Henry & Cath. Davis, married **A. Johnson**, 18, single, b. & residing Mid., dau. of Oney Johnson. Minister-James Kenner.
  29:06 - 20 Jan. 1874 - **W. T. Thrift**, 31, widower, farmer, b. & residing Mid., son of Ro. & Eliza Thrift, married **Mary A. Daniel**, 21, single, b. & residing Mid., dau. of Ellison & Mary Daniel. Minister-J. W. Ryland.
  29:07 - 10 Feb. 1874 - **Alex Midgett**, 24, single, lighthouse keeper, b. & residing Elizabeth City, North Carolina, son of John C. & Eliz. Midgett, married **A. Harrison**, 24, single, b. & residing Mid., dau. of W. M. & A. Harrison. Minister-John J. Boss.
  29:08 - 19 Feb. 1874 - **John Laws**, 36, widower, farmer, b. & residing Mid., son of Linsey & Coly, married **M. E. Bundy**, 22, single, b. & residing Mid., dau. of S. & M. Jane Bundy. Minister-James Kenner.
  29:09 - 27 Feb. 1874 - **Joseph Robinson**, 25, widower, farmer, b. & residing Mid., son of Polloda & R. Robinson, married **Ellen Gresham**, 18, single, b. King & Queen, residing Mid., dau. of [not given]. Minister-[not given].
  29:10 - 2 Mar. 1874 - **W. W. Wright**, 38, widower, sea captain, b. Accomack, residing Mid., son of Walter & St. E. Wright, married **E. Hundley**, 20, single, b. & residing Mid., dau. of Tho. H. & Eliz. Hundley. Minister-R. H. Crittenden.
  29:11 - 4 Mar. 1874 - **William Smith**, 21, single, farmer, b. & residing Lancaster, son of Wm. & H. Smith, married **Clara Blackwell**, 18, single, b. Lancaster, residing Mid., dau. of Oscar & W. Blackwell. Minister-James Kenner.
  29:12 - 13 Mar. 1874 - **S. Robinson**, 21, single, farmer, b. & residing Mid., son of P. & Rachel Robinson, married **F. A. Harris**, 23, single, b. & residing Mid., dau. of Eliza Harris. Minister-[not given].
  29:13 - 14 Mar. 1874 - **Joseph Corbin**, 21, single, farmer, b. & residing Mid., son of Joseph & Milly Corbin, married **Martha Boyd**, 20, single, b. & residing Mid., dau. of Thomas Boyd. Minister-J. W. Ryland.
  29:14 - 16 Mar. 1874 - **Daniel H. Nagle**, 29, single, farmer, b. York Co., Pennsylvania, residing Mid., son of

Michael & R. Nagle, married **Jane Chrisper**, 19, single, b. & residing Mid., dau. of J. P. & M. J. Chrisp<u>in</u>. Minister-Holland Walker.

29:15 - 24 Mar. 1874 - **A. C. Robinson**, 29, single, farmer, b. & residing Mid., son of John D. & Sarah Robinson, married **Ann L. Blake**, 31, widow, b. Gloucester, residing Mid., dau. of [not given]. Minister-Holland Walker.

29:16 - 28 Mar. 1874 - **J. W. Deagle**, 26, single, oysterman, b. & residing Mid., son of Henry & Nancy Deagle, married **Susan Hundley**, 20, single, b. & residing Mid., dau. of Tho. & Eliz. Hundley. Minister-R. H. Crittenden.

29:17 - 31 Mar. 1874 - **G. L. Johnson**, 25, single, laborer, b. & residing Mid., son of George & C. Johnson, married **Ann Vaughan**, 20, single, b. & residing Mid., dau. of C. & Sarah Vaughan. Minister-R. H. Crittenden.

29:18 - 3 Apr. 1874 - **W. H. Blake**, 34, widower, farmer, b. & residing Mid., son of W. S. & C. Blake, married **Mary J. Sadler**, 38, widow, b. & residing Mid., dau. of John C. & M. A. New. Minister-Holland Walker.

29:19 - 4 Apr. 1874 - **Lee Walker**, 60, widower, farmer, b. & residing Mid., son of Charles & Rachel Walker, married **M. Ann Kelly**, 19, single, b. & residing Mid., dau. of Richard & Jane Kelly. Minister-R. H. Crittenden.

29:20 - 15 Apr. 1874 - **James Orell**, 36, widower, seaman, b. King & Queen, residing Mid., son of Robert & Frances Orell, married **M. A. Weston**, 34, widow, b. Fredericksburg, residing Mid., dau. of T. & Almira Jenkins. Minister-John J. Boss.

29:21 - 22 Apr. 1874 - **Thos. H. Jenkins**, 24, widower, oysterman, b. Gloucester, residing Mid., son of Tho. & Mary Jenkins, married **V. H. Harris**, 16, single, b. Gloucester, residing Mid., dau. of John W. & Eliz. Harris. Minister-C. D. Crawley.

29:22 - 4 Jun. 1874 - **Richard Webb**, 23, widower, oysterman, b. & residing Mid., son of John & Harriet Webb, married **Caroline Johnson**, 18, single, b. King William, residing Mid., dau. of Christiana Johnson. Minister-James Kenner.

29:23 - 10 Jun. 1874 - **James W. Mayo**, 33, widower, shoemaker, b. King & Queen, residing Mid., son of J. D. F. [&] Ann Mayo, married **M. A. Enos**, 21, single, b. & residing Mid., dau. of W. H. & Eliz. Enos. Minister-Holland Walker.

29:24 - 12 Jun. 1874 - **J. W. Armstrong**, 23, single, farmer, b. & residing Mid., son of W. H. & M. A. Armstrong, married **Alice W. Davis**, 18, single, b. King & Queen, residing Mid., dau. of Stege D. & Eliz. Davis. Minister-W. W. Wood.

30:01 - 17 Jun. 1874 - **M. Page**, 24, single, farmer, b. King & Queen, residing Mid., son of Manuell & A. E. Page, married **E. Robinson**, 21, single, residing Mid., dau. of [not given]. Minister-J. W. Ryland.

30:02 - 17 Jun. 1874 - **Chas. Brockenbrough**, 19, single, oysterman, b. Gloucester, residing Mid., son of Lewis & Martha Brockenbrough, married **P. Robinson**, 32, single, b. King & Queen, residing Mid., dau. of Benj. & Eliz. Robinson. Minister-J. W. Ryland.

30:03 - 15 Jul. 1874 - **F. C. Southerland**, 21, single, oysterman, b. & residing Mid., son of Geo. Thos. & N. Southerland, married **M. E. King**, single, b. & residing Mid., dau. of Lewis & Jane King. Minister-James Kenner.

30:04 - 5 Sep. 1874 - **S. R. T. Rust**, 21, single, oysterman, b. & residing Mid., son of A. & W. Rust, married **Winnie Beady**, 21, single, b. & residing Mid., dau. of D. & M. Ready. Minister-Geo. W. Wood.

30:05 - 19 Sep. 1874 - **Manuel Green**, 21, single, oysterman, b. King & Queen, residing Mid., son of Manuel & Judy Green, married **Ellen Boyd**, 20, single, b. & residing Mid., dau. of Henry Boyd. Minister-Geo. W. Wood.

30:06 - 1874 - **Isaac Swanson**, single, laborer, b. King & Queen, residing Mid., son of [not given], married **Margaret Sears**, single, b. & residing Mid., dau. of Betsy Roane. Minister-Thos. B. Evans.

30:07 - 11 Oct. 1874 - **Herbert L. Smither**, 22, single, merchant, b. & residing Mid., son of Jos. E. & Lucy C. Smither, married **Fannie R. Gresham**, 20, single, b. & residing Mid., dau. of Rich'd T. A. & Lucy A. Gresham. Minister-W. W. Wood.

30:08 - 31 Oct. 1874 - **Burnett Lee**, 56, widower, farmer, b. King William, residing Mid., son of John & Anna Lee, married **Betsy Jackson**, 22, single, b. & residing Mid., dau. of [not given]. Minister-James Kenner.

30:09 - 1874 - **Alexander Trader**, 21, single, sailor, b. & residing Mid., son of Jas. H. & Susan Trader, married **Sarah G. Wilson**, 17, single, b. & residing Mid., son of Geo. W. & Sarah Wilson. Minister-John J. Boss.

30:10 - 22 Nov. 1874 - **Josiah C. Ailworth**, 21, single, mariner, b. & residing Mid., son of Josiah D. & Roberta Ailworth, married **Fanny B. Glenn**, 20, single, b. & residing Mid., dau. of Rich'd M. & Betty A. Glenn. Minister-M. W. Towill.

30:11 - 1 Dec. 1874 - **B. F. Hart**, 30, single, merchant, b. & residing Mid., son of B. F. & H. C. Hart, married **Sarah C. Eubank**, 21, single, b. & residing Mid., dau. of Jas. A. & C. Eubank. Minister-W. W. Wood.

30:12 - 2 Dec. 1874 - **Rich'd H. Bristow, Jr.**, 20,

single, blacksmith, b. & residing Mid., son of Rich'd H.
& Frances Bristow, married **Nanny T. Grennolds**, 16,
single, b. Maryland, residing Mid., dau. of Southy &
Mary Grennolds. Minister-C. D. Crawley.

30:13 - 17 Dec. 1874 - **Francis South**, 22, single,
farmer, b. & residing Mid., son of Jos. V. & Malica
South, married **Mary W. Clarke**, 21, single, b. & residing
Mid., dau. of John & Mary Clarke. Minister-Holland
Walker.

30:14 - 24 Dec. 1874 - **Jos. Robinson**, 23, single,
farmer, b. & residing King & Queen, son of Jack & Mary
Robinson, married **Useba Morris**, 22, single, b. &
residing Mid., dau. of Wm. & Mary Morris. Minister-
Chas. H. Harris.

30:15 - 24 Dec. 1874 - **Thomas Harris**, 22, single,
oysterman, b. & residing Mid., son of Robert & Fanny
Harris, married **Jane Lockley**, 22, single, b. & residing
Mid., dau. of Winney Lockley. Minister-John W. Scott.

30:16 - 26 Dec. 1874 - **Robert Willis**, 21, single,
laborer, b. & residing Mid., son of Thomas Jones & Fanny
Willis, married **George Anna Devenport**, 20, single, b.
Gloucester, residing Mid., dau. of George & Mira
Devenport. Minister-James Kenner.

30:17 - 29 Dec. 1874 - **David T. Evans**, 22, single,
sailor, b. Dorchester, Maryland, residing Mid., son of
Francis & Julia Ann Evans, married **Anna E. Ball**, 22,
single, b. St.[sic] George Co., Maryland, residing Mid.,
dau. of Rich'd T. & Eliza Ball. Minister-John J. Boss.

30:18 - Jan. 1875 - **Geo. Thomas Bull**, 23, single,
farmer, b. & residing Mid., son of Thomas A. & Mary A.
Bull, married **Sarah E. Davis**, 17, single, b. & residing
Mid., dau. of George W. Davis. Minister-John J. Boss.

30:19 - 29 Dec. 1874 - **Rich'd B. Seward**, 21, single,
farmer, b. & residing Mid., son of Robert & Ann Seward,
married **Mary E. Roane**, 21, single, b. & residing Mid.,
dau. of Wm. P. & Susan Roane. Minister-J. D. Hank.

30:20 - Jan. 1875 - **Thomas F. Hundley**, 22, single,
boatman, b. & residing Mid., son of Jas. & Elizabeth
Hundley, married **Sarah E. Kennard**, 21, single, b. Kent
Co., Maryland, residing Mid., dau. of James & Sarah E.
Kennard. Minister-M. W. Towill.

30:21 - 31 Dec. 1874 - **Isaac Hodges**, 21, single,
oysterman, b. Portsmouth, residing Mid., son of David &
Dianna Hodges, married **Fanny Robinson**, 18, single, b. &
residing Mid., dau. of Isaac & Polly Robinson.
Minister-James Kenner.

30:22 - 13 June 1874 - **Benj. Bundy**, 22, single,
farmer, b. Campbell Co., residing Mid., son of Benj'n &
Judy Bundy, married **Betty Carter**, 20, single, b. &
residing Mid., dau. of Martha Ann Carter. Minister-
Thos. B. Evans.

31:01 - 7 Jan. 1875 - **James Dillin**, 24, widower, farmer, b. Philadelphia, residing Mid., son of John & Ellen Dillin, married **Louise Blake**, 24, single, b. & residing Mid., dau. of Wm. J. & Sara Blake. Minister-Holland Walker.

31:02 - 7 Jan. 1875 - **Wm. A. Harrow**, 27, single, farmer, b. & residing Mid., son of An. J. Harrow, married **Missouri Tho. Clarke**, 21, single, b. & residing Mid., dau. of Wm. & Loi Ann Clarke. Minister-M. W. Towill.

31:03 - 9 Jan. 1875 - **Geo. Whiting**, 24, single, farmer, b. & residing Mid., son of Sam'l & Patsy Whiting married **Martha Daniel**, 16, single, b. & residing Mid., dau. of Carter & Betty Daniel. Minister-George W. Wood.

31:04 - 14 Jan. 1875 - **Christopher Robinson Jones**, 22, single, farmer, b. & residing Mid., son of Abraham & Louisa Jones, married **Mary Ellen Jackson**, 21, single, b. & residing Mid., dau. of Wm. & Martha Jackson. Minister-Holland Walker.

31:05 - 23 Jan. 1875 - **Dennis Page**, 22, single, oysterman, b. & residing Mid., son of Reubin & Molly Page, married **Jenetta Robinson**, 18, single, b. Richmond, residing Mid., dau. of [not given]. Minister-James Kenner.

31:06 - 27 Jan. 1875 - **Thos. C. Sibley**, 27, single, farmer, b. & residing Mid., son of Jas. D. & Susan Ann Sibley, married **Mary L. Major**, 21, single, b. & residing Mid., dau. of Robert S. Major. Minister-Holland Walker.

31:07 - 28 Jan. 1875 - **Wilinon C. Miller**, 23, single, farmer, b. & residing Mid., son of Christopher A. & Ellenor Miller, married **Amanda J. Sibley**, 24, single, b. & residing Mid., dau. of Norman C. & Mary E. Sibley. Minister-Holland Walker.

31:08 - 1 Feb. 1875 - **Philemon Gatewood**, 2, single, farmer, b. & residing Mid., son of Susan Gatewood, married **Sarah Miller**, 19, single, b. & residing Mid., dau. of Sarah Miller. Minister-George W. Wood.

31:09 - 3 Feb. 1875 - **M. P. Maxwell**, 29, single, merchant, b. New Castle Co., Delaware, residing Mid., son of Wm. & Rachel Maxwell, married **Juliet B. Hackney**, 28, single, b. & residing Mid., dau. of Jas. H. & Mary A. Hackney. Minister-J. D. Hank.

31:10 - 11 Feb. 1875 - **Wm. J. Powill**, 22, single, b. & residing Mid., son of Wm. & Martha Powill, married **Laura Ann Fleet**, 16, single, b. & residing Mid., dau. of Henry & Eliza Turner. Minister-James Kenner.

31:11 - 11 Feb. 1875 - **Jas. Wilson**, 49, widower, farmer, b. & residing Mid., son of Jas. & Milly Wilson, married **Louisa Burrell**, 45, widow, b. & residing Mid., dau. of Louis & Heney Peyton. Minister-George W. Wood.

31:12 - 11 Feb. 1875 - **Wm. T. Thornton**, 36, widower, mechanic, b. Gloucester, residing Mid., son of John & Catharine Thornton, married **Mary Jane Newcomb**, widow, b. & residing Mid., dau. of Wm. Johnson. Minister-J. W. Ryland.

31:13 - 13 Feb. 1875 - **Peter Jackson**, 21, single, farmer, Gloucester, residing Mid., son of John & Cordelia Jackson, married **Sarah Holmes**, 18, single, b. & residing Mid., dau. of Henry & Catharine Holmes. Minister-James Kenner.

31:14 - 23 Mar. 1875 - **Wm. S. Montague**, 33, single, machinist, b. Gloucester, residing Richmond, son of Thos. B. & Sarah Montague, married **Hattie Clegg**, 27, single, b. & residing Mid., dau. of Hillary Clegg. Minister-J. D. Hank.

31:15 - 30 Mar. 1875 - **Warner H. Shackelford**, 24, single, oysterman, b. Gloucester, residing Mid., son of John & Sarah Shackelford, married **Emma F. Walker**, 21, single, b. Gloucester, residing Mid., dau. of Peter & Louisa Walker. Minister-Thos. B. Evans.

31:16 - Apr. 1875 - **Jas. H. Powell**, 22, single, farmer, b. & residing Mid., son of Wm. & Martha Powill, married **Annie E. Taliaferro**, 16, single, b. Mathews, residing Mid., dau. of Benja. & Martha Taliaferro. Minister-M. W. Towill.

31:17 - 8 Apr. 1875 - **Zack Ward**, 23, single, farmer, b. & residing Mid., son of Zack & Adeline Ward, married **Betty Gardner**, 20, single, b. & residing Mid., dau. of Braxton & Adeline Gardner. Minister-George W. Wood.

31:18 - 14 Apr. 1875 - **James O. Healy**, 23, single, farmer, b. & residing Mid., son of Jas. T. & Mary F. Healy, married **Vashti Thurston**, 16, single, b. & residing Mid., dau. of James H. & Dorothy M. Thurston. Minister-Thos. B. Evans.

31:19 - Apr. 1875 - **Rich'd Burrly**, 24, single, farmer, b. & residing Mid., son of Ellick & Easter Burrly, married **Mary Lee**, 24, single, b. King & Queen, residing Mid., dau. of [not given]. Minister-James Kenner.

31:20 - 25 Apr. 1875 - **Lycus Nelson**, 24, single, hostler, b. & residing Gloucester, son of Lycus & Judy Nelson, married **Maria L. Bundy**, 20, single, b. & residing Mid., dau. of Sam'l & Jane Bundy. Minister-James Kenner.

31:21 - 15 May 1875 - **Jos. W. Ashbon**, 22, single, oysterman, b. & residing Lancaster, son of Griffin & Alicia Ashbon, married **Lucy T. Tullington**, 16, single, b. Gloucester, residing Mid., dau. of John E. & Rosa J. Tullington. Minister-J. W. Ryland.

31:22 - 18 May 1875 - **John F. Tompkins**, 37, single,

machinist, b. Essex, residing Mid., son of Joseph T. & Jane Tompkins, married **George Anne Smith**, 28, single, b. King & Queen, residing Mid., dau. of George Wm. & Amie F. Smith. Minister-J. W. Ryland.

31:23 - Feb. 1875 - **Geo. T. Bull**, 23, single, farmer, b. & residing Mid., son of Thos. R. & Mary A. Bull, married **Sarah E. Davis**, 17, single, b. & residing Mid., dau. of Geo. W. Davis. Minister-John J. Boss.

32:01 - 27 May 1875 - **Thomas Brooks**, 23, single, oysterman, b. & residing Mathews, son of Tama Broockes, married **Emily Walker**, 18, single, b. & residing Mid., dau. of Mary Roane.

32:02 - 10 Jun. 1875 -**Peter W. Revere**, 23, single, farmer, b. & residing King & Queen, son of Lawson & Leiga Revere, married **Georgia E. Lee**, 19, single, b. & residing Mid., dau. of O. & E. N. Lee. Minister-Thos. B. Evans.

32:03 - 26 Jun. 1875 - **Joshua Dudley**, 37, widower, oysterman, b. Gloucester, residing Mid., son of John & Fanny Dudley, married **Hannah Bush**, 22, widow, b. & residing Mid., dau. of Maria Bush. Minister-James Kenner.

32:04 - 1 Jul. 1875 - **Ro. H. Spencer**, widower, merchant, b. & residing King & Queen, son of Ro. M. & Harriet Spencer, married **Martha E. Evans**, single, b. & residing Mid., dau. of Thomas B. & Elizabeth Evans. Minister-Thos. B. Evans.

32:05 - 9 Jul. 1875 - **Sam'l Lewis, Jr.**, 23, single, farmer, b. & residing Mid., son of John Henry & Amy Lewis, married **Lucy Ann Holmes**, 24, single, b. & residing Mid., dau. of Wm. & Clara Holmes. Minister-George W. Wood.

32:06 - 22 Jul. 1875 - **Archibald Rust**, 50, widower, farmer, b. Lancaster, residing Mid., son of [not given], married **Molly Browne**, 50, widow, b. & residing Mid., dau. of George & Amy Rust. Minister-James Kenner.

32:07 - 31 Jul. 1875 - **Wm. Whitney**, 21, single, farmer, b. & residing Mid., son of Sam'l & Patsy Whiting, married **Lucy Davis**, 21, single, b. & residing Mid., dau. of Peter & Fanny Davis. Minister-James Kenner.

32:08 - 22 Aug. 1875 - **Wm. E. Pane**, 24, widower, farmer, b. Lancaster, residing Mid., son of Thom's & Catharine Pane, married **Lula B. French**, 16, single, b. & residing Mid., dau. of Thos. & Amanda French. Minister-not given].

32:09 - 18 Sep. 1875 - **Dilly F. Davis**, 22, single, oysterman, b. King & Queen, residing Mid., son of Hany & Margaret Davis, married **Maria Morris**, 21, single, b. &

residing Mid., dau. of George & Charlotte Morris. Minister-James Kenner.

32:10 - 26 Sep. 1875 - **Wm. Ball**, 45, single, farmer, b. King & Queen, residing Mid., son of Loui & Anny Ball, married **Martha Webb**, 27, single, b. King & Queen, residing Mid., dau. of Robin & Milly Webb. Minister-M. W. Towill.

32:11 - 23 Sep. 1875 - **John W. Daniel**, 61, widower, merchant, b. & residing Mid., son of John & Lucy Daniel, married **Mary E. Watton**, 25, single, b. King & Queen, residing Mid., dau. of Wm. & Sarah Watton. Minister-J. D. Hank.

32:12, - 9 Oct. 1875 - **Cary Ed. Burrus**, 23, single, laborer, b. James City, residing Mid., son of Henry & Harriet Burruss, married **Sarah Nelson**, 21, single, b. & residing Mid., dau. of James & Eliza Ann Nelson. Minister-M. W. Towill.

32:13 - 14 Oct. 1875 - **Jas. H. Johnson**, 23, single, farmer, b. & residing Mid., son of Henry & Betty Johnson, married **Martha George**, 18, single, b. & residing Mid., dau. of George & Fenton George. Minister-James Kenner.

32:14 - 9 Oct. 1875 - **James Bundy**, 26, single, farmer, b. & residing Mid., son of Sam'l J. & Mary Jane Bundy, married **Betty Nelson**, 21, single, b. & residing Mid., dau. of James & Eliza Ann Nelson. Minister-M. W. Towill.

32:15 - 14 Oct. 1875 - **Thos. E. Hammons**, 27, widower, farmer, b. Kent Co., Delaware, residing Mathews, son of Joseph & Mary Ann Hammonds, married **Matilda A. New**, 25, single, b. & residing Mid., dau. of John C. & Louisa A. New. Minister-Holland Walker.

32:16 - 16 Oct. 1875 - **Jas. Henry Braxton**, 43, widower, farmer, b. & residing Mid., son of Jerry & Polly Braxton, married **Sarah Ann Bagby**, 25, widow, b. King & Queen, residing Mid., dau. of Titus Bagby.

32:17 - 15 Oct. 1875 - **Abram L. Jones**, 37, widower, farmer, b. Caroline, residing Mid., son of Robert & Courtney Jones, married **Harriett Carr**, 23, single, b. & residing Mid., dau. of Burnett & Sarah Carr. Minister-J. W. Scott.

32:18 - 16 Oct. 1875 - **John Lewis**, 28, single, oysterman, b. & residing Mid., son of Tascoe & Clara Lewis, married **Lucy Upshaw**, 19, single, b. & residing Mid., dau. of Daniel & Frances Upshaw. Minister-James Kenner.

32:19 - 16 Oct. 1875 - **Israel Williams**, 25, single, farmer, b. Baltimore, Maryland, residing Mid., son of Henry & Mary Ellen Williams, married **Augusta Upshaw**, 21, single, b. & residing Mid., dau. of Daniel & Frances Upshaw. Minister-James Kenner.

32:20 - 21 Oct. 1875 - **Wm. Taliaferro**, 44, widower, farmer, b. Gloucester, residing Mid., son of Titus & Susan Williams, married **Matilda Robinson**, 41, widow, b. King & Queen, residing Mid., dau. of John & Jane Smith. Minister-James Kenner.

32:21 - 21 Oct. 1875 - **Churchill Taylor**, 21, oysterman, b. & residing Mid., son of Littleton & Betsy Taylor, married **Martha Wormley**, 18, single, b. & residing Mid., dau. of Rich'd & Louisa Wormley. Minister-James Kenner.

32:22 - Oct. 1875 - **James Iverson**, 21, single, oysterman, b. Caroline, residing Mid., son of Wm. & Maria Iverson, married **Venus Williams**, 23, single, b. & residing Mid., dau. of Chas. Williams. Minister-James Kenner.

33:01 - 10 Nov. 1875 - **Thos G. Jones**, 32, single, lawyer, b. & residing Mid., son of Lewis & Sally Jones, married **M. Alice Percifull**, 22, single, b. & residing Mid., dau. of Joseph & Mary A. Percifull. Minister-J. D. Hank.

33:02 - 10 Nov. 1875 - **George H. Weston**, 23, single, oysterman, b. Mathews, residing Mid., son of John & C. Weston, married **Columbia Kellum**, 20, single, b. & residing Mid., dau. of Rich'd H. & Bettie Kellum. Minister-Morris Montgomery.

33:03 - 9 Nov. 1875 - **Jos. E. Price**, 31, widower, carpenter, b. New Castle, Delaware, son of Sam'l & Ann Price, married **G. G. Glenn**, 22, single, b. & residing Mid., dau. of Rich'd & Bettie Glenn. Minister-M. W. Towill.

33:04 - 11 Nov. 1875 - **Rich'd M. Glenn**, 25, single, lighthouse keeper, b. Richmond Co., residing Mid., son of Rich'd M. & Bettie Glenn, married **Ann M. L. Blake**, 19, single, b. & residing Mid., dau. of John L. & Matilda E. Blake. Minister-M. W. Towill.

33:05 -25 Nov. 1875 - **Wm. T. Hall**, 24, single, blacksmith, b. & residing Mid., son of Thomas S. & Pelina J. Hall, married **Nannie A. Miller**, 20, single, b. & residing Mid., dau. of John D. & Mary Miller. Minister-[not given].

33:06 - 2 Dec. 1875 - **Franklin Meunderville**, 21, single, sailor, b. New York, residing Long Island, son of Nicolas & Elizabeth Meunderville, married **Columbia C. New**, 21, single, b. & residing Mid., dau. of Jas. W. & Lucy A. New. Minister-[not given].

33:07 - 16 Dec. 1875 - **S. Roszel Donohue**, 24, single, editor, b. London, residing West Point, Virginia, son of S. G. Donohue, married **Hela Eubank**, 21, single, b. & residing Mid., dau. of Jos. C. & E. B. Eubank. Minister-J. D. Hank.

33:08 - 15 Dec. 1875 - **Jesse B. Morris**, 24, single, farmer, b. Kent Co., Maryland, residing Mid., son of John W. & Mary R. Morris, married **Willie R. Selby**, 19, single, b. York Co., residing Mid., dau. of Jas. P. & Willie Selby. Minister-J. D. Hank.

33:09 - 23 Dec. 1875 - **Wm. Minor**, 21, single, laborer, b. & residing Mid., son of Henry & Nelly Minor, married **Lucy Ann Evans**, 21, single, b. & residing Mid., dau. of [not given]. Minister-George W. Wood.

33:10 - 23 Dec. 1875 - **Geo. Wm. Daniel**, 21, single, merchant, b. & residing Mid., son of Geo. W. & Mary A. Daniel, married **Annie L. Ingram**, 21, single, b. & residing Mid., dau. of Thos. & Mary Ingram. Minister-John J. Boss.

33:11 - 23 Dec. 1875 - **Buck Tunstall**, 21, single, farmer, b. King & Queen, residing Mid., son of Benja. & Milly Tunstall, married **Jane Bagby**, 21, single, b. King & Queen, residing Mid., dau. of Alcy Bagby. Minister-George W. Wood.

33:12 - 24 Dec. 1875 - **Thos. Harris**, 21, single, farmer, b. King & Queen, residing Mid., son of Ro. & Judy Harris, married **Jane Reed**, 20, single, b. & residing Mid., dau. of Lewis & Anny Brooking. Minister-[not given].

Transcriber's Note: From this point, the remaining persons listed in this Register are also entered in Marriage Register 2, 1876-1890 (which, for several years, does not contain the names of the ministers who performed the marriages, but does state the race of the parties). Therefore, the following records have been checked in both books, and any additional information contained in Marriage Register 2 has been added to this transcript of Marriage Register 1.

The race given in the marriage records will not always match the Census records. In the marriage records, the word "colored" was used to signify that the person was not white. "Colored" could mean African-American, Native American, a person of mixed blood (whatever the degree), or a Melungeon. It is impossible to determine to which of the above groups the persons belonged.

Whatever term was used in the original records for race identification is also used in this transcript:
   (C) - Colored
   (W) - White
   (B) - Black

33:13 - 30 Dec. 1875 - **Fred Dickinson**, 28, single, laborer, b. Essex, residing Mid., son of Wm. & Julia Dickinson, married **Laviny Lomax**, 20, single, b. &

residing Mid., dau. of Jas. [&] Eudora Lomax. (C) Minister-George W. Wood.

33:14 - 28 Dec. 1875 - **Geo. A. Ball**, 23, single, oysterman, b. Anne Arundel Co., Maryland, residing Mid., son of Rich'd & Elizabeth Ball, married **Estel V. Deagle**, 17, single, b. & residing Mid., dau. of Henry & Nancy Deagle. (W) Minister-John J. Boss.

33:15 - 28 Dec. 1875 - **Jas. Boyd**, 30, widower, b. & residing Mid., son of Phillip & Sally Boyd, married **Silvey Ann Churchhill**, 21, single, b. & residing Mid., dau. of Leroy & Jane Churchhill. (C) Minister-George W. Wood.

33:16 - 29 Dec. 1875 - **Columbus S. Burton**, 30, single, mechanic, b. Gloucester, residig Mid., son of Simon H. & Matilda Burton, married **Lucy L. Hackney**, 25, single, b. & residing Mid., James H. & Mary Hackney. (W) Minister-J. D. Hank.

33:17 - 30 Dec. 1875 - **Mingo Banks**, 59, widower, farmer, b. King & Queen, residing Mid., son of Mingo & Mary Banks, married **Dina Johnson**, 48, widow, b. & residing Mid., dau. of Jacob Johnson. (C) Minister-James Kenner.

33:18 - 30 Dec. 1875 - **Thos. H. Frazier**, 21, single, laborer, b. & residing Mid., son of Thos. & Eliza Frazier, married **Mary Eliz. Daniel**, 22, single, b. & residing Mid., dau. of [not given]. (C) Minister-James Kenner.

34:01 - 1 Jan. 1876 - **Wm. Williams**, 33, single, laborer, b. Essex, residing Mid., son of Wm. & Mary Williams, married **Margaret Boyd**, 23, single, b. & residing Mid., dau. of Phil & Sally Boyd. (C)

34:02 - 13 Jan. 1876 - **Thos H. Carter**, 23, single, sailor, b. & residing Mid., son of Addison & Sarah Carter, married **Etta B. Crittenden**, 17, single, b. & residing Mid., dau. of Thos. H. & Sally Crittenden. (W)

34:03 - 14 Jan. 1876 - **Hamilton Burwell**, 22, single, farmer, b. & residing Mid., son of [not given], married **Sallie Carter**, 25, single, b. & residing Mid., dau. of Jones & Martha Ann Carter. (C)

34:04 - 19 Jan. 1876 - **James T. Oliver**, 22, widower, farmer, b. Mid., residing Lancaster, son of Jesse & Mary Oliver, married **Eugenia Christopher**, 23, single, b. Northumberland, residing Mid., dau. of Rob't & Ann Christopher. (W)

34:05 - 18 Jan. 1876 - **Nathan L. Bristow**, 24, single, farmer, b. & residing Mid., son of Thos. & Eudora Bristow, married **Mary E. Hundley**, 18, single, b. & residing Mid., dau. of Rich'd H. & Amanda J. Hundley. (W)

34:06 - 27 Jan. 1876 - **Columbus R. Jackson**, 22, single, farmer, b. & residing Mid., son of Jeremiah & Amanda Jackson, married **Isabella I.** [or **Q.**] **Hart**, 17, single, b. & residing Mid., dau. of Jas. & Mary Harte. (W)

34:07 - 27 Jan. 1876 - **John C. Tellis**, 35, widower, farmer, b. Richmond Co., residing Lancaster, son of Jno. C. & Louisa Tellis, married **Laura Gibson**, 21, single, b. & residing Mid., dau. of [not given]. (W)

34:08 - 27 Jan. 1876 - **Jesse Hurd**, 29, single, farmer, b. Kent Co., Delaware, residing Mid., son of [not given], married **Ida V. Harrow**, 20, single, b. & residing Mid., dau. of [not given]. (W)

34:09 - 3 Feb. 1876 - **Ben Tucker**, 43, widower, farmer, b. & residing Mid., son of Jno. & Sally Tucker, married **Line Thornton**, 20, single, b. & residing Mid., dau. of Jas. & Cordelia Thornton. (C)

34:10 - 4 Feb. 1876 - **Maj. Banks**, 21, single, oysterman, b. & residing Mid., son of Mingo & Emily Banks, married **Lucy Brooks**, 22, single, b. & residing Mid., dau. of Jos. & Betty Brooks. (C)

34:11 - 10 Feb. 1876 - **Chas. Carter**, 21, single, oysterman, b. & residing Mid., son of [not given], married **Henrietta Evans**, 16, single, b. & residing Mid., dau. of Henry & Betty Johnson. (C)

34:12 - 10 Feb. 1876 - **Jacob Diggs**, 21, single, oysterman, b. & residing Mathews, son of Jos. & Dolly Diggs, married **Eliza Tabb**, 15, single, b. & residing Mid., dau. of Lewis & Betty Tabb. (C)

34:13 - 9 Mar. 1876 - **George H. Dunn**, 35, widower, farmer, b. & residing Essex, son of Jno. & Patsy A. Dunn, married **America E. Taylor**, 38, widow, b. Essex, residing Mid., dau. of Henry & Margaret M. Johnson. (W)

34:14 - 9 Mar. 1876 - **Wm. Greenwood**, 25, single, farmer, b. & residing Mid., son of Ransome & Grace Greenwood, married **Henrietta Braxton**, 16, single, b. & residing Mid., dau. of Henry & Betty Braxton. (C)

34:15 - 16 Mar. 1876 - **Ryland T. Mears**, 21, single, oysterman, b. & residing Lancaster, son of Jno. & Elizabeth Mears, married **Matilda Trader**, 21, widow, b. & residing Mid., dau. of Thos. Weston. (W)

34:16 - 8 Apr. 1876 - **Phillip Banks**, 30, widower, farmer, b. & residing Mid., son of Henry & Rebecca Banks, married **Elizabeth Fields**, 19, single, b. & residing Mid., dau. of Thos. & Annie Fields. (C)

34:17 - 10 Apr. 1876 - **Chas. Copeland Wright**, 34, single, teacher, b. Richmond City, residing Baltimore, Maryland, son of Jno. & Margaret C. Wight, married **Juliet A. Fauntleroy**, 30, single, b. & residing Mid., dau. of Thos. W. & Juliet A. Fauntleroy. (W)

34:18 - 1876 - **Isaac P. Revere**, single, married **Debra C. Walker**, single. (W) [No other information given.]

34:19 - 14 Apr. 1876 - **Thos. Street**, 21, single, farmer, b. & residing Mid., son of Jno. & Mary F. Street, married **Bettie A. Dillard**, 17, single, b. & residing Mid., dau. of Edmund L. Dillard. (W)

34:20 - 13 Apr. 1876 - **Abraham Bush**, 39, widower, oysterman, b. Gloucester, residing Mid., son of Aron & Louisa Bush, married **Margaret Fleet**, 19, single, b. & residing Mid., dau. of Lewis & Tabby Fleet. (C)

34:21 - 22 Apr. 1876 - **Geo. D. Tucker**, 30, single, cook, b. & residing Mid., son of Chas. & Rachel Tucker, married **Mary Price**, 25, single, b. & residing Mid., dau. of [not given]. (C)

34:22 - 2 May 1876 - **G. Thurston Williams**, 24, single, merchant, b. Liverpool, England, residing Mid., son of [not given], married **Sallie B. Nicolson**, 22, single, b. & residing Mid., dau. of Geo. L. & Nettie B. Nicolson. (W)

34:23 - 18 May 1876 - **James R. Jackson**, 30, single, farmer, b. & residing Mid., son of Jas. R. & Joice Jackson, married **Sarah Creighton**, 30, widow, b. Lancaster, residing Mid., dau. of Robert & Sarah Ingram. (W)

34:24 - 23 May 1876 - **Jas. Morris**, 25, single, oysterman, b. & residing Mid., son of Frank & Martha Morris, married **Matilda Gaines**, 22, single, b. & residing Mid., dau. of Benj. & Mary Gaines. (C)

35:01 - 3 Jun. 1876 - **Jerry Miles**, 30, widower, farmer, b. & residing Mid., son of Louis & Lucy Miller [Miles in Marriage Book 2], married **Martha Carter**, 20, single, b. & residing Mid., dau. of Samuel & Kate Carter. (C)

35:02 - 8 Jun. 1876 - **Jno. Davis**, 24, single, farmer, b. & residing Mid., son of Jno. & Mary Davis, married **Ann Thomas Whiting**, 22, single, b. & residing Mid., dau. of Beverly & Ann Whiting. (C)

35:03 - 20 Jun. 1876 - **George Coleman**, 23, single, farmer, b. & residing Mid., son of Arthur & Mary Coleman, married **Hannah B. Anderson**, 21, single, b. & residing Mid., dau. of Thos. & Saley B. Anderson. (C)

35:04 - 22 Jun. 1876 - **Harry Jackson**, 21, single, oysterman, b. & residing Mid., son of Jno. & Nancy Jackson, married **Mary Roy**, 19, single, b. & residing Mid., dau. of Mary Roy. (C)

35:05 - 28 Jun. 1876 - **Jno. A. Evans**, 26, single, mariner, married **Laura F. Hodges**, 24, widow, residing Mid., dau. of Wm. H. Kelly. (W)

35:06 - 6 Jul. 1876 - **Chas. E. Sears**, 33, single, editor, b. Gloucester, residing Kentucky, son of Edward

& Fannie C. Sears, married **Sallie E. Fauntleroy**, 29, single, b. & residing Mid., dau. of Thos. W. & Juliet A. Fauntleroy. (W)

35:07 - 13 Jul. 1876 - **Henry Lockley**, 26, widower, farmer, b. & residing Mid., son of Wm. & Winnie Lockley, married **Lucy Robinson**, 21, single, b. & residing Mid., dau. of Corbin & Emeline Robinson. (C)

35:08 - 5 Aug. 1876 - **Jacob Lomax**, 22, single, laborer, b. & residing Mid., son of Henry & Julia Lomax, married **Mary Moody**, 18, single, b. & residing Mid., dau. of Carter & Maria Moody. (C)

35:09 - 24 Aug. 1876 - **Walter Hill**, 25, single, farmer, b. King & Queen, residing Mid., son of Henry & Agnes Hill, married **Elenora Bates**, 25, widow, b. & residing Mid., dau. of Ro. & Lydia Tynius. (C)

35:10 - 7 Sep. 1876 - **Lewis Taliaferro**, 21, single, laborer, b. Mathews, residing Mid., son of Simon & Minerva Taliaferro, married **Rebecca Sales**, 19, single, b. & residing Mid., dau. of Peyton & Lucinda Sale. (C)

35:11 - 30 Aug. 1876 - **Jno. A. Booker**, 21, single, farmer, b. King & Queen, residing Mid., son of Leo & Malissa Booker, married **Malissa A. Milby**, 21, single, b. King & Queen, residing Mid., dau. of Frank & Ann Elisa Smith. (W)

35:12 - 21 Sep. 1876 - **Nathan T. Tomblinson**, 37, single, sailor, b. Gloucester, residing Mid., son of Wm. & Ann Eliza Tombilson, married **Eliza Roane**, 21, single, b. & residing Mid., dau. of Thos. & Mary Roane. (W)

35:13 - 27 Sep. 1876 - **Jos. F. Groom**, 30, widower, oysterman, b. Gloucester, residing Mid., son of Wm. & Eliza Groom, married **Eliza L. Parkes**, 23, single, b. & residing Mid., dau. of Abel & Eliza Parkes. (W)

35:14 - 11 Oct. 1876 - **Chas. H. Bray**, 23, single, farmer, b. & residing Mid., son of Thos. M. & Ophelia Bray, married **Mary A. Lee**, 22, single, b. & residing Mid., dau. of Obediah W. & Nettie Lee. (W)

35:15 - 4 Nov. 1876 - **Wm. J. Akes**, 26, single, mechanic, b. Princess Ann, residing Mid., son of Perry & Betsy Thomas, married **Lucy Vess**, 25, widow, b. King & Queen, residing Mid., dau. of Harrison & Cath. Holiway. (C)

35:16 - 18 Nov. 1876 - **Thos. Burrell**, 35, widower, farmer, b. & residing Mid., son of Caesar & Polly Burrell, married **Mary Ann Dabney**, 30, single, b. King & Queen, residing Mid., dau. of Peter & Malinda Dabney. (C)

35:17 - Dec. 1876 - **Joseph L. Conly**, 27, single, oysterman, b. & residing Lancaster, son of Wm. T. & Mary Conley, married **Rosa E. Rose**, 28, widow, b. & residing Mid., dau. of Ammon & Mary Didlake. (W)

35:18 - Dec. 1876 - **Jno. A. Payne**, 24, single, lumbering, b. & residing Lancaster, son of Thos. B. & Cathrine A. Payne, married **Minnie E. Gemmill**, 21, single, b. Kent Co., Maryland, residing Mid., dau. of Jno. H. & Wm. Geo. Anna Gemmill. (W)

35:19 - 10 Dec. 1876 - **Reubin Carter**, 20, single, oysterman, b. & residing Mid., son of Eliza Powell, married **Emma Bayton**, 17, single, b. & residing Mid., dau. of Richard & Cathrine Bayton. (C)

35:20 - 17 Dec. 1876 - **John Kellum**, 23, single, b. & residing Mid., son of Jas. & Harriet Kellum, married **Netta Wilson**, 16, single, b. & residing Mid., dau. of Jas. A. & Cath. Wilson. (W)

35:21 - 25 Dec. 1876 - **James Thomas Crittenden**, 23, single, farmer, b. & residing Mid., son of Jas. D. & Mary Crittenden, married **Lucy C. Dudley**, 17, single, b. & residing Mid., dau. of James & Sarah J. Dudley. (W)

35:22 - 25 Dec. 1876 - **Warner A. Blake**, 28, single, farmer, b. & residing Mid., son of Jno. L. & Margaret A. Blake, married **Cath. M. Hackney**, 27, single, b. & residing Mid., dau. of Jas. H. & Nancy Hackney. (W)

35:23 - 27 Dec. 1876 - **Rich'd T. Barrick**, 28, single, farmer, b. & residing Lancaster, son of David & Jane Barrick, married **Christa L. Seward**, 23, single, b. & residing Mid., dau. of Edward & Lucy A. Seward. (W)

35:24 - 28 Dec. 1876 - **Jno. Montague**, 24, single, farmer, b. & residing Mid., son of Alfred & Cath. Montague, married **Abby Taliaferro**, 19, single, b. & residing Mid., dau. of Wm. & Lucy Taliaferro. (C)

Index of Grooms

Abbott, Chas. C.	7:07		Bird, N. C.	4:07
Abram Key	19:38		Bird, Wm. A.	11:25
Abrech, Jacob W.	2:28		Blake, Apheus	5:12
Abrisch, J.	23:19		Blake, B. S.	27:08
Abrisch, Jacob W.	7:11		Blake, J. S.	4:11
Adams, Thos. D.	18:13		Blake, Jacob. S.	2:05
Ailworth, Ed.	3:19		Blake, Leo S.	26:42
Ailworth, Jos. D.	8:08		Blake, Rich'd H.	5:14
Ailworth, Jos. D.	3:03		Blake, Ro. M.	1:09
Ailworth, Josiah C.	30:10		Blake, W. H.	29:18
Ailworth, Ro. N.	11:42		Blake, Warner A.	35:22
Akes, Wm. J.	35:15		Blake, Wm. H.	8:02
Allen, Jas. B.	20:16		Blakey, J. A.	5:08
Alvis, Robert	1:28		Bohanon, Geo.	4:23
Amey, Jas.	28:06		Booker, Jno. A.	35:11
Anderton, C. H.	26:41		Boss, J. H.	8:04
Archibald, J. H.	26:26		Bowden, John H.	1:22
Armstrong, J. W.	29:24		Boyd, Jas.	33:15
Armstrong, Rich'd P.	25:12		Boyd, John	18:19
Ashbon, Jos. W.	31:21		Boyd, Wash.	18:24
Ashburn, Lewis E.	15:50		Bratten, Thos.	26:25
			Braxton, J. H.	28:02
Bagby, Titus	23:11		Braxton, Jas. Henry	32:16
Ball, Geo. A.	33:14		Bray, Chas. H.	35:14
Ball, Ro. R.	3:04		Brim, Lewis	12:11
Ball, Taswell	25:08		Brimm, Lewis	19:47
Ball, Wm.	32:10		Bristow, Andrew L.	2:04
Banks, Clay	23:02		Bristow, Calvin	13:07
Banks, John	18:18		Bristow, F. A.	17:09
Banks, Lewis	20:18		Bristow, Geo. T.	4:18
Banks, Lewis	20:21		Bristow, J. W.	27:12
Banks, Maj.	34:10		Bristow, Jos. A.	11:07
Banks, Mingo	33:17		Bristow, L. M.	5:10
Banks, Phillip	13:06		Bristow, L. S.	29:03
Banks, Phillip	34:16		Bristow,	
Barner, Daniel	17:25		L. S. , Sr.	14:44
Barnes, John W.	24:31		Bristow, Nathan L.	34:05
Barrell, Ric'd	20:24		Bristow, R. Braxton	11:14
Barrick, Jno. W.	19:35		Bristow, Richard T.	21:24
Barrick, Rich'd T.	35:23		Bristow,	
Barrick, Ro. H.	11:39		Rich'd H. , Jr.	30:12
Barrick, Wm. F.	2:02		Bristow, Walter	1:34
Bates, Henry	17:11		Bristow, Weston	24:28
Beale, J. H.	29:02		Bristow, Wm. C.	4:01
Beazley, Ed. W.	5:19		Bristow, Z. W.	10:07
Becket, Allen	23:09		Broach, Geo. W.	4:22
Bell, John	17:20		Broach, Rich'd	2:29
Bennett, John R.	13:05		Brockenbrough, Chas.	30:02
Birch, Chas.	4:25		Broocke, Geo. H.	6:02

Index of Grooms

Name	Ref	Name	Ref
Brooker, Allen	26:29	Chewning, James	4:03
Brooking, Allen	17:24	Chowning, F. S.	12:10
Brooks, Thomas	32:01	Chowning, Jas.	1:36
Browne, Ro.	14:29	Chowning, Jno.	27:09
Browne, Thos. S.	14:24	Chowning, Wm. B.	14:33
Browne, Thos. S.	8:12	Christopher, Thomas	4:15
Brushwood, L. C.	5:07	Clare, Wm. H.	11:02
Buckan, Sam. S.	3:10	Clarke, Jno. C.	11:03
Bull, Geo. T.	31:23	Clavel, Zadock	12:05
Bull, Geo. Thomas	30:18	Claybell, Elisha	8:09
Bundy, Benj.	30:22	Claybell, Zadock	8:10
Bundy, James	32:14	Clements, J. W.	13:16
Burke, Moses	20:11	Clements, Jno. W.	1:16
Burke, Wm., Jr.	26:35	Clements, Richard H.	5:01
Burrell, David	20:14	Cole, James M.	26:39
Burrell, Henry	14:23	Coleman, George	35:03
Burrell, J.	22:02	Conly, Joseph L.	35:17
Burrell, Jessee	15:53	Cook, Asey	23:08
Burrell, Rich.	13:03	Cooke, M. D.	4:17
Burrell, Robert	24:37	Cooke, Wm. H.	18:03
Burrell, Thos.	35:16	Cook, Thos. S.	3:11
Burrly, Rich'd	31:19	Cook, Warner T.	1:03
Burrus, Cary Ed.	32:12	Cooper, Rich'd	5:13
Burton, Columbus S.	33:16	Cooper, Rich'd	26:31
Burton, R'd C.	1:05	Corbin, Joseph	29:13
Burton, Thos. R.	1:17	Cornelius,	
Burwell, Hamilton	34:03	Bezabeel P.	5:03
Burwell, Wm.	25:23	Cornwell, C. C.	27:02
Bush, Abraham	34:20	Cottingham, Geo.	28:09
Bush, Chas.	21:13	Covington, Jos. G.	7:09
Butler, J. R.	4:29	Cox, James R.	3:22
Butler, J. R.	27:03	Crafton, Jas. S.	2:34
		Crask, Seldon F.	10:08
Calhoun, Thos.	11:36	Crittenden, Geo. W.	18:09
Campbell, Jas.	14:46	Crittenden, J. D.	4:20
Carr, Ro.	19:32	Crittenden,	
Carter, Chas.	34:11	James Thomas	35:21
Carter, Deaton	17:08	Croften, A. N.	11:11
Carter, Hiram	10:04	Croften, see Crafton	
Carter, Jas. W.	16:19	and Crofton	
Carter, Reubin	35:19	Crofton, Ro. F.	11:13
Carter, Ro. R.	4:16	Croxton, Jas. A.	27:20
Carter, Thos. H.	34:02	Cundiff, Griffin	9:04
Carter, Wm.	11:43	Cundiff, John	25:13
Cary, Sam'l B.	1:42	Cundiff, John F.	28:01
Castor, John	26:37	Curtis, Henry	12:12
Chamberlain, C.	23:05		
Chapman, Wm.	11:34	Dameral, Wm.	14:31
Charles, Cyrus	15:54	Daniel, E., Jr.	26:43

Index of Grooms

Daniel, El. B.	19:46		Easter, Henry	17:21
Daniel, Geo. W.	28:11		Easton, Noah	18:16
Daniel, Geo. Wm.	33:10		Eastwood, Wm. R.	5:18
Daniel, John W.	32:11		Edwards, John	3:12
Daniel, John W.	1:15		Epps, Marcus	26:38
Daniel, John W.	21:08		Evans, David T.	30:17
Daniel, Jos.	8:03		Evans, Jay	17:22
Daniel, K. R. S.	5:05		Evans, Jno. A.	35:05
Daniel, Ro.	2:45		Everett, Frank	21:23
Daniel, Ro.	18:06		Ewell, Wm.	26:28
Daniel, Wm. H.	10:01			
Daniel, Wm. J.	11:23		Farmer, Wm. P.	14:30
Davis, Dilly F.	32:09		Fauntleroy, Roy	27:05
Davis, Geo.	29:05		Ferneyhough, J. R.	14:38
Davis, Henry	20:23		Fields, Robert	21:22
Davis, Jas.	20:08		Fisher, Daniel	24:27
Davis, Jesse	25:17		Fitchett, James	13:17
Davis, Jno.	35:02		Fitchett, S. P.	3:13
Davis, Jos.	12:A		Fitchett,	
Davis, R. A.	5:21		Salathiel P.	1:33
Davis, Ro.	17:12		Fitchett, W.	26:33
Davis, Wm.	17:07		Fitzhugh, Jno. H.	1:19
Deagle, H. W.	3:15		Fleet, Rich'd L.	2:22
Deagle, Hiram	2:01		Fleet, Rob't	2:22
Deagle, J. W.	29:16		Fleet, Wm. C.	4:28
Deagle, James	4:04		Fogg, L. L.	2:44
Deagle, John	3:16		Fogg, Lewis L.	9:05
Deagle, John A.	7:06		Fones, R. P.	27:17
Deliever, Thomas	1:48		Foreman, B.	23:15
Dickinson, Fred	33:13		Forest, Isaiah	6:09
Didlake, Ammon	21:12		Forrest, N.	16:18
Didlake, Wm. R.	4:10		Foster, J. W.	19:28
Diggs, Jacob	34:12		Foster, Jas. R.	2:38
Dillard, Ed. S.	27:10		Foster, Phil	19:44
Dillin, James	25:04		Frazier, Thos. H.	33:18
Dillin, James	31:01		French, John R.	11:40
Doane, Edmund C.	2:11		French, William T.	5:02
Done, Edmund C.	2:11			
Donohue,			Gabor, John	1:32
S. Roszel	33:07		Gaines, Aron	28:21
Dudley, James	12:13		Gaines, Lewis	14:40
Dudley, Jas.	3:01		Gaines, Thos.	27:06
Dudley, Joshua	32:03		Gaines, Wm. H.	16:11
Dudley, Joshua	18:23		Gardner, A. B.	27:24
Dudley, Ro. E.	4:08		Gardner, Braxton	25:01
Dungee, Elijah	10:A		Gardner, Lewis M.	2:20
Dunlavy, J. J.	28:23		Gardner, Ro. T.	2:35
Dunn, Geo. H.	11:22		Garland, Ro. C.	19:26
Dunn, George H.	34:13		Garnett, Booker	8:07

Index of Grooms

Garrett, H. W.	10:03	Hart, B. F.	30:11
Gatewood, Cam. H.	1:04	Hart, Jas.	3:09
Gatewood, Philemon	31:08	Hart, Jno. W.	11:09
Glenn, Mathew	28:03	Hart, Rich'd H.	11:17
Glenn, Rich'd M.	33:04	Hart, Rich'd C.	2:13
Goldman, John	18:14	Hart, W. H.	23:21
Gore, Thomas	21:20	Healy, G. S.	28:07
Gouldman, John	3:05	Healy, James O.	31:18
Graham, Jas. R.	18:10	Healy, Julius E.	2:08
Green, Chas.	21:14	Healy, Thos. L.	16:22
Green, Manuel	30:05	Heany, Baldron	18:02
Green, Wilson	27:19	Hearn, Albert	2:26
Greenwood, Alpheus	17:01	Heath, G. H.	5:11
Greenwood, Ed.	3:02	Heath, Jos. S.	11:06
Greenwood, J. B.	2:30	Henry, Patric	23:03
Greenwood, Ransom	1:46	Henry, R. R.	25:07
Greenwood, Wm.	34:14	Hern, Wm.	13:08
Griffin, Ed.	15:52	Hill, Walter	35:09
Griffin, Green	17:02	Hilyard, R. H.	10:02
Grigry, Peter	20:20	Hodges, A. N.	11:20
Grimes, Charles	21:10	Hodges, Daniel	17:16
Groom, Andrew	24:32	Hodges, Isaac	30:21
Groom, Benj.	2:32	Holland, F.	16:14
Groom, J. F.	25:14	Holmes, John	13:10
Groom, Jos. F.	35:13	Horn, Everest	1:43
Groom, Robert	1:41	Hoskins, Thos.	19:30
Groom, Wm. H.	18:15	Howard, Samuel	12:B
		Howlet, Jas. W.	4:26
Hacket, Sam	25:02	Hughes, Jno. M.	27:15
Haile, Jos.	1:21	Humphreys, Rich'd T.	13:09
Hall, Addison	2:07	Hundley, J. T. C.	26:27
Hall, Gideon	3:17	Hundley, John A.	2:03
Hall, John A.	18:20	Hundley, Richard H.	2:10
Hall, Wm. T.	33:05	Hundley, Thomas F.	30:20
Hammonds, Tho. C.	28:04	Hurd, Jesse	34:08
Hammons, Thos. E.	32:15	Hurley, Sam'l H.	17:18
Hardy, John	8:11		
Harrington, Stuart	23:04	Ingram, James	1:47
Harris, D.	16:20	Ingram, Jas. E.	6:06
Harris, D. H.	23:10	Ingram, Loyd H.	19:34
Harris, Geo. H.	18:12	Ingram, Thos. E.	4:14
Harris, Geo. H.	28:19	Ingram, W. H.	11:26
Harris, Henry	24:30	Iverson, James	32:22
Harris, Henry L.	24:36		
Harris, Isaih	25:22	Jackson, Columbus R.	34:06
Harris, Oscar T.	20:07	Jackson, Harry	35:04
Harris, Thomas	30:15	Jackson, J. B.	23:06
Harris, Thos.	33:12	Jackson, J. H.	27:23
Harrow, Wm. A.	31:02	Jackson, James R.	34:23

Index of Grooms

Jackson, Jas. H.	1:06	Kinner, Henry	4:21
Jackson, Judge	20:09		
Jackson, Peter	31:13	Laurence, Ed.	17:23
Jackson, S.	25:21	Laws, Charles	15:47
Jackson, S.	26:40	Laws, John	29:08
Jackson, Sam'l R.	1:12	Laws, Miles C.	20:10
Jackson, Sam'l R.	1:44	Lawson, Thos. Y.	6:10
Jefferson, Thos. H.	25:20	Lee, Burnett	30:08
Jeffries, Jas. M.	9:02	Lee, George	29:04
Jenkins, Thos. H.	29:21	Lee, Lewis	15:51
Jinkins, Bev. W.	9:06	Lee, Moses	26:32
Johnson, Aug.	16:21	Lee, Obedia W.	1:02
Johnson, Ben.	21:02	Lewis, Alfred	17:05
Johnson, Benjamin	20:22	Lewis, Dinx	13:20
Johnson, Curtis	20:17	Lewis, Henry C.	21:09
Johnson, Doctor	14:26	Lewis, J. T.	28:22
Johnson, Frank	11:33	Lewis, Jas. T.	20:13
Johnson, G. L.	29:17	Lewis, John	32:18
Johnson, Henry	21:18	Lewis, Julius	17:13
Johnson, Jas. H.	32:13	Lewis, Ro. H.	20:05
Johnson, Moses	12:01	Lewis, Sam'l, Jr.	32:05
Johnson, Phil	18:01	Lewis, Thos.	7:10
Johnson, Ro.	13:15	Littlepage, Wilson	28:10
Johnson, Wm.	2:14	Lockley, Henry	14:34
Johnson, Wm.	17:04	Lockley, Henry	35:07
Jones, Abram L.	32:17	Lomax, F.	23:23
Jones, Christopher Robinson	31:04	Lomax, Jacob	35:08
Jones, George	21:11	Lomax, Moses	17:14
Jones, Oscar	20:01	Lumpkin, J. R.	3:06
Jones, Steven	18:05	Major, John M.	20:12
Jones, Thos. G.	33:01	Major, John M.	24:35
Jordan, Geo.	28:15	Major, L. O. B.	11:05
		Major, W. M.	1:23
Kain, Fred'k A.	6:08	Major, Walter M.	2:18
Keinningham, Jas. C.	11:41	Marchant, John R.	25:09
		Marchant, John W.	2:27
Keinningham, Julius G.	28:05	Marston, O. D.	25:03
Kellum, John	35:20	Mason, N.	10:11
Kellum, Rich'd H.	6:11	Mathews, Henry	21:19
Kellum, Wm.	13:04	Mathews, Joseph D.	5:22
Kembril, James	21:07	Maxwell, M. P.	31:09
Kemp, M. T.	28:18	Mayo, James W.	29:23
Kennard, Wm. J.	26:30	Mayo, Sam'l	19:43
Key, Geo.	4:19	McGeorge, John F.	1:39
Key, Walter H.	19:41	McKan, Ro. H.	12:09
Kidd, Jas.	4:09	McKenny, Jos. B.	18:17
King, Jas.	14:35	McTyre, An.	3:21
		Mears, Ryland T.	34:15

Index of Grooms

Mercer, Geo. W.	11:21	Norris, Geo.	7:05
Mercer, Jas. C.	16:04	Norris, Jas. Wm.	7:08
Meunderville, Franklin	33:06	Northam, Thomas H.	5:16
		Northern, Thos. H.	16:06
Mickelborough, Lewis	1:10	Norton, John	8:01
Mickleborough, Geo. W.	5:15	Norton, Wm. H.	2:40
Midgett, Alex	29:07	Oberg, William	1:31
Milbay, R.	27:22	Oliver, James T.	34:04
Milbey, Richard L.	15:48	Oliver, Jas.	28:08
Milby, Geo. W.	12:04	Orell, James	29:20
Miles, A. R.	16:08	Orell, Jas. H.	6:07
Miles, Jerry	11:44	Owen, John A.	15:49
Miles, Jerry	35:01	O'Brien, Ro.	6:01
Miller, John	26:44		
Miller, Wilinon C.	31:07	Pace, H. E.	23:14
Minor, Wm.	33:09	Page, Dennis	31:05
Moffitt, Ed. W.	18:07	Page, M.	30:01
Montague, E. B.	3:14	Page, Stephen	25:15
Montague, F.	26:34	Pall, Chas.	19:31
Montague, Geo. W.	4:12	Palmer, Alfred	1:24
Montague, Jno.	35:24	Palmer, Andrew J.	4:05
Montague, T. H.	11:12	Palmer, Jno. D.	1:08
Montague, Wm. S.	31:14	Pane, Wm. E.	32:08
Moody, Carter	16:13	Parish, Wm. F.	5:20
Moore, Jas.	11:19	Parker, Al. H.	27:18
Moore, Job	9:01	Parker, John	13:18
Moore, Wm.	25:11	Parker, Joseph R.	21:21
Morgan, B. H.	14:42	Parker, Sandy J.	25:10
Morris, Jas.	23:24	Parker, T. C.	1:37
Morris, Jas.	34:24	Parron, Rich'd H.	11:32
Morris, Jesse B.	33:08	Parrow, Thos. Henry	2:16
Morris, Silas	18:08	Payne, Jno. A.	35:18
Muire, Geo. H.	17:17	Payne, Wm. E.	26:46
Muse, Alfred	1:07	Penrod, Henry C.	19:39
Muse, Jos. A.	2:24	Perrin, Thos. Henry	2:16
Muse, Wm. A.	5:06	Peterson, Elijah	24:38
Nagle, Daniel H.	29:14	Peyton, Phillip	21:03
Nagle, John V.	20:04	Pines, Ro.	2:46
Nelson, Amus	21:16	Pippin, Edward A.	1:29
Nelson, J. H.	19:48	Pitman, Wm. W.	2:06
Nelson, John H.	13:21	Powell, Jas. H.	31:16
Nelson, Lycus	31:20	Powers, Wm.	18:11
Nelson, Ro.	11:35	Powill, Wm. J.	31:10
Newbill, John	4:06	Pratt, Wm.	17:26
Newcomb, Wm. F.	2:12	Price, Jos. E.	33:03
New, W. G.	23:12	Prince, Jas. R.	19:25
Nieman, Albrecht	11:16	Purkins, Ed. T.	1:18

Index of Grooms

Raddick, Rich'd	18:04		Segar, John E.	1:35
Reveer, Joel	11:18		Seward, Hiram A.	11:10
Revel, Geo.	14:45		Seward, M. A.	2:37
Revere, Isaac P.	34:18		Seward, Rich'd B.	30:19
Revere, Joel	9:03		Seward, Thos. C.	14:39
Revere, John M.	12:06		Shackelford,	
Revere, N. J.	3:18		Warner H.	31:15
Revere, Peter W.	32:02		Shaw, Lewis W.	1:14
Revere, Ro. V.	13:01		Shrieves, Geo. T.	6:04
Richards, Ed.	6:05		Shrieves, Wm. D.	19:42
Ridgwell, R.	10:14		Sibley, N. C.	2:23
Rilee, J. Lee	4:24		Sibley, S. D.	27:04
Rister, J.	23:20		Sibley, Thos. C.	31:06
Roane, Charles	11:15		Sibley, Wm. Jas.	1:11
Roane, Sam'l H.	7:04		Sibley, Wm. Jas.	4:27
Robinson, A. C.	29:15		Slaughter,	
Robinson, E. J.	3:08		Americus W.	22:01
Robinson, Geo.	13:12		Smither, E. S.	26:45
Robinson, J. H.	19:49		Smither, Herbert L.	30:07
Robinson, Jacob	14:41		Smith, G. H.	10:12
Robinson, Jos.	24:26		Smith, Geo. W.	13:11
Robinson, Jos.	30:14		Smith, Harry	28:20
Robinson, Joseph	29:09		Smith, James	11:30
Robinson, S.	29:12		Smith, James Micham	2:17
Robinson, Wm. C.	19:36		Smith, Jas.	13:14
Robins, S. W.	28:24		Smith, Phillip	11:27
Rock, Adolphus	2:33		Smith, Robert	6:03
Rock, Adolphus	13:02		Smith, Wash.	14:32
Rose, Hollis M.	11:08		Smith, William	29:11
Ross, J. R.	17:03		South, A. J.	1:38
Roy, Charles	26:48		South, Andrew S.	1:13
Roy, Jas.	23:22		Southerland, F. C.	30:03
Royster, Thos. F.	2:21		South, Francis	30:13
Ruffin, Griffin	28:12		Sparrow, Sam'l L.	25:19
Rust, Archibald	32:06		Spencer, R. B.	24:29
Rust, J. H.	19:29		Spencer, Ro. H.	32:04
Rust, S. R. T.	30:04		Sterling, Jas.	2:31
Ryland, Jno. W.	11:28		Stewart, Jos.	20:03
			Stewart, Jos.	2:48
Sadler, A. B.	1:40		Stiff, Jos. A.	13:19
Sadler, A. M.	16:16		Stiff, Thos. J.	27:07
Sale, Jas. H.	16:15		Stiff, W. H.	28:13
Sample, Geo.	17:19		Stone, Wm. W.	1:01
Sam'l Richeson	10:06		Street, Rich'd H.	11:29
Scott, Jas. H.	20:15		Street, Thos.	34:19
Scott, Jno. W.	16:17		Street, Wm. L.	26:36
Scott, Wm. H.	16:03		Stringer, J. A.	10:05
Sears, B.	25:24		Strother, David	19:40
Sears, Chas. E.	35:06		Summers, J. E.	2:25

Index of Grooms

Swanson, Isaac	30:06	Trader, Jas. D.	11:01
		Trader, Rich'd	8:06
Taff, Thomas F.	15:55	Trader, Thomas G.	2:09
Taliaferro,		Trevillilan, B.	1:27
Augustus	24:33	Trice, Ro. M.	16:07
Taliaferro, Lewis	35:10	Trice, Robt. N.	28:16
Taliaferro, Wm.	32:20	Trimyer, F. S.	5:17
Taper, Jos.	19:27	Trimyer, Wm. L.	17:10
Taylor, Archibald	7:02	Trymyer, Wm. S.	4:13
Taylor, Churchill	32:21	Tucker, Ben	34:09
Taylor, D. A.	25:18	Tucker, Geo. D.	34:21
Taylor, R. M.	2:39	Tunstall, Buck	33:11
Taylor, Ric'd	10:16	Turner, Henry	16:09
Taylor, Ro.	14:43	Tyson, John	16:01
Taylor, Ro. M.	14:27		
Taylor, Robert	25:05	Vaughan, Ves.	27:16
Taylor, W. W.	18:21	Vaughan, Wm. H.	27:14
Tellis, John C.	34:07		
Thomas,		Waites, Peter, Jr.	24:25
Alfred H. N.	21:17	Wake, Edmond	21:04
Thomas, Geo. W.	14:25	Wake, John J.	16:02
Thomas, J. H.	27:13	Walden, Enos	2:41
Thomas, Robert	21:06	Walden, H.	10:13
Thompson, Hardy	27:21	Walden, J. W.	23:16
Thornton, Ro. H.	12:02	Walden, Jos. H.	2:47
Thornton, W. T.	23:01	Walker, Chas.	19:33
Thornton, Wm. T.	31:12	Walker, H. H.	10:10
Thrift, James H.	24:34	Walker, H. W. F.	19:45
Thrift, James W.	1:25	Walker, Lee	29:19
Thrift, Jas. W.	11:04	Walker, Ro. H.	2:42
Thrift, R. T.	1:20	Walker, Rob. D.	13:22
Thrift, W. T.	29:06	Ward, Ad. H.	18:22
Thrift, Wm. T.	16:12	Ward, Sol.	11:37
Thurston,		Ward, Zack	31:17
Cornwell	27:11	Ware, Joseph H.	5:04
Thurston, Geo. W.	16:05	Wathen, Wm. G.	1:45
Thurston, J. H.	2:43	Watlington,	
Thurston, R. A.	11:31	Thos. R.	14:37
Thurston, Sam'l	20:02	Watson, Wm.	20:19
Thurston, Wm. B.	17:15	Webb, Jos.	12:03
Timons, G. W.	26:47	Webb, Richard	29:22
Tod, R. M.	10:15	Weston, George H.	33:02
Tomblinson,		Weston, Thos. D.	2:36
Nathan T.	35:12	White, Ro.	12:07
Tompkins, John F.	31:22	Whitheuse, John C.	2:19
Towill, M. F.	23:13	Whiting, Geo.	31:03
Towill, M. W.	3:07	Whitney, Wm.	32:07
Trader, Alexander	30:09	Wiatt, Thos. M.	1:26
Trader, C. H.	23:07	Wilkins, Ro. E.	28:17

Index of Grooms

Williams, G. Thurston	34:22	Wiston, John W.	8:05
Williams, Hen.	25:16	Wood, Chas.	23:18
Williams, Israel	32:19	Wood, Jas. A.	19:37
Williams, Jas. M.	20:06	Wood, John M.	14:36
Williamson, Jas. J.	11:45	Wood, N. S.	12:08
		Wood, Rich'd T.	2:15
		Woodward, Ro. R.	21:01
Williams, Wm.	34:01	Wood, Wm.	11:38
Willis, Robert	30:16	Worril, Joseph	1:30
Wilson, J. W.	23:17	Wortham, Wm. G.	1:45
Wilson, James	16:10	Wright, Chas. Copeland	34:17
Wilson, Jas.	13:13		
Wilson, Jas.	31:11	Wright, W. W.	29:10
Wilson, Joel C.	25:06	Wright, William	21:15
Wilson, N. G.	28:14	Wyatt, R. W.	10:09
Wilson, William	27:01		
Wilson, Wm. L.	17:06	Yates, James D.	4:02
Winder, Thos.	5:09	Yates, Ro.	3:20
Winkfield, Scipio	21:05	Yerby, Jas. T.	7:03
Winstead, Ferrol	11:24	Young, Aron	16:23
Wister, John W.	8:05	Young, Noah	14:28

Index of Brides

Name	Ref	Name	Ref
Ailworth, M. A.	4:18	Blake, Ann M. L.	33:04
Ailworth, Mary A.	3:20	Blake, C. E.	23:17
Ailworth, Sarah C.	4:21	Blake, Cath.	6:03
Allen, M. V.	27:01	Blake, E. A.	28:17
Alvace, Sarah	1:28	Blake, Eliz.	14:24
Amanda Petersen	11:34	Blake, Eliz. Ann	11:01
Anderson, Hannah B.	35:03	Blake, Emily S.	25:06
Anderson, Pre.	16:13	Blake, Frances S.	2:05
Armstead, Mary	19:41	Blake, Frances A.	11:04
Armstrong, Peggy	19:29	Blake, J. E.	10:10
Aytes, Mary	21:14	Blake, Joanna	1:43
		Blake, Louisa	20:13
Bagby, Jane	33:11	Blake, Louise	31:01
Bagby, Lucy F.	7:04	Blake, Ma. J.	16:16
Bagby, Sarah Ann	32:16	Blake, Mary L.	8:12
Bagby, Susan A.	26:44	Blake, Paulina	25:14
Ball, Anna E.	30:17	Blake, Sarah E.	23:13
Banks, F. A.	20:24	Bluefoot, Lucy A.	17:21
Banks, Joicy	4:20	Booth, Ellen Cath.	1:03
Barford, Sarah E.	7:08	Boss, Ann E.	2:32
Barrack, Mary E.	5:22	Boss, Anna H.	1:06
Barrick, Elizabeth	1:32	Boss, Jullia M.	27:16
Barrick, Nancy W.	27:14	Boss, Martha J.	28:04
Bates, Elenora	35:09	Boss, Mary E.	2:02
Bayton, Emma	35:19	Boss, Sarah E.	23:12
Beady, Winnie	30:04	Bourne, Maria E.	11:26
Beale, Maria	10:08	Bourrel, L.	28:22
Beazley, Henrietta A.	2:06	Boyd, Anna	28:15
		Boyd, Ellen	30:05
Beazley, Mary O.	11:05	Boyd, Margaret	34:01
Bennett, N. E.	10:12	Boyd, Martha	29:13
Bennett, S. J.	3:01	Braxton, C.	28:19
Berry, Ann E.	10:04	Braxton, Henrietta	34:14
Berry, Judith E.	5:14	Bray, Amanda	2:10
Berry, Mary V.	13:05	Bray, Frances E.	1:17
Berry, Nancy W.	11:39	Brinm, Mary A.	4:22
Beverly, Lou.	16:14	Bristow, Ann S.	14:39
Billups, Sally	29:02	Bristow, M. E.	21:08
Bird, Anna M.	15:49	Bristow, M. F.	26:26
Bird, Anna	18:11	Bristow, Maria A.	4:01
Bird, E.	3:05	Bristow, Martha A.	2:14
Bird, Jane	17:25	Bristow, Mira A.	1:15
Bird, Lea Ann	19:38	Bristow, Sarah E.	25:12
Bird, Susan A.	28:12	Broach, Elizabeth	4:06
Blackburn, J. E.	25:09	Broach, Lucie A.	12:11
Blackburn, S. D. E.	3:13	Broach, Mary	25:08
Blackley, Mary E.	2:13	Broach, V.	10:07
Blackwell, Clara	29:11	Broocke, Julia	5:21
Blake, Ann L.	29:15	Brooks, Lucy	34:10

Index of Brides

Brook, Vir. E.	17:09		Chowning, Mary L.	28:13
Browne, Mary E.	13:18		Chrisper, Jane	29:14
Browne, Molly	32:06		Chrispin, Jane	29:14
Bruce, Eliz. J.	23:06		Christopher, Emily	4:04
Bruce, Mary J.	8:09		Christopher, Eugenia	34:04
Bryant, Va.	2:46		Christopher, F. A.	28:08
Buckner, H. P.	3:18		Christopher, M.	10:11
Buckner, Mary L.	5:05		Christopher,	
Bull, A. E.	13:19		Sarah E.	14:31
Bullitt, Harriet	1:19		Churchill,	
Bull, Mary A.	4:16		Silvey Ann	33:15
Bundy, Anna	12:13		Clare, Elizabeth	1:10
Bundy, Betty Ann	23:03		Clare, Leonora E.	2:24
Bundy, M. E.	29:08		Clarke, Hester A.	1:16
Bundy, Maria L.	31:20		Clarke, Mary W.	30:13
Burch, Rosarelia	11:10		Clarke,	
Burke, D.	23:22		Missouri Tho.	31:02
Burrell, Agnes	24:26		Clarke, Sarah J.	16:02
Burrell, Louisa	31:11		Clegg, Hattie	31:14
Burrell, Mary	25:15		Clements, Lucinda	8:01
Burrell, Sena	14:28		Clements, Mary M.	1:25
Burrell, Virginia	24:25		Clements, Orinda	1:27
Bush, Hannah	32:03		Cole, Columbia F.	18:09
Bushwood, Eliza B.	16:04		Coleman, Lucy	11:44
			Coleman, Rosa	14:40
Callis, India	24:29		Cole, Vic. A.	16:19
Callis, Mary M.	7:06		Cook, Eliz.	17:08
Callis, Sarah	2:26		Cook, Nancy	10:A
Callis, Willie A.	21:21		Corbin, Betsy	19:40
Camey, Roxanah	6:09		Corbin, Sarah	18:08
Campbell, Lucy C.	25:03		Corr, Arabella	10:01
Campbell, M. A.	18:02		Corr, Levinia	14:27
Carlton, Frances	2:03		Creighton, Sarah	34:23
Carlton, Martha F.	2:03		Crittenden, E. P.	1:07
Carlton, Mary F.	15:55		Crittenden, Etta B.	34:02
Carr, Harriett	32:17		Crittenden,	
Carr, Lucy	21:03		Sallie E.	8:08
Carter, Betty	30:22		Croswell, Rachel	1:31
Carter, Frances E.	2:11		Cundiff, E. Vir.	16:11
Carter, Lucy A.	12:12		Cundiff, Mary E.	11:42
Carter, Martha	35:01		Cundiff, S. J.	27:06
Carter, S. A.	4:08		Curtis, Martha E.	20:07
Carter, Sallie	34:03			
Carter, Susan	13:15		Dabney, Betty	26:48
Carter, Winney	17:05		Dabney, Mary Ann	35:16
Cary, Frances	21:06		Daniel, A. E.	21:12
Cauthen, Sarah F.	8:02		Daniel, Betsy	17:24
Chapman, Mary	13:11		Daniel, Betty	11:24
Chesley, Ann H.	2:25		Daniel, Dorothy A.	7:03

Index of Brides

Daniel, Jane	5:16	
Daniel, Lucy B.	2:45	
Daniel, M. M.	3:08	
Daniel, Martha	31:03	
Daniel, Mary E.	15:54	
Daniel, Mary L.	27:04	
Daniel, Mary Eliz.	33:18	
Daniel, Mary A.	29:06	
Daniel, Mary Ann	23:04	
Daniel, Milly	11:38	
Daniel, Robinet	21:15	
Daniel, S. C.	2:39	
Davis, Alice W.	29:24	
Davis, Elizabeth	1:46	
Davis, Elizabeth W.	2:04	
Davis, Emily A.	4:05	
Davis, Fanny	25:23	
Davis, Grace	23:02	
Davis, Laura	18:18	
Davis, Lucy	32:07	
Davis, Mary F.	1:08	
Davis, Sarah E.	30:18	
Davis, Sarah E.	31:23	
Dawson, Betsy	16:10	
Deagle, Cor. F.	18:10	
Deagle, Estel V.	33:14	
Deagle, Lucy A.	25:07	
Deagle, Mariah R.	21:17	
Deagle, Martha	15:50	
Deagle, Sarah E.	5:03	
Dean, Jane	17:26	
Devenport, George Anna	30:16	
Dickinson, J. F.	10:03	
Didlake, Ellen	11:08	
Didlake, Mary J.	20:04	
Dillard, Bettie A.	34:19	
Dudley, A. F.	3:03	
Dudley, F. A. E.	3:04	
Dudley, Lucy E.	11:31	
Dudley, Lucy C.	35:21	
Dudley, Sarah A.	18:17	
Dudley, Sarah	17:23	
Dugan, Co.	3:21	
Dugan, Otera	2:47	
Dunaway, Maria	23:15	
Dunn, Alice R.	27:20	
Dunnaway, Mary E.	18:05	
Dunn, R. H.	3:22	
Dutton, Harriet J.	11:15	
Edmunds, Vir.	19:45	
Enos, M. A.	29:23	
Epps, Ann	11:30	
Eubank, Fannie A.	27:07	
Eubank, Hela	33:07	
Eubank, L. E.	5:08	
Eubank, Mary E.	10:09	
Eubank, Mary E.	1:35	
Eubank, S. V.	3:14	
Eubank, Sarah C.	30:11	
Evans, F. H.	4:29	
Evans, Henrietta	34:11	
Evans, L. R.	27:03	
Evans, Lucy Ann	33:09	
Evans, Martha E.	32:04	
Fauntleroy, Juliet A.	34:17	
Fauntleroy, Marg.	14:43	
Fauntleroy, Martha	7:02	
Fauntleroy, Sallie E.	35:06	
Fields, Elizabeth	34:16	
Fisher, Elizabeth H.	2:20	
Fisher, Mary W.	2:35	
Fisher, Vir. F.	27:24	
Fitchett, Mary Susan	2:17	
Fitchett, Melvina	5:04	
Fitchett, Mil. G.	20:08	
Fleet, Julia	18:15	
Fleet, Laura Ann	31:10	
Fleet, Margaret	34:20	
Fleet, Mary J.	18:06	
Fleet, Mary E.	16:09	
Fleet, Sallie A.	6:10	
Foster, A. H.	10:15	
Foster, Elizabeth H.	2:20	
Foster, Hannah	17:20	
Foster, M. A.	26:38	
Foster, Mary A.	11:35	
French, E. J.	11:40	
French, Lula B.	32:08	
Gaines, M. A.	29:03	
Gaines, Matilda	34:24	
Gaines, Mira A.	18:21	
Gaines, Sally	12:B	

Index of Brides

Name	Ref	Name	Ref
Gale, Ann E.	5:11	Haise, F. B.	25:17
Gale, Maria F.	11:45	Hall, Martha	24:32
Garder, Isabella	1:14	Hardy, M. J.	3:10
Gardner, Betty	31:17	Harrington, M. A.	28:03
Gardner, Euzalia	1:02	Harris, F. A.	29:12
Gardner, Nancy	1:20	Harris, Melinda	21:22
Garland, E. B.	5:07	Harrison, A.	29:07
Garland, Louisa	1:45	Harris, V. H.	29:21
Garland, Lucia H.	17:18	Harrow, E. D. H.	2:40
Garrett, Betsy A.	14:33	Harrow, Eliz.	19:27
Gatewood, Ann E.	8:07	Harrow, Ida V.	34:08
Gatewood, Lucie B.	9:02	Harrow, Irena	2:38
Gatewood, S. C.	28:07	Harrow, Rosetta	26:25
Gemmill, Minnie E.	35:18	Hart, Ann E.	4:15
George, Martha	32:13	Hart, Isabella	34:06
Gibbs, Eliza C.	20:05	Hart, Sarah E.	8:06
Gibson, Laura	34:07	Hart, Susan	26:42
Gibson, Va. S.	19:42	Hart, Virginia F.	25:04
Gipson, Leonora	6:06	Healy, K. A.	16:20
Gipson, Mary C.	6:04	Healy, Louisa E.	20:06
Glenn, Fanny B.	30:10	Healy, Mary F.	16:22
Glenn, G. G.	33:03	Hearne, F. E.	3:15
Goode, Juliza	5:13	Heath, Ann E.	7:10
Gordy, Anna	23:20	Henry, Liney	21:19
Green, Farsulie	11:25	Henry, Mary	23:10
Greenwood, Miriam	2:19	Henry, Sally	18:23
Greenwood, Mirianna	2:19	Hill, Alice	11:37
Grennolds, Nanny T.	30:12	Hodges, Laura F.	35:05
Gresham, Cordelia	20:17	Holloway, Mary	17:16
Gresham, Ellen	29:09	Holmes, Emma	12:A
Gresham, Fannie R.	30:07	Holmes, Fanny	17:07
Gressett, Virginia	6:02	Holmes, Lucy Ann	32:05
Gressitt, Mary A.	14:42	Holmes, Milly	13:21
Griffin, Eliza	13:13	Holmes, Sarah	31:13
Griffin, Haz.	19:33	Horsley, L. A.	25:24
Griffin, Lucy B.	20:15	Hoskins, Susan	17:04
Griffin, Nancy	24:38	Hudgins, Eu. F.	13:02
Grimes, Cath.	20:03	Hudgins, Mary F.	2:33
Groom, Martha E.	1:11	Hudgins, Millie H.	28:05
Gwyn, Mary F.	3:11	Hudgins, Sarah A.	8:10
		Hundley, Ann	9:04
Hackney, Cath. M.	35:22	Hundley, E.	29:10
Hackney, Juliet B.	31:09	Hundley, Em.	11:36
Hackney, Lucy L.	33:16	Hundley, Lidia A.	20:11
Hackney, Mary E.	13:07	Hundley, Lucy A.	11:22
Haile, F. B.	26:43	Hundley, Manda J.	27:12
Haile, Lu. A.	16:12	Hundley, Martha J.	26:30
Haile, Mary E.	19:46	Hundley, Mary E.	34:05
Haile, Rebecca	8:05	Hundley, Sally B.	5:17

Index of Brides

Hundley, Sarah S.	17:10	
Hundley, Susan	29:16	
Huntington, Nannie	17:06	
Ingram, Annie L.	33:10	
Ingram, Mary	4:14	
Ingram, Mary E.	26:27	
Ingram, R. B. B.	28:24	
Ingram, S. F.	28:23	
Jackson, Amanda	11:17	
Jackson, Betsy	30:08	
Jackson, Cath.	24:36	
Jackson, Eudora	20:18	
Jackson, Frances A.	4:13	
Jackson, Louisa	27:19	
Jackson, Lucy C.	2:27	
Jackson, M.	23:09	
Jackson, Mary A.	20:20	
Jackson, Mary Ellen	31:04	
Jackson, Rosanna	4:07	
Jackson, Sarah	13:08	
Jackson, Tamer	20:14	
Jenkins, Mary A.	2:36	
Johnson, A.	29:05	
Johnson, Amanda	13:12	
Johnson, Ann E.	10:16	
Johnson, Caroline	29:22	
Johnson, Dina	33:17	
Johnson, Eliz.	19:43	
Johnson, Eliza	16:03	
Johnson, Eliza	13:20	
Johnson, Lucy	14:41	
Johnson, M. A.	3:19	
Johnson, M. J. M.	16:15	
Johnson, Mary Jane	2:12	
Johnson, Oney	19:32	
Johnson, Sarah	12:05	
Jones, Betty H.	1:18	
Jones, Catharine	28:10	
Jones, E. M.	16:21	
Jones, Eliza	18:12	
Jones, Fanny	25:21	
Jones, Lucinda E.	11:14	
Kelley, J.	28:01	
Kellum, Columbia	33:02	
Kellum, Harriet	14:45	
Kellum, M. J.	10:13	

Kelly, E. P.	27:23	
Kelly, Ida A.	27:15	
Kelly, Laura	11:20	
Kelly, M. Ann	29:19	
Kennard, Sarah E.	30:20	
Kenningham, M. S.	1:38	
Kenningham, Sary	9:06	
Key, Amelia/Camelia	7:05	
Key, Espe	14:46	
Key, Mary A.	4:19	
Key, Polly	6:05	
Key, Rusey	23:08	
Kidd, Eliz. C.	1:37	
Kidd, Lucy A.	6:08	
King, M. E.	30:03	
King, Maria	21:11	
King, Sallie	21:07	
Kinningham, Cath.	5:19	
Laws, Cath.	23:11	
Layton, B. E.	27:02	
Layton, Cor. T.	5:20	
Lee, Ellen	19:44	
Lee, Georgia E.	32:02	
Lee, Hannah E.	21:13	
Lee, Julia A.	14:32	
Lee, Lucy B.	20:01	
Lee, Maria L.	1:39	
Lee, Mary	31:19	
Lee, Mary A.	35:14	
Lewis, Ann E.	14:36	
Lewis, Cath.	25:16	
Lewis, Frances	19:48	
Lewis, L.	29:04	
Lewis, M. C.	1:30	
Lewis, M. E.	23:24	
Lewis, Mar. A.	14:35	
Lewis, Sarah B.	2:28	
Lockley, Frances A.	16:05	
Lockley, Jane	30:15	
Lockley, Mary	14:29	
Lomax, Laviny	33:13	
Lomax, Maria	15:52	
Lomax, Nancy	20:21	
Long, Betty	1:41	
Long, M. F.	25:19	
Madison, Lucy A.	15:51	
Major, Hen.	27:18	

Index of Brides

Major, Lucie A.	13:09		Newcomb, Ann C.	28:16
Major, Lucy Ellen	17:15		Newcomb, Lucy F.	16:07
Major, Mary L.	31:06		Newcomb, Mary Jane	31:12
Major, Missouri E.	12:04		New, Emily S.	25:10
Martin, Fannie E.	23:14		New, Lucy E.	2:23
Mason, Anna F.	4:23		New, Mary A.	14:25
Mathews, Mary A.	5:06		New, Mary Jane	1:40
McCarty, Winifred E.	1:42		New, Matilda A.	32:15
McKan, Isabella F.	1:01		Nichols, A. A.	27:13
McTyre, Lucetta E.	7:07		Nicolson, Sallie B.	34:22
Meigs, Frances	18:14		Noel, Mildred	21:23
Mercer, Louisa	2:41		Norris, Cornelia	11:19
Mickelborough, C. B.	11:12		Norris, Maria	28:02
Milby, D. M.	2:43		Northam, L. B.	10:06
Milby, Malissa A.	35:11		Northan, Ida M.	24:28
Miles, Milly	24:37		Norton, Evaline	18:07
Miller, C. A.	27:08		Norton, M.	23:19
Miller, C. W.	15:48			
Miller, Nannie A.	33:05		Oakes, M. A.	3:12
Miller, Sarah	31:08			
Montague, Cath.	13:17		Pace, A. M.	3:07
Montague, Eusabia N.	1:04		Page, Lucy	26:47
Montague, F. H.	27:09		Palmer, Ann E.	13:01
Montague, Maria	13:14		Palmer, Ed. C.	17:03
Montague, Mary J.	2:22		Palmer, Ellen F.	20:12
Montague, Sarah F.	11:16		Palmer, L. C.	3:06
Montgomery, Mary A.	17:12		Palmer, V. S.	28:09
Moody, Mary	35:08		Parkes, Eliz.	9:03
Moore, Julia Ann	25:13		Parkes, Eliza L.	35:13
Moore, Sarah B.	2:31		Parks, Ann R.	4:02
Morris, Alice	17:13		Parks, Har. C.	19:37
Morris, Amelia	1:48		Parron, Lucy E.	16:06
Morris, Julia	12:03		Parry, Geo. Anna	20:19
Morris, Maria	32:09		Patterson, Lucinda	25:02
Morris, Mary A.	25:11		Patterson, Margiana	8:04
Morris, Useba	30:14		Percifull, M. Alice	33:01
Mossey, Eliz. F.	4:26		Peterson, Amanda	28:06
Moton, Elvina	21:10		Peterson, Hester	15:53
Murcer, Cath.	1:33		Pittman, M. S.	27:17
Muse, Henrietta A.	2:08		Powers, L. A.	2:44
Muse, Lucy	19:30		Price, Mary	34:21
Muse, Matilda	23:07		Prince, Emily J.	11:40
			Prince, Lucy C.	3:02
Neale, Sarah E.	1:09		Prince, Mary	26:46
Nelson, Betty	32:14		Pritchett, Loui'a	6:07
Nelson, Sarah	32:12		Purkins, M. L.	2:30
Newbill, Emma J.	24:34			
Newbill, Rosa B.	19:47		Ransome, Frances B.	19:35
New, Columbia C.	33:06		Reade, Matilda	23:05

Index of Brides

Reade, Virginia	20:23	Saunders, Eli'th	8:11
Ready, Winnie	30:04	Saunders, Lucy E.	21:24
Reed, Jane	33:12	Schrieves, Fran. C.	19:31
Revere, Leti'a A.	3:17	Scott, Virginia	24:30
Revere, Lucy H.	18:20	Sears, Margaret	30:06
Revere, Mary J.	17:01	Seaward,	
Richardson, Rosie E.	18:13	Mary Elizabeth	2:18
Richeson, Cath.	26:33	Segar, In. C.	14:38
Ricks, Julia	18:16	Segar, Sarah C.	1:26
Rilie, Hester	16:01	Selby, Willie R.	33:08
Rilie, M. C.	26:39	Seward, Almade	11:02
Risby, Tamar	20:22	Seward, Ann C.	14:44
Roane, Eliza	35:12	Seward, Christa L.	35:23
Roane, Emily F.	4:17	Seward, Fanny A.	24:35
Roane, Eudora	18:22	Seward, Frances A.	10:02
Roane, Julia A.	1:22	Seward, Mary F.	14:37
Roane, Lucy D.	4:28	Seward, Mira C.	4:24
Roane, Lucy F.	11:28	Seward, Ophelia	5:01
Roane, M. E.	11:11	Seward, Ro. Ann	19:39
Roane, Mary E.	30:19	Seward, S. A.	2:37
Roane, Mary M.	11:07	Seward, Sarah	7:09
Roane, Ozela A.	11:13	Shackleford, Sarah F.	4:12
Roberts, Elizabeth	2:01	Shrieves, Elizabeth	1:47
Robinson, Betty	22:02	Sibley, Amanda J.	31:07
Robinson, E.	30:01	Sibley, Eliz.	19:25
Robinson, Eliz. A.	8:03	Sibley, H. F.	23:16
Robinson, Fanny	30:21	Sibley, Marg. F.	19:49
Robinson, Jenetta	31:05	Sibley, Mary E.	13:16
Robinson, Julia	27:21	Slaughter, Emma J.	22:01
Robinson, Lucie H.	13:22	Smith, Anne E.	4:03
Robinson, Lucy	20:02	Smith, Car. F.	21:01
Robinson, Lucy	35:07	Smither, Ann L.	5:12
Robinson, Matilda	32:20	Smither, B. E.	26:45
Robinson, P.	30:02	Smith, George Anne	31:22
Robinson, Polly	26:29	Smith, Har.	16:17
Robinson, Sallie	27:22	Smith, Harriet	11:33
Rose, Rosa E.	35:17	Smith, Mary	24:27
Roy, Amanda	14:34	Smith, Mary	11:43
Roy, Mary	35:04	Smith, Mary	26:28
Royster, Eliza	4:09	Smith, Sallie E.	14:30
Rust, Eliza	21:04	Smith, Sarah	12:06
		South, Mary B.	2:34
Sadler, Mary J.	29:18	South, Mary A.	7:11
Sadler, Rebecca	2:48	South, S. F.	4:10
Sadler, Sophronia	1:24	Sparrow, Cath.	19:28
Sadler, V. E.	26:36	Sparrow, Sarah	19:34
Sales, Alice	25:05	Spencer, Mary E.	1:36
Sales, Rebecca	35:10	Spillman, Mary E.	28:11
Saunders, A. E.	25:18	Stiff, O. A.	16:08

Index of Brides

Street, Alice	27:10		Upton, Maria	26:34
Sutton, Lucy L.	11:41			
Sutton, M. E.	23:21		Vaughan, Ann	29:17
			Vaughn, Martha E.	1:29
Tabb, Betsy	20:09		Vess, Lucy	35:15
Tabb, Eliza	34:12			
Taliaferro, Abby	35:24		Waddle, Ann E.	1:13
Taliaferro, Annie E.	31:16		Waites, Anna	17:14
Taliaferro, Char.	12:01		Wake, Kittie	11:27
Taliaferro, Grace	17:19		Wake, Madlund	12:02
Taliaferro, N.	26:32		Wake, Martha	6:11
Taper, Mary C.	4:27		Walden, Lucy	11:21
Taylor, America E.	34:13		Walden, M. S.	3:16
Taylor, Eliz. C.	1:23		Walden, Mary	2:09
Taylor, Hannah Cath.	2:16		Walden, Rebecca	1:21
Taylor, Mary	5:18		Walker, Ann M.	2:07
Taylor, Netta	14:23		Walker, Ar. N.	19:36
Taylor, Sarah V.	13:03		Walker, Debra C.	34:18
Taylor, Virg'a H.	11:29		Walker, Emily	32:01
Thomas, Aman.	14:26		Walker, Emma F.	31:15
Thomas, Elnora	17:11		Walker, Julia F.	2:42
Thompson, Rosa M.	20:16		Walker, Margaret E.	1:05
Thornton, A.	5:15		Walker, Saphronia	1:44
Thornton, E. J.	6:01		Ward, Julia	18:19
Thornton, Line	34:09		Ward, Milly	23:23
Thornton, Louisa	24:31		Ware, Malvina J.	11:06
Thornton, Maria	26:37		Ware, Sarah	1:28
Thurston, Ann	12:09		Washington, Adelia	25:01
Thurston, D. M.	9:05		Washington, Margaret	28:20
Thurston, Elizabeth	2:15		Washington, Vio.	15:47
Thurston, Jane	18:01		Washington, Violet	25:20
Thurston, Martha E.	23:01		Watkins, Edna E.	5:02
Thurston, Sarah	27:05		Watkins, Mary W.	11:09
Thurston, Vashti	31:18		Watton, Mary E.	32:11
Topping, Am. E.	19:26		Watts, Mary E.	10:05
Topping, Eliz. A.	11:03		Watts, Va. A.	2:29
Tousley, S. E.	26:40		Webb, Chris.	18:24
Towill, Mary E. A.	1:12		Webb, Clara	12:07
Towill, S. V.	28:18		Webb, Fanny	24:33
Trader, M. E.	10:14		Webb, Martha	32:10
Trader, Mary	11:18		Webstead, Eliza	13:06
Trader, Matilda	34:15		Weston, M. A.	29:20
Trader, S. E.	28:14		Weston, M. E.	3:09
Trice, Mary L.	26:41		Weston, Matilda S.	17:17
Tullington, Lucy T.	31:21		Wheeler, Sarah E.	17:22
			Wheely, Mary	2:21
Upshaw, Augusta	32:19		Whiting, Ann Thomas	35:02
Upshaw, Frances	20:10		Wiatt, Adeline	1:34
Upshaw, Lucy	32:18		Wiggins, Ann E.	21:20

Index of Brides

Williams, Ada	23:18	Winkfield, M.	21:05
Williams, Cora A.	12:08	Wood, Ann E.	26:31
Williams, Emma G.	11:32	Wood, Christiana	27:11
Williams, Julia A.	9:01	Wood, D. E.	4:11
Williams, Julia	25:22	Wood, Dianna	21:16
Williams, Laura	28:21	Wood, Ellen	26:35
Williams, M. E.	5:10	Wood, Frances A.	4:25
Williams, M. J.	21:09	Wood, Julia A.	21:02
Williams, Venus	32:22	Wood, Louisa	16:23
Wilson, Alice	13:04	Woodward, Ann C.	12:10
Wilson, E. P.	5:09	Wormley, Martha	32:21
Wilson, Eliz.	16:18	Wormley, Martha	13:10
Wilson, Netta	35:20		
Wilson, Sarah G.	30:09	Yerby, Judith	17:02
Wilson, Sarah	18:03	Young, Betty	21:18
Winder, Eliz. P.	11:23	Young, Ellen	18:04

Marriage Register 2, 1876-1890
Transcribed by
Carolyn H. Jett

There are only three marriages per page recorded in this book. Letters A, B and C have been appended to the page number to identify the location of the marriage record on the page.

All the marriages recorded on the first 18 pages of this book, plus two marriages on the 19th page, are also in Register of Marriages, 1853-1876. Therefore, this transcription of Marriage Register 2, 1876-1890 will begin with the third marriage on page 19, identified as 19C.

As in the last records in Register of Marriages, 1853-1876, the race of the principals is given. They are transcribed here just as they were entered in the original records, as follows:
- (B) - Black
- (C) - Colored
- (W) - White

It is important to remember that in this period the term "colored" was applied to African-Americans, and often to Native-Americans and Melungeons as well.

For interpretation of other abbreviations used, see the introduction to Register of Marriages, 1853-1876.

19C - Dec. 1876 - **Alfred W. Ruark**, 26, single, mariner, b. Maryland, residing Hoopers Island, Maryland, son of Major and Ruark, married **Ju. V. Bull**, 20, single, b. & residing Mid., dau. of Thos. R. & Mary A. Bull. (W)

20A - Dec. 1876 - **Vanness Nonan**, 19, single, mariner, b. & residing Jersey Co., Maryland, son of [not given], married **Mary J. Bulle**, 22, single, b. & residing Mid., dau. of Thos. R. & Mary A. Bull. (W)

20B - 18 Jan. 1877 - **Obediah Norris**, 25, single, farmer, b. & residing Mid., son of Frank & Martha Norris, married **Percilla Smith**, 27, single, b. & residing Mid., dau. of [not given]. (C)

20C - 20 Jan 1877 - **Henry Bundy**, 21, single, farmer, b. & residing Mid., son of Fanny Bundy, married **Cath. Conway**, 21, single, b. & residing Mid., dau. of W. & Emeline Conway. (C)

21A - 23 Jan. 1877 - **Matthew E. Graves**, 23, single, farmer, b. Gloucester, residing Mid., son of Wm. H. & Mary Graves, married **Mary A. Blake**, 18, single b. & residing Mid., dau. of Berkley & Susan Blake. (W)

21B - 25 Jan. 1877 - **John Pollard**, 73, widower, attorney at law, b. Goochland, residing King & Queen, son of Joseph & Cath. Pollard, married **Eugenia A. Purkins**, 53, single, b. & residing Mid., dau. of Carter Purkins. (W)

21C - 28 Jan. 1877 - **Richard Burrell**, 30, farmer, b. & residing Mid., married **Hester Wilson**, 21, b. & residing Mid. (C) [No other information given.]

22A - 7 Feb. 1877 - **Lewis S. Garrett**, 30, single, mechanic, b. King & Queen, residing Mid., son of Thos. H. & Elizabeth Garrett, married **Mary A. Smither**, 23, single, b. King & Queen, residing Mid., dau. of Ribon M. & Cath. W. Smither. (W)

22B - 8 Feb. 1877 - **Carter A. Key**, 32, single, farmer, b. & residing Mid., son of Thos. & Cath. Key, married **Roberta Key**, 31, single, b. & residing Mid., dau. of Jas. & Eliza Key. (C)

22C - 22 Feb. 1877 - **Jacob Peter Franz**, 25, single, sailor, b. Heligoland, residing Mid., son of Peter J. & Mary E. Franz, married **Mary Alice Ingram**, 18, single, b. & residing Mid., dau. of Charles & Emmie Ingram. (W)

23A - 22 Feb. 1877 - **John P. Bristow**, 77, widower, farmer, b. & residing Mid., son of Benjamin & Ann Bristow, married **Adeline Gwyn**, 37, widow, b. Gloucester, residing Mid., dau. of Robinson C. & Rosa Bridges. (W)

23B - 28 Feb. 1877 - **Cyrus Nelson**, 22, single, oysterman, b. & residing Mid., son of Washington & Venus Nelson, married **Maria McCauley**, 25, widow, b. Lancaster, residing Mid., dau. of Fleet & Ann McCauley. (C)

23C - 6 Mar. 1877 - **Thomas A. Saunders**, 24, single, farmer, b. & residing Mid., son of John H. & Sarah A. Saunders, married **Cath. Jackson**, 19, single, b. & residing Mid., dau. of Jas. & Malvina Jackson. (W)

24A - 14 Mar. 1877 - **John B. Smith**, 28, single, farmer, b. & residing Mid., son of John R. & Sarah S. Smith, married **Mary S. Slaughter**, 26, single, b. & residing Mid., dau. of George B. & Eliz. Slaughter. (W)

24B - Mar. 1877 - **Samuel Norris**, 21, single, sailor, b. & residing Mid., son of James & Virginia Norris, married **Rachel Hurley**, 17, single, b. Maryland, residing Mid., dau. of David & Jane Hurley. (W)

24C - 15 Mar. 1877 - **Alonzo Lewis**, 25, single, farmer, b. King & Queen, residing Mid., son of Samuel & Marie Jane Lewis, married **Elizabeth Lewis**, 25, single, b. & residing Mid., dau. of Albert & Grace Lewis. (C)

25A - 14 Apr. 1877 - **Wm. S. Holoway**, 32, widower, farmer, b. King & Queen, residing Mid., son of Harrison & Catherine Holoway, married **Lavinia Williams**, 20, single, b. King & Queen, residing Mid., dau. of Frances Williams. (C)

25B - 18 Apr. 1877 - **Fer. H. Hall**, 29, single, teacher, b. Lancaster, residing Mid., son of Addison & Cath. C. Hall, married **Maryanna D. Pitt**, 26, single, b. & residing Mid., dau. of Douglas & Ann C. Pitt. (W)

25C - 17 Apr. 1877 - **Wm. H. Green**, 24, single, farmer, b. Hanover, residing Mid., son of Wm. & Matilda Green, married **Betty Keinningham**, 28, single, b. & residing Mid., dau. of Wm. Keinningham. (W)

26A - 19 Apr. 1877 - **Elias Waites**, 25, single, farmer, b. & residing Mid., son of Peter & Sally Waites, married **Elmira Jones**, 37, widow, b. King & Queen, residing Mid., dau. of Sam'l & Catharine Jones. (C)

26B - 25 May 1877 - **Wm. G. New**, 31, widower, carpenter, b. & residing Mid., son of John C. & Louisa M. New, married **Anne Good**, 28, single, b. & residing Mid., dau. of John C. & Ann Good. (W)

26C - 29 May 1877 - **Moses Burk**, 27, widower, farmer, b. & residing Mid., son of Edward & Mollie Burk, married **Roberta Uptsier**, 21, single, b. & residing Mid., dau. of Harry & Frances Uptsier. (C)

27A - 27 Jun. 1877 - **George W. Grimes**, 19, single, farmer, b. & residing Mid., son of George & Alsey Grimes, married **Martha Tabb**, single, b. & residing Mid., dau. of [not given]. (C)

27B - 6 Jul. 1877 - **James Johnson**, 25, single, farmer, b. & residing Mid., son of Moses & Rachel Johnson, married **Emma Braxton**, 26, single, b. & residing Mid., dau. of Elijah & Rose Braxton. (C)

27C - 2 Aug. 1877 - **Frank Reed**, 22, single, farmer, b. & residing Mid., son of Austin & Matilda Reed, married **Hester Ann Curtis**, 18, single, b. & residing Mid., dau. of Ellick & Charlotte Curtis. (C)

28A - Aug. 1877 - **Lambeth Evans**, 22, single, seaman, b. & residing Accomack, son of Elijah & Matilda Evans, married **Lola M. Harrow**, 20, single, b. & residing Mid., dau. of Jeremiah & Catharine Harrow. (W)

28B - 13 Sep. 1877 - **Vanburen Morris**, 24, single, farmer, b. & residing Mid., son of Linsey & Jane Morris, married **Malvina Morris**, 21, single, b. & residing Mid., dau. of Cornelius & Ann Morris. (C)

28C - 13 Sep. 1877 - **Thos. H. Gwyns**, 21, single, oysterman, b. Mathews, residing Mid., son of Jas. H. & Sarah Gwyn, married **Martha Dunaway**, 18, single, b. & residing Mid., dau. of Jas. Dunaway. (C)

29A - 17 Sep. 1877 - **Wm. H. Healy**, 20, single, farmer, b. & residing Mid., son of Jas. T. & Mary F. Healy, married **Mary C. Armstrong**, 24, single, b. & residing Mid., dau. of Wm. H. & Martha A. Armstrong.(W)

29B - 8 Oct. 1877 - **Charles P. Layton**, 35, single, farmer, b. & residing Mid., son of Henry L. & Sarah V.

Layton, married **Ellen H. Gatewood**, 33, widow, b. Tappahannock, Essex, residing Urbanna, Middlesex, dau. of James R. & Ellen H. Micou. (W)

29C - 13 Oct. 1877 - **Henry Hill**, 24, single, oysterman, b. & residing Mid., son of Harrold & Betsy Hill, married **Sarah Linkius**, 22, single, b. & residing Mid., dau. of Washington & Alsey Lorimore [sic]. (C)

30A - 31 Oct. 1877 - **R. W. Franklin**, 25, single, sailor, b. Essex, residing Mid., son of R. W. & Ann Franklin, married **Carrie E. Crittenden**, 24, single, b. King & Queen, residing Mid., dau. of John & Mary Crittenden. (W)

30B - 29 Nov. 1877 - **Charles Carter**, 22, single, farmer, b. & residing Mid., son of Robert & Cordelia Carter, married **Betty Floyd**, 21, single, b. King & Queen, residing Mid., dau. of Albert & Fanny Floyd. (C)

30C - 29 Nov. 1877 - **Jerome Mickelborough**, 29, single, farmer, b. & residing Mid., son of James & Ann Mickelborough, married **Isabella P. Holliday**, 19, single, b. Spotsylvania, residing Mid., dau. of Tabnur W. Holliday. (W)

31A - 17 Dec. 1877 - **Charles Henry Lomax**, 63, widower, farmer, b. King & Queen, residing Mid., son of Benja. & Violett Lomax, married **Fanny Davis**, 46, widow, b. Essex, residing Mid., dau. of Jos. & Anny Ransome. (C)

31B - 19 Dec. 1877 - **W. H. Parks**, 22, single, farmer, b. & residing Mid., son of Abel & Ann E. Parks, married **Elivira J. Blake**, 17, single, b. & residing Mid., dau. of Wm. S. & Catharine Blake. (W)

31C - 22 Dec. 1877 - **George Johnson**, 25, single, farmer, b. & residing Mid., son of Daniel & Eliza Johnson, married **Nancy Wingfield**, 24, single, b. & residing Mid., dau. of Thos. Field & Sally Wingfield. (C)

32A - 22 Dec. 1877 - **George Minor**, single, farmer, b. & residing Mid., son of Jefferson & Sarah Minor, married **Susan Foster**, single, b. & residing Mid., dau. of George & Hannah Foster. (C)

32B - 31 Dec. 1877 - **Beverly Wormley**, 21, single, farmer, b. King & Queen, residing Mid., son of Beverly & Isabelle Wormley, married **Emeline Lee**, 18, single, b. & residing Mid., dau. of Ellen Foster. (C)

32C - 26 Jan. 1878 - **John South**, 22, single, farmer, b. & residing Mid., son of Thomas & Katy South, married **Polly Braxton**, 16, single, b. & residing Mid., dau. of Henry & Betsy Braxton. (C)

33A - 31 Jan. 1878 - **Joseph E. Price**, 33, widower, b. Newcastle Co., Delaware, residing Mid., son of Samuel &

Annah Price, married **Nannie E. Gordy**, 19, single, b. & residing Mid., dau. of Nutter & Anna Gordy. (W)

33B - 2 Feb. 1878 - **Isaac Reed**, 34, single, farmer, b. Gloucester, residing Mid., son of Jacob & Eliz. Reed, married **Fanny Laws**, 36, single, b. & residing Mid., dau. of John & Anna Laws. (C)

33C - Feb. 1878 - **Wm. W. Hundley**, 22, single, seaman, b. & residing Mid., son of Thos. & Bettie Hundley, married **Maria S. Mason**, 17, single, b. & residing Mid., dau. of Lemuel & Susan Mason. (W)

34A - 9 Feb. 1878 - **Ralph Burrell**, 24, single, farmer, b. & residing Mid., son of Edward & Molley Burrell, married **Patsy Howe**, 17, single, b. & residing Mid., dau. of Jack & Molley Howe. (C)

34B - 14 Feb. 1878 - **Cornelius Morris**, 29, single, farmer, b. & residing Mid., son of Lorenza & Jane Morris, married **Elmira Key**, 21, single, b. & residing Mid., dau. of Eliza Key. (C)

34C - 5 Mar. 1878 - **George W. Milby**, 38, widower, farmer, b. King & Queen, residing Mid., son of [not given], married **Elizabeth Slaughter**, 29, single, b. & residing Mid., dau. of Richeson Slaughter. (W)

35A - 12 Mar. 1878 - **John Wesly Freeman**, 28, single, oysterman, b. & residing Gloucester, son of Math. & Margaret Freeman, married **Sarah Ellen Morris**, 16, single, b. & residing Mid., dau. of Wm. & Mary Morris. (C)

35B - 21 Mar. 1878 - **Robin Robinson**, 23, widower, farmer, b. & residing Mid., son of Harry & Sally Robinson, married **Anna Fitchett**, 21, widow, b. & residing Mid., dau. of Jas. Fitchett. (C)

35C - 27 Mar. 1878 - **George R. Finch**, 23, single, merchant, b. King & Queen, residing Mid., son of George R. & Ann H. Finch, married **Mattie Chowning**, 21, single, b. & residing Mid., dau. of Wm. N. & Cath. Chowning. (W)

36A - 28 Mar. 1878 - **Geo. Taylor Wood**, 21, single, oysterman, b. & residing Mid., son of Geo. Wood & Anna Wood, married **Martha Peterson**, 18, single, b. & residing Mid., dau. of Wm. Peterson. (C)

36B - 6 Apr. 1878 - **James Ruffin**, 27, single, wagoner, b. Essex, residing Mid., son of Jesse & Adeline Ruffin, married **Mary Reed**, 18, single, b. & residing Mid., dau. of Lewis & Eliza Reed. (C)

36C - Apr. 1878 - **Solomon Fields**, 36, widower, farmer, b. & residing Mid., son of [not given], married **Molley Roy**, 15, single, b. & residing Mid., dau. of Jane Roy. (C)

37A - 16 Apr. 1878 - **Martin Jacobson**, 25, single, sailor, b. Stockholm, Sweden, residing New York, son of Anderson & Louisa Jacobson, married **Louisa B. Trader**,

17, single, b. & residing Mid., dau. of Geo. T. & Mary Trader. (W)

37B - 1878 - **James Jackson**, residing Mid., married **Frances Young**, residing Mid. (C) [No other information given.]

37C - 20 Apr. 1878 - **Wyatt Dangerfield**, 23, single, farmer, b. & residing Mid., son of Richard & Lydia Dangerfield, married **Rosa Motley**, 21, single, b. & residing Mid., dau. of Moses & Hannah Motley. (C)

38A - 24 Apr. 1878 - **Peter B. Hall**, 30, single, farmer, b. & residing Mid., son of Gideon & Anna Hall, married **Julia May Walden**, 18, single, b. & residing Mid., dau. of Enos & Louisa Walden. (W)

38B - 27 Apr. 1878 - **Isaih Townley**, 21, single, oysterman, b. & residing Mid., son of Geo. & Sarah Ann Townley, married **Harriet Thurston**, 21, single, b. & residing Mid., dau. of Beverly & Lucy Thurston. (C)

38C - May 1878 - **John L. Montgomery**, 21, single, seaman, b. & residing Mid., son of Jas. T. & Elizabeth Montgomery, married **Mary Ann Kellum**, 18, single, b. & residing Mid., dau. of James & Harriet Kellum. (W)

39A - 1878 - **Ellis Jackson**, single, farmer, residing Mid., son of [not given], married, **Grace Roane**, 23, single, residing Mid., dau. of [not given]. (C)

39B - May 1878 - **John W. Tabb**, 22, single, farmer, b. & residing Mid., son of [not given], married **Susan Jackson**, 21, single, b. & residing Mid., dau. of [not given]. (C)

39C - 23 May 1878 - **John A. Carr**, 24, single, farmer, b. & residing Mid., son of Burrell & Sarah E. Carr, married **Tama Jackson**, 24, single, b. & residing Mid., dau. of John & Cordelia Jackson. (C)

40A - 29 May 1878 - **Warner H. Shackleford**, 28, widower, oysterman, b. Gloucester, residing Mid., son of John & Sarah Shackleford, married **Mary C. Stringer**, 30, widow, b. & residing Mid., dau. of James & Fanny Watts. (W)

40B - 3 Jun. 1878 - **Jas. H. Richeson**, 44, widower, sailor, b. Maryland, residing Mid., son of Henry & Julia A. Richeson, married **Courtney Blake**, 34, single, b. & residing Mid., dau. of Thomas M. & Courtney Blake. (W)

40C - 16 Jun. 1878 - **Sam'l Lecount**, 23, single, sailor, b. & residing Somerset Co., Maryland, son of William & Jane Lecount, married **Courtney S. Blake**, 16, single, b. & residing Mid., dau. of Jacob & Doratha E. Blake. (W)

41A - 22 Jun. 1878 - **Joseph Henry Brooks**, 25, single, laborer, b. & residing Mid., son of Jesse & Betty Brooks, married **Anna Johnson**, 21, single, b. & residing Mid., dau. of Johnson & Eliza. (C)

41B - 17 Jul. 1878 - **Wm. Ed. Barrick**, 39, widower, builder, b. Mid., residing Richmond, son of John & Emeline Barrick, married **Bettie C. Northam**, 22, single, b. & residing Mid., dau. of Henry C. & Susan A. Northam. (W)

41C - 31 Jul. 1878 - **Wm. H. Armstrong**, 58, widower, farmer, b. Essex, residing Mid., son of Perkins & Mary Armstrong, married **Sarah Creswell**, 30, widow, b. Caroline, residing Mid., dau. of Philip & Lucy Estis. (W)

42A - 8 Aug. 1878 - **Charles H. Frazier**, 23, single, farmer, b. King & Queen, residing Mid., son of West & Charlotte Frazier, married **Eliza Ann Boyd**, 19, single, b. & residing Mid., dau. of Allen & Judy Boyd. (C)

42B - 15 Aug. 1878 - **Rich'd H. Sibley**, 24, married **Mary S. Massey**, 17. (W) [No other information given.]

42C - 14 Aug. 1878 - **John W. Adams**, 21, single, mechanic, b. King & Queen, residing Mid., son of [not given], married **Georgia A. Groom**, 21, single, b. & residing Mid., dau. of Ro. M. & Mary E. Groom. (W)

43A - 20 Aug. 1878 - **Robert Burrell**, 23, widower, farmer, b. & residing Mid., son of John & Cordelia Burrell, married **Josephine King**, 20, single, b. & residing Mid., dau. of Lewis & Jane King. (C)

43B - 28 Aug. 1878 - **Richard H. Sibly**, 24, single, farmer, b. & residing Mid., son of Narbon C. & Mary E. Sibly, married **Mary S. Massey**, 17, single, b. Gloucester, residing Mid., dau. of Robert & Mary Massey. (W)

43C - 5 Sep. 1878 - **Joshua Burnett**, 21, single, laborer, residing Mid., married **Mary E. Cook**, 30, single, residing Mid. (C) [No other information given.]

44A - 19 Sep. 1878 - **James Rawley**, 25, single, oysterman, b. Surrey, North Carolina, residing Mid., son of Gabriel & Matilda Rawley, married **Louisa Barns**, 23, widow, b. & residing Mid., dau. of Benja. & Mary Thornton. (C)

44B - 25 Sep. 1878 - **John J. Montague**, 27, single, farmer, b. Gloucester, residing Mid., son of Thos. B. & Sarah H. Montague, married **Rebecca West**, 18, single, b. Gloucester, residing Mid., dau. of Isaac M. West. (W)

44C - 24 Oct. 1878 - **Philip H. Sadler**, single, farmer, b. & residing Mid., son of Jas. H. & Mary Sadler, married **Annie Laura Gipson**, single, b. Lancaster, residing Mid., dau. of Sarah J. Gipson. (W)

45A - 7 Nov. 1878 - **Beverly Louden**, 45, widower, farmer, b. & residing Gloucester, son of Richard & Fannie Louden, married **Martha Dabney**, 25, single, b. King & Queen, residing Mid., dau. of Peter & Malinda

Dabney. (C)
45B - 7 Nov. 1878 - **Marcus Harris**, 21, single, farmer, b. & residing Mid., son of Geo. & Lucy Harris, married **Cordelia Wood**, 22, single, b. & residing Mid., dau. of William Wood. (C)
45C - 20 Nov. 1878 - **Jas. M. Street**, 33, single, merchant, b. & residing Mid., son of Zack & Ursula Street, married **Mary E. Gresham**, 20, single, b. & residing Mid., dau. of R. T. A. & Lucy A. Gresham. (W)
46A - 4 Dec. 1878 - **John H. Taliaferro**, 22, single, farmer, b. & residing Mid., son of Wm. & Kitty Taliaferro, married **Nillintina Cook**, 20, single, b. & residing Mid., dau. of Jame & Louisa Cook. (C)
46B - 18 Dec. 1878 - **Otho A. Saunders**, 25, single, merchant, residing Mid., son of R. & B. M. Saunders, married **Lela A. Rouzie**, 22, single, b. & residing Mid., dau. of R. F. & Maria Rouzie. (W)
46C - 15 Dec. 1878 - **Lewis S. Bristow**, 30, widower, merchant, b. & residing Mid., son of Larkin S. & Cath. S. Bristow, married **Nellie B. Gaines**, 18, single, b. & residing Mid., dau. of John T. & Mary F. Gaines. (W)
47A - 17 Dec. 1878 - **James C. Grey**, 27, single, farmer, b. Newport, Rhode Island, residing Mid., son of Edward & Josephine Grey, married **E. Florance Parrish**, 17, single, b. & residing Mid., dau. of Wm. F. & Cordelia T. Parrish. (W)
47B - 24 Dec. 1878 - **James T. Revere**, 27, single, farmer, b. & residing Mid., son of Joel & Sarah Revere, married **Fannie E. Revere**, 24, single, b. & residing Mid., dau. of Jas. & Pach. F. Revere. (W)
47C - 26 Dec. 1878 - **Alfred Montague**, 25, single, farmer, b. & residing Mid., son of Alfred & Cath. Montague, married **Bettie Lee**, 19, single, b. Essex, residing Mid., dau. of Mary Lee. (C)
48A - 25 Dec. 1878 - **John H. Morris**, 22, single, farmer, b. & residing Mid., son of George & Charlotte Morris, married **Mollie Wicks**, 20, single, b. & residing Mid., dau. of Ralph & Mary Wicks. (C)
48B - 25 Dec. 1878 - **Frank Minor**, 21, single, farmer, b. & residing Mid., son of Jefferson & Sarah Minor, married **Martha Motley**, 26, single, b. & residing Mid., dau. of Moses & Hannah Motley. (C)
48C - 25 Dec. 1878 - **General Perrill**, 23, single, farmer, b. Essex, residing Mid., son of Richard & Isabella [no surname given], married **Maria Powell**, 24, single, b. & residing Mid., dau. of Wm. & Martha Powi̲ll. (C)
49A - 25 Dec. 1878 - **James Campbell**, 22, single, farmer, b. & residing Mid., son of Warner & Easther Campbell, married **Sophia Burrell**, 21, single, b. &

residing Mid., dau. of Thomas & Peggy Burrell. (C)
49B - 25 Dec. 1878 - **Ro. Henry Evans**, 23, single, miller, b. & residing Mid., son of Mary Foster, married **Cath. Morris**, 19, single, b. & residing Mid., dau. of Wm. & Betty Morris. (C)
49C - 31 Dec. 1878 - **Griffin E. Thurston**, 30, widower, farmer, b. & residing Mid., son of Thackery & Nancy Thurston, married **Alice A. Blackley**, 35, single, b. & residing Mid., dau. of Ro. C. & Nancy Blackley. (W)
50A - 2 Jan. 1879 - **Samuel Lomax**, 23, single, farmer, b. King & Queen, residing Mid., son of Jas. & Dorah Lomax, married **Louisa Ward**, 18, single, b. & residing Mid., dau. of Zack & Martha Ward. (C)
50B - 9 Jan. 1879 - **Warner Gresham**, 23, single, oysterman, b. & residing Mid., son of Daniel & Jane Gresham, married **Sarah Jones**, 21, single, b. & residing Mid., dau. of Ed. & Emily Jones. (C)
50C - 9 Jan. 1879 - **Thos. H. Wormley**, 23, single, oysterman, b. & residing Mid., son of Thos. & Isabella Wormley, married **Emeline Washington**, 22, single, b. & residing Mid., dau. of Geo. & Lucy Anne Washington. (C)
51A - 18 Jan. 1879 - **Henry Minor**, 24, single, farmer, b. & residing Mid., son of Henry & Nelly Minor, married **Mary Harris**, 21, single, b. & residing Mid., dau. of Sam & Jenny Coleman. (C)
51B - 25 Jan. 1879 - **Wm. Braxton**, 20, single, farmer, b. & residing Mid., son of Wm. Braxton, married **Phenton Carter**, 18, single, b. & residing Mid., dau. of [not given]. (C)
51C - 23 Jan. 1879 - **Marcus A. Seward**, 47, widower, farmer, b. & residing Mid., son of Walter F. & Elvira Seward, married **Lucy C. Wheeler**, 28, single, b. & residing Mid., dau. of Carter & Virginia Wheeler. (W)
52A - 22 Jan. 1879 - **Wm. R. Apsley**, 27, single, merchant, b. Kent, Maryland, residing Mid., son of Wm. R. & Mary A. Apsley, married **Maggie F. Slaughter**, 20, single, b. & residing Mid., dau. of Richeson & Ann Slaughter. (W)
52B - 30 Jan. 1879 - **Philmore Henry**, 27, single, farmer, b. & residing Mid., son of Patrick & Louisa Henry, married **Fanny Jackson**, 19, single, b. & residing Mid., dau. of Edward Jackson. (C)
52C - 14 Feb. 1879 - **Charles Liveley**, 26, single, oysterman, b. & residing Mid., son of Zack & Milley Livel_y_, married **Virginia Cook**, 17, single, b. & residing Mid., dau. of Frank & Mary Cook. (C)
53A - 30 Jan. 1879 - **Washington Lee**, 24, single, oysterman, b. & residing Mid., son of Canton & Anna Lee, married **Mary Ellen Banks**, 23, single, b. & residing

Mid., dau. of Mingo & Emily Banks. (C)
    53B - 6 Feb. 1879 - **Geo. Aug. Diggs**, 23, single, farmer, b. Mathews, residing Mid., son of Isaih & Eliz. Diggs, married **Felicia Wake**, 22, single, b. & residing Mid., dau. of Ed. & Elenora Wake. (C)
    53C - Feb. 1879 - **Ephraim Young**, 36, single, seaman, b. Accomac, residing Mid., son of Ro. & Amelia Young, married **Mary Carter**, 23, single, b. & residing Mid., dau. of Geo. H. & Sarah Carter. (W)
    54A - 1879 - **William Cooke**, 21, single, oysterman, b. Gloucester, residing Mid., son of Frank & Mary Cooke, married **Mara E. Holmes**, 24, single, b. Gloucester, residing Mid., dau. of Martha Roy Holmes. (C)
    54B - 27 Feb. 1879 - **Joshua Townsend**, 28, single, farmer, b. Gloucester, residing Mid., son of Kendall & Elizabeth Townsend, married **Lucy E. Armstrong**, 16, single, b. & residing Mid., dau. of Wm. H. & Martha A. Armstrong. (W)
    54C - 6 Mar. 1879 - **Geo. Randsom**, 23, single, oysterman, b. & residing Mid., son of Mary Randsom, married **Betsy Cary**, 22, single, b. & residing Mid., dau. of Henry & Celey Cary. (C)
    55A - 1879 - **Wellington Purkins**, 60, widower, farmer, b. & residing Mid., son of Venus Purkins, married **Lucy Taliaferro**, 40, widow, b. & residing Mid., dau. of Isaac & Lettie Forcet. (C)
    55B - 27 Mar 1879 - **Lewis Nelson**, 22, single, oysterman, b. & residing Mid., son of Wm. & Milly Nelson, married **Ada Laws Wilson**, 21, single, b. & residing Mid., dau. of Jas. & Joanna Wilson. (C)
    55C - 20 Mar. 1879 - **Hammitt Weathers**, 22, single, farmer, b. King & Queen, residing Mid., son of Merry & Eliza Weathers, married **Nanny Davis**, 20, single, b. Essex, residing Mid., dau. of Peter & Matilda Davis. (C)
    56A - 6 Mar. 1879 - **Jack T. Harris**, 24, single, farmer, b. & residing Mid., son of Sam'l & Jane Harris, married **Sarah Ruffin**, 21, single, b. & residing Mid., dau. of Lewis & Caroline Ruffin. (C)
    56B - Apr. 1879 - **Herbert White**, 26, single, seaman, b. Accomack, residing Mid., son of Napoleon & Merry White, married **Georgia Sibley**, 19, single, b. & residing Mid., dau. of William & Mary Sibley. (W)
    56C - 24 Apr. 1879 - **Thos. Gwynn**, 21, single, farmer, b. Mathews, residing Mid., son of Robert & Mary Gwynn, married **Marg. Holmes**, 20, single, b. & residing Mid., dau. of Catharine Holmes. (C)
    57A - 24 Apr. 1879 - **Phillip F. McKan**, 37, single, farmer, b. & residing Mid., son of Henry & Ellen McKan, married **Sallie Evans**, 20, single, b. & residing Mid.,

dau. of Mort. & Jane R. Evans. (W)
57B - 24 Apr. 1879 - **Thos. H. Holmes**, 22, single, farmer, b. & residing Mid., son of Wm. & Clora Ella Holmes, married **Lydia D. Wells**, 20, single, b. & residing Mid., dau. of [not given]. (C)
57C - 24 Apr. 1879 - **George Carter**, 26, single, oysterman, b. & residing Mid., son of Anderson Taylor & Cordelia Carter, married **Lizzie Burrell**, 23, single, b. & residing Mid., dau. of Jacob & Rachel Burrell. (C)
58A - 1879 - **Joseph A. Clair**, 23, single, farmer, b. & residing Mid., son of Ro. & Virginia Clair, married **Ida Martin**, 21, single, b. & residing Mid., dau. of H. C. & Emily Martin. (W)
58B - 1879 - **Bartlett Davis**, 45, widower, oysterman, b. Lancaster, son of Jesse & Eliza Davis, married **Eliza Kellum**, 40, single, b. & residing Mid., dau. of Abel & Frances Kellum. (W)
58C - 30 Apr. 1879 - **Jas. P. Holliway**, 21, single, farmer, b. Fredericksburg, residing Mid., son of Ro. & Susan Holliway, married **Mira Payton**, single, b. & residing Mid., dau. of Phil Payton. (C)
59A - 4 May 1879 - **John W. Wood**, 24, single, farmer, b. & residing Mid., son of John T. & Eliz. Wood, married **Sarah Edwards**, 26, single, b. & residing Mid., dau. of Jas. & Rosa A. Edwards. (W)
59B - May 1879 - **Sam'l Christopher**, 21, single, b. & residing Mid., son of Riley & Fanny Christopher, married **Olivia Davis**, 18, single, b. & residing Mid., dau. of Bartlett & Bettie Davis. (W)
59C - May 1879 - **Wm. R. Evans**, 26, single, seaman, b. Accomack, residing Norfolk, son of Revel & Eliza Evans, married **Sarah Carter**, 21, single, b. & residing Mid., dau. of Geo. A. & Sarah Carter. (W)
60A - 8 May 1879 - **Henry Carey**, 48, widower, farmer, b. & residing Mid., son of [not given], married **Louisa Taliaferro**, 28, single, b. & residing Mid., dau. of Phil & Nancy Taliaferro. (C)
60B - 8 May 1879 - **Nicholas Wood**, 23, oysterman, b. & residing Mid., son of Minnie & Louisa Wood, married **Cath. Cook**, 24, single, b. & residing Mid., dau. of Jas. & Louisa Cook. (C)
60C - May 1879 - **Jas. A. Sadler**, 24, single, oysterman, b. & residing Mid., son of Jas. H. & Mary Eliz. Sadler, married **Mary Dunlevy**, 23, single, b. & residing Mid., dau. of Wm. B. & Mary Dunlevy. (W)
61A - 14 May 1879 - **John L. Jackson**, 44, widower, farmer, b. & residing Mid., son of Jno. & Lucy Jackson, married **Sallie Ailworth**, 34, widow, b. Mathews, residing Mid., dau. of Boyd & Nancy Ailworth. (W)
61B - May 1879 - **James Peade**, 25, single, oysterman,

b. Mathews, residing Mid., son of Jas. & Pattie Peade, married **Cleopatra Hundley**, 18, single, b. & residing Mid., dau. of Thomas & Elizabeth Hundley. (W)
  61C - 22 May 1879 - **Ro. H. Mercer**, 25, single, farmer, b. & residing Mid., son of Jas. C. & Ellenora Mercer, married **Edda J. Major**, 21, single, b. & residing Mid., dau. of Ro. S. & Lucy Major. (W)
  62A - May 1879 - **James Ingram**, 45, widower, oysterman, b. Lancaster, residing Mid., son of James & Leasey Ingram, married **Livia Daniel**, 23, single, b. & residing Mid., dau. of George & Mary Daniel. (W)
  62B - 29 May 1879 - **Wm. Andrew Jackson**, 23, single, oysterman, b. & residing Mid., son of Jos. & Jane Jackson, married **Eliz. Weems**, 21, single, b. Lancaster, residing Mid., dau. of [not given]. (C)
  62C - 14 Jun. 1879 - **William Foster**, 24, single, farmer, b. & residing Mid., son of Philip & Amanda Foster, married **Mary F. Carter**, 22, single, b. & residing Mid., dau. of James & Mollie Carter. (C)
  63A - Jul. 1879 - **Cuffy Washington**, 57, widower, farmer, b. & residing Mid., son of Cuffy and Lucy Washington, married **Eliz. Henry**, 32, single, b. & residing Mid., dau. of Richard & Milly Washington. (C)
  63B - 24 Jul. 1879 - **Ro. M. Blake**, 49, widower, farmer, b. & residing Mid., son of John B. & Nancy Blake, married **Geo. Anna Slaughter**, 28, single, b. Gloucester, residing Mid. (W)
  63C - 28 Aug. 1879 - **W. W. Keinningham**, 25, single, farmer, b. & residing Mid., son of [not given], married **Mary E. Edwards**, 21, single, b. & residing Mid., dau. of Jas. & Rosa Edwards. (W)
  64A - 27 Aug. 1879 - **Elijah Banks**, 30, single, laborer, b. & residing Mid., son of York & Lucinda Banks, married **Nancy Ann Ackiss**, 24, single, b. Norfolk Co., residing Mid., dau. of [not given]. (C)
  64B - 2 Sep. 1879 - **Wm. Powers**, 42, widower, farmer, b. & residing Mid., son of Robert & Charity Powers, married **Mary Harris**, 20, single, b. & residing Mid., dau. of Robert & Fannie Harris. (C)
  64C - 1879 - **Wm. V. Brownley**, 24, single, b. & residing Mathews, son of Jas. R. & Mary F. Brownley, married **Amanda E. Dunlevy**, 19, single, b. & residing Mid., dau. of Wm. B. & Mary Dunlevy. (W)
  65A - 5 Oct. 1879 - **Richard H. Trader**, 22, single, sailor b. & residing Mid., son of James & Susan Trader, married **Hester Christopher**, 22, single, b. & residing Mid., dau. of Nathan & Mary Christopher. (W)
  65B - 1879 - **Wm. R. Taylor**, 22, single, laborer, b. Gloucester, residing Mid., son of Wm. R. & Sally Ann Taylor, married **Mahaley Jones**, 21, single, b. & residing

Mid., dau. of Abram Jones. (C)
65C - 9 Oct. 1879 - **John W. Morgan**, 29, widower, sailor, b. & residing Mathews, son of Persilla Morgan, married **Gertrude Hart**, 21, single, b. Statton [sic] Island, residing Mid., dau. of Mary Hart. (C)
66A - Oct. 1879 - **Peter Guthrey**, 24, single, oysterman, b. Gloucester, residing Mid., son of Epy [or Essy] & Betsy Guthrey, married **Esta Johnston**, 18, single, b. & residing Mid., dau. of Henry & Betsey Johnston. (C)
66B - 23 Oct. 1879 - **Andrew W. Stiff**, 25, single, merchant, b. Mid., son of Andrew & Eliz. Stiff, married **Emma J. Walker**, 23, single, b. Princess Ann, Norfolk Co., residing Mid., dau. of O. M. & S. J. Walker. (W)
66C - 23 Oct. 1879 - **Ro. L. Scott**, 23, single, farmer, b. King & Queen, residing Mid., son of Harrison & Sally Scott, married **Coley Carter**, 22, single, b. & residing Mid., dau. of Lewis & Nancy Carter. (C)
67A - 3 Nov. 1879 - **Walter Forest**, 22, single, sailor, b. & residing Mathews, son of [not given], married **Lucy South**, 19, single, b. & residing Mid., dau. of Jos. & Felicia South. (W)
67B - 13 Nov. 1879 - **Nelson Thurston**, 21, single, oysterman, b. & residing Mid., son of Daniel & Jane Thurston, married **Molly Goldman**, 18, single, b. & residing Mid., dau. of Eliza [sic] & Jane Goldman. (C)
67C - 16 Nov. 1879 - **Richard Billups**, 46, widower, farmer, b. & residing Gloucester, son of George & Betsey Billups, married **Jane Pratt**, 35, widower, b. & residing Mid., dau. of Peter & Lucy Dean. (C)
68A - Nov. 1879 - **Simon D. Sable**, 23, single, sailor, b. Maryland, residing Mid., son of A. J. & Sarah Sable, married **Cathrine Paul**, 22, widow, b. & residing Mid., dau. of Wm. & Louisa Shrieves. (W)
68B - 11 Dec. 1879 - **Ed. T. Mason**, 22, single, waterman, b. Gloucester, residing Mid., son of John & Ann D. Mason, married **Nancy E. Dunlevy**, 25, single, b. & residing Mid., dau. of Wm. B. & Mary Dunlevy. (W)
68C - 1879 - **Geo. Wood**, 20, single, oysterman, b. & residing Mid., son of Wm. & Cordry Wood, married **Margaret Purkins**, 18, single, b. & residing Mid., dau. of Wellington & Betty Purkins. (C)
69A - 27 Nov. 1879 - **Lewis Lee**, 36, widower, farmer, b. & residing Mid., son of Kenton & Hennie Lee, married **Lucy Lee**, 21, single, b. & residing Mid., dau. of Charles Lee. (C)
69B - 18 Dec. 1879 - **Pharoah Purkins**, 22, single, oysterman, b. & residing Mid., son of Wellington & Betty Purkins, married **Sarah Burrell**, 18, single, b. & residing Mid., dau. of John Burrell. (C)

69C - 18 Dec. 1879 - **Moses Johnson**, 30, single, farmer, b. & residing Mid., son of Doctor & Jane Johnson, married **Eliza Ann Webb**, 21, single, b. & residing Mid., dau. of John & Betsey Webb. (C)
70A - 18 Dec. 1879 - **William Burrell**, 21, single, farmer, b. & residing Mid., son of Kinsey & Charlotte Burrett, married **Fannie Mosby**, 21, single, b. South Carolina, residing Mid., dau. of Mosby. (C)
70B - 18 Dec. 1879 - **John Prior**, 28, single, farmer, b. & residing Gloucester, son of Richard & Fanny Prior, married **Charlott Holmes**, 37, widow, b. & residing Mid., dau. of [not given]. (C)
70C - 18 Dec. 1879 - **John H. Jackson**, 25, single, waterman, b. & residing Mid., son of Joseph & Isabella Jackson, married **Julia Wormley**, 18, single, b. & residing Mid., dau. of Thos. & Isabella Wormley. (C)
71A - License issued Dec. 1879, marriage date not given - **Wm. H. Budds**, 29, widower, sailor, b. North Bridgewater, Massachusetts, residing Mid., son of William & Lucy Budds, married **Grace L. C. Mears**, 22, single, b. & residing Mid., dau. of John W. & Amanda Mears. (W)
71B - License issued Dec. 1879, marriage date not given - **John A. Davis**, 22, single, sailor, b. Suffolk Co., New York, residing Mid., son of Alfred & Ellen Davis, married **Saphronia A. Mears**, 18, single, b. & residing Mid., dau. of John W. & Amanda Mears. (W)
71C - License issued Dec. 1879, marriage date not given - **John C. Miller**, 27, single, farmer, b. & residing Mid., son of John D. & Mary E. Miller, married **Hattie Slaughter**, 22, single, b. & residing Mid., dau. of Burruss & Ann Slaughter. (W)
72A - License issued Dec. 1879, marriage date not given - **John R. Parks**, 25, single, oysterman, b. & residing Mid., son of Curtis & Frances Parks, married **Sarah E. Revere**, 21, single, b. & residing Mid., dau. of Joel & Sarah Revere. (W)
72B - License issued Dec. 1879, marriage date not given - **Lewis H. Perkins**, 24, single, oysterman, b. & residing Mid., son of Walington & Lucinda Perkins, married **Matty Robinson**, 21, single, b. & residing Mid., dau. of Walter & Louisa Robinson. (C)
72C - License issued Dec. 1879, marriage date not given - **Edwin West**, 21, single, oysterman, b. & residing Mid., son of Alexander & Carolina West, married **Betty Burk**, 20, single, b. & residing Mid., dau. of Harry & Letty Ann Burk. (C)
73A - 28 Dec. 1879 - **Richard Morris**, 23, single, farmer, b. & residing Mid., son of Cornelius & Ann Morris, married **Farley Ellen Dungey**, 21, single, b. &

residing Mid., dau. of E. A. & Julia Dungey. (C)
   73B - 6 Jan. 1880 - **Edward Cary Percifull**, 21, single, farmer, b. & residing Mid., son of Jos. & Mary A. Percifull, married **Eddie B. Eubank**, 22, single, b. & residing Mid., son of Jos. C. & Eliz. Eubank. (W)
   73C - Jan. 1880 - **Muscoe R. Ailworth**, 21, single, sailor, b. & residing Mid., son of Josiah D. & Amanda Ailworth, married **Anna Greenwood**, 21, single, b. & residing Mid., dau. of Ransome & Bettie Greenwood. (W)
   74A - 8 Jan. 1880 - **Caesar Anderson**, 21, single, farmer, b. & residing Mid., son of Thos. & Sally Anderson, married **Elizabeth Carter**, 22, widow, b. & residing Mid., dau. of Betsy Cook. (C)
   74B - 9 Jan. 1880 - **Sam'l R. Blake**, 22, single, tailor, b. & residing Mid., son of Jacob S. Blake, married **Elizabeth South**, single, b. & residing Mid., dau. of Jas. South. (W)
   74C - 13 Jan. 1880 - **Jas. H. Atkins**, 29, single, blacksmith, b. Essex, residing King & Queen, son of R. H. & Pricilla Atkins, married **Mary Anna Hall**, 23, single, b. & residing Mid., dau. of Gid. G. W. Hall. (W)
   75A - 15 Jan. 1880 - **Ro. F. Ransome**, 27, single, farmer, b. & residing Mid., son of Ro. F. & Eliz. Ransome, married **Emma V. Jackson**, 23, single, b. & residing Mid., dau. of Sam'l R. & Mary Jackson. (W)
   75B - Jan. 1880 - **James Sable**, 26, single, sailor, b. Maryland, residing Mid., son of A. J. & Sarah Sable, married **Ginia Perry**, 21, single, b. & residing Mid., dau. of Elisha & Mary Perry. (W)
   75C - 17 Jan. 1880 - **Moses Harris**, 30, single, farmer, b. & residing Mid., son of Sam'l & Jane Harris, married **Nancy Holmes**, 24, single, b. & residing Mid., dau. of Wm. & Clora Holmes. (C)
   76A - 22 Jan. 1880 - **Daniel Wormley**, 21, single, oysterman, b. & residing Mid., son of Thos. & Isabella Wormley, married **Sarah Thornton**, 18, single, b. & residing Mid., dau. of Mary Thornton. (C)
   76B - 25 Jan. 1880 - **Henry Wormley**, 24, single, farmer, b. & residing King & Queen, son of Washington & Martha Wormley, married **Lucy Jane Smith**, 24, single, b. & residing Mid., dau. of Austine Smith. (C)
   76C - 27 Jan. 1880 - **Jas. H. Pollard**, 25, single, oysterman, b. King & Queen, residing Mid., son of Solomon & Mary Pollard, married **Mary Ward**, 23, single, b. & residing Mid., dau. of Zack & Martha Ward. (C)
   77A - 29 Jan. 1880 - **Joseph Harris**, 24, single, oysterman, b. & residing Mid., son of Ro. & Fanny Harris, married **Adeline Corr**, 21, single, b. & residing Mid., dau. of Wm. & Adeline Corr. (C)

77B - 1880 - **Wm. Washington**, 22, single, oysterman, b. & residing Mid., son of Geo. & Lucy Ann Washington, married **Rebecca Sutherlin**, 18, single, b. & residing Mid., dau. of Thos. & Nelly Sutherlin. (C)
77C - 30 Jan. 1880 - **Washington Fitchett**, 33, widower, farmer, b. & residing Mid., son of Jas. & Mollie Fitchett, married **Elizabeth Baker**, 20, single, b. & residing Mid., dau. of James & Betsy Baker. (C)
78A - Feb. 1880 - **Peter Smith**, 30, single, laborer, b. Mathews, residing Mid., son of James & Susan Smith, married **Nancy Robinson**, 21, single, b. & residing Mid., dau. of King & Lucy Robinson. (C)
78B - 11 Feb. 1880 - **Carter Moody**, 22, single, oysterman, b. & residing Mid., son of Mortimer & Charlotte Moody, married **Louisa Gresham**, 18, single, b. King & Queen, residing Mid., dau. of Samuel & Anna Gresham. (C)
78C - 11 Feb. 1880 - **Henry Ross**, 23, single, oysterman, b. & residing Mid., son of George & Ellen Ross, married **Rosella Croxton**, 19, single, b. Essex, residing Mid., dau. of John & Judy Croxton. (C)
79A - 1880 - **Emmit Franklin Topping**, 24, single, farmer, b. & residing Mid., son of Edward & Kesiah Topping, married **Mollie F. Purcell**, 21, single, b. & residing Mid., dau. of John & Hester Purcell. (W)
79B - 22 Feb. 1880 - **Henly W. Smith**, 28, single, merchant, b. Mid., residing Essex, son of Geo. W. & Ann F. Smith, married **Betsy A. Christian**, 24, single, b. & residing Mid., dau. of Wm. S. & Hellen E. Christian. (W)
79C - 4 Mar. 1880 - **James S. Marchant**, 25, single, oysterman, b. Mathews, residing Mid., son of Christopher & Dedemia Marchant, married **Maria Lou. West**, 16, single, b. Gloucester, residing Mid., dau. of John M. & Martha West. (W)
80A - 9 Mar. 1880 - **Wm. Henry Lomax**, 28, single, farmer, b. King & Queen, residing Mid., son of Jas. & Eudora Lomax, married **Fanny Floyd**, 21, single, b. & residing Mid., dau. of Floyd. (C)
80B - Mar. 1880 - **Andrew J. Sable**, 22, single, sailor, b. Maryland, residing Mid., son of A. J. & Sarah Sable, married **Vandelia Perry**, 21, single, b. & residing Mid., dau. of Elisha & Mary F. Perry. (W)
80C - 11 Mar. 1880 - **Fuller Walker**, 31, single, farmer, b. & residing Mid., son of Joel T. & Mary C. Walker, married **Mary E. Stiff**, 30, single, b. & residing Mid., dau. of Wm. Stiff. (W)
81A - 18 Mar. 1880 - **Zachary Street**, 24, single, farmer, b. & residing Mid., son of Zack & Ursula Street, married **Marg. Eliz. Folliard**, 20, single, b. King &

Queen, residing Mid., dau. of John P. & Susan Folliard. (W)
   81B - 18 Mar. 1880 - **Wm. H. Payne**, 22, single, laborer, b. & residing Mid., son of Jacob & Eliza Payne, married **Rosetta Lewis**, 16, single, b. & residing Mid., dau. of Betsy Lewis. (C)
   81C - 20 Mar. 1880 - **Richard Brockenbrough**, 20, single, sailor, b. & residing Mid., son of Newman & Silla Brockenbrough, married **Frances Jackson**, 18, single, b. & residing Mid., dau. of Jas. & Mary Jane Jackson. (C)
   82A - 18 Apr. 1880 - **William Corbin**, 22, single, farmer, b. & residing Mid., son of Geo. & Sarah Corbin, married **Malinda Chamberlain**, 23, widow, b. & residing Mid., dau. of Washington & Bessy Read. (C)
   82B - 21 Apr. 1880 - **John Lockley**, 21, single, oysterman, b. & residing Mid., son of George & Anna Lockley, married **Sarah Ann Harris**, 18, single, b. & residing Mid., dau. of Phil W. & Mary Eliz. Harris. (C)
   82C - 28 Apr. 1880 - **Major Parker Grenels**, 23, single, farmer, b. Accomack, residing Mid., son of Southey & Mary Grenels, married **Irene Harrow**, 20, single, b. & residing Mid., dau. of Wm. M. & Almedia Harrow. (W)
   83A - 29 Apr. 1880 - **Robert Webb**, 24, single, oysterman, b. & residing Mid., son of John & Betsey Webb, married **Sarah Wormley**, 20, single, b. & residing Mid., dau. of Richard & Louisa Wormley. (C)
   83B - 6 May 1880 - **Jas. H. Robinson**, 22, single, oysterman, b. & residing Mid., son of Richard & Jane Robinson, married **Belle Jones**, 21, single, b. & residing Mid., dau. of Beverly & Chaney Jones. (C)
   83C - 11 May 1880 - **Baylor Smith**, 23, single, b. & residing Mid., son of John & Willa Ann Smith, married **Violet Ruffin**, 19, single, b. & residing Mid., dau. of John & Violet Ruffin. (C)
   84A - May 1880 - **Alonzo Harrow**, 30, single, sailor, b. & residing Mid., son of Wm. & Amelia Harrow, married **Hattie Cavenaugh**, 21, single, b. Maryland, residing city of Baltimore, dau. of James & Priscilla Cavenaugh. (W)
   84B - 20 May 1880 - **John W. Topping**, 29, single, merchant, b. & residing Mid., son of Edward & Kesiah Topping, married **Jessie W. Daniel**, 22, single, b. & residing Mid., dau. of John W. & M. A. Daniel. (W)
   84C - 25 May 1880 - **Jas. H. Bohannon**, 24, single, merchant, b. Mathews, residing Mid., son of Geo. W. & Lucy H. Bohannon, married **Vio. D. Parrish**, 17, single, b. & residing Mid., dau. of Wm. F. & Cordelia T. Parrish. (W)
   85A - 27 May 1880 - **Oswald Snead**, 26, single, oysterman, b. Accomack, residing Mid., son of John L. &

Tabitha Snead, married **Mary B. Carlow**, 23, single, b. & residing Mid., dau. of Alex. & Sarah Carlow. (W)

85B - 8 Jun. 1880 - **John Rich'd Browne**, 37, widower, farmer, b. Mid., residing Gloucester, son of Smith W. & Susan N. Browne, married **Ruth W. Prince**, 25, single, b. King & Queen, residing Mid., son of Henry D. & Sarah Ann Prince. (W)

85C - 11 Jun. 1880 - **Chas. Henry Lomax**, 17, single, farmer, b. & residing Mid., son of Henry & Frances Lomax, married **Fanny Burrell**, 21, single, b. & residing Mid., dau. of Robert & Jane Burrell. (C)

86A - 1880 - **Sheppard Scarbrough**, 23, single, b. Accomac, residing Mid., son of Dan'l & Mary Scarbrough, married **Elmetina Boyton**, single, b. & residing Mid., dau. of Richard & Catherine Boyton. (C)

86B - 16 Jun. 1880 - **Lewis Griffin**, 24, single, oysterman, b. & residing Mid., son of Richard & Anne Griffin, married **Cath. Henry**, 18, single, b. & residing Mid., dau. of Thos. & Martha E. Henry. (C)

86C - 24 Jun. 1880 - **Addison Wake**, 62, widower, farmer, b. & residing Mid., son of Ransome & Mary Wake, married **Harriet Wormley**, 30, widow, b. Gloucester, residing Mid., dau. of Wormley. (C)

87A - 28 Jul. 1880 - **Walter Macklane**, 28, single, oysterman, b. Gloucester, residing Mid., son of Wm. & Elizabeth Macklane, married **Bettie T. Mickelborough**, 21, single, b. & residing Mid., dau. of John Mickelborough. (W)

87B - Jul. 1880 - **Samuel Mason**, 21, single, sailor, b. & residing Mid., son of Lemuel & Susan Mason, married **Susan Trader**, 21, single, b. & residing Mid., dau. of James & Susan Trader. (W)

87C - 24 Aug. 1880 - **John Wm. Davis**, 21, single, blacksmith, b. Portsmouth, residing Mid., son of John R. & Mary J. Davis, married **Saphronia Dodges**, 21, single, b. Essex, residing Mid., dau. of Jas. & Martha Hodges. (W)

88A - 30 Sep. 1880 - **Alexander Curtis**, 60, widower, farmer, b. & residing Mid., son of Wm. & Fanny Curtis, married **Betsey Hill**, 45, widow, b. & residing Mid., dau. of Washington & Alsey Lorimer.

88B - 3 Oct. 1880 - **Richard Burrell**, 38, white, farmer, b. King & Queen, residing Mid., son of Lewis & Barbary Burrell, married **Rebecca Reed**, 24, single, b. & residing Mid., dau. of Lewis & Eliza. Reed. (C)

88C - 12 Oct. 1880 - **Richard Fuller Bristow**, 35, widower, farmer, b. & residing Mid., married **Emma V. Ailworth**, 21, single, b. & residing Mid., dau. of Josiah D. & Roberta Ailworth. (W)

89A - 25 Oct. 1880 - **Clarance S. Montague**, 20,

single, farmer, b. & residing Mid., son of George & Sarah F. Montague, married **Mary C. Bristow**, 20, single, b. & residing Mid., dau. of Henry C. & Frances Bristow. (W)

89B - Nov. 1880 - **James Christopher**, 23, single, oysterman, b. & residing Mid., son of Nathan & Hattie Christopher, married **Adie** [or **Cidie**] **Bird**, 22, single, b. & residing Mid., dau. of Nathaniel & Rosanna Bird. (W)

89C - 6 Nov. 1880 - **Wm. Walker**, 22, single, farmer, b. Lancaster, residing Mid., son of Wm. & Eliza Walker, married **Jane Lockley**, 21, single, b. & residing Mid., dau. of Lockley. (C)

90A - 2 Dec. 1880 - **Harry Robinson**, 24, single, oysterman, b. Mathews, residing Mid., son of Kit & Maria Robinson, married **Emily Henry**, 23, single, b. & residing Mid., dau. of Nathan & Charlotte Henry. (C)

90B - 1880 - **John Henry Campbell**, single, farmer, b. & residing Mid., son of Campbell, married **Hester L. Bayton**, 21, single, b. & residing Mid., dau. of Richard T. Bayton. (C)

90C - 16 Dec. 1880 - **Jos. Harris**, 21, single, farmer, b. & residing Mid., son of George & Eliza Harris, married **Jane Washington**, 19, single, b. & residing Mid., dau. of Moses & Frances Washington. (C)

91A - 16 Dec. 1880 - **Wm. Jas. French**, 27, single, farmer, son of Wm. T. & Amanda French, married **Ida Sue Hall**, 23, single, b. & residing Mid., dau. of Addison & Nanie M. Hall. (W)

91B - 23 Dec. 1880 - **Samuel Amy**, 25, single, farmer, b. Tennessee, residing Mid., son of Henry & Eliza Amy, married **Susan Jones**, 20, single, b. & residing Mid., dau. of Beverly & Chaney Jones. (C)

91C - 23 Dec. 1880 - **James H. Horsley**, 23, single, mechanic, b. Gloucester, residing Mid., son of Keinningham & Martha Ann Horsley, married **Adeline Bristow**, 38, widow, b. Gloucester, residing Mid., dau. of (not given]. (W)

92A - 28 Dec. 1880 - **Jos. Thos. Worrel**, 23, single, oysterman, b. Mid., residing King & Queen, son of Jos. & Mary Worrell, married **Mary A. Brizentine**, 19, single, b. Essex, residing Mid., dau. of John Wm. Brizentine. (W)

92B - 30 Dec. 1880 - **Benja. C. Sibley**, 30, single, farmer, b. & residing Mid., son of Benj. B. & Louisa Sibley, married **Mary E. Smith**, 30, single, b. & residing Mid., dau. of John B. & Sarah Smith. (W)

92C - 28 Dec. 1880 - **Norman R. Blake**, 24, single, farmer, b. & residing Mid., son of Berkley R. & Susanna Blake, married **Mary C. Williams**, 27, single, b. Kent Co., Maryland, residing Mid., dau. of Jos. T. & Hannah

H. Williams. (W)

93A - 29 Dec. 1880 - **John Ro. Hundley**, 21, single, farmer, b. & residing Mid., son of Richard & Amanda Hundley, married **Georgia Ella Brown**, 17, single, b. King & Queen, residing Mid., dau. of George & Willie Ann Brown. (W)

93B - 1 Jan. 1881 - **Jessee Norris**, 57, widower, farmer, b. Lancaster, residing Mid., son of [not given], married **Lizie Johnson**, 25, single, b. & residing Mid., dau. of [not given]. (C)

93C - 6 Jan. 1881 - **Richard Fauntleroy**, 21, single, farmer, b. & residing Mid., son of Sarah Fauntleroy, married **Mary Richeson**, 16, single, b. & residing Mid., dau. of Susan Richeson. (C)

94A - 16 Jan. 1881 - **Robert Bundy**, 22, single, oysterman, b. & residing Mid., son of Fanny Bundey, married **Catharine Robinson**, 22, single, b. & residing Mid., dau. of Matilda Robinson. (C)

94B - 22 Jan. 1881 - **Ro. H. Montague**, 60, widower, farmer, b. & residing Mid., son of Thos. H. & Eliz. Montague, married **F. H. Schools**, 26, single, b. Essex, residing Mid., dau. of Adolphos & Lucy Schools. (W)

94C - 1881 - **John C. Robinson**, 30, single, house carpenter, b. & residing Mid., son of John S. & Alice E. Robinson, married **Jennie Purcell**, 27, single, b. & residing Mid., dau. of John & Hester Purcell. (W)

95A - Jan. 1881 - **David W. Wilson**, 23, single, oysterman, b. & residing Mid., son of Jas. L. & Cath. Wilson, married **Anna Ailworth**, 21, widow, b. & residing Mid., dau. of Ransome & Bettie Greenwood. (W)

95B - 17 Feb. 1881 - **Wm. Thornton**, 21, single, oysterman, b. & residing Mid., son of Benja. & Mary Thornton, married **Roberta Corr**, 20, single, b. & residing Mid., dau. of William & Adeline Corr. (C)

95C - 20 Feb. 1881 - **Willie Reed**, 22, single, oysterman, b. Gloucester, residing Mid., son of Carter & Matilda Braxton, **Fannie Fields**, 18, single, b. & residing Mid., dau. of Fielding & Julia Fields. (C)

96A - 24 Feb. 1881 - **Thos. Henry Waller**, 21, single, farmer, b. Essex, residing Mid., son of Clay & Cath. Waller, married **Annice Stalia Ross**, 21, single, b. & residing Mid., dau. of George & Ellen Ross. (C)

96B - 1881 - **Allen Major**, 26, single, farmer, b. & residing Mid., son of Iverson & Martha Major, married **Mary Wake**, 21, single, b. & residing Mid., dau. of Minnie & Mary Wake. (C)

96C - 3 Mar. 1881 - **Daniel Bright**, 27, single, sailor, b. Gloucester, residing Mid., son of Wm. & Susan Bright, married **Hester Williams**, 16, single, b. &

residing Mid., dau. of Thos. & Milley Williams. (C)
  97A - 10 Mar. 1881 - **Manuel Green**, 24, widower,
oysterman, b. & residing Mid., son of Manuel & Judith
Green, married **Louisa Robinson**, 20, single, b. &
residing Mid., dau. of Isaac & Polly Robinson. (C)
  97B - 22 Mar. 1881 - **Wm. H. Lanning**, 49, widower,
carpenter, b. Oneida, New York, residing Mid., son of
Henry & Abigail Lanning, married **Lucilla J. Hale**, 24,
single, b. & residing Mid., dau. of Wm. & Anna Hale.
(W)
  97C - 29 Mar. 1881 - **Wm. Mahone**, 28, single, farmer,
b. & residing Essex, son of Rich'd Mahone, married **Annis Croxton**, 21, single, b. Essex, residing Mid., dau. of
Claiborne & Susan Croxton. (W)
  98A - 24 Mar. 1881 - **Alexander Wilson**, 21, single,
farmer, b. & residing Mid., son of Jas. & Joanna Wilson,
married **Rebecca Taliaferro**, 24, single, b. & residing
Mid., dau. of Wm. & Lucy Taliaferro. (C)
  98B - 27 Mar. 1881 - **Ed. W. Corr**, 25, single, farmer,
b. & residing Mid., son of Wm. & Adeline Corr, married
Willie Ann Ellis, 21, single, b. & residing Mid., dau.
of Carter & Martha Ellis. (C)
  98C - 14 Apr. 1881 - **Wm. H. Wormley**, 22, single,
oysterman, b. & residing Mid., son of Julia Wormley,
married **Ailsey Henry**, 18, single, b. & residing Mid.,
dau. of Thos. & Martha E. Henry. (C)
  99A - 21 Apr. 1881 - **Erastus Harris**, 25, single,
oysterman, b. & residing Mid., son of John & Betsey
Harris, married **Hattie Curtis**, 27, single, b. & residing
Mid., dau. of Alexander & Charlotte Curtis. (C)
  99B - 28 Apr. 1881 - **Riter Carr Chamberlayne**, 24,
single, farmer, b. Essex, residing Mid., son of John &
Ellen Chamberlayne, married **Auta J. Cauthern**, 18,
single, b. Essex, residing Mid., dau. of Thos. & Lucy
Cauthern. (C)
  99C - 28 Apr. 1881 - **Harry C. Cook**, 24, single,
farmer, b. & residing Mid., son of Ralph & Betsy A.
Cook, married **Sally Smith**, 21, single, b. & residing
Mid., dau. of Thomas & Margaret Smith. (C)
  100A - May 1881 - **John H. Christopher**, 26, single,
sailor, b. & residing Mid., son of Malichi & Sallie
Christopher, married **Gennia Hurley**, 23, single, b.
Maryland, residing Mid., dau. of David & Jane Hurley.
(W)
  100B - 17 May 1881 - **Frank Haynes**, 23, single,
oysterman, b. Maine, residing Richmond Co., son of
Marion & Julia Haynes, married **Columbia A. Dunn**, 21,
single, b. Essex, residing Mid., dau. of Thos. H. & Mary
E. Dunn. (W)
  100C - May 1881 - **James R. Davis**, 35, widower,

oysterman, b. & residing Mid., son of Bartlett & Nancy Davis, married **Porter Didlake**, 35, widow, dau. of David & Bettie Wilson. (W)

101A - 16 Jun. 1881 - **Frederick Williams**, 22, single, oysterman, b. Gloucester, residing Mid., son of Daniel & Delpia Williams, married **Mary Burk**, 17, single, b. & residing Mid., dau. of Geo. Powers & Ellen Burk. (B)

101B - 15 Jun. 1881 - **Ro. W. Blake**, 25, single, lumberman, b. Gloucester, residing Mid., son of John & Nancy Blake, married **Maria Hale**, 22, single, b. & residing Mid., dau. of Wm. H. & Anna Hale. (W)

101C - Jun. 1881 - **Daniel Scarborough**, 45, widower, laborer, b. Accomack, residing Mid., son of Geo. & Racheal Scarborough, married **Betty Jackson**, 35, single, b. & residing Mid., dau. of John & Nancy Jackson. (C)

102A - 6 Aug. 1881 - **James Preston White**, 21, single, farmer, b. King & Queen, residing Mid., son of Arasmus & Elizabeth White, married **Mira Brockenbrough**, 21, single, b. King & Queen, residing Mid., dau. of Brockenbrough. (C)

102B - 21 Aug. 1881 - **Jno. Amos Burrell**, 21, single, farmer, b. & residing Mid., son of John & Nancy Burrell, married **Maggie Davis**, 19, single, b. Essex, residing Mid., dau. of Peter & Matilda Davis. (C)

102C - 23 Aug. 1881 - **John D. Gressitt, Jr.**, single, merchant, b. & residing Mid., son of J. D. Gressitt, married **Ada B. Faulkner**, 19, single, b. Charlotte, residing Mid., dau. of J. B. & Silester Faulkner. (W)

103A - 15 Sep. 1881 - **Wm. C. Broocke**, 40, widower, farmer, b. Gloucester, residing Mid., son of Geo. Thos. & Julia Ann Broocke, married **Mary J. Walden**, 20, single, b. & residing Mid., dau. of John & Sarah Walden. (W)

103B - 22 Sep. 1881 - **John Benjamin Franklin**, 21, single, farmer, b. Caroline, residing Mid., son of Richard & Mary Eliz. Franklin, married **Sarah Eliza Royster**, 21, single, b. & residing Mid., dau. of Thos. Franklin & Mary A. Royster. (W)

103C - 1881 - **James F. Vandergrift**, 26, single, farmer, b. Cecil Co., Maryland, residing Mid., son of John Vandergrift, married **Letitia Hall**, 19, single, b. & residing Mid., dau. of Gideon G. W. & Letitia Hall. (W)

104A - 23 Oct. 1881 - **Benjamin Johnson**, 20, single, laborer, b. & residing Mid., son of Benja. & Oney Johnson, married **Net. Ruffin**, 22, single, b. & residing Mid., dau. of Ruffin. (C)

104B - 21 Oct. 1881 - **Elijah Banks**, 21, single, oysterman, b. & residing Mid., son of A. Gabel & Nancie Banks, married **Anna Wormley**, 18, single, b. & residing Mid., dau. of Thomas & Isabella Wormley. (C)

104C - 1 Nov. 1881 - **Anthony Peterson**, 61, widower,

farmer, b. Mid., residing Essex, son of Wm. & Nancy Peterson, married **Susan Miller**, 45, single, b. Essex, residing Mid., dau. of Amy Miller. (C)

105A - 1 Nov. 1881 - **Rich. H. Griffin**, 21, single, oysterman, b. & residing Mid., son of Richard & Annah Griffin, married **Louisa Jones**, 17, single, b. & residing Mid., dau. of Edward & Eliza Jones. (C)

105B - 6 Nov. 1881 - **Ed. C. Walker**, 53, widower, farmer, b. Mid., residing King George, son of Holland & Debra Walker, married **Charlotte M. Muse**, 48, single, b. & residing Mid., dau. of Neilsen & Louisa Muse. (W)

105C - 10 Nov. 1881 - **John R. Morris**, 24, single, oysterman, b. & residing Mid., son of Cornelius & Ann Morris, married **Rosa Taliaferro**, single, b. & residing Mid., dau. of Sally Taliaferro. (C)

106A - 10 Nov. 1881 - **John Madison**, 23, single, oysterman, b. King & Queen, residing Mid., son of John & Lucy Madison, married **Patsey Robinson**, 18, single, b. & residing Mid., dau. of Corbin & Cordry Robinson. (C)

106B - 14 Nov. 1881 - **John A. Webb**, 23, single, oysterman, b. & residing Mid., son of John & Betsy Webb, married **Ellen Cook**, 19, single, b. & residing Mid., dau. of Ralph & Rebecca Cook. (C)

106C - 20 Nov. 1881 - **Marion T. Mayo**, 25, single, shoemaker, b. King & Queen, residing Mid., son of John D. & Franklin A. E. Mayo, married **Fannie Miller**, 24, single, b. & residing Mid., dau. of John D. & Mary E. Miller. (W)

107A - 23 Nov. 1881 - **Jas. B. Verlander**, 29, single, farmer, b. & residing Essex, son of Jas. & Elizabeth Verlander, married **Ada M. Saunders**, 21, single, b. & residing Mid., dau. of Thomas T. T. & Mary M. Saunders. (W)

107B - 24 Nov. 1881 - **Samuel Ferguson**, 23, single, sailor, b. Baltimore, Maryland, residing Mid., son of Wm. & Margaret Ferguson, married **Ida Webb**, 19, single, b. Lancaster, residing Mid., dau. of Virginia Webb. (W)

107C - 29 Nov. 1881 - **John T. Williams**, 26, single, farmer, b. Kent Co., Maryland, residing Mid., son of Joseph & Hannah A. Williams, married **Florance A. Daniel**, 16, single, b. & residing Mid., dau. of Joseph & Eliza Daniel. (W)

108A - 8 Dec. 1881 - **Ellis T. Curtis**, 24, single, oysterman, b. & residing Mid., son of Alex & Charlotte Curtis, married **Martha J. Gaines**, 23, single, b. Essex, residing Mid., dau. of Thomas L. & Robinett Gaines. (C)

108B - 7 Dec. 1881 - **Coleman Johnson**, 20, single, oysterman, b. & residing Mid., son of George & Cornelia Johnson, married **Bettie Peterson**, 18, single, b. & residing Mid., dau. of Henry & Hester Peterson. (C)

108C - 10 Dec. 1881 - **Wm. Gatewood**, 60, widower, farmer, b. King & Queen, residing Mid., son of Phil. & Mary Gatewood, married **Susan Churchill**, 35, widow, b. King & Queen, residing Mid., dau. of Garrett. (C)
109A - 10 Dec. 1881 - **Richard Page**, 21, single, farmer, b. & residing Mid., son of Manuel & Ann Eliza Page, married **Hester Ann Laws**, 19, single, b. & residing Mid., dau. of John & Caty Laws. (C)
109B - 13 Dec. 1881 - **Joshua N. Gregg**, 25, single, merchant, b. King & Queen, residing Mid., son of Peter & Martha Gregg, married **Cath. E. Fleet**, 24, single, b. & residing Mid., dau. of Ro. L. & Mary J. Fleet. (W)
109C - 25 Dec. 1881 - **Henry Stokes**, 24, single, oysterman, b. Gloucester, residing Mid., son of Christopher & Ann Stokes, married **Lettie Gardner**, 22, single, b. King & Queen, residing Mid., dau. of Judy Gardner. (C)
110A - 21, Dec. 1881 - **Wm. H. Fitchett**, single, b. & residing Mid., son of Wm. H. Fitchett, married **Iva Blake**, 17, single, b. & residing Mid.. (W) [No other information given.]
110B - 22 Dec. 1881 - **Lewis Burke**, 25, single, oysterman, b. & residing Mid., son of Wm. & Susan Burke, married **Eliza Robinson**, 16, single, b. & residing Mid., dau. of Matilda Robinson. (C)
110C - 22 Dec. 1881 - **Rolly Banks**, 22, single, farmer, b. King & Queen, residing Mid., son of Latiny & Susan Banks, married **Emma Washington**, 26, single, b. & residing Mid., dau. of George & Matilda Washington. (C)
111A - 22 Dec. 1881 - **Joseh** [sic - **Joseph** or **Josiah**?] **Madison**, 21, single, oysterman, b. King & Queen, residing Mid., son of John & Lucy Madison, married **Rexanna Goin**, 18, single, b. & residing Mid., dau. of John Goin & Betty. (C)
111B - 25 Dec. 1881 - **Robert B. Slaughter**, 21, single, farmer, b. & residing Mid., son of Geo. B. & Ann Slaughter, married **Elizabeth Hall**, 21, single, b. & residing Mid., dau. of Gid. G. W. & Letitia Hall. (W)
111C - 28 Dec. 1881 - **John W. Hurst**, 25, single, sailor, b. & residing Mathews, son of John W. & Maria J. Hurst, married **Vir. Ella Daniel**, 22, single, b. & residing Mid., dau. of Nath. C. Daniel. (W)
112A - 28 Dec. 1881 - **James H. Jackson**, 23, single, farmer, residing Mid., son of [not given], married **Barbara A. Mitchell**, 21, single, residing Mid., dau. of [not given]. (C)
112B - Dec. 1881 - **Charles Harte**, 21, single, oysterman, b. & residing Mid., son of James & Mary Harte, married **Emma Henley**, 17, single, b. Maryland, residing Mid., dau. of David & June Hen_ly_. (W)

112C - 3 Jan. 1882 - **James Ailworth**, 21, single, oysterman, b. & residing Mid., son of Josiah & Amanda Ailworth, married **Georgia Weston**, 21, single, b. & residing Mid., dau. of Thos. D. & Sarah Weston. (W)
113A - 28 Dec. 1881 - **Charles Davis**, 24, single, oysterman, b. Mathews, residing Mid., son of George & Fanny Davis, married **Mary Kemp**, 27, single, b. Richmond City, residing Mid., dau. of Stephen & Rebecca Kemp. (C)
113B - 28 Dec. 1881 - **Wm. E. Thomas**, 22, single, sailor, b. & residing Mathews, son of George A. & Lucy V. Thomas, married **Julia A. Blake**, 22, single, b. & residing Mid., dau. of Jacob & Dorothy E. Blake. (W)
113C - 29 Dec. 1881 - **John Hurbert Blake**, 22, single, oysterman, b. Gloucester, residing Mid., son of John & Louisa Blake, married **Mary Woollard**, 23, single, b. Richmond Co., residing Mid., dau. of Woollard. (W)

114A - Jan. 1882 - **Wm. Burke, Sr.**, 55, widower, farmer, b. & residing Mid., son of Edward & Betty Burke, married **Julia Wormley**, 40, single, b. Gloucester, residing Mid., dau. of Solomon Wormley. (C)
114B - 31 Dec. 1881 - **Chas. B. Wood**, 22, single, farmer, b. & residing Mid., son of Charles & Mary Wood, married **Louisa Conway**, 21, single, b. & residing Mid., dau. of Wm. & Emeline Conway. (C)
114C - 19 Jan. 1882 - **Thomas Harris**, 26, widower, farmer, b. & residing Mid., son of Robert & Fanny Harris, married **Fannie Lockley**, 19, single, b. & residing Mid., dau. of Sam'l & Delphia Lockley. (C)
115A - 18 Jan. 1882 - **Benjamin Griffin**, 21, single, farmer, b. & residing Mid., son of Wm. & Eliza Griffin, married **Lavenia Taliaferro**, 21, single, b. & residing Mid., dau. of Wm. & Lucy Taliaferro. (C)
115B - 19 Jan. 1882 - **John M. West**, 50, widower, farmer, b. Gloucester, residing Mid., son of Isaac & Harriett West, married **Josephine Newbill**, 33, single, b. King & Queen, residing Mid., dau. of John Newbill. (W)
115C - 26 Jan. 1882 - **Wm. H. Daniel**, 62, widower, farmer, b. & residing Mid., son of Ro. & Hannah Daniel, married **Anna Corr**, 50, single, b. & residing Mid., dau. of Braxton & Mary Corr. (W)
116A - 2 Feb. 1882 - **Columbus F. Walton**, 23, single, farmer, b. & residing Mid., son of Wm. & Sarah Walton, married **Ella Carlton**, 22, single, b. King & Queen, residing Mid., dau. of Jas. & Mary Carlton. (W)
116B - 5 Feb. 1882 - **Columbus S. Ison**, 32, single, farmer, b. King & Queen, residing Mid., son of John & Mary Ison, married **Indianna Major**, 28, single, b. Gloucester, residing Mid., dau. of Benjamin & Fanny

Major. (W)

116C - 5 Feb. 1882 - **Richard Bagby**, 22, single, farmer, b. & residing Mid., son of Titus & Catharine Bagby, married **Henrietta Tucker**, 22, single, b. & residing Mid., dau. of Richard & Frances Tucker. (C)

117A - Feb. 1882 - **John W. Marchant**, 24, single, oysterman, b. Mathews, residing Mid., son of Christopher C. & Tadenia Marchant, married **Rebecca Montague**, 21, widow, b. Gloucester, residing Mid., dau. of John M. & Martha West. (W)

117B - 11 Feb. 1882 - **Alexander Roane**, 20, single, farmer, b. & residing King & Queen, son of James & Nancy Roane, married **Betty Boyd**, 19, single, b. & residing Mid., dau. of Allen & Judy Boyd. (C)

117C - 15 Feb. 1882 - **Geo. W. Revere**, 31, single, sailor, b. & residing Mid., son of George B. & Letitia Revere, married **Sarah V. Revere**, 28, single, b. & residing Mid., dau. of Isaac N. & Martha A. Revere. (W)

118A - 21 Feb. 1882 - **Benjamin F. Dobson**, 32, widower, sailor, b. Gloucester, residing Mid., son of John & Eliza Dobson, married **Virginia Gardner**, widow, b. & residing Mid., dau. of Jas. & Elizabeth Fisher. (W)

118B - Feb. 1882 - **Ro. Gwynn**, 58, widower, farmer, b. & residing Mid., son of Gwynn, married **Nancy Upshaw**, 38, widow, b. & residing Mid., dau. of Upshaw. (C)

118C - 15 Mar. 1882 - **James C. Sibley**, 26, single, farmer, b. & residing Mid., son of Stage D. & Ann F. Sibley, married **Martha A. Morris**, 22, single, b. Kent Co., Maryland, residing Mid., dau. of John W. & Rebecca Morris. (W)

119A - 16 Mar. 1882 - **Lewis Thurston**, 21, single, oysterman, b. & residing Mid., son of Daniel & Jane Thurston, married **Emma Boss**, 21, single, b. King & Queen, residing Mid., dau. of Peter & Julianna Boss. (C)

119B - 23 Mar. 1882 - **Walter Davis**, 21, single, farmer, b. & residing Mid., son of John & Mary Davis, married **Susan Taliaferro**, 20, single, b. & residing Mid., dau. of Wm. & Lucy Taliaferro. (C)

119C - 28 Mar. 1882 - **John R. Smith**, 21, single, farmer, b. & residing King & Queen, son of Thos. & Milly Ann Smith, married **Maria Louisa Campbell**, 19, single, b. & residing Mid., dau. of Lee & Louisa Campbell. (C)

120A - 30 Mar. 1882 - **Isaac Braxton**, 21, single, oysterman, b. Essex, residing Mid., son of Carter & Alcy Braxton, married **Sarah Reed**, 21, single, b. & residing Mid., dau. of George & Petina Reed. (C)

120B - No complete record in this area. The following date and name were entered, then marked through: 12 Apr. 1882 - **James E. Walden**.

120C - 2 Apr. 1882 - **Jas. H. Kemp**, 25, single, oysterman, b. & residing Mid., son of James & Disa Kemp, married **Patsy J. Burrell**, 20, single, b. & residing Mid., dau. of Thos. & Mary Jane Burrell. (C)
121A - 13 Apr. 1882 - **Lewis Dunn**, 71, widower, farmer, b. Essex, residing Mid., son of Iverson & Mary Dunn, married **Virginia A. Cox**, 34, single, b. Essex, residing Mid., dau. of George & Agnes Cox. (W)
121B - 23 Apr. 1882 - **James Genmill**, 24, single, farmer, b. Kent Co., Maryland, residing Mid., son of John H. & W. G. R. Genmill, married **Mary L. Blake**, 21, single, b. & residing Mid., dau. of John L. & Matilda Blake. (W)
121C - 4 May 1882 - **John Fields**, 27, single, farmer, b. & residing Mid., son of Fielding & Cath. Fields, married **Percilla Robinson**, 17, single, b. & residing Mid., dau. of Robbin & Millie Robinson. (C)
122A - 18 May 1882 - **Joseph Dudley**, 22, single, farmer, b. & residing Mid., son of Ransome & Anna Dudley, married **Susan Robinson**, 23, single, b. & residing Mid., dau. of Matilda Robinson. (C)
122B - 18 May 1882 - **Austin Wilson**, 21, single, farmer, b. & residing Mid., son of Jas. & Sally Wilson, married **Sally Ann Braxton**, 20, single, b. & residing Mid., dau. of Carter & Mary Braxton. (C)
122C - May 1882 - **Henry Clarke**, 21, single, farmer, b. & residing Mid., son of Clarke, married **Lillie A. Lanning**, 21, single, b. Oneida, New York, residing Mid., dau. of Wm. H. & Almira Lanning. (W)
123A - 15 Jun. 1882 - **Griffin Cundiff**, 63, single [marriage license says widower], farmer, b. & residing Mid., son of Griffin & Mary Cundiff, married **Orintha C. Foster**, 34, single [marriage license says widow], b. Accomack, residing Mid., dau. of David & Cath. Sparrow. (W)
123B - 13 Jul. 1882 - **Moses Robinson**, 28, single, farmer, b. & residing Mid., son of Christopher [&] Maria Robinson, married **Mary Sutherlin**, 22, single, b. & residing Mid., dau. of Thos. & Nellie Sutherlin. (C)
123C - 19 Jul. 1882 - **Elijah Williams**, 22, single, farmer, b. & residing Mid., son of Chas. & Sally Williams, married **Sally Johnson**, 17, single, b. & residing Mid., dau. of John & Betty Johnson. (C)
124A - 27 Jul. 1882 - **Henry Corbin**, 22, single, farmer, b. & residing Mid., son of Jeff. & Milly Corbin, married **Letty Carter**, widow, b. & residing Mid., dau. of [not given]. (C)
124B - 3 Aug. 1882 - **Wm. O. Mitchell**, 24, single, farmer, b. Dorchester, Maryland, residing Mid., son of Wm. M. & Araminta Mitchell, married **Mary E. Daniel**, 21,

single, b. & residing Mid., dau. of Kembill & Laura E. Daniel. (W)
124C - 6 Sep. 1882 - **Albert Schools**, 39, widower, farmer, b. Essex, residing Mid., son of Dorsen & Lucy Schools, married **Louisa Norton**, 33, single, b. & residing Mid., dau. of John T. & Sarah Norton. (W)
125A - 7 Sep. 1882 - **Walter Rust**, 24, single, farmer, b. & residing Mid., son of Archibald & Winney Rust, married **Lucy Smith**, 31, widow, b. & residing Mid., dau. of Thos. & Margaret Smith. (C)
125B - 21 Sep. 1882 - **Joseph Keiser**, 21, single, laborer, b. Richmond Co., residing Mid., son of Eliza Keiser, married **Fanny Robinson**, 18, single, b. & residing Mid., dau. of Corbin & Eliza Robinson. (C)
125C - 12 Oct. 1882 - **Christopher Burk**, 21, single, oysterman, b. & residing Mid., son of Wm. & Susan Burk, married **Sarah Smith**, 21, single, b. & residing Mid., dau. of Cath. Smith. (C)
126A - 26 Oct. 1882 - **Richard Montague**, 23, single, farmer, b. & residing Mid., son of Catharine Montague, married **Agness Bundy**, 21, single, b. King & Queen, residing Mid., dau. of Ro. & Pinky Bundy. (C)
126B - Nov. 1882 - **Walter P. Hill**, 31, single, farmer, b. King & Queen, residing Mid., son of Henry & Agnes Hill, married **Lucy Jackson**, 21, single, b. & residing Mid., dau. of William & Martha Jackson. (C)
126C - 16 Nov. 1882 - **John J. Bennett**, single, farmer, b. & residing Mid., son of Wm. J. Bennett, married **Mary A. Bristow**, 22, single, b. & residing Mid., dau. of Lewis S. & Octavia Bristow. (W)
127A - 15 Nov. 1882 - **John S. Waples**, 25, single, merchant, b. & residing Accomack, son of Edward B. & Sarah A. Waples, married **Liz. T. Woodward**, 24, single, b. & residing Mid., dau. of P. T. & Mary E. Woodward. (W)
127B - 23 Nov. 1882 - **Jas. Henry Nelson**, 21, single, farmer, b. & residing Mid., son of Wm. & Milley Nelson, married **Lottie Bayton**, 17, single, b. & residing Mid., dau. of Rich'd Bayton. (C)
127C - 22 Nov. 1882 - **Hardy Thomas**, 30, widower, oysterman, b. Norfolk, residing Mid., son of Henry & Maria Thomas, married **Sally Vena**, 30, single, b. & residing Mid., dau. of Vena. (C)
128A - 23 Nov. 1882 - **Wm. Corbin**, 21, single, oysterman, b. & residing Mid., son of Wm. & Milly Corbin, married **Ella Fisher**, 21, single, residing Mid., dau. of Clara Fisher. (C)
128B - 25 Nov. 1882 - **Allen Reed**, 23, single, oysterman, b. & residing Mid., son of Austin & Fanny Reed, married **Louisa Robinson**, 21, single, b. & residing

Mid., dau. of Lewis & Mary Robinson. (C)
128C - 25 Nov. 1882 - **Henry Harris**, 36, widower, blacksmith, b. & residing Mid., son of Henry & Margaret Harris, married **Addie Jackson**, 55, widow, b. Essex, residing Mid., dau. of [not given]. (C)
129A - 30 Nov. 1882 - **Wm. Henry Revere**, 34, single, farmer, b. & residing Mid., son of Isaac N. & Martha A. Revere, married **Emma J. Hall**, 22, single, b. & residing Mid., dau. of Thomas & Pelena Hall. (W)
129B - 29 Nov. 1882 - **Moat A. Jackson**, 27, single, farmer, b. & residing Mid., son of James H. & Anna H. Jackson, married **Emma A. Martin**, 22, single, b. & residing Mid., dau. of Henry C. & Emily Martin. (W)
129C - 30 Nov. 1882 - **Geo. E. Sibley**, 26, single, farmer, b. & residing Mid., son of Daniel & Sarah Sibley, married **Cath. E. Sibley**, 25, single, b. & residing Mid., dau. of B. B. & Ellenor Sibley. (W)
130A - 6 Dec. 1882 - **Jas. Walter Broach**, 24, single, carriage maker, b. Essex, residing Mid., son of Robert & Martha Broach, married **Lulie Daniel**, 21, single, b. & residing Mid., dau. of Carpenter C. Daniel. (W)
130B - 10 Dec. 1882 - **Richard Ed. Thrift**, 30, single, farmer, b. & residing Mid., son of Robert & Elizabeth Thrift, married **Lucy A. Smither**, 22, single, b. & residing Mid., dau. of Ribon & Cath. Smither. (W)
130C - 13 Dec. 1882 - **Thos. R. Goulding**, 26, single, farmer, b. & residing Caroline, son of Thos. W. & Louisa E. Goulding, married **Nannie W. Hall**, 19, single, b. & residing Mid., dau. of Addison & Nannie M. Hall. (W)
131A - 14 Dec. 1882 - **Nelson Lockley**, 23, single, farmer, b. & residing Mid., son of Jas. & Molley Lockley, married **Sallie A. Cook**, 18, single, b. & residing Mid., dau. of Ralph & Betsy Cook. (C)
131B - 26 Dec. 1882 - **G. T. B. Miller**, 23, single, farmer, b. & residing Mid., son of John D. & Mary E. Miller, married **Josephine Q. Dunlevy**, 23, single, b. & residing Mid., dau. of Wm. B. & Mary E. Dunlevy. (W)
131C - 21 Dec. 1882 - **Adolphus Morris**, 25, single, farmer, b. & residing Mid., son of Lorenza & Jane Morris, married **Janetta Morris**, 19, single, b. & residing Mid., dau. of Wm. 7 Jane Morris. (C)
132A - 20 Dec. 1882 - **John Williams**, 22, single, oysterman, b. King & Queen, residing Mid., son of Thomas & Mary Williams, married **Cora Harris**, 21, single, b. & residing Mid., dau. of Rose Harris. (C)
132B - 25 Dec. 1882 - **Joseph A. Townsend**, 24, single, merchant, b. Gloucester, residing Mid., son of Kendall & Elizabeth Townsend, married **Mattie E. Bristow**, 23, single, b. & residing Mid., dau. of Thos. & Eudora Bristow. (W)

132C - 23 Dec. 1882 - **Charles Hamilton**, 22, single, farmer, b. & residing Essex, son of Lewis & Ann Hamilton, married **Willintina Harris**, 30, single, b. & residing Mid., dau. of Henry & Cordry Harris. (C)

133A - 29 Dec. 1882 - **Millard F. Ruark**, 24, single, mariner, b. Dorchester, Maryland, residing Maryland, son of Thomas & Sarah Ruark, married **Willis F. Carter**, 22, single, b. & residing Mid., dau. of Robert & Mary Carter. (W)

133B - 28 Dec. 1882 - **Scipio Davis**, 26, single, farmer, b. & residing Mid., son of John & Mary Davis, married **Mary Wormley**, 20, single, b. & residing Mid., dau. of Richard & Louisa Wormley. (C)

133C - 7 Jan. 1883 - **Charles Conley**, 22, single, farmer, b. & residing Mid., son of Wm. & Emeline Conley, married **Judy Nest**, 20, single, b. & residing Mid., dau. of Judy Nest. (C)

134A - 28 Dec. 1882 - **Thos. H. Cook**, 23, single, farmer, b. & residing Mid., son of Ralph & Betsy Cook, married **Laura Morris**, 18, single, b. & residing Mid., dau. of Wm. & Betsy Morris. (C)

134B - Dec. 1882 - **Albert Perry**, 23, single, sailor, b. & residing Mid., son of Elisha & Mary F. Perry, married **Clarissa Trader**, 21, single, b. & residing Mid., dau. of Richard & Permelia Trader. (W)

134C - 4 Jan. 1883 - **Wm. S. Lewis**, 23, single, oysterman, b. King & Queen, residing Mid., son of Samuel & Maria June Lewis, married **Ida B. Johnson**, 22, single, b. & residing Mid., dau. of Frank & Harriet Johnson. (C)

135A - 10 Jan. 1883 - **Joseph Josias**, 20, single, farmer, b. Gloucester, residing Mid., son of Wm. Street & Lucy Thurston, married **Mary Johnson**, 16, single, b. & residing Mid., dau. of Spencer & Adeline Johnson. (C)

135B - 17 Jan. 1883 - **William Dunlevy, Jr.**, single, farmer, b. & residing Mid., son of Wm. & Mary Dunlevy, married **Macy Mercer**, single, b. & residing Mid., dau. of John & Lucy Mercer. (W)

135C - 25 Jan. 1883 - **John W. Bohannon**, 36, single, sailor, b. Mathews, residing Mid., son of Geo. W. & Lucy Bohannon, married **India Browne**, 30, single, b. Gloucester, residing Mid., dau. of Browne. (W)

136A - 1 Feb. 1883 - **Joseph T. Wood**, 22, single, farmer, b. & residing Mid., son of George & Anna Wood, married **Elizabeth Robinson**, 21, single, b. & residing Mid., dau. of Walter Robinson. (C)

136B - 1 Feb. 1883 - **Armstead Williams**, 21, single, oysterman, b. Lancaster, residing Mid., son of Armstead & Sarah Williams, married **Ada Henry**, 18, single, b. &

residing Mid., dau. of Thos & Martha Henry. (C)
      136C - 8 Feb. 1883 - **Joseph P. Slaughter**, 30, single,
farmer, b. & residing Mid., son of Richeson & Ann
Slaughter, married **Rachel E. Mason**, 17, single, b. &
residing Mid., dau. of John W. & Andrella Mason. (W)
      137A - 13 Feb. 1883 - **Daniel Sibley**, 22, single,
oysterman, b. & residing Mid., son of Norman & Lucy
Sibley, married **Margaret Robinson**, 32, widow, b. &
residing Mid., dau. of Daniel & Sarah Robinson. (W)
      137B - 20 Feb. 1883 - **Fayette Burton**, 34, widower,
sailor, b. & residing Gloucester, son of Thomas & Jane
Burton, married **Lucy Carter**, 22, single, b. Gloucester,
residing Mid., dau. of Lucy Carter. (C)
      137C - 20 Feb. 1883 - **Albert Parker**, 30, single,
oysterman, b. Prince Edward, residing Mid., son of Peter
& Sally Parker, married **Tela Ann Lewis**, 30, widow, b. &
residing Mid., dau. of Zack & Frances Crittenden. (C)
      138A - 22 Feb. 1883 - **James Fitchett**, 23, single,
oysterman, b. & residing Mid., son of Allen & Lucy Ann
Fitchett, married **Susan Griffin**, 19, single, b. &
residing Mid., dau. of Richard & Anna Griffin. (C)
      138B - 27 Feb. 1883 - **Joshua Lewis**, 24, single,
oysterman, b. & residing Mid., son of John Peterson &
Elizabeth Lewis, married **Hester Latine**, 19, single, b. &
residing Mid., dau. of [not given]. (C)
      138C - 1 Mar. 1883 - **Richard Beverly**, 40, widower,
farmer, b. & residing Mid., son of Ellick & Easter
Beverly, married **Nancy Washington**, 35, widow, b. &
residing Mid., dau. of George & Matilda Washington. (C)
      139A - 8 Mar. 1883 - **Eugene G. Schools**, 23, single,
farmer, b. Essex, residing Mid., son of Leonard & Martha
A. Schools, married **Ella S. Staigal**, 19, single, b.
Halifax, residing Mid., dau. of John D. & Sarah M.
Staigal. (W)
      139B - 8 Mar. 1883 - **John Reed**, 28, single,
oysterman, b. & residing Mid., son of Austin & Matilda
Reed, married **Ella Hill**, 26, single, b. & residing Mid.,
dau. of James & Betsey Hill. (C)
      139C - 13 Mar. 1883 - **Charles Jones**, 23, single,
oysterman, b. King & Queen, residing Mid., son of
Charles & Winny Jones, married **Mary J. Smith**, 20,
single, b. & residing Mid., dau. of John & Jane Smith.
(C)
      140A - 11 Mar. 1883 - **Richard P. Baker**, 27, single,
sailor, b. & residing New York, son of John & Mary E.
Baker, married **Mary T. Trader**, 21, single, b. & residing
Mid., dau. of Mary Trader. (W)
      140B - 15 Mar. 1883 - **John Jones**, 62, widower,
oysterman, b. Lancaster, residing Mid., son of Robin &
Hannah Jones, married **Mary Jane Wilson**, 18, single, b. &

residing Mid., dau. of Julius & Mary Wilson. (C)
    140C - 22 Mar. 1883 - **Wm. F. Ward**, 22, single, carpenter b. Northampton, residing Mid., son of Henry & Eliza Ward, married **Fannie Hurley**, 23, single, b. Cambridge, Maryland, residing Mid., dau. of John H. & Margaret Hurley. (W)
    141A - 24 Mar. 1883 - **James M. Gwynn**, 31, single, oysterman, b. King & Queen, residing Mid., son of Chas. E. & Cordelia A. Gwynn, married **Effie M. Mickleborough**, 21, single, b. & residing Mid., dau. of John Mickleborough. (W)
    141B - 24 Mar. 1883 - **John Wm. Lightfoot**, 22, single, oysterman, b. & residing Mid., son of Wm. & Maria Lightfoot, married **Alice Cook**, 18, single, b. & residing Mid., dau. of Edgar & Lucy Cook. (C)
    141C - 7 Apr. 1883 - **Eli Whiting**, 26, single, oysterman, b. & residing Mid., son of Beverly & Mary Whiting, married **Ada Johnson**, 16, single, b. & residing Mid., dau. of George & Matilda Johnson. (C)
    142A - 26 Apr. 1883 - **George Henry**, 20, single, oysterman, b. & residing Mid., son of Richard & Roberta Henry, married **Sarah Payton**, 16, single, b. & residing Mid., dau. of Robert & Catharine Payton. (C)
    142B - 10 May 1883 - **Pearley Ransome**, 27, single, sailor, b. & residing Mid., son of Robert & Eliz. Ransome, married **Anndelusia Revere**, 21, single, b. & residing Mid., dau. of Isaac N. & Martha A. Revere. (W)
    142C - 14 Apr. 1883 - **Thomas Henry Harris**, 26, single, oysterman, b. & residing Mid., son of Jacob & Elizabeth Harris, married **Cherry Burrell**, 20, single, b. & residing Mid., dau. of Thomas & Mary J. Burrell. (C)
    143A - 29 Apr. 1883 - **Wm. H. Healy**, 25, widower, lumberman, b. & residing Mid., son of Jas. T. & Mary F. Healy, married **Mary E. Thomas**, 17, single, b. Kent Co., Maryland, residing Mid., dau. of Geo. W. & Caroline Thomas. (W)
    143B - 3 May 1883 - **William Kidd**, 29, single, oysterman, b. & residing Mid., son of James & Betsy Kidd, married **Nancy Morris**, 24, single, b. & residing Mid., dau. of William & Mary Morris. (C)
    143C - 3 May 1883 - **Samuel Boyd**, 23, single, oysterman, b. & residing Mid., son of Allen & Nancy Boyd, married **Fannie Burrell**, 22, single, b. & residing Mid., dau. of Thomas & Peggy Burrell. (C)
    144A - 10 May 1883 - **Joseph Thos. Harris**, 22, single, oysterman, b. King & Queen, residing Mid., son of Thomas & Betsey Harris, married **Lucy Morris**, 20, single, b. & residing Mid., dau. of Cornelius & Ann Morris. (C)
    144B - 15 May 1883 - **John Jones**, 29, single, oysterman, b. New Kent, residing James City Co., son of

John & Lucy Jones, married **Lucy Ann Washington**, 22, single, b. & residing Mid., dau. of [not given]. (C)
144C - 16 May 1883 - **John W. Larkin**, 27, single, oysterman, b. Gloucester, residing Mid., son of George & Maria Larkin, married **Roberta A. Gardner**, 22, single, b. & residing Mid., dau. of Lewis W. & Elizabeth H. Gardner. (W)
145A - 16 May 1883 - **Jas. Henry Ferguson**, 21, single, waterman, b. Baltimore, Maryland, residing Mid., son of Wm. H. & Marg't Ferguson, married **Betty Aug. Fitchett**, 21, single, b. & residing Mid., dau. of S. P. & Sarah E. Fitchett. (W)
145B - None.
145C - 30 May 1883 - **Beauregard Turner**, 22, single, farmer, b. & residing Hanover, son of Thos. G. & Margaret Turner, married **Nannie E. Healy**, 21, single, b. & residing Mid., dau. of Julius E. & Henrietta E. Healy. (W)
146A - 31 May 1883 - **Oliver Brockenbrough**, 22, single, oysterman, b. & residing Mid., son of Jacob & Annah Brockenbrough, married **Barbary A. Smith**, 19, single, b. Essex, residing Mid., dau. of Austin & Nancy Smith. (C)
146B - 7 Jun. 1883 - **Washington Johnson**, 52, widower, farmer, b. King & Queen, residing Mid., son of Martin & June Johnson, married **Blanche Payton**, 21, single, b. & residing Mid., dau. of Solomon & Fanny Payton. (C)
146C - 12 Jun. 1883 - **W. W. Wood**, 23, single, farmer, b. & residing Mid., son of Richard & Bettie Wood, married **Lulie L. Dillard**, 21, single, b. & residing Mid., dau. of Ed. L. & Elizabeth Dillard. (W)
147A - 13 Jun. 1883 - **John A. Jackson**, 21, single, farmer, b. & residing Mid., son of Jas. R. & Malvina Jackson, married **Ella Daniel**, 16, single, b. & residing Mid., dau. of Geo. W. & Mary Daniel. (W)
147B - 1883 - **Robert Carr**, 23, single, residing Mid., married **Rose Dawson**, 22, single, residing Mid. (C) [No other information given.]
147C - 3 Jul. 1883 - **Wm. E. Barrick**, 45, widower, mechanic, b. Mid., residing Lunenberg, son of John & Emeline Barrick, married **Sarah B. Northam**, 29, single, b. & residing Mid., dau. of Henry C. & Susan H. Northam. (W)
148A - 18 Jul. 1883 - **James Dudley**, 22, single, farmer, b. & residing Mid., son of James & Sarah Dudley, married **Elizabeth Callis**, 21, single, b. Mathews, residing Mid., dau. of Thos. & Elizabeth Callis. (W)
148B - 19 Jul. 1883 - **Alexander Perrin**, 21, single, farmer, b. Gloucester, residing Mid., son of Ellick & Mary Perrin, married **Mary Jackson**, 18, single, b.

Caroline, residing Mid., dau. of Andrew & Grace Jackson. (C)

148C - 21 Jul. 1883 - **Jas. Payne Williams**, 21, single, farmer, b. & residing Mid., son of Zack & Charity Williams, married **Chaney Davis**, 20, single, b. Essex, residing Mid., dau. of Peter & Matilda Davis. (C)

149A - 25 Jul. 1883 - **Isaac A. Cole**, 34, single, mechanic, b. Chesterfield, residing Mid., son of Geo. W. & Mary Susan Cole, married **Johona Gardner**, 19, single, b. & residing Mid., dau. of Thomas & Jane Gardner. (W)

149B - 2 Aug. 1883 - **Chas. W. Moss**, 25, single, farmer, b. & residing Mid., son of Stephen & Matilda Moss, married **Martha E. Campbell**, 18, single, b. & residing Mid., dau. of Warner & Easter Campbell. (C)

149C - 14 Aug. 1883 - **Gabriel Goldenberg**, 25, single, farmer, b. Russia, residing Mid., son of Isreal & Bessie Goldenberg, married **Lena Magedman**, 21, single, b. Russia, residing Mid., dau. of Solomon & Ruthga Magedman. (W)

150A - 13 Aug. 1883 - **Samuel Davis**, 65, widower, farmer, b. & residing Mid., son of Abram & Beckey Davis, married **Virginia Greenwood**, 40, widow, b. & residing Mid., dau. of Greenwood. (C)

150B - 19 Aug. 1883 - **John R. Carter**, 23, single, farmer, b. & residing Mid., son of David & Milly Carter, married **Mary Robinson**, 19, single, b. & residing Mid., dau. of Lucy Robinson. (C)

150C - 16 Aug. 1883 - **Jacob Harris**, 23, single, farmer, b. & residing Mid., son of Jacob & Betsey Harris, married **Alice Reed**, 18, single, b. & residing Mid., dau. of Wm. & Martha Reed.

151A - 1883 - **R. W. Southerlin**, 24, single, farmer, b. & residing Mid., son of Thos. & Nellie Southerlin, married **Eliza Payton**, 17, single, b. & residing Mid., dau. of Ro. & Catherine Payton. (C)

151B - 11 Sep. 1883 - **Jas. T. Parks**, 24, single, oysterman, b. & residing Mid., son of Abel & Elizabeth Parks, married **Louisa Bridges**, 21, single, b. Mathews, residing Mid., dau. of Peter & Francis. (W)

151C - 25 Sep. 1883 - **Gouvernear Thos. Greenlaw**, 23, single, farmer, b. & residing Stafford, son of Price & Virginia Greenlaw, married **Sallie E. Montague**, 19, single, b. & residing Mid., dau. of Robert & Fannie Montague. (W)

152A - 11 Oct. 1883 - **John Wm. Jackson**, 22, single, oysterman, b. Gloucester, residing Mid., son of Johan & Cordelia Ann Jackson, married **Mary Ross**, 18, single, b. King & Queen, residing Mid., dau. of Taliaferro & Ross.

152B - 11 Oct. 1883 - **James Bundy**, 21, single,

oyserman, b. & residing Mid., son of June Bundy, married **Eliza Key**, 21, single, b. & residing Mid., dau. of Cath. Key. (C)

152C - 15 Oct. 1883 - **John Jones, Jr.**, 23, single, oysterman, b. & residing Mid., son of John & Laura Jones, married **Mary Carter**, 22, single, b. & residing Mid., dau. of Reubin & Anna Carter. (C)

153A - 25 Oct. 1883 - **Preston B. White**, 24, single, oysterman, b. Accomack, residing Mid., son of Napolean & Catharine White, married **Malvina V. Jackson**, 21, single, b. & residing Mid., dau. of John L. & Malvina Jackson. (W)

153B - 24 Oct. 1883 - **Wm. Hall**, 24, single, farmer, b. & residing King & Queen, son of Hall, married **Lucy Walton**, 22, single, b. Essex, residing Mid., dau. of Wm. & Sarah A. Walton. (W)

153C - 31 Oct. 1883 - **Edmund Baytop**, 21, single, farmer, b. Gloucester, residing Mid., son of Jacob Baytop, married **Florence Wilson**, 21, single, b. & residing Mid., dau. of James & Eliza Wilson. (C)

154A - 1883 - **Ellick (Alexander) Cook**, 25, single, residing Mid., married **Anne Burrell**, 17, single, residing Mid. (C) [No other information given.]

154B - 8 Nov. 1883 - **John Adams**, widower, mechanic, b. King William, residing Mid., son of Adams, married **Luella Schools**, 16, single, b. & residing Mid., dau. of Leonard & Martha Schools. (W)

154C - 13 Nov. 1883 - **Andrew J. Brown**, 34, widower, farmer, b. & residing King & Queen, son of Wm. W. & Mary F. Brown, married **Lucie E. Thurston**, 32, widow, b. & residing Mid., dau. of Charles & Jane Dudley. (W)

155A - 15 Nov. 1883 - **Thomas H. Corbin**, 21, single, oysterman, b. & residing Mid., son of George & Sarah Conley, married **Ella Browne**, 21, single, b. & residing Mid., dau. of Ellick & Maria Ann Browne. (C)

155B - 15 Nov. 1883 - **Oscar Holliday**, 21, single, oysterman, b. Powhatan, residing Mid., son of Robert & Susan Holliday, married **Fanny Lewis**, 16, single, b. & residing Mid., dau. of Albert & Isabella Lewis. (C)

155C - Dec. 1883 - **Benjamin Landing**, 22, single, oysterman, b. & residing Mathews, son of Eziel & Emily Landing, married **Dorothy Taper**, 21, single, b. Mathews, residing Mid., dau. of [not given]. (W)

156A - 1 Dec. 1883 - **Sims Burrell**, 23, single, oysterman, b. & residing Gloucester, son of Jackson & Arrena Burrell, married **Ellinora Tunstall**, 19, single, b. & residing Mid., dau. of Ben. & Nelly Tunstall. (C)

156B - Dec. 1883 - **Hernius Jackson**, 23, single, oysterman, b. & residing Mid., son of Noah & Anna Jackson, married **Alice Kellum**, 30, widow, b. & residing

Mid., dau. of Jos. L. & Cath. Wilson. (W)
    156C - Dec. 1883 - **Sam'l R. Jackson**, 25, single, oysterman, b. & residing Mid., son of James R. & Malvina Jackson, married **Bertha A. Ailworth**, 17, single, b. & residing Mid., dau. of Josiah D. & Sallie Ailworth. (W)
    157A - 13 Dec. 1883 - **Jas. E. Redd**, 38, widower, farmer, b. & residing King & Queen, son of Thos. W. & Mary Redd, married **Josephine West**, 34, widow, b. King & Queen, residing Mid., dau. of John & Eliza Newbill. (W)
    , B - 20 Dec. 1883 - **Wm. Mason**, 23, single, farmer, b. & residing Mid., son of John W. & Andinella Mason, married **Sue E. Enos**, 21, single, b. & residing Mid., dau. of Wm. H. & Mary E. Enos. (W)
    , C - Dec. 1883 - **John T. Lush**, 41, widower, carpenter, b. Brooklyn, New York, residing Mid., son of Geo. W. & Letta Lush, married **Rosetta Bratton**, 30, widow, b. & residing Mid., dau. of Wm. & Almeda Harrow. (W)
    158A - 20 Dec. 1883 - **Ro. H. Wood**, 25, single, oysterman, b. & residing Mid., son of Geo. W. & Anna Wood, married **Hester Ann Morris**, 21, single, b. & residing Mid., dau. of Betty Morris. (C)
    158B - 23 Dec. 1883 - **Jefferson Peterson**, 22, single, oysterman, b. & residing Mid., son of Henry & Hester Peterson, married **Mat. Carter**, 22, single, b. & residing Mid., dau. of Carter. (C)
    158C - 25 Dec. 1883 - **John R. Sadler**, 22, single, oysterman, b. & residing Mid., son of Arther & Mary J. Sadler, married **Emma Schools**, 17, single, b. King & Queen, residing Mid., dau. of Charles Schools. (W)
    159A - 27 Dec. 1883 - **Charles H. Carlow**, 21, single, oysterman, b. & residing Mid., son of Alex & Sarah Carlow, married **Sarah Blake**, 21, single, b. & residing Mid., dau. of John Blake. (W)
    159B - 27 Dec. 1883 - **Harry C. Cooke**, 27, widower, farmer, b. & residing Mid., son of Ralph & Betsy Cooke, married **Mary E. Morris**, 22, single, b. & residing Mid., dau. of Noah & Cath. Morris. (C)
    159C - 28 Dec. 1883 - **Lindsay Bagby**, 23, single, oysterman, b. & residing Mid., son of Armstead Bagby, married **Lucie Tucker**, 19, single, b. & residing Mid., dau. of Richard & Frances Tucker. (C)

    160A - 2 Jan. 1884 - **Jas. Ed. Banks**, 22, single, farmer, b. & residing Mid., son of John Henry & Eliza Ann Banks, married **Lea Winfield**, 21, single, b. & residing Mid., dau. of Scipio & Milley Winfield. (C)
    160B - 12 Jan. 1884 - **Menser Robinson**, 21, single, farmer, b. King & Queen, residing Mid., son of Squire & Ellen Robinson, married **Julia Carr**, 17, single, b. &

residing Mid., dau. of Robert & Oney Carr. (C)
160C - 17 Jan. 1884 - **Jackson Thos. Montgomery**, 21, single, oysterman, b. Fredericksburg, residing Mid., son of Seth & Mary Montgomery, married **Ellen M. Major**, 16, single, b. & residing Mid., dau. of L. O. B. & Mary Major. (W)
161A - 1884 - **John Johnson**, 24, single, residing Mid., son of [not given], married **Rosa Carter**, 19, single, residing Mid., dau. of Parker & Carter. (C)
161B - Jan. 1884 - **Beverly Belle**, 21, single, oysterman, b. & residing Mid., son of John & Amy Bell, married **Eliz. Harris**, 21, single, b. & residing Mid., dau. of Robert & Fanny Harris. (C)
161C - 3 Feb. 1884 - **Richard Nickolson, Sr.**, 51, widower, farmer, b. King William, residing Mid., son of Milly Roy, married **Lizzie Moody**, 19, single, b. Essex, residing Mid., dau. of Emily Moody. (C)
162A - 17 Feb. 1884 - **John M. George**, 23, single, sailor, b. Stafford, residing Mid., son of Jas. M. & Margaret R. George, married **Liz. E. Rains**, 22, single, b. Stafford, residing Mid., dau. of Rains. (W)
162B - 27 Feb. 1884 - **John Wm. Morris**, 22, single, farmer, b. Kent Co., Maryland, residing Mid., son of John W. & Rebecca Morris, married **Mary Sibley**, 23, single, b. & residing Mid., dau. of Jane Sibley. (W)
162C - 27 Feb. 1884 - **Josiah Travis**, 22, single, farmer, b. Dorchester, Maryland, residing Mid., son of Daniel Saunders & Lavinia Travers, married **Harriet Griffin**, 21, single, b. & residing Mid., dau. of Wm. & Eliza Griffin. (C)
163A - 28 Feb. 1884 - **Rich. T. Snead**, 36, single, oysterman, b. Northampton, residing Mid., son of John L. & Tabatha Snead, married **Miria C. Blake**, 24, widow, b. & residing Mid., dau. of Wm. H. & Anna Hale. (W)
163B - 6 Mar. 1884 - **Adolphus Beedles**, 21, single, oysterman, b. Lancaster, residing Mid., son of Wm. Y Virginia Beedles, married **Rosella Courtney**, 21, single, b. King & Queen, residing Mid., dau. of Wm. & Jane Courtney. (C)
163C - 9 Mar. 1884 - **Peter Blake**, 23, single, farmer, b. & residing Mid., son of John L. & Matilda Blake, married **Margaret A. Kennard**, 17, single, b. & residing Mid., dau. of Wm. J. Kennard. (W)
164A - 16 Mar. 1884 - **Geo. A. Parks**, 25, single, oysterman, b. & residing Mid., son of Abe & Betty Parks, married **Sarah Thos. Cook**, 22, single, b. & residing Mid., dau. of Clayvin & Cath. Cook. (W)
164B - 20 Mar. 1884 - **Charles Smith**, 22, single, oysterman, b. Gloucester, residing Mid., son of Sanker & Eliza Thurston, married **Mary Ellin Latanie**, 17, single,

b. & residing Mid., dau. of Fanny Latinie. (C)
  164C - 27 Mar. 1884 - **Marius Jordon**, 38, single, painter, b. King & Queen, residing Essex, son of Walker & Mary Jordon, married **Harriet Faucett**, 22, single, b. & residing Mid., dau. of John R. & Sarah Faucett. (W)
  165A - 30 Mar. 1884 - **Lewis N. Powell**, 23, single, sailor, b. Mathews, residing Mid., son of John & Betty Powell, married **Lucie E. B. Montague**, 17, single, b. & residing Mid., dau. of Thos. H. & Columbia Montague. (W)
  165B - 20 Apr. 1884 - **David Baylor**, 22, single, oysterman, b. Essex, residing Mid., son of Thos. & Eliz. Baylor, married **Acy Morris**, 21, single, b. & residing Mid., dau. of Julius & Mary Morris. (C)
  165C - 19 Apr. 1884 - **Carter Braxton**, 24, single, farmer, b. & residing Mid., son of Carter & Susan Braxton, married **Betty Carter**, 23, single, b. & residing Mid., dau. of James & Mary Carter. (C)
  166A - 24 Apr. 1884 - **Thos. Williams**, 21, single, oysterman, b. & residing Mid., son of Thomas & Mary Williams, married **Lena Harris**, 21, single, b. & residing Mid., dau. of Harris. (C)
  166B - 5 May 1884 - **Geo. Wash. Bird**, 30, single, oysterman, b. King & Queen, residing Mid., son of Wash. & Louisa Bird, married **Caroline Mitchil**, 22, single, b. King & Queen, residing Mid., dau. of Niel & Marial Mitchil. (C)
  166C - 2 May 1884 - **Stepnie Page**, 26, widower, oysterman, b. King & Queen, residing Mid., son of Stepnie & Elener Page, married **Polly Ann Nicolson**, 27, single, b. King & Queen, residing Mid., dau. of James & Oney Nicolson. (C)
  167A - 8 May 1884 - **Cornelius Jones**, 42, widower, farmer, b. King & Queen, residing Mid., son of Sam'l & Kate Jones, married **Sarah Miller**, 30, single, b. Gloucester, residing Mid., dau. of John & Betsy Miller. (C)
  167B - 29 May 1884 - **Wm. J. Taylor**, 23, single, sailor, b. Accomack, residing Mid., son of Wm. & Macy Taylor, married **Mary A. Clayville**, 19, single, b. & residing Mid., dau. of Elisha & Mary Clayville. (W)
  167C - 27 May 1884 - **Geo. E. Taylor**, 34, single, merchant, b. King & Queen, residing Richmond, son of John M. & Frances Taylor, married **Fannie M. Hackney**, 25, single, b. & residing Mid., dau. of James H. & Mary Hackney. (W)
  168A - 31 May 1884 - **Virginius Frazier**, 23, single, farmer, b. King & Queen, residing Mid., son of West & Charlotte Frazier, married **Eliz. Courtney**, 21, single, b. King & Queen, residing Mid., dau. of John R. & Maria

Courtney. (C)
168B - 24 May 1884 - **Lewis Foster**, 45, widower, farmer, b. High Co., North Carolina, residing Mid., son of James & Sally Foster, married **Eddie Straughter** [**Strother**], 27, single, b. & residing Mid., dau. of David & Amanda Straughter. (C)
168C - 4 Jun. 1884 - **Moses Pendleton**, 22, single, farmer, b. & residing Mid., son of George P. & Peggie Pendleton, married **Hattie Johnson**, 19, single, b. & residing Mid., dau. of Benjamin & Oney Johnson. (C)
169A - 19 Jun. 1884 - **John R. Lumpkin**, 24, single, sailor, b. & residing Mid., son of John R. & Lucy C. Lumpkin, married **Mary Sue Jackson**, 21, single, b. & residing Mid., dau. of James & Mary Jackson. (W)
169B - 1 Jul. 1884 - **Francis B. Hudson**, 24, single, merchant, b. Delaware, residing West Point, King William Co., son of C. W. & Mary Hudson, married **Sarah F. Evans**, 28, single, b. & residing Mid., dau. of John M. & Ellen Evans. (W)
169C - 8 Jul. 1884 - **John T. Armstrong**, 40, widower, farmer, residing Mid., son of Jno. P. & Malissa Armstrong, married **Cora A. Wood**, 40, widow, residing Mid., dau. of Christopher & Anna Wood. (W)
170A - 29 Jul. 1884 - **Homer Grigg**, 24, single, merchant, b. Mid., residing Gloucester, son of Peter J. & Martha Grigg, married **Mary Louisa Fleet**, 23, single, b. & residing Mid., dau. of Ro. Logan & Mary Jesse. (W)
170B - 31 Jul. 1884 - **John Henry Roane**, 24, single, oysterman, b. & residing Mid., son of Henry & Jane Roane, married **Anna Thornton**, 21, single, b. & residing Mid., dau. of Ribon Thornton. (C)
170C - 19 Aug. 1884 - **Richard Trader**, 26, widower, sailor, b. & residing Mid., son of James & Susan Trader, married **Mary Greenwood**, 21, single, b. & residing Mid., dau. of Ransome & Bettie Greenwood. (W)
171A - 13 Aug. 1884 - **Edward Taylor Johnson**, 21, single, oysterman, b. & residing Mid., son of George & Cornelia Johnson, married **Eliz. Banks**, single, b. & residing Mid., dau. of Richard & Mary Banks. (C)
171B - 14 Aug. 1884 - **Geo. H. Heath**, 47, widower, farmer, b. Gloucester, residing Mid., son of Joseph & Frances Heath, married **Mary E. Creswell**, 15, single, b. King & Queen, residing Mid., dau. of Job & Sarah Creswell. (W)
171C - 19 Aug. 1884 - **Geo. Taylor Wood**, 27, widower, farmer, b. & residing Mid., son of Geo. W. & Anna Wood, married **Marg. Smith**, 25, single, b. & residing Mid., dau. of Thomas & Marg. Smith. (C)
172A - 23 Aug. 1884 - **Zack Lee**, 26, single, doctor,

b. & residing Mid., son of Jefferson & Cordelia Lee, married **Mary Carter**, 26, single, b. King & Queen, residing Mid., dau. of Rachel Carter. (C)
    172B - 3 Sep. 1884 - **Corbin Robinson**, 53, widower, farmer, b. & residing Mid., son of Harry & Fanny Robinson, married **Kitty Smith**, 30, widow, b. & residing Mid., dau. of Addison & Patsy Wake. (C)
    172C - Sep. 1884 - **James S. Payne**, 41, widower, farmer, b. Lancaster, residing Mid., son of Thos. E. Payne, married **Martha E. Carter**, 36, widow, b. & residing Mid., dau. of John P. & Martha E. Christopher. (W)
    173A - 13 Sep. 1884 - **Wm. Armstrong**, 20, single, oysterman, b. Prince George, residing Mid., son of Armstrong & Peggy Armstrong, married **Margaret Harris**, 21, single, b. & residing Mid., dau. of Jacob & Betsy Harris. (C)
    173B - 16 Sep. 1884 - **Wm. H. Treackle**, 27, widower, sailor, b. Lancaster, residing Mid., son of Wm. & Eliza Treakle, married **Emretta Gaines**, 24, single, b. & residing Mid., dau. of Richard & Ester Gaines. (W)
    173C - 20 Sep. 1884 - **Joshua Braxton**, 45, widower, farmer, b. & residing Mid., son of Jerry & Polly Braxton, married **Lucy Ellen Taylor**, 21, single, b. & residing Mid., dau. of Robert & Mary Taylor. (C)
    174A - 2 Oct. 1884 - **Cin. C. Ward**, 22, single, oysterman, b. Northampton, residing Mid., son of Henry & Eliza Ward, married **Sally L. Hurley**, 22, single, b. Maryland, residing Mid., dau. of Jos. & Margaret Hurley. (W)
    174B - 7 Oct. 1884 - **John R. Segar, Sr.**, 48, widower, merchant, b. Essex, residing Mid., son of Cyrus & Maria Segar, married **Nannie Lee Evans**, 27, single, b. & residing Mid., dau. of A. B. Evans. (W)
    174C - 8 Oct. 1884 - **Fred Holmes**, 22, single, oysterman, b. & residing Mid., son of Billy & Milly Holmes, married **Ella Holliday**, 18, single, b. & residing Mid., dau. of [not given]. (C)
    175A - 9 Oct. 1884 - **Alexander Perrin**, 22, widower, oysterman, b. Gloucester, residing Mid., son of Alex & Mary Perrin, married **Rena Davis**, 23, single, b. & residing Mid., dau. of John & Mary Davis. (C)
    175B - 23 Oct. 1884 - **Ro. H. Holliday**, 25, single, oysterman, residing Mid., son of Ro. & Susan Holliday, married **Addie Davis**, 23, single, b. & residing Mid., dau. of Temple & Mary Davis. (C)
    175C - 23 Oct. 1884 - **Joseph Pratt**, 23, single, oysterman, b. & residing Mid., son of Wm. & Julia Pratt, married **Emeline Davis**, 18, single, b. & residing Mid., dau. of Peter & Fanny Davis. (C)

176A - 28 Oct. 1884 - **Floyd L. Roane**, 22, single, merchant, b. & residing King & Queen, son of Chas. A. & Matilda F. Roane, married **Emma E. Shackelford**, 18, single, b. Richmond, residing Mid., dau. of Wm. & Ann E. Shackelford. (W)

176B - Oct. 1884 - **Andrew F. Bristow**, 22, single, farmer, b. & residing Mid., son of Andrew L. & Eliz. W. Bristow, married **Ella N. Mercer**, 23, single, b. & residing Mid., dau. of James Mercer. (W)

176C - 9 Nov. 1884 - **Charles Duster**, 21, single, laborer, b. & residing Mid., son of [not given], married **Mary Matthews**, 21, single, b. Accomack, residing Mid., dau. of Lea Matthews. (C)

177A - 11 Nov. 1884 - **Major Walter Smith**, 21, single, oysterman, b. Essex, residing Mid., son of Wm. & Eliza Smith, married **Eliz. Robinson**, 19, single, b. & residing Mid., dau. of Alexander & Isabella Robinson. (C)

177B - 13 Nov. 1884 - **Richard Bird**, 37, widower, farmer, b. Gloucester, residing Mid., son of Sam'l & Amy Bird, married **Julia Lomax**, 17, single, b. & residing Mid., dau. of Henry & Judy Lomax. (C)

177C - 26 Nov. 1884 - **Francis B. Sadler**, 24, single, oysterman, b. & residing Mid., son of James A. & Mary E. Sadler, married **Susan M. Mason**, 21, single, b. Gloucester, residing Mid., dau. of John W. & Andrella Mason. (W)

178A - 4 Dec. 1884 - **Isaih Gatewood**, 28, single, farmer, b. & residing King & Queen, son of James & Rosetta Gatewood, married **Emma Delever**, 22, single, b. & residing Mid., dau. of Thomas & Amelia Delever. (C)

178B - Dec. 1884 - **George W. Daniel**, 45, widower, farmer, b. & residing Mid., son of Christopher & Bettie Daniel, married **Martha Fisher**, 21, single, b. Mathews, residing Mid., dau. of "unknown." (W)

178C - 16 Dec. 1884 - **Wm. E. Shackelford**, 25, single, b. Richmond, residing Mid., son of Wm. & Elizabeth Shackelford, married **Nanie B. Anderton**, 25, single, b. & residing Mid., dau. of John G. & Annie W. Anderton. (W)

179A - 17 Dec. 1884 - **Jacob Peterson**, 21, single, oysterman, b. & residing Mid., son of Anthony & Susan Peterson, married **Nancy Cauthon**, 18, single, b. & residing Mid., dau. of George Cauthon & Lucilla Smith. (C)

179B - 21 Dec. 1884 - **William W. Mason**, 21, single, merchant, b. Accomack, residing Lancaster, son of Riley & Mary Mason, married **Louisa V. Cornelius**, 18, single, b. & residing Mid., dau. of Bezliel & Betty Cornelius. (W)

179C - 18 Dec. 1884 - **John Taylor**, 25, single, oysterman, b. & residing Mid., son of Anderson & Luanda

Taylor, married **Mary J. Morris**, 19, single, b. & residing Mid., dau. of George & Charlotte Morris. (C)

180A - 18 Dec. 1884 - **Peter Carey**, 50, widower, minister, b. King & Queen, residing Mid., son of Thomas & Sally Carey, married **Emma Carter**, 23, single, b. & residing Mid., dau. of George & Lucy Carter. (C)

180B - 20 Dec. 1884 - **Thomas Segar**, 22, single, b. & residing Lancaster, married **Mary Carter**, 21, single, b. & residing Mid., dau. of Wm. & Eliza Carter.

180C - 21 Dec. 1884 - **Henry Walden**, 41, residing Mid., son of Edward & Rebecca, married **Nellie Owens**, 22, single, residing Mid. (W) [No other information given.]

181A - 20 Dec. 1884 - **Edward [Edmund] Jones**, 45, widower, farmer, b. Mid., residing King & Queen, son of Samuel & Maria Jones, married **Emeline Lee**, 40, widow, b. & residing Mid., dau. of John & Jane Smith. (C)

181B - 25 Dec. 1884 - **Squire Conway**, 21, single, oysterman, b. & residing Mid., son of Wm. & Emeline Conway, married **Mary Fitchett**, 26, single, b. & residing Mid., dau. of Jas. & Cath. Fitchett (C)

181C - 24 Dec. 1884 - **John A. Revere**, 36, single, sailor, b. & residing Mid., son of George & Letitia A. Revere, married **Mary T. Walker**, 26, single, b. & residing Mid., dau. of T. Monroe & Walker. (W)

182A - 11 Jan. 1885 - **Wm. F. Daniel**, 27, single, farmer, b. & residing Mid., son of Nathaniel C. & Martha Daniel, married **Sally Pittman**, 26, single, b. & residing Mid., dau. of John F. & Caroline Pittman. (W)

182B - 14 Jan. 1885 - **Thomas H. Palmer**, 32, single, farmer, b. & residing Mid., son of Thos. J. & Emily Palmer, married **Virginia F. Pittman**, 29, single, b. Caroline, residing Mid., dau. of John F. & Caroline Pittman. (W)

182C - Jan. 1885 - **Joseph W. Bristow**, 54, widower, farmer, b. & residing Mid., son of Zack W. & Maria Bristow, married **Lelia Bristow**, 15, single, b. & residing Mid., dau. of Walter & Adeline Bristow. (W)

183A - 1 Feb. 1885 - **Thos. Montgomery**, 23, single, oysterman, b. & residing Mid., son of James & Eliza Montgomery, married **Linie Cloville**, 20, single, b. & residing Mid., dau. of Elijah & Mary Cloville. (W)

183B - 25 Feb. 1885 - **J. B. Harrow**, 29, single, oysterman, b. & residing Mid., son of Wm. M. & Amelia Harrow, married **Betty Grinils**, 16, single, b. & residing Mid., dau. of Southey & Mary Grinils. (W)

183C - 26 Feb. 1885 - **Leonard W. Davis**, 26, single, brickmaker, b. New York, residing Mid., son of Wm. H. & Lucy A. Davis, married **Ada Bohannon**, 21, single, b.

Gloucester, residing Mid., dau. of Chas. & Sarah E. Bohannon. (W)

184A - Mar. 1885 - **Scipio Jackson**, 27, widower, farmer, b. & residing Mid., son of Wm. & Martha Jackson, married **Julia A. Laws**, 22, single, b. & residing Mid., dau. of Wm. & Fanny Laws. (C)

184B - 22 Mar. 1885 - **Pollard Wood**, 21, single, oysterman, b. & residing Mid., son of Wm. & Cordy Wood, married **Annah Johnson**, 21, single, b. & residing Mid., dau. of Gip & Emeline Johnson. (C)

184C - 31 Mar. 1885 - **Wm. Henry Taliaferro**, 23, single, oysterman, b. Mid., residing [not given], son of Robert & Patsy Taliaferro, married **Roberta Burk**, 24, widow, b. & residing Mid., dau. of Hester [surname not given]. (C)

185A - 5 Apr. 1885 - **John H. Jackson**, 31, widower, farmer, b. & residing Mid., son of Jos. & Jane A. Jackson, married **Coley Laws**, 20, single, b. & residing Mid., dau. of John & Anna Laws. (C)

185B - 2 Apr. 1885 - **Andrew Crittenden**, 23, single, oysterman, b. York Co., residing Mid., son of Geo. W. & Ellen Crittenden, married **Susan Harris**, 24, single, b. & residing Mid., dau. of Major & Mary Harris. (C)

185C - 1885 - **R. W. Major**, 25, single, farmer, b. & residing Mid., son of Walter M. & Mary E. Major, married **Blanche Muse**, 21, single, b. & residing Mid., dau. of Joseph & Nora Muse. (W)

186A - 8 Apr. 1885 - **Geo. H. Roane**, single, farmer, b. & residing Mid., son of Thos. N. & Mary N. Roane, married **Willie L. Maxwell**, widow, residing Mid., dau. of John F. & Caroline Pittman. (W)

186B - 14 Apr. 1885 - **Jefferson D. White**, 25, single, farmer, b. & residing Mathews, son of Bartlett B. & Eliza E. White, married **Dorothy Blake**, 19, single, b. & residing Mid., dau. of Jacob S. & Eliz. E. Blake. (W)

186C - 23 Apr. 1885 - **Anthony Thornton**, 28, single, oysterman, b. Gloucester, residing Mid., son of Anthony & Eliza Thornton, married **Nancy Going**, 17, single, b. & residing Mid., dau. of John H. & Etta Going. (C)

187A - 29 Apr. 1885 - **John W. Cropper**, 33, single, farmer, b. & residing Mid., son of John S. & Matilda A. Cropper, married **Mary Jane Blake**, 34, single, b. & residing Mid., dau. of Jacob S. & Lucy W. Blake. (W)

187B - 30 Apr. 1885 - **William Thornton**, 28, single, oysterman, b. Gloucester, residing Mid., son of Anthony & Ann Eliza Thornton, married **Susan Carter**, 21, single, b. & residing Mid., dau. of George & Lucy Carter. (C)

187C - 17 May 1885 - **George Davis**, 24, single, oysterman, b. Somerset, Maryland, son of George & Fanny Davis, married **Alice W. Bundey**, 26, single, b. &

residing Mid., dau. of Sam'l & Mary Jane Bundey. (C)
   188A - 21 May 1885 - **J. Walter Hurley**, 22, single, merchant, b. Dorchester Co., Maryland, residing Mid., son of Jos. H. & Margaret Hurley, married **Amanda Wagner**, 18, single, b. & residing Mid., dau. of D. Van & Emily Wagner. (W)
   188B - 13 May 1885 - **Thomas Frazier**, 25, widower, farmer, b. & residing Mid., son of Thos. & Elizabeth Frazier, married **Sarah Daniel**, 23, single, b. & residing Mid., dau. of Betsey Daniel. (C)
   188C - 24 Jun. 1885 - **R. M. Glenn**, 55, widower, merchant, b. Gloucester, residing Mid., son of Mathew & Frances E. M. Glenn, married **Sallie E. Jackson**, 45, widow, b. Mathews, residing Mid., dau. of Boyd & Ann Winder. (W)
   189A - 21 Jun. 1885 - **Johnston G. Blake**, 24, single, farmer, b. & residing Mid., son of John L. & Matilda A. E. Blake, married **Fannie B. Ailworth**, 29, widow, b. & residing Mid., dau. of Rich'd M. & Bettie Glenn. (W)
   189B - 1 Jul. 1885 - **Wm. G. Jeffries**, 56, widower, physician, b. & residing Essex, son of Orville & Mary Jeffries, married **Eugenia A. Pollard**, 60, widow, b. & residing Mid., dau. of Carter & Purkins. (W)
   189C - 15 Jul. 1885 - **George L. Blackburn**, 38, single, farmer, b. & residing Mid., son of Paulin A. & Nancy S. Blackburn, married **Hattie A. Shuman**, 32, single, b. London, residing Mid., dau. of George W. & Harriet Shuman. (W)
   190A - 12 Jul. 1885 - **Robert Clayton**, 22, single, oysterman, b. Gloucester, residing Mid., son of Robert & Nancy Clayton, married **Easter Johnson**, widow, b. Lancaster, residing Mid., dau. of [not given]. (C)
   190B - 18 Jul. 1885 - **Ro. G. Douglas**, 22, single, merchant, b. Essex, residing Mid., son of Rich'd T. & Ellen Douglas, married **Mattie L. Sleet**, 20, single, b. Mathews, residing Mid., dau. of Yancey & Anna Sleet. (W)
   190C - 22 Jul. 1885 - **Beverly C. Clarkston**, [**Taliaferro**, according to marriage license - see 192B.] 22, single, oysterman, b. & residing Mid., son of Simon & Minerva Taliaferro, married **Maggie Robinson**, 18, single, b. & residing Mid. (C)
   191A - 25 Jul. 1885 - **Henry Lewis**, 45, widower, farmer, b. Gloucester, residing Mid., son of Warner & Maria Lewis, married **Sally Buckner**, 40, widow, residing Mid., dau. of [not given]. (C)
   191B - 4 Oct. 1885 - **Robert Carter**, 27, widower, oysterman, b. Gloucester, residing Mid., son of Peter & Caroline Carter, married **Emily Roy**, 22, single, b. Gloucester, residing Mid., dau. of Joshua & Martha Roy. (B)

191C - 1 Oct. 1885 - **Carter Williams**, 72, widower, farmer, b. & residing Mid., son of Carter & Ann Williams, married **Louisa F. Bristow**, 44, widow, b. & residing Mid., dau. of Zack & Maria Bristow. (W)

192A - 6 Oct. 1885 - **Joseph W. Harwood**, 26, single, oysterman, b. Charles City Co., residing New Kent, son of Joseph C. & Susan S. B. Harwood, married **Sallie J. Purkins**, 25, single, b. & residing Mid., dau. of Ed. T. & Betty Purkins. (W)

192B - Repeat of 190C - as **Beverly C. Taliaferro** instead of Clarkston. [Marriage license gives his surname as Taliaferro.]

192C - 19 Nov. 1885 - **James Key**, 21, single, farmer, b. & residing Mid., son of Carter & Catharine Key, married **Feeby Conoway**, 21, single, b. & residing Mid., dau. of Wm. & Emeline Conway. (C)

193A - 26 Nov. 1885 - **Rich'd Bev. Segar**, 24, single, farmer, b. & residing Mid., son of John E. & Mary C. Segar, married **Hattie L. Chowning**, 22, single, b. & residing Mid., dau. of James & Ann E. Chowning. (W)

193B - 26 Nov. 1885 - **John H. Robinson**, 22, single, oysterman, b. & residing Mid., son of Henry & Eliza Robinson, married **Mary Morris**, 17, single, b. & residing Mid., dau. of Obediah & Precilla Morris. (C)

193C - 29 Nov. 1885 - **James Dickenson**, 22, single, oysterman, b. Accomack, residing Mid., son of David & Rosanna Dickenson, married **Carrie Bree**, 21, single, b. & residing Mid., dau. of Amanda Bree. (C)

194A - 1 Dec. 1885 - **Robert Daniel**, 24, single, oysterman, b. & residing Mid., son of Carter & Betsy Daniel, married **Maria Washington**, 26, widow, b. & residing Mid., dau. of Rachel [surname not given]. (C)

194B - 8 Dec. 1885 - **George E. Beale**, 35, widower, tinner, b. Suffolk Co., New York, residing Williamsburg, son of D. B. & Mary Beale, maried **Isabella J. Daniel**, 28, single, b. & residing Mid., dau. of John W. & Marian A. Daniel. (W)

194C - 12 Dec. 1885 - **Jos. C. Wallace**, 22, single, oysterman, b. Norfolk, residing Mid., son of Isaac & Lucy A. Wallace, married **Cordelia Whiting**, 20, single, b. & residing Mid., dau. of Robert & Lucy Whiting. (C)

195A - 17 Dec. 1885 - **George F. Walker**, 28, single, farmer, b. & residing Mid., son of M. J. M. & Sarah F. Walker, married **Georgia S. Hall**, 24, single, b. & residing Mid., dau. of Addison & Nannie M. Hall. (W)

195B - 17 Dec. 1885 - **Philip Jones**, 44, widower, farmer, b. King & Queen, residing Essex, son of Philip & Sidna Jones, married **Amanda Amy**, 29, widow, b. & residing Mid., dau. of Anthony & Susan Peterson. (C)

195C - 20 Dec. 1885 - **R. C. Harrow**, 21, single,

oysterman, b. & residing Mid., son of J. J. & Cath. Harrow, married **Mary Jackson**, 18, single, b. & residing Mid., dau. of John L. & Malvina Jackson. (W)

196A - 23 Dec. 1885 - **John F**. Hooks, 22, single, oysterman, residing Mid., son of Hooks, married **Mariah Jones**, 20, single, b. & residing Mid., dau. of [not given]. (C)

196B - 23 Dec. 1885 - **Geo. S. Chowning**, 26, single, farmer, b. & residing Mid., son of James & Anne E. Chowning, married **Lulie O. Beazley**, 20, single, b. & residing Mid., dau. of George P. & India Beazley. (W)

196C - 24 Dec. 1885 - **Andrew Brockenbrough**, 22, single, oysterman, b. King & Queen, residing Mid., son of Jacob & Anna Brockenbrough, married **Martha J. Wood**, 18, single, b. & residing Mid., dau. of Geo. W. & Anna Wood. (C)

197A - 24 Dec. 1885 - **Thomas W. Redd**, 27, single, farmer, b. & residing King & Queen, son of Geo. S. & Susan N. Redd, married **Lucy G. Kain**, 17, single, b. & residing Mid., dau. of F. A. & Lucy A. Kain. (W)

197B - 24 Dec. 1885 - **Robert Waller**, 23, single, oysterman, b. & residing Essex, son of Clay & Cath. Waller, married **Geo. Anna Lockley**, 21, single, b. & residing Mid., dau. of George & Anna Lockley. (C)

197C - 24 Dec. 1885 - **Wm. Ellis Jones**, 23, widower, farmer, b. Essex, residing Mid., son of Wm. & Martha Jones, married **Polly Washington**, 24, single, b. & residing Mid., dau. of George & Matilda Washington. (C)

198A - 4 Jan. 1886 - **Jas. Ro. Jones**, 23, single, farmer, b. & residing Mid., son of Cornelius & Saphronia Jones, married **Hellen Wake**, 14, single, b. & residing Mid., dau. of Hannah Wake. (C)

198B - 29 Dec. 1885 - **Paul D. Franke**, 26, single, carpenter, b. Milwaukee, Wisconsin, residing King & Queen, married **Etta Callis**, 29, single, b. & residing Mid., dau. of John D. & Virginia A. Callis. (W)

198C - Repeat of 197C.

199A - 29 Dec. 1885 - **Ro. V. Revere**, 46, widower, farmer, b. & residing Mid., son of Geo. B. & Lucy H. Revere, married **Sarah E. Stiff**, 34, single, b. & residing Mid., dau. of Wm. & Nancy Stiff. (W)

199B - 29 Dec. 1885 - **Richard H. Burton**, 23, single, farmer, b. & residing King & Queen, son of Richard & Margaret Burton, married **Martha C. Smither**, 18, single, b. & residing Mid., dau. of Ribon & Cath. Smither. (W)

199C - Dec. 1885 - **Thos J. Kellum**, 21, single, oysterman, b. & residing Mid., son of Henry & Martha Kellum, married **Annie M. Marchant**, 18, single, b. Mathews, residing Mid., dau. of John W. & Cath. Marchant. (W)

200A - 30 Dec. 1885 - **Thos. C. Callis**, 22, single, oysterman, b. Mathews, residing Mid., son of Thos. & Eliz. Callis, married **Mary E. Davis**, 19, single, b. & residing Mid., dau. of Bartlett & Bettie Davis. (W)
200B - 31 Dec. 1885 - **Lewis Wilson**, 28, single, farmer, b. King & Queen, residing Mid., son of Jas. & Mary Wilson, married **Christianna Thurston**, 35, widow, b. & residing Mid., dau. of Wm. Wood. (C)
200C - 31 Dec. 1885 - **Robert Johnson**, 22, single, oysterman, b. & residing Mid., son of Nelson & Betty Johnson, married **Maria Jones**, 22, single, b. King & Queen, residing Mid., dau. of Lucy Jones. (C)
201A - 14 Jan. 1886 - **Cornelius Morris**, 22, single, laborer, b. & residing Mid., son of Noah & Kitty Morris, married **Harriet E. Webb**, 20, single, b. & residing Mid., dau. of John & Betty Webb. (C)
201B - 21 Jan. 1886 - **James M. Durham**, 21, single, farmer, b. & residing Essex, son of Ambrose & Sarah Durham, married **Ella H. Thurston**, 18, single, b. & residing Mid., dau. of Ro. & Lucy Thurston. (W)
201C - 21 Jan. 1886 - **Wm. H. Banks**, 24, single, oysterman, b. King & Queen, residing Mid., son of George & Winney Banks, married **Alice V. Lockley**, 19, single, b. Washington, D. C., residing Mid., dau. of Lockley. (C)
202A - 28 Jan. 1886 - **John Washington**, 22, single, oysterman, b. & residing Mid., son of Geo. & Lucy Ann Washington, married **Mary Robinson**, 21, single, b. & residing Mid., dau. of Corbin & Cordry Robinson. (C)
202B - 28 Jan. 1886 - **Wm. Delever**, 23, single, oysterman, b. & residing Mid., son of Thomas & Amelia Deleaver, married **Cath. Morris**, 21, single, b. & residing Mid., dau. of Cornelius & Ann Morris. (C)
202C - 1886 - **Jas. Ed. Ransome**, 36, widower, oysterman, b. Gloucester, residing Mid., son of John W. & Mary Ransome, married **Mary Cath. Lemon**, 21, single, b. Gloucester, residing Mid., dau. of Wm. & Elizabeth Lemon. (W)
203A - 18 Feb. 1886 - **Westley Dunlevy**, 22, single, farmer, b. & residing Mid., son of Wm. & Mary Dunlevy, married **Corada Mason**, 18, (W), b. & residing Mid., dau. of J. W. & Indiana Mason. (W)
203B - 1886 - **C. Weslie Ridgell**, 21, single, oysterman, b. St. Mary's Co., Maryland, residing Mid., son of Cornelius & Mary Ellen Ridgell, married **Annie Stunt**, 22, single, b. Crisfield, Maryland, residing Mid., dau. of Sam'l & Jane Stunt. (W)
203C - 18 Feb. 1886 - **James H. Didlake**, 24, single, farmer, b. & residing Mid., son of Wm. R. & Sarah F. Didlake, married **Anna R. Clare**, 19, single, b. &

residing Mid., dau. of Wm. H. & A. C. Clare. (W)
 204A - 25 Feb. 1886 - **James S. Marchant**, 31, widower, merchant, b. Mathews, residing Mid., son of Christopher & Didema Marchant, married **M. A. V. Hale**, 19, single, b. & residing Mid., dau. of Robert & Saphrona Hale. (W)
 204B - 11 Mar. 1886 - **Thomas E. Dungey**, 22, widower, farmer, b. & residing Mid., son of Elias Ad. & Julia Dungee, married **Lee Anna Campbell**, 25, single, b. & residing Mid., dau. of Leroy & Louisa Campbell. (C)
 204C - 16 Mar. 1886 - **Pope H. French**, 25, widower, merchant, b. & residing Mid., son of Wm. T. & Edna E. French, married **Florence B. French**, 18, single, b. & residing Mid., dau. of John R. & E. J. French. (W)
 205A - 18 Mar. 1886 - **Joshua Roane**, 21, single, oysterman, b. King & Queen, residing Mid., son of James H. & Nancy Roane, married **Winney Fauntleroy**, 26, single, b. & residing Mid., dau. of Sarah Fauntleroy. (C)
 205B - 24 Mar. 1886 - **Thos. Robinson**, 26, single, farmer, b. & residing Mid., son of Robinson, married **Kittura Ates**, 30, widow, b. & residing Mid., dau. of Landus & Jane Reed. (C)
 205C - 15 Apr. 1886 - **Isaiah Wake**, 22, single, oysterman, b. & residing Mid., son of Minnie & Mary Wake, married **Lucy Carter**, 21, single, b. & residing Mid., dau. of Carter. (C)
 206A - 25 Apr. 1886 - **Edward W. Bristow**, 25, single, merchant, b. & residing Mid., son of George T. & Mary Bristow, married **Lydia Ailworth**, 16, single, b. & residing Mid., dau. of Ro. N. & Mary E. Ailworth. (W)
 206B - 27 Apr. 1886 - **Eugene C. Field**, 25, single, merchant, b. & residing Baltimore, Maryland, son of Charles C. & Harriet Field, married **Lelia W. Shackleford**, 24, single, b. Gloucester, residing Mid., dau. of Wm. & Ann E. Shackelford. (W)
 206C - 5 May 1886 - **Peter Revere**, 28, single, oysterman, b. & residing Mid., son of Joel & Sarah Revere, married **Sara M. Mason**, 23, single, b. Gloucester, residing Mid., dau. of J. W. & Indianna Mason. (W)
 207A - 29 Apr. 1886 - **Thomas C. Hurley**, 23, single, merchant, b. Kent Co., Maryland, residing Mid., son of David & Jane Hurley, married **Viola Norris**, 20, single, b. & residing Mid., dau. of John W. & Sarah E. Norris. (W)
 207B - 2 May 1886 - **Chas. H. Roy**, 21, single, farmer, b. & residing Mid., son of Henry & Chris. Roy, married **Mary Jane Young**, 25, single, b. & residing Mid., dau. of Peggy Young. (C)
 207C - 19 May 1886 - **Southey S. Grinels**, 23, single, farmer, b. Accomack, residing Mid., son of Southey &

Mary Grinels, married **Lorelia B. Hall,** 21, single, b. & residing Mid., dau. of Thos. & Lina Hall. (W)

208A - 19 May 1886 - **John Dawson,** 30, single, oysterman, b. Norfolk, residing Mid., son of Everett & Harriet Dawson, married **Mary Wood,** 19, single, b. & residing Mid., dau. of William & Mildred Wood. (C)

208B - 27 May 1886 - **Erastus Jones,** 26, single, farmer, residing Mid., married **Mary Williams,** 22, single, residing Mid. (C) [No other information given.]

208C - None.

209A - 15 Jun. 1886 - **R. H. Parrow,** 40, widower, farmer, b. & residing Mid., son of Parrow, married **Sue C. Derieux,** 39, single, b. Essex, residing Mid., dau. of Derieux. (W)

209B - 10 Jun. 1886 - **John Brim,** 72, widower, farmer, b. & residing Mid., son of Leonard Brim, married **Catharine Kidd,** 35, single, b. & residing Mid., dau. of Chowning & Cath. Kidd. (W)

209C - 24 Jun. 1886 - **Casper T. Marston,** 25, single, merchant, b. & residing Mid., son of Oliver & Margaret A. Marston, married **Lucy G. Healy,** 20, single, b. & residing Mid., dau. of Robert & Georgeanna Healy. (W)

210A - 24, Jun. 1886 - **Samuel M. Simmons,** 23, single, mariner, b. & residing Dorchester Co., Maryland, son of Wm. & Frances Simmons, married **Maggie L. Ruark,** 21, single, b. Dorchester Co., Maryland, residing Mid., dau. of Major & Frances Ruark. (W)

210B - 2 Sep. 1886 - **Jas. A. Braxton,** 23, single, farmer, b. & residing Mid., son of Albert & Maria Braxton, married **Anna Crittenden,** 23, single, b. Essex, residing Mid., dau. of Zack & Frances Crittenden. (C)

210C - 2 Sep. 1886 - **Willie B. Keinningham,** 18, single, farmer, b. & residing Mid., son of Jas. B. & Mary Keinningham, married **Trible Lee,** 18, single, b. & residing Mid., dau. of Obediah W. & Netta Lee. (W)

211A - Sep. 1886 - **David Stormont,** 27, single, vet. surgeon, b. Louisiana, residing Mid., son of Stormont, married **Victoria A. Bristow,** 19, single, b. & residing Mid., dau. of Jos. A. & Mary M. Bristow. (W)

211B - 12 Sep. 1886 - **Charles R. Evans,** 21, single, farmer, b. & residing Essex, son of James B. & Mary F. Evans, married **Eugenie E. Wiese,** 26, widow, b. King & Queen, residing Mid., dau. of Jas. S. & Eugenia E. Bristow. (W)

211C - 23 Sep. 1886 - **Wm. Philip Buckner,** 25, single, oysterman, b. & residing Mid., son of Phil & Sally Buckner, married **Lucy Jackson,** 19, single, b. & residing Mid., dau. of Betty Jackson. (C)

212A - 26 Sep. 1886 - **William Bayton,** 23, single, oysterman, b. & residing Mid., son of Richard Bayton, married **Sarah J. Weeks**, 19, single, b. & residing Mid., dau. of Charles & Sarah Weeks. (C)

212B - 30 Sep. 1886 - **Sterling Thornton**, 24, single, oysterman, b. Gloucester, residing Mid., son of Anthony & Elisa Thornton, married **Mary Dudley**, 18, single, b. & residing Mid., dau. of Ransome & Anna Dudley. (C)

212C - 4 Sep. 1886 - **Samuel J. Lewis**, 33, widower, farmer, b. & residing Mid., son of Frank & Anny Lewis, married **Mary Ann Banks**, 30, single, b. King & Queen, residing Mid., dau. of [not given]. (C)

213A - 7 Oct. 1886 - **Major Holmes**, 21, single, farmer, b. & residing Mid., son of Mary Ann Dabney, married **Charlotte Lomax**, 16, single, b. & residing Mid., dau. of Henry & Judy Lomax. (C)

213B - 11 Oct. 1886 - **John Dillard**, 22, single, farmer, b. Sussex, residing Norfolk Co., son of Lewis & Sarah Dillard, married **Alice Jones**, 18, single, b. & residing Mid., dau. of Stephen & Mary Jones. (C)

213C - 20 Oct. 1886 - **Chas. Ellis Taylor**, 23, single, farmer, b. King & Queen, residing Mid., son of Thos. J. & Sarah J. Taylor, married **Betty Slaughter**, 24, widow, b. & residing Mid., dau. of Gid. G. W. & Letitia Hall. (W)

214A - 24 Oct. 1886 - **Moses Motley**, 21, single, farmer, b. & residing Mid., son of Griffin & Julia Motley, married **Nancy Withers**, 30, widow, b. Essex, residing Mid., dau. of Matilda Davis. (C)

214B - 26 Oct. 1886 - **Richard Jeter Palmer**, 29, single, merchant, b. Mid., residing West Point [Prince William Co.], son of John D. & Mary F. Palmer, married **Lelia A. Blake**, 22, single, b. & residing Mid., dau. of R. L. & Marg. Blake. (W)

214C - 30 Oct. 1886 - **Charles King**, 23, single, oysterman, b. Gloucester, residing Mid., son of Wm. & Eliz. King, married **Betty Robinson**, 21, single, b. & residing Mid., dau. of Barbara Wilson. (C)

215A - 28 Oct. 1886 - **Lorenzo Crittenden**, 23, single, laborer, b. Essex, residing Mid., son of Zack & Frances Crittenden, married **Mira Robinson**, 21, single, b. King & Queen, residing Mid., dau. of Ellen Robinson. (C)

215B - 3 Nov. 1886 - **Allen Peterson**, 23, single, farmer, b. & residing Mid., son of Robert & Susan Peterson, married **Ella Tucker**, 21, single, b. & residing Mid., dau. of Benj'n & Susan Tucker. (C)

215C - 18 Nov. 1886 - 18 Nov. 1886 - **Richard Morris**, 24, single, farmer, b. & residing Mid., son of George & Charlotte Morris, married **Maggie Harris**, 19, single, b. & residing Mid., dau. of Maria Harris. (C)

216A - Nov. 1886 - **Armstead Lockley**, 26, single, oysterman, b. & residing Mid., son of Sam'l & Delphia

Lockley, married **Louisa Braxton**, 24, single, b. & residing Mid., dau. of Susan Braxton. (C)

216B - 24 Nov. 1886 - **Jeter G. Mitchell**, 39, widower, oysterman, b. New Kent Co., Maryland, residing Mid., son of John G. & Eliza Mitchell, married **Laura Pitts**, 21, single, b. James City, residing Mid., dau. of Allen & Mary Pitts. (W)

216C - 2 Dec. 1886 - **Caleb Lewis**, 21, single, farmer, b. & residing Mid., son of Moses & Anna Lewis, married **Mary Davis**, 19, single, b. & residing Mid., dau. of Peter & Fanny. (C)

217A - 16 Dec. 1886 - **Samuel Morris**, 21, single, laborer, b. & residing Mid., son of George & Charlotte Morris, married **Matilda Ruffin**, 17, single, b. & residing Mid., dau. of Lewis & Caroline Ruffin. (C)

217B - 17 Dec. 1886 - **Thomas Nelson**, 21, single, b. & residing Mid., married **Martha E. Taliaferro**, 21, single, b. & residing Mid. (C) [No other information given.]

217C - Dec. 1886 - **Thomas Carr**, 26, single, residing Mid., married **Willintina Minnafield**, 22, single, residing Mid. (C) [No other information given.]

218A - 20 Dec. 1886 - **Rich'd Glenn Richardson**, 34, single, farmer, b. & residing Gloucester, son of Joseph & Mary Richeson, married **Grace Waller**, 27, single, b. King & Queen, residing Mid., dau. of Wm. & Rachel Waller. (C)

218B - 26 Dec. 1886 - **Burley Waller**, 22, single, oysterman, b. Mid., residing Essex, son of Clay & Cath. Waller, married **Lucy Ruffin**, 21, single, b. & residing Mid., dau. of Anna Ruffin. (C)

218C - 29 Dec. 1886 - **Edwin Burke**, 20, single, oysterman, b. & residing Mid., son of Harry & Lettie Burke, married **Victoria Bates**, 19, single, b. & residing Mid., dau. of Emma Johnson. (C)

219A - 28 Dec. 1886 - **Charles W. Smither**, 35, single, farmer, b. & residing Mid., son of Ribon M. & Cath. W. Smither, married **Emma T. Davis**, 30, widow, b. King & Queen, residing Mid., dau. of Thomas & Fanny E. Bristow. (W)

219B - 28 Dec. 1886 - **Elijah Goldman**, 24, single, oysterman, b. & residing Mid., son of Elijah & Milley Goldman, married **Frances Williams**, 18, single, b. & residing Mid., dau. of Thomas & Mary Williams. (C)

219C - 6 Jan. 1887 - **Milton Braxton**, 21, single, laborer, residing Mid., married **Levinia Laws**, 21, single, residing Mid. (C) [No other information given.]

220A - 30 Dec. 1886 - **James Davis**, 22, single, farmer, b. King & Queen, residing Mid., son of James & Anna Davis, married **Mary Ann Sorrell**, 16, single, b. &

residing Mid., dau. of George & Eliza Sorrell. (C)

220B - 6 Jan. 1886 [sic - should be 1887] - **Iveson Roy**, 28, single, oysterman, b. King & Queen, residing Mid., son of Jasper & Betsey Roy, married **Ida Washington**, 19, single, b. & residing Mid., dau. of George & Susan Washington. (C)

220C - Jan. 1887 - **Sylvanna Hand**, 26, single, sailor, b. New York, son of Timothy & Phelebit Hand, married **Livinia Cornelius**, 18, single, b. & residing Mid., dau. of Bez & Cornelius. (W)

221 A - 13 Jan. 1887 - **Benjamin Ellis**, 25, single, oysterman, b. & residing Mid., son of Carter & Martha Ellis, married **Virginia Harris**, 23, single, b. & residing Mid., dau. of Jacob & Eliz. Harris. (C)

221B - 20 Jan. 1887 - **W. H. Norton**, 24, single, oysterman, b. & residing Mid., son of W. H. & Evy Moffit [sic - license says Norton, not Moffit], married **Olivia Ailworth**, 20, single, b. & residing Mid., dau. of Ro. N. & M. E. Ailworth. (W)

221C - Jan. 1887 - **Wm. C. Johnson**, 22, single, farmer, b. & residing Mid., son of William & Chloe Johnson, married **Louisa Curtis**, 21, single, b. Gloucester, residing Mid., dau. of James & Mary Curtis. (C)

222A - 10 Feb. 1887 - **Thomas H. Harrow**, 26, single, oysterman, b. & residing Mid., son of Jeremiah & Cath. Harrow, married **Hattie Hurley**, 19, single, b. & residing Mid., dau. of David & Eliz. Hurley. (W)

222B - 9 Feb. 1887 - **Edward H. Sibley**, 30, widower, farmer, b. & residing Mid., son of Jas. D. & Susan Sibley, married **Julia E. Lanning**, 18, single, b. Ohio, residing Mid., dau. of Wm. H. Lanning. (W)

222C - 15 Feb. 1887 - **Addison Hall**, 30, single, farmer, b. & residing Mid., son of Thomas & Lina Hall, married **Julia Lee Hudgins**, 24, single, b. & residing Mid., dau. of Wm. & Mildred Hudgins. (W)

223A - 16 Feb. 1887 - **Andrew West**, 50, widower, farmer, b. & residing King & Queen, son of James & Harriet West, married **Eliz. Smith**, 38, single, b. & residing Mid., dau. of Phenton & Benjamin Lee. (C)

223B - 24 Feb. 1887 - **Peter Ruffin**, 27, single, farmer, b. & residing Mid., son of Louis & Caroline Ruffin, married **Nancy Taliaferro**, 29, widow, b. & residing Mid., dau. of Peter & Malinda Dabney. (C)

223C - 3 Feb. 1887 - **Rich'd Lewis Wormley**, 22, single, farmer, b. & residing Mid., son of Mack & Barbary Wormley, married **Frances Carter**, 18, single, b. & residing Mid., dau. of Pierce & Martha Ann Carter. (C)

224A - 2 Mar. 1887 - **Thomas Burrell**, 45, widower, farmer, b. & residing Mid., son of Caesar & Polly Burrell, married **Mattie Burrell**, 26, single, b. & residing Mid., dau. of Burrell. (C)
224B - Mar. 1887 - **Moses Carr**, 22, single, farmer, b. & residing Mid., son of Burrell & Mary Carr, married **Elnora Booth**, 21, single, b. & residing Mid., dau. of Robert C. Booth. (C)
224C - 1 Mar. 1887 - **Wm. S. Lewis**, 23, single, laborer, b. & residing Mid., son of Moses & Anna Lewis, married **Marie Banner**, 18, single, b. & residing Mid., dau. of Daniel & Jane Bonner. (C)
225A - 8 Mar. 1887 - **Wm. Franklin Gale**, 25, single, farmer, b. & residing Mid., son of Wm. & Eliza Gayle, married **Beaula A. Major**, 20, single, b. & residing Mid., dau. of L. O. B. & Mary Major. (W)
225B - 9 Mar. 1887 - **George H. Shrieves**, 24, single, oysterman, b. & residing Mid., son of Geo. T. & Mary C. Shrieves, married **Vivian E. Norris**, 21, single, b. & residing Mid., dau. of John D. & Sally Norris. (W)
225C - 10 Mar. 1887 - **Elijah Goodman Boyd**, 23, single, oysterman, b. & residing Mid., son of Joseph & Emily Boyd, married **Martha Smallwood**, 22, single, b. Washington, residing Mid., dau. of Wm. & Elizabeth Smallwood. (C)
226A - 24 Mar. 1887 - **John Norton**, 24, single, oysterman, b. & residing Mid., son of Henry & Evy Norton, married **Cora Gaines**, 16, single, b. & residing Mid., dau. of William & Jane Gaines. (W)
226B - Mar. 1887 - **Wm. Roy**, 23, single, farmer, b. King & Queen, residing Mid., son of Jasper & Martha Roy, married **Buela Johnson**, 24, single, b. & residing Mid., dau. of John & Elizabeth Johnson. (C)
226C - 31 Mar. 1887 - **J. F. Selby**, 38, widower, farmer, b. Kent Co., Maryland, residing Mid., son of J. P. & Wilmina Selby, married **Edith P. Jackson**, 32, widow, b. & residing Mid., dau. of Wm. H. & Nancey Kelly. (W)
227A - 2 Apr. 1887 - **James Henry Curtis**, 20, single, farmer, b. & residing Mid., son of John H. & Lucy Ann Curtis, married **Sarah Ann Braxton**, 22, single, b. & residing Mid., dau. of Carter & Susan Braxton. (C)
227B - 2 Apr. 1887 - **Walter Johnson**, 21, single, farmer, b. Princess Anne, residing Mid., son of Edward & Henrietta Johnson, married **Sena Baker**, 25, single, b. & residing Mid., dau. of James & Eliz. Baker. (C)
227C - 7 Apr. 1887 - **John Morton**, 23, single, oysterman, b. & residing Mid., son of John & Maria Morton, married **Maggie Lewis**, 19, single, b. & residing Mid., dau. of Alley & Winnie Lewis. (C)

228A - 14 Apr. 1887 - **Dandridge Lorimer**, 22, single, farmer, b. & residing Mid., son of John Lori<u>mo</u>re, married **Bell Jones**, 18, single, b. & residing Mid., dau. of [not given]. (C)
228B - Entry crossed out.
228C - 16 Apr. 1887 - **Anderson Washington**, 22, single, farmer, b. & residing Mid., son of George & Matilda Washington, married **Mildred Ann Scott**, 23, single, b. King & Queen, residing Mid., dau. of Scott. (C)
229A - 4 May 1887 - **Geo. W. Cauthorn**, 50, single, farmer, b. & residing Essex, son of Cauthorn, married **Virginia Street**, 38, widow, b. Essex, residing Mid., dau. of Ann McKan. (W)
229B - 6 May. 1887 - **Thos. Robinson**, 25, single, oysterman, b. Washington, D. C., residing Mid., son of James & Agnes Robinson, married **Eliz. Davis**, 22, single, b. King & Queen, residing Mid., dau. of John Davis. (C)
229C - 8 May 1887 - **Carlos Z. Keyser**, 29, single, farmer, b. Northumberland, residing Mid., son of Andrew B. & Eliza Keyser, married **Willie A. Lipscomb**, 28, widow, b. King & Queen, residing Mid., dau. of [not given]. (W)
230A - 12 May 1887 - **Wm. Montague**, 40, widower, farmer, b. & residing Mid., son of Alfred & Catharine Montague, married **Virginia Harris**, 22, single, b. & residing Mid., dau. of Maria Harris. (C)
230B - 15 May 1887 - **Charles H. Wood**, 24, single, oysterman, b. & residing Mid., son of Wm. & Milley Wood, married **Hester Burrell**, 21, single, b. & residing Mid., dau. of John & Kesiah Burrell. (C)
230C - 15 May 1887 - **Charles West**, 24, single, oysterman, b. & residing Mid., son of Alexander & Caroline West, married **Mary Jane Carr**, 21, single, b. & residing Mid., dau. of Burrell & Sarah <u>K</u>arr. (C)
231A - 14 May 1887 - **Thomas Boyd**, 23, single, farmer, b. & residing Mid., son of Allen & Judy Boyd, married **Rosa Bird**, 21, single, b. & residing Mid., dau. of Robert & Jane Bird. (C)
231B - 20 May 1887 - **Christian H. Hansen**, 27, single, clerk, b. Germany, residing Mid., son of Hans C. & Anna M. Hansen, married **Ada B. Payne**, 20, single, b. Lancaster, residing Mid., dau. of Jas. S. & Mary E. Payne. (W)
231C - 5 Jun. 1887 - **Charles Fauntleroy**, 30, single, laborer, b. & residing Mid., son of Washington & Sarah Fauntleroy, married **Juliet Washington**, 21, single, b. & residing Mid., dau. of Charles & Susan Washington. (C)
232A - 12 Jun. 1887 - **Edward Ingram**, 22, single, oysterman, b. & residing Lancaster, son of Wm. &

Margaret Ingram, married **Luly Shrieves**, 17, single, b. & residing Mid., dau. of Geo. T. & Sarah Shrieves. (W)

232B - 1887 - **John H. Walden**, 19, single, farmer, b. & residing Mid., son of Henry & Martha Walden, married **Lessie F. Jackson**, 22, single, b. & residing Mid., dau. of Noah & Ann F. Jackson. (W)

232C - 27 Jun. 1887 - **Henry Handy**, 29, single, farmer, b. Richmond Co., residing Mid., son of Henry & Eliza Handy, married **Lucy Griffin**, 21, single, b. Lancaster, residing Mid., dau. of George & Lucy Griffin. (C)

233A - 30 Jun. 1887 - **Jas. Wm. Daniel**, 27, single, merchant, b. & residing Mid., son of Wm. A. & Matilda J. Daniel, married **Mary S. Baughan**, 23, single, b. Essex, residing Mid., dau. of Theo. P. & Margaret Baughan. (W)

233B - 30 Jun. 1887 - **Alphus Payton**, 22, single, oysterman, b. Mathews, residing Mid., son of Mann & Lucy Payton, married **Julia Burrell**, 17, single, b. & residing Mid., dau. of Lewis & Betsy Burrell. (C)

233C - 16 Jul. 1887 - **Thomas Mitchel**, 45, widower, farmer, b. King & Queen, residing Mid., son of Benj'n & Mary Mitchel, married **Rose Dangerfield**, 30, widow, b. & residing Mid., dau. of Griffin Motley. (C)

234A - 19 Jul. 1887 - **Philip London** married **Sarah E. Smith**. (C) [No other information given. See 235C.]

234B - 25 Jul. 1887 - **Walter J. Pitt**, 29, single, merchant, b. & residing Mid., son of Douglass & Cath. Pitt, married **Alice V. Mann**, 18, single, b. & residing Mid., dau. of John & Andrewilla E. Mann. (W)

234C - 28 Jul. 1887 - **Joseph Adkins**, 21, single, farmer, b. Henrico, residing Mid., son of Wm. & Emily Adkins, married **Peggy Taylor**, 21, single, b. King & Queen, residing Mid., dau. of Thornton & Sarah Taylor. (C)

235A - 17 Aug. 1887 - **Julius Healy**, 21, single, merchant, b. & residing Mid., son of Julius & Henrietta E. Healy, married **Lucelia C. Hilliard**, 20, single, b. & residing Mid., dau. of Richard D. & Frances A. Hilliard. (W)

235B - 25 Aug. 1887 - **Wm. King**, 17, single, oysterman, b. King & Queen, residing Mid., son of James & Cath. King, married **Alice Lockley**, 19, single, b. & residing Mid., dau. of Henry & Lucy Lockley. (C)

235C - 25 Aug. 1887 - **Philip London**, 20, single, oysterman, b. & residing Mid., son of Jacob London, married **Sarah Smith**, 18, single, b. & residing Mid., dau. of Jas. L. & Maria Smith. (C)

236A - 8 Sep. 1887 - **Herbert Daniel**, 23, single, farmer, b. & residing Mid., son of N. C. & Martha Daniel, married **Alice E. Stringer**, 21, single, b. &

residing Mid., dau. of Mary Stringer. (W)
    236B - 27 Sep. 1887 - **Andrew S. Brown**, 24, single, merchant, b. Mathews, residing Norfolk, son of Andrew C. & Virginia C. Brown, married **Mary M. Segar**, 20, single, b. & residing Mid., dau. of John R. & Sally Segar. (W)
    236C - 29 Sep. 1887 - **Moses King**, 28, married **Mary Thomas**. (C) [No other information given. See 239C.]
    237A - 13 Oct. 1887 - **Benjamin Carter**, 27, single, oysterman, b. York Co., residing Mid., son of Hannah Carter, married **Bettie Bundy**, 25, widow, b. & residing Mid., dau. of Martha Ann Carter. (C)
    237B - 26 Oct. 1887 - **Wm. Washington Johnson**, 21, single, oysterman, b. & residing Mid., son of Benja. & Lucy Johnson, married **Mary A. Swanson**, 21, single, b. & residing Mid., dau. of Isaac & Margaret Swanson. (C)
    237C - 27 Oct. 1887 - **Thos. Edwy Bray**, 30, single, farmer, b. & residing Mid., son of Thos. M. & Ophelia Bray, married **Sarah E. Smither**, 25, single, b. & residing Mid., dau. of Ribon M. & Catharine Smither. (W)
    238A - 6 Nov. 1887 - **Christopher Wiatt**, 23, single, oysterman, b. Gloucester, residing Mid., son of William & Louisa Wiatt, married **Mary A. Roane**, 21, single, b. & residing Mid., dau. of Mary A. Roane. (C)
    238B - 10 Nov. 1887 - **James Dickerson**, 23, widower, oysterman, b. Accomack, residing Mid., son of David & Rosa Ann Dickerson, married **Lucy Crump**, 19, single, b. & residing Mid., dau. of Henry & Mollie Crump. (C)
    238C - 24 Nov. 1887 - **Roscoe C. Travilian**, 26, single, farmer, b. & residing Gloucester, son of Roscoe & Arrinda Travilian, married **Emma A. Sibley**, 24, single, b. & residing Mid., dau. of Stage D. & Francis E. Sibley. (W)
    239A - 24 Nov. 1887 - **Moses Lewis** [sic- marriage license says **Moses King**], 28, single, farmer, b. & residing Mid., son of Lewis & Jane King, married **Arametta Thomas**, 19, single, b. & residing Mid., dau. of Thom. & Martha A. Thomas. (C)
    239B - 3 Dec. 1887 - **Little Coleman**, 23, single, farmer, b. Richmond City, residing Mid., son of Rubin & Maria Coleman, married **Harriet Thurston**, 22, single, b. Lancaster, residing Mid., dau. of Samuel & Harriet Thurston. (C)
    239C - 5 Dec. 1887 - **Charles Braxton**, 18, single, farmer, b. & residing Mid., son of Carter & Braxton, married **Maria L. King**, 20, single, b. & residing Mid., dau. of Adam & Mary King. (C)
    240A - 15 Dec. 1887 - **Wm. H. Wormley**, 22, single, laborer, b. King & Queen, residing Mid., son of Ralph & Mary Ann Wormley, married **Nancy Laws**, 21, single, b. &

residing Mid., dau. of Frank & Fanny Laws. (C)
   240B - 17 Dec. 1887 - **Rich'd Robinson**, 59, widower, farmer, b. & residing Mid., son of Richard & Eliza Robinson, married **Martha Holmes**, 30, widow, b. King & Queen, residing Mid., dau. of Peter Holmes. (C)
   240C - 18 Dec. 1887 - **Thomas H. Burrell**, 24, single, farmer, b. & residing Mid., son of Thomas & Margaret Burrell, married **Sarah Young**, 21, single, b. & residing Mid., dau. of Joshua & Mary Young. (C)
   241A - 25 Dec. 1887 - **Joshua Gowin**, 21, single, oysterman, b. & residing Mid., son of William & Cordelia Gowin, married **Alice Smith**, 16, single, b. & residing Mid., dau. of James & Maria Smith. (C)
   241B - 22 Dec. 1887 - **Ro. E. Ingram**, 41, single, farmer, b. King & Queen, residing Mid., son of Geo. W. & Nancy Ingram, married **Savina Jackson**, 34, single, b. King & Queen, residing Mid., dau. of Jno. V. & Maria Jackson. (W)
   241C - 25 Dec. 1887 - **Robert Braxton**, 21, single, farmer, b. & residing Mid., son of Peter & Sally Braxton, married **Pinkey Ann Burrell**, 21, single, b. & residing Mid., dau. of Lewis & Judy Burrell. (C)
   242A - Record crossed out - for **Walter T. Morris** & **Susan Ann Prince**. (W)
   242B - 27 Dec. 1887 - **Fleming Roy**, 21, single, farmer, b. Essex, residing Mid., son of Thos. & Alcie Roy, married **Margaret Williams**, 21, single, b. & residing Mid., dau. of Zack & Charity Williams. (C)
   242C - 27 Dec. 1887 - **George Roy**, 30, widower, farmer, b. Essex, residing Mid., son of Thos. & Alice Roy, married **Lucie Williams**, 23, single, b. & residing Mid., dau. of Zack & Charity Williams. (C)
   243A - [License issued Dec. 1887 - marriage date not given] - **John F. Cooper**, 23, single, farmer & oysterman, b. Stafford, residing Mid., son of George & Betty Cooper, married **Eliza C. Abbott**, 22, single, b. Deals Island, Maryland, residing Mid., dau. of [not given]. (W)
   243B - 29 Dec. 1887 - **Christopher Brown**, 32, single, farmer, b. & residing Mid., son of Wm. & Judy Brown, married **Sarah Fisher**, 19, single, b. & residing Mid., dau. of Rhoda Robinson. (C)
   243C - 28 Dec. 1887 - **Geo. F. Copper**, 24, single, butcher, b. Kent Co., Maryland, residing Mid., son of Wm. & Elizabeth Copper, married **Susan A. Prince**, 18, single, b. & residing Mid., dau. of Jas. Ro. & Elizabeth A. Prince. (W)
   244A - 29 Dec. 1887 - **Thomas B. Mitchell**, 24, single, farmer, b. King & Queen, residing Mid., son of [not given], married **Rosa M. Bristow**, 18, single, b.

Gloucester, residing Mid., dau. of Edward & Eliza Bristow. (W)

244B - 4 Jan. 1888 - **Charles D. Milby**, 35, single, carpenter, b. & residing Mid., son of Ro. & Dorothy M. Milby, married **Mary L. Trice**, 18, single, b. & residing Mid., dau. of Ro. M. & Elizabeth Trice. (W)

244C - 8 Jan. 1888 - **Wm. W. Hundley**, 31, widower, farmer, b. & residing Mid., son of Thos. & Elizabeth Hundley, married **Emma J. Hart**, 23, widow, b. & residing Mid., dau. of David & Jane Hurley. (W)

245A - 11 Jan. 1888 - **Austie Creighton**, 21, single, oysterman, residing Mid., son of Wm. M. & Susan M. Creighton, married **Cleo. Peade**, 25, widow, b. & residing Mid., dau. of Thos. & Eliz. Hundley. (W)

245B - 8 Jan. 1888 - **Henry C. Walter**, 47, widower, farmer, b. Caroline, residing Mid., son of Ap. & Chaney Waller, married **Catharine Harris**, 30, widow, b. Essex, residing Mid., dau. of Eliza Gowin. (C)

245C - 8 Jan. 1888 - **Strann Lewis**, 21, single, oysterman, b. & residing Mid., son of Thomas & Martha Lewis, married **Louisa Tucker**, 19, single, b. & residing Mid., dau. of Richard & Frances Tucker. (C)

246A - Jan. 1888 - **James A. Beale**, 38, widower, oysterman, b. & residing Mid., son of Robert & Mary Beale, married **Aurenia Banks**, 23, single, b. & residing Mid., dau. of [not given]. (C)

246B - 19 Jan. 1888 - **Smith Thornton**, 21, single, oysterman, b. & residing Mid., son of Ribon & Martha Thornton, married **Lucy Johnson**, 17, single, b. & residing Mid., dau. of Doctor & Amanda Johnson. (C)

246C - 19 Jan. 1888 - **George Meggs**, 22, single, oysterman, b. Gloucester, residing Mid., son of Peter & Tena Meggs, married **Maria Becket**, 34, widow, b. & residing Mid., dau. of John & Nancy Jackson. (C)

247A - 26 Jan. 1888 - **David Carter**, 40, widower, farmer, b. Essex, residing Mid., son of Zachariah & Martha Carter, married **Mary E. Ware**, 21, single, b. & residing Mid., dau. of Robert & Catharine E. Ware. (W)

247B - 1 Feb. 1888 - **Ro. Boss**, 24, single, farmer, b. & residing Mid., son of Robert & Bettie Boss, married **Nettie Carter**, 21, single, b. & residing Mid., dau. of Addison A. Carter. (W)

247C - 2 Feb. 1888 - **Frank Anderson**, 22, single, farmer, b. King & Queen, residing Mid., son of David & Rachel Anderson, married **Jane Johnson**, 19, single, b. & residing Mid., dau. of Doctor & Amanda Johnson. (C)

248A - 9 Feb. 1888 - **William Deleaver**, 26, widower, oysterman, b. & residing Mid., son of Thomas & Amelia Deleaver, married **Rosa Morris**, 21, single, b. & residing

Mid., dau. of Cornelius & Ann Morris. (C)
    248B - 9 Feb. 1888 - **Mack. Wormley,** 37, single, oysterman, b. & residing Mid., son of Mack & Barbary Wormley, married **Maria Davis,** 21, single, b. & residing Mid., dau. of Rachel Davis. (C)
    248C - 12 Feb. 1888 - **Lewis Burrell,** 22, single, farmer, b. & residing Mid., son of Lewis & Betsey Burrell, married **Mary Garnett,** 16, single, b. & residing Mid., dau. of John T. & Sally Garnett. (C)
    249A - 14 Feb. 1888 - **Wm. Francis Miller,** 23, single, merchant, b. Gloucester, residing Mid., son of Robert & Maria Miller, married **Emma G. Jones,** 20, single, b. & residing Mid., dau. of Lewis & Maria Jones. (W)
    249B - 23 Feb. 1888 - **Mark W. Tinsley,** 40, widower, farmer, b. Hanover, residing Mid., son of Sam'l H. & Sarah K. Tinsley, married **Fannie B. Towill,** 17, single, b. & residing Mid., dau. of Mark W. & Amanda M. Towill. (W)
    249C - 4 Mar. 1888 - **Edwin Thomas George,** 23, single, sailor, b. Lancaster, residing Mid., son of Jas. M. & Marg. R. George, married **Adelade Rains,** 22, single, b. Stafford, residing Mid., dau. of Wm. R. & Rebecca Rains. (W)
    250A - 15 Mar. 1888 - **William Morris,** 39, single, oysterman, b. & residing Mid., son of Frank & Martha Morris, married **Amanda Reed,** 30, single, b. & residing Mid., dau. of Austin & Matilda Read. (C)
    250B - 18 Mar. 1888 - **Harvey Ruffin,** 29, single, oysterman, b. & residing Essex, son of Hugan & Luisa Ruffin, married **Fannie B. Reed,** 22, single, b. & residing Mid., dau. of Silas & Mary E. Reed. (C)
    250C - 25 Mar. 1888 - **R. J. Major,** 23, single, sailor, b. Mid., residing Stafford, son of Wm. M. & Bettie Major, married **Martha A. Muse,** 17, single, b. & residing Stafford, dau. of Jos. A. & Nora Muse. (W)
    251A - 1 Apr. 1888 - **Wm. Richardson,** 21, single, oysterman, b. Essex, residing Mid., son of Susan Ann Bird, married **Rosetta Chamberlin,** 19, single, b. & residing Mid., dau. of Saphronia Ross. (C)
    251B - 29 Mar. 1888 - **Andrew N. Hanson,** 37, single, carpenter, residing Mid., son of Hans C. & Anna M. Hanson, married **Elvira I. Parks,** 27, widow, b. & residing Mid., dau. of Wm. S. & Catharine Blake. (W)
    251C - 5 Apr. 1888 - **Thomas Deleaver, Jr.,** 24, single, oysterman, b. & residing Mid., son of Thomas & Amelia Deleaver, married **Clara Croxton,** 25, single, b. Essex, residing Mid., dau. of John Croxton. (C)
    252A - 5 Apr. 1888 - **Otis J. Palmer,** 27, single, sailor, b. & residing Mid., son of John D. & Mary F. Palmer, married **Lucy E. Clements,** 21, single, b. &

residing Mid., dau. of Richard M. & Ophelia V. Clements. (W)

252B - 1888 - **Wm. T. Sherman Kies**, 23, single, farmer, b. Maryland, residing Mid., son of Wm. T. & Louisa Kies, married **Eliz. T. Husk** [or **Hush**], 17, single, b. Maryland, residing Mid., dau. of San'l C. & Hannah M. Husk. (W)

252C - 12 Apr. 1888 - **Berkley S. Richardson**, 22, single, merchant, b. King & Queen, residing Mid., son of Wm. T. & Sarah Richardson, married **Fannie G. Northam**, 21, single, b. & residing Mid., dau. of Henry C. & Susan Northam. (W)

253A - 18 Apr. 1888 - **Geo. W. Callis**, 21, single, oysterman, b. Mathews, residing Mid., son of Thomas C. & Elizabeth Callis, married **Mary Liz Trader**, 20, single, b. Mathews, residing Mid., dau. of Richard & Elizabeth Trader. (W)

253B - 14 Apr. 1888 - **Wm. Ruffin**, 21, single, laborer, b. & residing Mid., son of Jesse & Adeline Ruffin, married **Martha Ellen Johnson**, 18, single, b. & residing Mid., dau. of David & Mary Johnson. (C)

253C - 16 Apr. 1888 - **Wm. A. Faucett**, 24, single, farmer, b. & residing Mid., son of John R. & Sarah C. Faucett, married **Mary J. Street**, 21, single, b. & residing Mid., dau. of Richard H. & Virginia H. Street. (W)

254A - 18 Apr. 1888 - **Harry Robinson**, 50, widower, farmer, b. & residing Mid., son of Harry & Sally Robinson, married **Lois Mathews**, 30, widow, b. Maryland, residing Mid., dau. of Davis. (C)

254B - 1888 - **Isaac Davis**, 45, widower, mechanic, b. & residing King & Queen, son of John & Hannah Davis, married **Louisa King**, 38, widow, b. & residing Mid., dau. of Richard & Easter Beverly. (C)

254C - 10 May 1888 - **Walter M. Major, Jr.**, 26, single, farmer, b. & residing Mid., son of Walter M. & Eliz. Major, married **Belle Mercer**, 23, single, b. & residing Mid., dau. of John Mercer. (W)

255A - 13 May 1888 - **Wm. E. Payne**, 23, single, mechanic, b. Lancaster, residing Mid., son of Jas. S. & Mary E. Payne, married **Mary E. Callis**, 22, single, b. Mathews, residing Mid., dau. of Geo. L. & Judy Callis. (W)

255B - 2 Jun. 1888 - **Ed. Thos. Jones**, 21, single, farmer, b. Gloucester, residing Mid., son of Edmund & Margaret Jones, married **Lucy Carr**, 17, single, b. & residing Mid., dau. of Ro. & Oney Carr. (C)

255C - 7 Jun. 1888 - **J. Frank Smith**, 56, widower, physician, b. King & Queen, son of Frank & Caroline Smith, married **Caroline F. Woodward**, 43, widow, b.

Gloucester, residing Mid., dau. of Wm. & Ann F. Smith. (W)

256A - 25 Oct. 1888 - **Walter C. Palmer**, 26, single, merchant, b. Mid., residing Baltimore, Maryland, son of Andrew J. & Emily Palmer, married **Roberta L. Marston**, 19, single, b. & residing.Mid., dau. of Oliver J. & Margaret Marston. (W)

256B - 1888 - **George Smith**, 27, single, oysterman, b. & residing Mid., son of Phil & Susan Smith, married **Mary White**, 21, single, b. & residing Mid., dau. of John & Martha White. (C)

256C - 10 Jul. 1888 - **Holland M. Walker**, 38, single, farmer, b. & residing Mid., son of M. J. M. & Sarah F. Walker, married **Louisa M. Barrick**, single, b. & residing Mid., dau. of Wm. H. & Frances Barrick. (W)

257A - 18 Jul. 1888 - **Geo. Ed. Sadler**, 32, single, carpenter, b. & residing Mid., son of James A. & Mary Sadler, married **Irena J. Taylor**, 19, single, b. Northumberland, residing Mid., dau. of Sam'l & Martha Taylor. (W)

257B - 6 Sep. 1888 - **Jeter W. Blake**, 22, single, oysterman, b. & residing Mid., son of Alpheus & Ann Lewis Blake, married **Henrietta Haynes**, 21, single, b. Gloucester, residing Mid., dau. of Geo. H. & Frances F. Haynes. (W)

257C - 16 Aug. 1888 - **Julius Harris**, 24, single, oysterman, b. & residing Mid., son of Wm. & Lucy Harris, married **Ellen Morris**, 20, single, b. & residing Mid., dau. of William & Betty Morris. (C)

258A - 13 Sep. 1888 - **Frank Ben Davis**, 24, single, printer, b. New York, residing Chicago, Illinois, son of Julius & Laura Davis, married **Ella Florence Hewett**, 20, single, b. Maine, residing Mid., dau. of Mark L. & Sarah E. Hewett. (W)

258B - 23 Sep. 1888 - **Beverly Smith**, 23, widower, oysterman, b. Gloucester, residing Mid., son of John & Charlotte Smith, married **Adelade Aytes**, 19, single, b. & residing Mid., dau. of John & Chary Aytes. (C)

258C - 4 Oct. 1888 - **Sam'l Henry Webb**, 24, single, oysterman, b. & residing Mid., son of John & Betsy Webb, married **Copia Lewis**, 18, single, b. & residing Mid., dau. of Julius & Alice Lewis. (C)

259A - 9 Oct. 1888 - **Magruder Browne**, 24, single, oysterman, b. Gloucester, residing Mid., son of Seaymor & Sarah J. Browne, married **Lucy A. Chandler**, 26, single, b. & residing Mid., dau. of Silas Chandler. (W)

259B - 16 Oct. 1888 - **Cincinatus C. Ward**, 23, widower, carpenter, b. Northampton, residing Mid., son of Harry & Eliza Ward, married **Mary F. Lyle**, 18, single, b. Gloucester, residing Mid., dau. of Wm. J. & Adeline

Lyle. (W)
259C - 25 Oct. 1888 - **John A. Blake**, 42, widower, book agent, b. & residing Mid., son of Berkley R. & Susan Blake, married **Bettie T. Green**, 30, widow, b. & residing Mid., dau. of Wm. Keiningham. (W)
260A - 25 Oct. 1888 - **Ribon Thornton**, 23, single, oysterman, b. Essex, residing Mid., son of Ribon & Margaret Thornton, married **Hester Boyd**, 23, single, b. Philadelphia, residing Mid., dau. of Henry & Henrietta Boyd. (C)
260B - 10 Nov. 1888 - **Wellington Davis**, 24, single, farmer, b. & residing Mid., son of John & Mary Davis, married **Mary Ellen Jones**, 30, widow, b. & residing Mid., dau. of [not given]. (C)
260C - 29 Nov. 1888 - **Thos. H. Wood**, 24, single, oysterman, b. & residing Mid., son of Geo. W. & Anna Wood, married **Maggie Thornton**, 18, single, b. & residing Mid., dau. of Benjamin & Mary Thornton. (C)
261A - 2 Dec. 1888 - **Henry Boyd**, 21, single, oysterman, b. & residing Mid., son of Robert & Nancy Gwynn, married **Rebecca Anderson**, 22, single, b. King & Queen, residing Mid., dau. of Rachel Anderson. (C)
261B - Dec. 1888 - **Edward McEntire**, 26, single, sailor, b. Maine, residing Mid., son of Enock & Ella McEntire, married **C. E. Moore**, 25, widow, b. & residing Mid., dau. of James H. & Virginia A. Norris. (W)
261C - 14 Dec. 1888 - **Geo. D. Thomas**, 25, single, oysterman, b. Mathews, residing Mid., son of Rev. Geo. E. & Lucy E. Thomas, married **Martha South**, 22, single, b. & residing Mid., dau. of South. (W)
262A - 16 Dec. 1888 - **R. W. Cook**, 27, single, oysterman, b. & residing Mid., son of James H. & Louise Cook, married **Martha A. Robinson**, 25, single, b. & residing Mid., dau. of George Robinson. (C)
262B - 20 Dec. 1888 - **Geo. H. Griffin**, 23, single, oysterman, b. North Carolina, residing Mid., son of Taylor & Mary Griffin, married **Christianna Fleet**, 25, single, b. & residing Mid., dau. of Eliz. Fleet. (C)
262C - 25 Dec. 1888 - **Benjamin Jones**, 21, single, oysterman, b. & residing King & Queen, son of John & Judy Jones, married **Josie Courtney**, 21, single, b. King & Queen, residing Mid., dau. of Wm. & Jane Courtney. (C)
263A - 23 Dec. 1888 - **Robert J. Hale**, 27, single, farmer, b. & residing Mid., son of Ro. W & Saphronia Hale, married **Hattie A. Marchant**, 22, single, b. Mathews, residing Mid., dau. of Christopher Marchant. (W)
263B - 23 Dec. 1888 - **James C. Carter**, 22, single, oysterman, b. & residing Mid., son of Wm. & Louisa

Carter, married **Kitty A. Laws**, 21, single, b. & residing Mid., dau. of John Laws. (C)

263C - 26 Dec. 1888 - **Isaih Washington**, 23, single, farmer, b. & residing Mid., son of George & Matilda Washington, married **Eliza Cook**, 17, single, b. & residing Mid., dau. of India Cook. (C)

264A - 24 Dec. 1888 - **Thos. Jeff. Lewis**, 25, single, farmer, b. & residing Mid., son of Thos. & Mary Lewis, married **Mary L. Stiff**, 35, widow, b. & residing Mid., dau. of Wm. N. & Eliz. Chowning. (W)

264B - 30 Dec. 1888 - **Benjamin Robinson**, 24 single, farmer, b. & residing Mid., son of Benj'n & Isabella Robinson, married **Charity A. Smith**, 22, single, b. & residing Mid., dau. of Eliza Smith. (C)

264C - 26 Dec. 1888 - **James Munroe**, 21, single, oysterman, son of Patsy Washington, married **Rebecca Williams**, 20, single, b. & residing Mid., dau. of Albert Williams. (C)

265A - 27 Dec. 1888 - **John B. Holmes**, 26, single, oysterman, b. King & Queen, residing Mid., son of Patrick & Laura Holmes, married **Nannie E. Carter**, 21, single, residing Mid., dau. of Lewis & Ellen Carter. (C)

265B - 27 Dec. 1888 - **Robert Thomas**, 26, widower, oysterman, b. & residing Lancaster, son of James & Elizabeth Thomas, married **Virgin Kenner**, 21, single, b. Washington, residing Mid., dau. of James & Kissiah Kinner. (C)

265C - 17 Jan. 1889 - **Wm. H. Holmes**, 23, single, oysterman, b. & residing Mid., son of Wm. & Clory Holmes, married **Mary Johnson**, 21, single, b. & residing Mid., dau. of Robert & Susan Johnson. (C)

266A - 16 Jan. 1889 - **Braxton Gardner**, 54, widower, farmer, b. King & Queen, residing Mid., son of Moses & Winney Gardner, married **Rachel Davis**, 36, single, b. & residing Mid., dau. of Samuel Davis. (C)

266B - 16 Jan. 1889 - **Augustin Bird**, 48, widower, farmer, b. & residing King & Queen, son of Iveson & Rosa A. Bird, married **Margaret Muse**, 35, single, b. King & Queen, residing Mid., dau. of Harriet Muse. (C)

266C - 24 Jan. 1889 - **John F. Hale**, 34, widower, farmer, b. & residing Mid., son of Robert & Saphronia Hale, married **Mary Alice Broach**, 27, single, b. & residing Mid., dau. of Richard & Virginia Broach. (W)

267A - 24 Jan. 1889 - **Geo. B. Taylor**, 23, single, oysterman, b. & residing Mid., son of Anderson & Lucinda Taylor, married **Mary E. Jones**, 21, single, b. & residing Mid., dau. of Wallace & Martha Jones. (C)

267B - 25 Jan. 1889 - **Charles Walker, Jr.**, 21,

single, oysterman, b. & residing Mid., son of Charles & Tina Walker, married **Rebecca Johnson**, 18, single, b. & residing Mid., dau. of John & Betty Johnson. (C)

267C - 1889 - **Early Goldman**, 21, single, oysterman, b. & residing Mid., son of Elijah & Jane Goldman, married **Columbia Carter**, 21, single, b. & residing Mid., dau. of David & Milly Carter. (C)

268A - 6 Feb. 1889 - **George S. Davis**, 29, single, farmer, b. & residing Mid., son of George S. & Sarah E. Davis, married **Ellen B. Evans**, 30, single, b. & residing Mid., dau. of John M. & Ellen Evans. (W)

268B - 7 Feb. 1889 - **William E. Walker**, 30, single, merchant, b. & residing Mid., son of Francis M. & Elizabeth Walker, married **Estelle Bristow**, 20, single, b. & residing Mid., dau. of Calvin & [Mary penned in] Bristow. (W)

268C - 13 Feb. 1889 - **Philip H. Fitzhugh**, 31, single, merchant, b. Gloucester, residing Washington, D. C., son of P. H. & Mary S. Fitzhugh, married **Mary T. Purkins**, single, b. & residing Mid., dau. of Ed. T. & Betty H. Purkins. (W)

269A - 13 Feb. 1889 - **Muscoe R. Booker**, 31, single, miller, b. Gloucester, residing Mid., son of Lewis T. & Lucy F. Booker, married **Kate E. Taylor**, 19, single, b. King & Queen, residing Mid., dau. of Thomas & Sarah J. Taylor. (W)

269B - 13 Feb. 1889 - **Chas. B. Dunlevy**, 24, single, farmer, b. & residing Mid., son of Wm. B. & Mary Dunlevy, married **Sarah A. Mears**, 21, single, b. & residing Mid., dau. of John W. & Amanda Mears. (W)

269C - 14 Feb. 1889 - **Geo. Thos. Robinson**, 23, single, oysterman, b. & residing Mid., son of Harry & Malea Robinson, married **Queen Vic. Mathews**, 19, single, b. Accomack, residing Mid., dau. of Mathews. (C)

270A - 19 Feb. 1889 - **R. G. Blake**, 28, single, farmer, b. & residing Mid., son of R. L. & M. A. Blake, married **Matie T. Baughan**, 20, single, b. Essex, residing Mid., dau. of T. P. & M. A. Baughan. (W)

270B - 17 Feb. 1889 - **Zack C. Bristow**, 27, single, farmer, b. & residing Mid., son of Thos. S. & Eudora Bristow, married **Mary L. Taylor**, 17, single, b. & residing Mid., dau. of Martha J. Taylor. (W)

270C - Feb. 1889 - **Robert Henry Thornton**, 21, single, oysterman, b. & residing Mid., son of Henry & Madland Thornton, married **Mary Nelson**, 19, single, b. & residing Mid., dau. of James & Eliza A. Nelson. (C)

271A - 7 Mar. 1889 - **Ellick Boyd**, 22, single, oysterman, b. & residing Mid., son of Thos. & Mary Boyd, married **Mattie L. Roane**, 17, single, b. & residing Mid., dau. of Wm. F. & Sarah Roane. (C)

271B - 10 Mar. 1889 - **Augustus Fields**, 23, single, oysterman, b. Gloucester, residing Mid., son of Edward & Eliza Fields, married **Sarah Foster**, 21, single, b. & residing Mid., dau. of Mary Ann Foster. (C)

271C - 20 Mar. 1889 - **John R. Ferneyhough**, 45, widower, farmer, b. Essex, residing Mid., son of Robert & Frances Ferneyhough, married **Ida B. Eubank**, 29, single, b. & residing Mid., dau. of James A. & Cornelia Eubank. (W)

272A - 24 Mar. 1889 - **Andrew W. Carter**, single, farmer, b. & residing Mid., son of Geo. A. Carter, married **Maggie A. Taylor**, 17, single, b. Accomack, residing Mid., dau. of Ro. S. & Vernetta Taylor. (W)

272B - 24 Mar. 1889 - **Richard Page**, 26, single, farmer, b. & residing Mid., son of Manuel & Eliza Page, married **Harriet Foster**, 19, single, b. & residing Mid., dau. of Phil & Ellen Foster. (C)

272C - 1889 - **Jno. W. A. Tabor**, 19, single, oysterman, b. & residing Mid., son of Jos. & Betty Tabor, married **Ennie E. Davis**, 17, single, b. & residing Mid., dau. of Jas. R. Davis. (W)

273A - 28 Mar. 1889 - **John Jackson**, 21, single, oysterman, b. & residing Mid., son of Agnes Jackson, married **Nora Conway**, 17, single, b. & residing Mid., dau. of Wm. & Emiline Conway. (C)

273B - Record crossed out.

273C - Record crossed out.

274A - 6 Apr. 1889 - **Toney Beverly**, 29, single, farmer, b. Caroline, residing Mid., son of Anderson & Ann Beverly, married **Nancy Carter**, 23, single, b. & residing Mid., dau. of Davy & Milly Carter. (C)

274B - 18 Apr. 1889 - **Milton Johnson**, 27, single, farmer, b. King & Queen, residing Mid., son of Dandridge & Anna Johnson, married **Roberta Muse**, 22, single, b. King & Queen, residing Mid., dau. of Ira & Lettie Muse. (C)

274C - 18 Apr. 1889 - **Jeff. Curtis**, 22, single, farmer, b. & residing Gloucester, son of Wm. & Betty Curtis, married **Grace Laws**, 19, single, b. & residing Mid., dau. of Frank & Fanny Laws. (C)

275A - 2 May 1889 - **Thomas Williams**, 24, widower, oysterman, b. & residing Mid., son of Thos. & Mary Williams, married **Marg't Robinson**, 23, single, b. & residing Mid., dau. of Wm. Robinson. (C)

275B - 20 May 1889 - **Abram Smith**, 22, single, laborer, b. & residing Mid., son of Phil. & Kitty Smith, married **Sallie Upshaw**, 19, single, b. & residing Mid., dau. of Augustine Upshaw. (C)

275C - 23 May 1889 - **Green Griffin**, 44, widower, farmer, b. South Carolina, residing Mid., son of Hiram &

Judy Griffin, married **Fanny Jones**, 22, single, b. & residing Mid., dau. of Augustine & Frances Jones. (C)

276A - 30 May 1889 - **Christopher Anderson**, 21, single, farmer, b. King & Queen, residing Mid., son of David & Rachel Anderson, married **Crissella Baker**, 21, single, b. & residing Mid., dau. of James & Betsy Baker. (C)

276B - 13 Jun. 1889 - **Richard F. Jarvis**, 21, single, clerk, b. Mathews, residing Mid., son of F. P. & Sarah Jarvis, married **Mary A. Haynes**, 18, single, b. Gloucester, residing Mid., dau. of Geo. H. & Lucy F. Haynes. (W)

276C - 19 Jun. 1889 - **John A. Wilson**, 38, single, farmer, b. King & Queen, residing Mid., son of Warner & Ann Wilson, married **Lucy A. Campbell**, 36, single, b. & residing Mid., dau. of Lee & Louisa Campbell. (C)

277A - 26 Jun. 1889 - **George S. Blake**, 40, widower, mechanic, b. & residing Mid., son of Jacob S. & Lucy Blake, married **Lucy B. Schools**, 20, widow, b. Gloucester, residing Mid., dau. of Thomas & Bettie Brown. (W)

277B - 4 Jul. 1889 - **Jas. T. Hart**, 23, widower, oysterman, b. & residing Mid., son of James H. & Mary Hart, married **Lilly M. Owens**, 17, single, b. Mathews, residing Mid., dau. of Wm. & Mary Owen. (W)

277C - 6 Jul. 1889 - **Lewin N. Kennard**, 26, single, sailor, b. Kent Co., Maryland, residing Mid., son of Wm. J. & Mary Ann Kennard, married **Etta Powell**, 21, single, b. Lancaster, residing Mid., dau. of Ro. C. Powell. (W)

278A - Jul. 1889 - **John S. Burrell**, 22, single, farmer, b. & residing Mid., son of Thos. & Peggy Burrell, married **Martha Thurston**, 17, single, b. & residing Mid., dau. of Geo. & Lucy Thurston. (C)

278B - 14 Ju. 1889 - **Nathan Henry**, 23, single, oysterman, b. & residing Mid., son of Nathan & Charlotte Henry, married **Jenny Bundy**, 23, single, b. & residing Mid., dau. of Sam'l & Jane Bundy. (C)

278C - 16 Jul. 1889 - **Spencer Johnson**, 70, widower, farmer, b. & residing Mid., son of Spencer & Polly Johnson, married **Milley Wood**, 46, widow, b. & residing Mid., dau. of Thomas Frazier. (C)

279A - 27 Jul. 1889 - **Jas. W. Booker**, 21, single, laborer, b. Hampton, residing Mid., son of Richard & Frances Booker, married **Cath. Jones**, 21, single, b. Gloucester, residing Mid., dau. of Eliza Jones. (C)

279B - 31 Jul. 1889 - **James A. Fitchett**, 22, single, farmer, b. & residing Mid., son of S. P. & Sally Fitchett, married **Correna D. Bristow**, 16, single, b. & residing Mid., dau. of Walter & Adeline Bristow. (W)

279C - 10 Aug. 1889 - **James G. Laws**, 22, single,

oysterman, b. & residing Mid., son of John & Anna Laws, married **Mary Ann Banks**, 18, single, b. & residing Mid., dau. of Lewis & Eudora Banks. (C)

280A - 23 Aug. 1889 - **George Thurston, Sr.**, widower, farmer, b. & residing Mid., married **Hannah Street**, 24, single, b. & residing Mid. (C) [No other information given.]

280B - 8 Sep. 1889 - **Chas. Henry Banks**, 20, single, oysterman, b. & residing Mid., son of Mingo & Emily Banks, married **Ellen Monroe**, 18, single, b. & residing Mid., dau. of Albert & Anna Monroe. (C)

280C - 12 Sep. 1889 - **Major E. Fountain**, 24, single, oysterman, b. & residing Mid., son of Geo. & Maria Fountain, married **Sally Robinson**, 21, single, b. & residing Mid., dau. of Matilda Robinson. (C)

281A - 26 Sep. 1889 - **M. P. Maxwell**, 43, widower, farmer, b. New Castle Co., Delaware, residing Mid., son of Wm. & Rachel Maxwell, married **Sarah F. Hudson**, 33, widow, b. & residing Mid., dau. of John M. & Ellen Evans. (W)

281B - 24 Sep. 1889 - **John H. Adams**, 23, single, blacksmith, b. & residing Baltimore, Maryland, son of Jas. B. & Fannie P. Adams, married **Lelia V. Stiff**, 21, single, b. & residing Mid., dau. of George & Mary Stiff. (W)

281C - 31 Oct. 1889 - **Ed. B. Richards**, 24, single, farmer, b. & residing Mid., son of Edmund & Polly Richards, married **Laura A. Bagby**, 20, single, b. & residing Mid., dau. of Washington & Polly Bagby. (C)

282A - 13 Nov. 1889 - **Robert Linson**, 24, single, farmer, b. & residing Mid., son of Sciaras & Violet Linson, married **Cilitan Howard**, 20, single, b. & residing Mid., dau. of Sam'l & Sally Howard. (C)

282B - 20 Nov. 1889 - **Geo. E. Sibley**, 33, widower, farmer, b. & residing Mid., son of Daniel B. & Sarah Sibley, married **Fannie C. Lewis**, 16, single, b. & residing Mid., dau. of Jas. T. & Louisa J. Lewis. (W)

282C - Nov. 1889 - **A. J. Sable**, 70, widower, farmer, b. St. Marys Co., Maryland, residing Mid., son of John & Catherine Sable, married **Susan Coates**, 22, single, b. Westmoreland, residing Mid., dau. of Coates. (W)

283A - 28 Nov. 1889 - **William Browne**, 23, single, oysterman, b. & residing Mid., son of Martha E. Browne, married **Emma Bird**, 18, single, b. & residing Mid., dau. of Anna Bird. (C)

283B - 25 Dec. 1889 - **R. B. Evans**, 28, single, farmer, b. & residing Essex, son of Jas. B. & Mary F. Evans, married **M. L. Dickinson**, 17, single, b. & residing Mid., dau. of L. H. & Lucy E. Dickinson. (W)

283C - 28 Nov. 1889 - **Lewis Carter**, 24, single,

farmer, b. Washington, D. C., residing Mid., son of Lewis & Ella Carter, married **Mary E. Wormley**, 22, single, b. & residing Mid., dau. of Archy & Mary Wormley. (C)

284A - 1 Dec. 1889 - **Charles H. Walker**, 46, widower, farmer, b. & residing Mid., son of Lee & Maria Walker, married **Louisa J. Thurston**, 20, single, b. & residing Mid., dau. of George & Frances Thurston. (C)

284B - 5 Dec. 1889 - **Carter Conway**, 27, single, farmer, b. & residing Mid., son of William & Emeline Conway, married **Anna Reed**, 21, single, b. & residing Mid., dau. of Isaac & Fannie Reed. (C)

284C - 25 Apr. 1889 - **Reubin Ward**, 25, single, farmer, b. & residing Mid., son of Zack & Martha Ward, married **Mariah Gresham**, 23, single, b. & residing Mid., dau. of Robert Gresham. (C)

285A - 12 Dec. 1889 - **R. H. Clements**, 27, single, blacksmith, b. & residing Mid., son of Rich'd H. & Ophelia V. Clements, married **Mary E. Bristow**, 25, single, b. & residing Mid., dau. of Andrew & E. W. Bristow. (W)

285B - 26 Dec. 1889 - **A. F. Smither**, 36, single, oyster dealer, b. Essex, residing West Point, King William, son of Geo. K. & Cordelia Smither, married **Lulie W. Lee**, 24, single, b. & residing Mid., dau. of D. W. & Netta Lee. (W)

285C - 26 Dec. 1889 - **Caesar Williams**, 27, single, oysterman, b. & residing Mid., son of Chap. & Ada Williams, married **Alice Wormley**, 21, single, b. & residing Mid., dau. of Archy & Mary Ann Wormley. (C)

286A - 25 Dec. 1889 - **James E. Harris**, 24, single, oysterman, b. & residing Mid., son of Philip & Mary Harris, married **Emma L. Lincoln**, 21, single, b. & residing Mid., dau. of Syrus & Violet Lincoln. (C)

286B - 25 Dec. 1889 - **Wm. Elliott**, 26, single, bricklayer, b. Norfolk Co., residing Norfolk, son of Henry & June Elliott, married **Amy Burrell**, 23, single, b. & residing Mid., dau. of Lewis & Judy Burrell. (C)

286C - 26 Dec. 1889 - **George Jackson**, 22, single, farmer, b. King & Queen, residing Mid., son of George & Caroline Jackson, married **Alice Reed**, 19, single, b. & residing Mid., dau. of Isaac & Catharine Reed. (C)

287A - 26 Dec. 1889 - **Joseph Smith**, 22, single, oysterman, b. & residing Lancaster, son of James & Mary J. Smith, married **Rebecca Yates**, 21, single, b. & residing Mid., dau. of John & Chillery Yates. (C)

287B - Repeat of 287A.

287C - 29 Dec. 1889 - **Gowing Robinson**, 23, single, oysterman, b. & residing Mid., son of Alex & Adeline Robinson, married **Mattie K. Reed**, 19, single, b. &

residing Mid., dau. of Jesse & Laura Reed. (C)

288A - 2 Jan. 1890 - **Daniel Johnson**, 26, single, farmer, b. King & Queen, residing Mid., son of Daniel & Martha Johnson, married **Lucy Scott**, 22, single, b. Gloucester, residing Mid., dau. of Manerva Scott. (C)

288B - 7 Jan. 1890 - **Richard Johnson**, 24, single, farmer, b. & residing Mid., son of Simon & Matilda Johnson, married **Laura Jones**, 16, single, b. & residing Mid., dau. of Oscar & Lucy Jones. (C)

288 C - 9 Jan. 1890 - **Frank M. Carter**, 28, single, farmer, b. King & Queen, residing Mid., son of Frank & Judith Carter, married **Lelia Keiningham**, 28, single, b. & residing Mid., dau. of James & Mary Keiningham. (W)

289A - 9 Jan. 1890 - **Virginius Thornton**, 25, single, oysterman, b. & residing Mid., son of Benjamin & Mary Thornton, married **Alice Mosley**, 19, single, b. Halifax, residing Mid., dau. of George & Alice Mosley. (C)

289B - 16 Jan. 1890 - **Harry Carter**, 31, single, oysterman, b. & residing Mid., son of George & Lucy Carter, married **Anna B. Owen**, 23, single, b. King & Queen, residing Mid., dau. of Lewis & Mima Owen. (C)

289C - 6 Feb. 1890 - **Ro. Franklin Meggs**, 26, single, farmer, b. King & Queen, residing Mid., son of Walker & Frances Meggs, married **Juna Holliway**, 30, widow, b. King & Queen, residing Mid., dau. of Frances Williams. (C)

290A - 31 Aug. 1890 - **Wm. B. Carter**, 21, single, oysterman, b. & residing Mid., son of Deaton & Lizzie Carter, married **Nellie G. Taylor**, 18, single, b. & residing Mid., dau. of Allen & Eliza Taylor. (C)

290B - Feb. 1890 - **Jacob Washington**, 33, single, oysterman, b. Gloucester, residing Mid., son of George & Winney, married **Fanny Chamberlane**, 26, single, b. & residing Mid., dau. of George & Matilda Chamberlane. (C)

290C - 27 Feb. 1890 - **Robert Campbell**, 21, single, farmer, b. & residing Mid., son of James & Esperella Campbell, married **Susan M. Smith**, 21, single, b. & residing Mid., dau. of John & Emma Smith. (C)

291A - 12 Mar. 1890 - **James T. Waller**, 23, single, oysterman & farmer, b. & residing Mid., son of Clay & Catherin Waller, married **Agnes Reeds**, 18, single, b. & residing Mid., dau. of Geo. & Lena Reeds. (C)

291B - Repeat of 291A.

291C - 13 Mar. 1890 - **Stephen Fields**, 24, single, oysterman, b. Gloucester, residing Mid., son of Edward & Eliza Fields, married **Maria Smith**, 19, single, b. & residing Mid., dau. of Kitty Smith. (C)

292A - 20 Mar. 1890 - **Frederick Robinson**, 20, single, farmer, b. King & Queen, residing Mid., son of Leonard & Ann Robinson, married **Susan Scott**, 19, single, b. &

residing Mid., dau. of Sallie Ann Scott. (C)
  292B - 20 Mar. 1890 - **Wm. Wallace Jones**, 26, single, oysterman, b. & residing Mid., son of Walace & Martha E. Jones, married **Maria Weeks**, 22, single, b. & residing Mid., dau. of Ralph & Mary Weeks. (C)
  292C - 23 Mar. 1890 - **Thornton Chandler**, 29, single, farmer, b. Essex, residing Mid., son of Archy & Margaret Chandler, married **Catharine Johnson**, 20, single, b. & residing Mid., dau. of Simon & Matilda Johnson. (C)
  293A - 2 Apr. 1890 - **Sam'l R. Rilee**, 30, single, blacksmith, b. & residing Mid., son of George D. & Sarah Rilee, married **Mattie Lee Johnson**, 14, single, b. Essex, residing Mid., dau. of J. W. & Lotta Johnson. (W)
  293B - 9 Apr. 1890 - **Lucius Bates**, 22, single, residing Mid., son of [not given], married **Agnes Nelson**, 19, single, b. & residing Mid., dau. of Robert Nelson. (C)
  293C - 10 Apr. 1890 - **Frank C. Knapp**, 44, single, cooper, b. Oniver Co., New York, residing Mid., son of John & Mary Knapp, married **Eliza C. Gayle**, 31, widow, b. York Co, residing Mid., dau. of James & Eliza Chandler. (W)
  294A - 22 Apr. 1890 - **Richard Bristow**, single, laborer, b. & residing Mid., son of [not given], married **Rebecca Johnson**, 18, single, b. & residing Mid., dau. of Benjamin Johnson. (C)
  294B - 24 Apr. 1890 - **Janiel West**, 37, widower, laborer, b. King & Queen, residing Mid., son of Nelson & Catharine West, married **Matilda A. Pollard**, 23, single, b. & residing Mid., dau. of Wm. Z. B. & Car. Upshaw. (C)
  294C - 1 May 1890 - **John Furgusson**, 38, widower, oysterman, b. & residing Mathews, son of Wm. & Maria Furgusson, married **Ann Churchill**, 23, single, b. & residing Mid., dau. of Leroy & Ann Churchill. (C)
  295A - 12 May 1890 - **Albert Armstead**, 24, single, oysterman, b. Gloucester, residing Mid., son of Andrew & Patsy Armstead, married **Mary Gaines**, 18, single, b. & residing Mid., dau. of Lewis & Rose Gaines. (C)
  295B - 18 May 1890 - **Geo. Wash. Holmes**, 26, single, oysterman, b. & residing Mid., son of Kit & Anna Holmes, married **Hettey B. Chamberlain**, 24, single, b. & residing Mid., dau. of Geo. & Mary Chamberlain. (C)
  295C - 18 May 1890 - **Thos. H. Burke**, 26, single, oysterman, b. & residing Mid., son of William & Susan Burke, married **Lucinda Upshaw**, 21, single, b. & residing Mid., dau. of Belle Upshaw. (C)
  296A - 20 May 1890 - **Emmitt Thurston**, 22, single, oysterman, b. & residing Mid., son of Daniel & Jane Thurston, married **Caroline Lee**, 16, single, b. & residing Mid., dau. of Wm. B. & Eliz. Lee. (C)

296B - 1 Jun. 1890 - **Wm. H. Roane**, 22, single, oysterman, b. Gloucester, residing Mid., son of Wm. F. & Sarah Roane, married **Precilla Johnson**, 22, single, b. King & Queen, residing Mid., dau. of Rosetta Johnson. (C)

296C - 5 Jun. 1890 - **Taylor Griffin**, 45, widower, farmer, b. & residing Mid., son of George & Frances Griffin, married **Mary Fauntleroy**, 28, widow, b. & residing Mid., dau. of Susan Richardson. (C)

297A - 5 Jun. 1890 - **A. C. Powell**, 23, single, oysterman, b. Baltimore, Maryland, residing Mid., son of A. W. & A. Powell, married **Louise Parker**, 18, single, b. King & Queen, residing Mid., dau. of Jos. & Willie A. Parker. (W)

297B - 12 Jun. 1890 - **George Becket**, 21, single, oysterman, b. & residing Mid., son of Allen & Maria Becket, married **Susan Roy**, 15, single, b. & residing Mid., dau. of Jos. & Dianna Roy. (C)

297C - 15 Jun. 1890 - **William H. Hart**, 22, single, wheelwright, b. & residing Mid., son of John W. & Mary W. Hart, married **Augusta E. Calhoun**, 21, single, b. & residing Mid., dau. of Thomas & Emma Calhoun. (W)

298A - 22 Jun. 1890 - **Sam'l Jones**, 22, single, oysterman, b. & residing Mid., son of Cornelius & Saphronia Jones, married **Martha Henry**, 18, single, b. & residing Mid., dau. of Thos. & Martha Ellen Henry. (C)

298B - Jul. 1890 - **Paul Williams**, 21, single, oysterman, b. & residing Mid., son of Williams, married **Aida Jarvis**, 21, single, b. & residing Mid., dau. of Jarvis. (C)

298C - 3 Jul. 1890 - **James Thornton**, 21, single, oysterman, b. & residing Mid., son of Ribon & Margaret Thornton, married **Sallie Johnson**, 17, single, b. & residing Mid., dau. of Doctor & Amanda Johnson. (C)

299A - 15 Jul. 1890 - **John Travis**, 22, single, b. & residing Gloucester, son of Carl & Judy Travis, married **Maggie Morris**, 20, single, b. & residing Mid., dau. of Carter Morris. (C)

299B - 13 Aug. 1890 - **Robert F. Sibley**, 30, single, farmer, b. & residing Mid., son of Stage D. & Ann F. Sibley, married **Ida V. Morris**, 21, single, b. & residing Mid., dau. of John W. & Rebecca Morris. (W)

299C - 14 Aug. 1890 - **Richard Gresham**, single, oysterman, b. & residing Mid., son of Gresham, married **Jessie Powell**, 21, single, b. & residing Mid., dau. of Wm. & Martha Powell. (C)

300A - Aug. 1890 - **Chas. W. Ridgel**, 24, widower, oysterman, b. St. Marys Co., Maryland, residing Mid., son of Cornelius & Mary Ridgel, married **Missouri Hull**, 22, single, b. York Co., residing Mid., dau. of [not given]. (W)

300B - Sep. 1890 - **Major Burrell**, 26, single, oysterman, b. Gloucester, residing Mid., son of Coleman & Eliza Burrell, married **Anna E. Morris**, 17, single, b. & residing Mid., dau. of Julious & Mary Morris. (C)

300C - 24 Sep. 1890 - **George Massey**, 33, single, farmer, b. King & Queen, residing Mid., son of Wm. & Mary Massey, married **Ella Hundley**, 25, widow, b. King & Queen, residing Mid., dau. of [not given]. (W)

301A - 4 Oct. 1890 - **John Whiting**, 21, single, oysterman, b. & residing Mid., son of Robert & Clay Whiting, married **Willie Smith**, 21, single, b. & residing Mid., dau. of Benjamin & Lucy Smith. (C)

301B - 7 Oct. 1890 - **George Wright**, 39, widower, b. Essex, residing Richmond,, son of Dr. Edw'd L. & Mary A. Wright, married **Loulie B. Evans**, 23, single, b. & residing Mid., dau. of Dr. J. M. & Ellen Evans. (W)

301C - 18 Sep. 1890 - **James Taliaferro**, 21, single, oysterman, b. & residing Mid., son of Martha Taliaferro, married **Sarah C. Bayton**, 20, single, b. & residing Mid., dau. of Richard & Hannah Bayton. (C)

302A - 18 Oct. 1890 - **Thomas Johnson**, 40, widower, b. & residing King & Queen, son of David & Martha Johnson, married **Winnie Banks**, 46, widow, b. King & Queen, residing Mid., dau. of Thos. & Lucy Holmes. (C)

302B - Oct. 1890 - **Geo. H. Powell**, 35, widower, oysterman, b. & residing Mid., son of Wm. & Martha Powell, married **Sue Burrell**, 18, single, b. & residing Mid., dau. of Henry & Netta Burrell. (C)

302C - 4 Jun. 1890 - **Chas. W. Mercer**, 36, single, residing Mid., son of John L. & Louisa Mercer, married **Mary E. Garland**, 17, single, b. & residing Mid., dau. of Ro. C. & Amanda Garland. (W)

Index of Grooms

Name	Ref	Name	Ref
Adams, John	154B	Blake, Johnston G.	189A
Adams, John H.	281B	Blake, Norman R.	92C
Adams, John W.	42C	Blake, Peter	163C
Adkins, Joseph	234C	Blake, R. G.	270A
Ailworth, James	112C	Blake, Ro. M.	63B
Ailworth, Muscoe R.	73C	Blake, Ro. W.	101B
Amy, Samuel	91B	Blake, Sam'l R.	74B
Anderson, Caesar	74A	Bohannon, Jas. H.	84C
Anderson, Christopher	276A	Bohannon, John W.	135C
Anderson, Frank	247C	Booker, Jas. W.	279A
Apsley, Wm. R.	52A	Booker, Muscoe R.	269A
Armstead, Albert	295A	Boss, Ro.	247B
Armstrong, John T.	169C	Boyd, Samuel	143C
Armstrong, Wm. H.	41C	Boyd, Thomas	231A
Armstrong, Wm.	173A	Boyd, Elijah Goodman	225C
Atkins, Jas. H.	74C	Boyd, Ellick	271A
		Boyd, Henry	261A
Bagby, Lindsay	159C	Braxton, Carter	165C
Bagby, Richard	116C	Braxton, Charles	239C
Baker, Richard P.	140A	Braxton, Isaac	120A
Banks, Chas. Henry	280B	Braxton, Jas. A.	210B
Banks, Elijah	64A	Braxton, Joshua	173C
Banks, Elijah	104B	Braxton, Milton	219C
Banks, Jas. Ed.	160A	Braxton, Robert	241C
Banks, Rolly	110C	Braxton, Wm.	51B
Banks, Wm. H.	201C	Bray, Thos. Edwy	237C
Barrick, Wm. E.	147C	Bright, Daniel	96C
Barrick, Wm. Ed.	41B	Brim, John	209B
Bates, Lucius	293B	Bristow, Andrew F.	176B
Baylor, David	165B	Bristow, Edward W.	206A
Bayton, William	212A	Bristow, John P.	23A
Baytop, Edmund	153C	Bristow, Joseph W.	182C
Beale, George E.	194B	Bristow, Lewis S.	46C
Beale, James A.	246A	Bristow, Richard	294A
Becket, George	297B	Bristow Richard Fuller	88C
Beedles, Adolphus	163B	Bristow, Zack C.	270B
Belle, Beverly	161B	Broach, Jas. Walter	130A
Bennett, John J.	126C	Brockenbrough, Andrew	196C
Beverly, Richard	138C	Brockenbrough, Oliver	146A
Beverly, Toney	274A	Brockenbrough, Richard	81C
Billups, Richard	67C	Broocke, Wm. C.	103A
Bird, Geo. Wash.	166B	Brooks, Joseph Henry	41A
Bird, Augustin	266B	Brown, Andrew J.	154C
Bird, Richard	177B	Brown, Andrew S.	236B
Blackburn, George L.	189C	Brown, Christopher	243B
Blake, George S.	277A	Browne, John Rich'd	85B
Blake, Jeter W.	257B	Browne, Magruder	259A
Blake, John A.	259C	Browne, William	283A
Blake, John Hurbert	113C	Brownley, Wm. V.	64C

73

Index of Grooms

Buckner, Wm. Philip	211C	Carter, Lewis	283C
Budds, Wm. H.	71A	Carter, Robert	191B
Bundy, Henry	20C	Carter, Wm. B.	290A
Bundy, James	152B	Cauthorn, Geo. W.	229A
Bundy, Robert	94A	Chamberlayne,	
Burk, Christopher	125C	Riter Carr	99B
Burk, Moses	26C	Chandler, Thornton	292C
Burke, Edwin	218C	Chowning, Geo. S.	196B
Burke, Lewis	110B	Christopher, James	89B
Burke, Thos. H.	295C	Christopher, John H.	100A
Burke, Wm., Sr.	114A	Christopher, Sam'l	59B
Burnett, Joshua	43C	Clair, Joseph A.	58A
Burrell, Jno. Amos	102B	Clarke, Henry	122C
Burrell, John S.	278A	Clarkston, Beverly C.	190C
Burrell, Lewis	248C	Clayton, Robert	190A
Burrell, Major	300B	Clements, R. H.	285A
Burrell, Ralph	34A	Cole, Isaac A.	149A
Burrell, Richard	21C	Coleman, Little	239B
Burrell, Richard	88B	Conley, Charles	133C
Burrell, Robert	43A	Conway, Carter	284B
Burrell, Sims	156A	Conway, Squire	181B
Burrell, Thomas	224A	Cook, Ellick	154A
Burrell, Thomas H.	240C	Cook, Harry C.	99C
Burrell, William	70A	Cook, R. W.	262A
Burton, Fayette	137B	Cook, Thos. H.	134C
Burton, Richard H.	199B	Cooke, Harry C.	159B
		Cooke, William	54A
Callis, Geo. W.	253A	Cooper, John F.	243A
Callis, Thos. C.	200A	Copper, Geo. F.	243C
Callis, Geo. W.	253A	Corbin, Thomas H.	155A
Campbell, John Henry	90B	Corbin, Wm.	128A
Campbell, James	49A	Corbin, Henry	124A
Campbell, Robert	290C	Corbin, William	82A
Carey, Henry	60A	Corr, Ed. W.	98B
Carey, Peter	180A	Creighton, Austie	245A
Carlow, Charles H.	159A	Crittenden, Andrew	185B
Carr, John A.	39C	Crittenden, Lorenzo	215A
Carr, Moses	224B	Cropper, John W.	187A
Carr, Robert	147B	Cundiff, Griffin	123A
Carr, Thomas	217C	Curtis, Alexander	88A
Carter, Andrew W.	272A	Curtis, Ellis T.	108A
Carter, Benjamin	237A	Curtis, James Henry	227A
Carter, Charles	30B	Curtis, Jeff.	274C
Carter, David	247A		
Carter, Frank M.	288C	Dangerfield, Wyatt	37C
Carter, George	57C	Daniel, George W.	178B
Carter, Harry	289B	Daniel, Herbert	236A
Carter, James C.	263B	Daniel, Jas. Wm.	233A
Carter, John R.	150B	Daniel, Robert	194A

Index of Grooms

Daniel, Wm. F.	182A	Ferguson, Jas. Henry	145A
Daniel, Wm. H.	115C	Ferguson, Samuel	107B
Davis, Bartlett	58B	Ferneyhough, John R.	271C
Davis, Charles	113A	Field, Eugene C.	206B
Davis, Frank Ben	258A	Fields, Augustus	271B
Davis, George	187C	Fields, John	121C
Davis, George S.	268A	Fields, Solomon	36C
Davis, Isaac	254B	Fields, Stephen	291C
Davis, James	220A	Finch, George R.	35C
Davis, James R.	100C	Fitchett, James	138A
Davis, John A.	71B	Fitchett, James A.	279B
Davis, John Wm.	87C	Fitchett, Washington	77C
Davis, Leonard W.	183C	Fitchett, Wm. H.	110A
Davis, Samuel	150A	Fitzhugh, Philip H.	268C
Davis, Scipio	133B	Forest, Walter	67A
Davis, Walter	119B	Foster, Lewis	168B
Davis, Wellington	260B	Foster, William	62C
Dawson, John	208A	Fountain, Major E.	280C
Deleaver, Thomas, Jr.	251C	Franke, Paul D.	198B
Deleaver, William	248A	Franklin, John Benj.	103B
Delever, Wm.	202B	Franklin, R. W.	30A
Dickenson, James	193C	Franz, Jacob Peter	22C
Dickerson, James	238B	Frazier, Charles H.	42A
Didlake, James H.	203C	Frazier, Thomas	188B
Diggs, Geo. Aug.	53B	Frazier, Virginius	168A
Dillard, John	213B	Freeman, John Wesly	35A
Dobson, Benjamin F.	118A	French, Pope H.	204C
Douglas, Ro. G.	190B	French, Wm. Jas.	91A
Dudley, James	148A	Furgusson, John	294C
Dudley, Joseph	122A		
Dungey, Thomas E.	204B	Gale, Wm. Franklin	225A
Dunlevy, Chas. B.	269B	Gardner, Braxton	266A
Dunlevy, Westley	203A	Garrett, Lewis S.	22A
Dunlevy, William, Jr.	135B	Gatewood, Isaih	178A
Dunn, Lewis	121A	Gatewood, Wm.	108C
Durham, James M.	201B	Genmill, James	121B
Duster, Charles	176C	George, Edwin Thomas	249C
		George, John M.	162A
Elliott, Wm.	286B	Goldenberg, Gabriel	149C
Ellis, Benjamin	221A	Goldman, Elijah	219B
Evans, Charles R.	211B	Goldman, Early	267C
Evans, Lambeth	28A	Goulding, Thos. R.	130C
Evans, R. B.	283B	Gowin, Joshua	241A
Evans, Ro. Henry	49B	Graves, Matthew E.	21A
Evans, Wm. R.	59C	Green, Manuel	97A
		Green, Wm. H.	25C
Faucett, Wm. A.	253C	Greenlaw,	
Fauntleroy, Charles	231C	Gouverneur Thos.	151C
Fauntleroy, Richard	93C	Gregg, Joshua N.	109B

Index of Grooms

Grenels, Major Parker	82C	
Gresham, Richard	299C	
Gresham, Warner	50B	
Gressitt, John D., Jr.	102C	
Grey, James C.	47A	
Griffin, Benjamin	115A	
Griffin, Geo. H.	262B	
Griffin, Green	275C	
Griffin, Lewis	86B	
Griffin, Rich. H.	105A	
Griffin, Taylor	296C	
Grigg, Homer	170A	
Grimes, George W.	27A	
Grinels, Southey S.	207C	
Guthrey, Peter	66A	
Gwynn, James M.	141A	
Gwynn, Ro.	118B	
Gwynn, Thos.	56C	
Gwyns, Thos. H.	28C	
Hale, John F.	266C	
Hale, Robert J.	263A	
Hall, Addison	222C	
Hall, Fer. H.	25B	
Hall, Peter B.	38A	
Hall, Wm.	153B	
Hamilton, Charles	132C	
Hand, Sylvanna	220C	
Handy, Henry	232C	
Hansen, Christian H.	231B	
Hanson, Andrew N.	251B	
Harris, Erastus	99A	
Harris, Henry	128C	
Harris, Jack T	56A	
Harris, Jacob	150A	
Harris, James E.	286A	
Harris, Jos.	90C	
Harris, Joseph	77A	
Harris, Joseph Thos.	144A	
Harris, Julius	257C	
Harris, Marcus	45B	
Harris, Moses	75C	
Harris, Thomas	114C	
Harris, Thomas Henry	142C	
Harrow, Alonzo	84A	
Harrow, J. B.	183B	
Harrow, R. C.	195C	
Harrow, Thomas H.	222C	
Hart, Jas. T.	277B	
Hart, William H.	297C	
Harte, Charles	112B	
Harwood, Joseph W.	192A	
Haynes, Frank	100B	
Healy, Julius	235A	
Healy, Wm. H.	29A	
Healy, Wm. H.	143A	
Heath, Geo. H.	171B	
Henry, George	142A	
Henry, Nathan	278B	
Henry, Philmore	52B	
Hill, Henry	29C	
Hill, Walter, P.	126B	
Holliday, Oscar	155B	
Holliday, Ro. H.	175B	
Holliway, Jas. P.	58C	
Holmes, Fred	174C	
Holmes, Geo. Wash.	295B	
Holmes, John B.	265A	
Holmes, Major	213A	
Holmes, Thos. H.	57B	
Holmes, Wm. H.	265C	
Holoway, Wm. S.	25A	
Hooks, John F.	196A	
Horsley, James H	91C	
Hudson, Francis B.	169B	
Hundley, John Ro.	93A	
Hundley, Wm. W.	33C	
Hundley, Wm. W.	244C	
Hurley, J. Walter	188A	
Hurley, Thomas C.	207A	
Hurst, John W.	111C	
Ingram, Edward	232A	
Ingram, James	62A	
Ingram, Ro. E.	241B	
Ison, Columbus S.	116B	
Jackson, Ellis	39A	
Jackson, George	286C	
Jackson, Hernius	156B	
Jackson, James	37B	
Jackson, James H.	112A	
Jackson, John	273A	
Jackson, John A.	147A	
Jackson, John H.	70C	
Jackson, John H.	185A	
Jackson, John L.	61A	

Index of Grooms

Jackson, John Wm.	152A	Kemp, Jas. H.	120C
Jackson, Moat A.	129B	Kennard, Lewin N.	277C
Jackson, Sam'l R.	156C	Key, Carter A.	22B
Jackson, Scipio	184A	Key, James	192C
Jackson, Wm. Andrew	62B	Keyser, Carlos Z.	229C
Jacobson, Martin	37A	Kidd, William	143B
Jarvis, Richard F.	276B	Kies,	
Jeffries, Wm. G.	189B	Wm. T. Sherman	252B
Johnson, Benjamin	104A	King, Charles	214C
Johnson, Coleman	108B	King, Moses	236C
Johnson, Daniel	288A	King, Moses	239A
Johnson,		King, Wm.	235B
Edward Taylor	171A	Knapp, Frank C.	293C
Johnson, George	31C		
Johnson, James	27B	Landing, Benjamin	155C
Johnson, John	161A	Lanning, Wm. H.	97B
Johnson, Milton	274B	Larkin, John W.	144C
Johnson, Moses	69C	Laws, James G.	279C
Johnson, Richard	288B	Layton, Charles P.	29B
Johnson, Robert	200C	Lecount, Sam'l	40C
Johnson, Spencer	278C	Lee, Lewis	69A
Johnson, Thomas	302A	Lee, Washington	53A
Johnson, Walter	227B	Lee, Zack	172A
Johnson, Washington	146B	Lewis, Alonzo	24C
Johnson, Wm. C.	221C	Lewis, Caleb	216C
Johnson,		Lewis, Henry	191A
Wm. Washington	237B	Lewis, Joshua	138B
Jones, Benjamin	262C	Lewis, Moses	239A
Jones, Charles	139C	Lewis, Samuel J.	212C
Jones, Cornelius	167A	Lewis, Strann	245C
Jones, Ed. Thos.	255B	Lewis, Thos. Jeff.	264A
Jones, Edward	181A	Lewis, Wm. S.	134C
Jones, Erastus	208B	Lewis, Wm. S.	224C
Jones, Jas. Ro.	198A	Lightfoot, John Wm.	141B
Jones, John	140B	Linson, Robert	282A
Jones, John	144B	Liveley, Charles	52C
Jones, John, Jr.	152C	Lockley, Armstead	216A
Jones, Philip	195B	Lockley, John	82B
Jones, Sam'l	298A	Lockley, Nelson	131A
Jones, Wm. Ellis	197C	Lomax, Charles Henry	31A
Jones, Wm. Wallace	292B	Lomax, Chas. Henry	85C
Jordon, Marius	164C	Lomax, Samuel	50A
Josias, Joseph	135A	Lomax, Wm. Henry	80A
		London, Philip	234A
Keinningham, W. W.	63C	London, Philip	235C
Keinningham,		Lorimer, Dandridge	228A
Willie B.	210C	Louden, Beverly	45A
Keiser, Joseph	125B	Lumpkin, John R.	169A
Kellum, Thos. J.	199C	Lush, John T.	157C

Index of Grooms

Macklane, Walter	87A	Morgan, John W.	65C
Madison, John	106A	Morris, Adolphus	131C
Madison, Joseh	111A	Morris, Cornelius	34B
Mahone, Wm.	97C	Morris, Cornelius	201A
Major Allen	96B	Morris, Cornelius	201A
Major, R. W.	185C	Morris, John H.	48A
Major, R. J.	250C	Morris, John R.	105C
Major, Walter M., Jr.	254C	Morris, John Wm.	162B
Marchant, James S.	79C	Morris, Richard	73A
Marchant, James S.	204A	Morris, Richard	215C
Marchant, John W.	117A	Morris, Samuel	217A
Marston, Casper T.	209C	Morris, Vanburen	28B
Mason, Ed. T.	68B	Morris, Walter T.	242A
Mason, Samuel	87B	Morris, William	250A
Mason, Wm.	157B	Morton, John	227C
Mason, William W.	179B	Moss, Chas. W.	149B
Massey, George	300C	Motley, Moses	214A
Maxwell, M. P.	281A	Munroe, James	264C
Mayo, Marion T.	106C		
McEntire, Edward	261B	Nelson, Cyrus	23B
McKan, Phillip F.	57A	Nelson, Jas. Henry	127B
Meggs, George	246C	Nelson, Lewis	55B
Meggs, Ro. Franklin	289C	Nelson, Thomas	217B
Mercer, Ro. H.	61C	New, Wm. G.	26B
Mercer, Chas. W.	302C	Nickolson,	
Mickelborough, Jerome	30C	Richard, Sr.	161C
Milby, Charles D.	244B	Nonan, Vanness	20A
Milby, George W.	34C	Norris, Jessee	93B
Miller, G. T. B.	131B	Norris, Obediah	20B
Miller, John C.	71C	Norris, Samuel	24B
Miller, Wm. Francis	249A	Norton, John	226A
Minor, George	32A	Norton, W. H.	221B
Minor, Frank	48B		
Minor, Henry	51A	Page, Richard	109A
Mitchell, Jeter G.	216B	Page, Richard	272B
Mitchell, Thomas B.	244A	Page, Stepnie	166C
Mitchel, Thomas	233C	Palmer, Otis J.	252A
Mitchell, Wm. O.	124B	Palmer, Richard Jeter	214B
Montague, Alfred	47C	Palmer, Thomas H.	182B
Montague, Clarance S.	89A	Palmer, Walter C.	256A
Montague, John J.	44B	Parker, Albert	137C
Montague, Richard	126A	Parks, Geo. A.	164A
Montague, Ro. H.	94B	Parks, Jas. T.	151B
Montague, Wm.	230A	Parks, John R.	72A
Montgomery,		Parks, W. H.	31B
Jackson T.	160C	Parrow, R. H.	209A
Montgomery, John L.	38C	Payne, James S.	172C
Montgomery, Thos.	183A	Payne, Wm. E.	255A
Moody, Carter	78B	Payne, Wm. H.	81B

Index of Grooms

Payton, Alphus	233B		Richardson, Rich'd G.	218A
Peade, James	61B		Richardson, Wm.	251A
Pendleton, Moses	168C		Richeson, Jas. H.	40B
Percifull, Edward Cary	73B		Ridgell, C. Weslie	203B
Perkins, Lewis H.	72B		Ridgel, Chas. W.	300A
Perrill, General	48C		Rilee, Sam'l R.	293A
Perrin, Alexander	148B		Roane, Alexander	117B
Perrin, Alexander	175A		Roane, Floyd L.	176A
Perry, Albert	134B		Roane, Geo. H.	186A
Peterson, Allen	215B		Roane, John Henry	170B
Peterson, Allen	215B		Roane, Joshua	205A
Peterson, Anthony	104C		Roane, Wm. H.	296B
Peterson, Jacob	179A		Robinson, Benjamin	264B
Peterson, Jefferson	158B		Robinson, Corbin	172B
Pitt, Walter J.	234B		Robinson, Frederick	292A
Pollard, Jas. H.	76C		Robinson, Geo. Thos.	269C
Pollard, John	21B		Robinson, Gowing	287C
Powell, A. C.	297A		Robinson, Harry	90A
Powell, Geo. H.	302B		Robinson, Harry	254A
Powell, Lewis N.	165A		Robinson, Jas. H.	83B
Powers, Wm.	64B		Robinson, John C.	94C
Pratt, Joseph	175C		Robinson, John H.	193B
Price, Joseph E.	33A		Robinson, Menser	160B
Prior, John	70B		Robinson, Moses	123B
Purkins, Pharoah	69B		Robinson, Rich'd	240B
Purkins, Wellington	55A		Robinson, Robin	35B
			Robinson, Thos.	205B
R. M. Glenn	188C		Robinson, Thos.	229B
Randsom, Geo.	54C		Ross, Henry	78C
Ransome, Jas. Ed.	202C		Roy, Chas. H.	207B
Ransome, Pearley	142B		Roy, Fleming	242B
Ransome, Ro. F.	75A		Roy, George	242C
Rawley, James	44A		Roy, Iveson	220B
Redd, Jas. E.	157A		Roy, Wm.	226B
Redd, Thomas W.	197A		Ruark, Alfred W.	19C
Reed, Allen	128B		Ruark, Millard F.	133A
Reed, Frank	27C		Ruffin, Harvey	250B
Reed, Isaac	33B		Ruffin, James	36B
Reed, John	139B		Ruffin, Peter	223B
Reed, Willie	95C		Ruffin, Wm.	253B
Revere, Geo. W.	117C		Rust, Walter	125A
Revere, James T.	47B			
Revere, John A.	181C		Sable, Andrew	80B
Revere, Peter	206C		Sable, A. J.	282C
Revere, Ro. V.	199A		Sable, James	75B
Revere, Wm. Henry	129A		Sable, Simon D.	68A
Richardson,			Sadler, Francis B.	177C
Berkley S.	252C		Sadler, Geo. Ed.	257A
Richards, Ed. B.	281C		Sadler, Jas. A.	60C

Index of Grooms

Sadler, John R.	158C	Stormont, David	211A
Sadler, Philip H.	44C	Street, Jas. M.	45C
Saunders, Otho A.	46B	Street, Zachary	81A
Saunders, Thomas A.	23C		
Scarborough, Daniel	101C	Tabb, John W.	39B
Scarbrough, Sheppard	86A	Tabor, Jno. W. A.	272C
Schools, Albert	124C	Taliaferro,	
Schools, Eugene G.	139A	Beverly C.	192B
Scott, Ro. L.	66C	Taliaferro,	
Segar, John R., Sr.	174B	Beverly C.	190C
Segar, Rich'd Bev.	193A	Taliaferro, James	301C
Segar, Thomas	180B	Taliaferro, John H.	46A
Selby, J. F.	226C	Taliaferro, Wm. Henry	184C
Seward, Marcus A.	51C	Taylor, Chas. Ellis	213C
Shackleford, Warner H.	40A	Taylor, Geo. B.	267A
Shackelford, Wm. E.	178C	Taylor, Geo. E.	167C
Shrieves, George H.	225B	Taylor, John	179C
Sibley, Benja. C.	92B	Taylor, Wm. J.	167B
Sibley, Daniel	137A	Taylor, Wm. R.	65B
Sibley, Edward H.	222B	Thomas, Geo. D.	261C
Sibley, Geo. E.	129C	Thomas, Hardy	127C
Sibley, Geo. E.	282B	Thomas, Robert	265B
Sibley, James C.	118C	Thomas, Wm. E.	113B
Sibley, Rich'd H.	42B	Thornton, Anthony	186C
Sibley, Robert F.	299B	Thornton, James	298C
Sibly, Richard H.	43B	Thornton, Ribon	260A
Simmons, Samuel M.	210A	Thornton,	
Slaughter, Joseph P.	136C	Robert Henry	270C
Slaughter, Robert B.	111B	Thornton, Smith	246B
Smith, Abram	275B	Thornton, Sterling	212B
Smith, Baylor	83C	Thornton, Virginius	289A
Smith, Beverly	258B	Thornton, Wm.	95B
Smith, Charles	164B	Thornton, William	187B
Smith, George	256B	Thrift, Richard Ed.	130B
Smith, Henly W.	79B	Thurston, Emmitt	296A
Smith, J. Frank	255C	Thurston, George, Sr.	280A
Smith, John B.	24A	Thurston, Griffin E.	49C
Smith, John R.	119C	Thurston, Lewis	119A
Smith, Joseph	287A	Thurston, Nelson	67B
Smith, Peter	78A	Tinsley, Mark W.	249B
Smith, Major Walter	177A	Topping,	
Smither, A. F.	285B	Emmit Franklin	79A
Smither, Charles W.	219A	Topping, John W.	84B
Snead, Oswald	85A	Townley, Isaih	38B
Snead, Rich. T.	163A	Townsend, Joseph A.	132B
South, John	32C	Townsend, Joshua	54B
Southerlin, R. W.	151A	Trader, Richard	170C
Stiff, Andrew W.	66B	Trader, Richard H.	65A
Stokes, Henry	109C	Travilian, Roscoe C.	238C

Index of Grooms

Travis, John	299A	West, John M.	115B
Travis, Josiah	162C	White, Herbert	56B
Treackle, Wm. H.	173B	White, James Preston	102A
Turner, Beauregard	145C	White, Jefferson D.	186B
		White, Preston B.	153A
Vandergrift, James F.	103C	Whiting, Eli	141C
Verlander, Jas. B.	107A	Whiting, John	301A
		Wiatt, Christopher	238A
Waites, Elias	26A	Williams, Armstead	136B
Wake, Addison	86C	Williams, Caesar	285C
Wake, Isaiah	205C	Williams, Carter	191C
Walden, Henry	180C	Williams, Elijah	123C
Walden, James E.	120B	Williams, Frederick	101A
Walden, John H.	232B	Williams, Jas. Payne	148C
Walker, Charles, Jr.	267B	Williams, John	132A
Walker, Charles H.	284A	Williams, John T.	107C
Walker, Ed. C.	105B	Williams, Paul	298B
Walker, Fuller	80C	Williams, Thos.	166A
Walker, George F.	195A	Williams, Thomas	275A
Walker, Holland M.	256C	Wilson, Alexander	98A
Walker, William E.	268B	Wilson, Austin	122B
Walker, Wm.	89C	Wilson, John A.	276C
Wallace, Jos. C.	194C	Wilson, David W.	95A
Waller, Burley	218B	Wilson, Lewis	200B
Waller, James T.	291A	Wood, Chas. B.	114B
Waller, Robert	197B	Wood, Charles H.	230B
Waller, Thos. Henry	96A	Wood, Geo.	68C
Walter, Henry C.	245B	Wood, Geo. Taylor	36A
Walton, Columbus	116A	Wood, Geo. Taylor	171C
Waples, John S.	127A	Wood, John W.	59A
Ward, Cin. C.	174A	Wood, Joseph T.	136A
Ward, Cincinatus C.	259B	Wood, Nicholas	60B
Ward, Reubin	284C	Wood, Pollard	184B
Ward, Wm. F.	140C	Wood, Ro. H.	158A
Washington, Anderson	228C	Wood, Thos. H.	260C
Washington, Curry	63A	Wood, W. W.	146C
Washington, Isaih	263C	Wormley, Beverly	32B
Washington, Jacob	290B	Wormley, Daniel	76A
Washington, John	202A	Wormley, Henry	76B
Washington, Wm.	77B	Wormley, Mack.	248B
Weathers, Hammitt	55C	Wormley, Rich'd Lewis	223C
Webb, John A.	106B	Wormley, Thos. H.	50C
Webb, Robert	83A	Wormley, Wm. H.	98C
Webb, Sam'l Henry	258C	Wormley, Wm. H.	240A
West, Andrew	223A	Worrel, Jos. Thos.	92A
West, Charles	230C	Wright, George	301B
West, Edwin	72C		
West, Janiel	294B	Young, Ephraim	53C

Index of Brides

Abbott, Eliza C.	243A		Blake, Mary Jane	187A
Ackiss, Nancy Ann	64A		Blake, Mary A.	21A
Ailworth, Anna	95A		Blake, Mary L.	121B
Ailworth, Bertha	156C		Blake, Miria C.	163A
Ailworth, Emma V.	88C		Blake, Sarah	159A
Ailworth, Fannie B.	189A		Bohannon, Ada	183C
Ailworth, Lydia	206A		Booth, Elnora	224B
Ailworth, Olivia	221B		Boss, Emma	119A
Ailworth, Sallie	61A		Boyd, Betty	117B
Amy, Amanda	195B		Boyd, Eliza Ann	42A
Anderson, Rebecca	261A		Boyd, Hester	260A
Anderton, Nanie B.	178C		Boyton, Elmetina	86A
Armstrong, Lucy E.	54B		Bratton, Rosetta	157C
Armstrong, Mary C.	29A		Braxton, Emma	27B
Ates, Kittura	205B		Braxton, Louisa	216A
Aytes, Adelade	258B		Braxton, Polly	32C
			Braxton, Sally Ann	122B
Bagby, Laura A.	281C		Braxton, Sarah Ann	227A
Baker, Crissella	276A		Bree, Carrie	193C
Baker, Elizabeth	77C		Bridges, Louisa	151B
Baker, Sena	227B		Bristow, Adeline	91C
Banks, Aurenia	246A		Bristow, Correna D.	279B
Banks, Eliz.	171A		Bristow, Estelle	268B
Banks, Mary Ellen	53A		Bristow, Lelia	182C
Banks, Mary Ann	212C		Bristow, Louisa F.	191C
Banks, Mary Ann	279C		Bristow, Mary A.	126C
Banks, Winnie	302A		Bristow, Mary C.	89A
Banner, Marie	224C		Bristow, Mary E.	285A
Barns, Louisa	44A		Bristow, Mattie E.	132B
Barrick, Louisa M.	256C		Bristow, Rosa M.	244A
Bates, Victoria	218C		Bristow, Victoria A.	211A
Baughan, Mary S.	233A		Brizentine, Mary A.	92A
Baughan, Matie T.	270A		Broach, Mary Alice	266C
Bayton, Hester L.	90B		Brockenbrough, Mira	102A
Bayton, Lottie	127B		Browne, Ella	155A
Bayton, Sarah C.	301C		Browne, India	135C
Beazley, Lulie O.	196B		Brown, Georgia Ella	93A
Becket, Maria	246C		Buckner, Sally	191A
Bird, Adie [or Cidie]	89B		Bulle, Mary J.	20A
Bird, Emma	283A		Bull, Ju. V.	19C
Bird, Rosa	231A		Bundey, Alice W.	187C
Blackley, Alice A.	49C		Bundy, Agness	126A
Blake, Courtney S.	40B		Bundy, Bettie	237A
Blake, Courtney	40B		Bundy, Jenny	278B
Blake, Dorothy	186B		Burk, Betty	72C
Blake, Elivira J.	31B		Burk, Mary	101A
Blake, Iva	110A		Burk, Roberta	184C
Blake, Julia A.	113B		Burrell, Amy	286B
Blake, Lelia A.	214B		Burrell, Anne	154A

Index of Brides

Burrell, Cherry	142C	
Burrell, Fannie	143C	
Burrell, Fanny	85C	
Burrell, Hester	230B	
Burrell, Julia	233B	
Burrell, Lizzie	57C	
Burrell, Mattie	224A	
Burrell, Patsy J.	120C	
Burrell, Pinkey Ann	241C	
Burrell, Sarah	69B	
Burrell, Sophia	49A	
Burrell, Sue	302B	
Calhoun, Augusta E.	297C	
Callis, Elizabeth	148A	
Callis, Etta	198B	
Callis, Mary E.	255A	
Campbell, Lee Anna	204B	
Campbell, Lucy A.	276C	
Campbell, Maria Louisa	119C	
Campbell, Martha E.	149B	
Carlow, Mary B.	85A	
Carlton, Ella	116A	
Carr, Julia	160B	
Carr, Lucy	255B	
Carr, Mary Jane	230C	
Carter, Betty	165C	
Carter, Coley	66C	
Carter, Columbia	267C	
Carter, Elizabeth	74A	
Carter, Emma	180A	
Carter, Frances	223C	
Carter, Letty	124A	
Carter, Lucy	137B	
Carter, Lucy	205C	
Carter, Martha E.	172C	
Carter, Mary	152C	
Carter, Mary	172A	
Carter, Mary F.	62C	
Carter, Mary	180B	
Carter, Mary	53C	
Carter, Mat.	158B	
Carter, Nancy	274A	
Carter, Nannie E.	265A	
Carter, Nettie	247B	
Carter, Phenton	51B	
Carter, Rosa	161A	
Carter, Sarah	59C	
Carter, Susan	187B	
Carter, Willis F.	133A	
Cary, Betsy	54C	
Cauthern, Auta J.	99B	
Cauthon, Nancy	179A	
Cavenaugh, Hattie	84A	
Chamberlain, Hettey B.	295B	
Chamberlain, Malinda	81A	
Chamberlane, Fanny	290B	
Chamberlin, Rosetta	251A	
Chandler, Lucy A.	259A	
Chowning, Hattie L.	193A	
Chowning, Mattie	35C	
Christian, Betsy A.	79B	
Christopher, Hester	65A	
Churchill, Ann	294C	
Churchill, Susan	108C	
Clare, Anna R.	203C	
Clayville, Mary A.	167B	
Clements, Lucy E.	252A	
Cloville, Linie	183A	
Coates, Susan	282C	
Conoway, Feeby	192C	
Conway, Cath.	20C	
Conway, Louisa	114B	
Conway, Nora	273A	
Cook, Alice	141B	
Cook, Cath.	60B	
Cook, Eliza	263C	
Cook, Ellen	106B	
Cook, Mary E.	43C	
Cook, Nillintina	46A	
Cook, Sallie A.	131A	
Cook, Sarah Thos.	164A	
Cook, Virginia	52C	
Cornelius, Livinia	220C	
Cornelius, Louisa V.	179B	
Corr, Adeline	77A	
Corr, Anna	115C	
Corr, Roberta	95B	
Courtney, Eliz.	168A	
Courtney, Josie	262C	
Courtney, Rosella	163B	
Cox, Virginia A.	121A	
Creswell, Mary E.	171B	
Creswell, Sarah	41C	
Crittenden, Anna	210B	
Crittenden, Carrie E.	30A	

Index of Brides

Croxton, Annie	97C	Edwards, Mary E.	63C
Croxton, Clara	251C	Edwards, Sarah	59A
Croxton, Rosella	78C	Ellis, Willie Ann	98B
Crump, Lucy	238B	Enos, Sue E.	157B
Curtis, Hattie	99A	Eubank, Eddie B.	73B
Curtis, Hester Ann	27C	Eubank, Ida B.	271C
Curtis, Louisa	221C	Evans, Ellen B.	268A
		Evans, Loulie B.	301B
Dabney, Martha	45A	Evans, Nannie Lee	174B
Dangerfield, Rose	233C	Evans, Sallie	57A
Daniel, Ella	147A	Evans, Sarah F.	169B
Daniel, Florance A.	107C		
Daniel, Isabella J.	194B	Faucett, Harriet	164C
Daniel, Jessie W.	84B	Faulkner, Ada B.	102C
Daniel, Livia	62A	Faultleroy, Winney	205A
Daniel, Lulie	130A	Fauntleroy, Mary	296C
Daniel, Mary E.	123B	Fields, Fannie	95C
Daniel, Sarah	188B	Fisher, Ella	128A
Daniel, Vir. Ella	111C	Fisher, Martha	178B
Davis, Addie	175B	Fisher, Sarah	243B
Davis, Chaney	148C	Fitchett, Anna	35B
Davis, Eliz.	229B	Fitchett, Betty Aug.	145A
Davis, Emeline	175C	Fitchett, Mary	181B
Davis, Emma T.	219A	Fleet, Cath. E.	109B
Davis, Ennie E.	272C	Fleet, Christianna	262B
Davis, Fanny	31A	Fleet, Mary Louisa	170A
Davis, Maggie	102B	Floyd, Betty	30B
Davis, Maria	248B	Floyd, Fanny	80A
Davis, Mary	216C	Folliard, Marg. Eliz.	81A
Davis, Mary E.	200A	Foster, Harriet	272B
Davis, Nanny	55C	Foster, Orintha C.	123A
Davis, Olivia	59B	Foster, Sarah	271B
Davis, Rachel	266A	Foster, Susan	32A
Davis, Rena	175A	French, Florence B.	204C
Dawson, Rose	147B		
Delever, Emma	178A	Gaines, Cora	226A
Derieux, Sue C.	209A	Gaines, Emretta	173B
Dickinson, M. L.	283B	Gaines, Martha J.	108A
Didlake, Porter	100C	Gaines, Mary	295A
Dillard, Lulie L.	146C	Gaines, Nellie B.	46C
Dodges, Saphronia	87C	Gardner, Johona	149A
Dudley, Mary	212B	Gardner, Lettie	109C
Dunaway, Martha	28C	Gardner, Roberta A.	144C
Dungey, Farley Ellen	73A	Gardner, Virginia	118A
Dunlevy, Amanda E.	64C	Garland, Mary E.	302C
Dunlevy, Josephine Q.	131B	Garnett, Mary	248C
Dunlevy, Mary	60C	Gatewood, Ellen H.	29B
Dunlevy, Nancy E.	68B	Gayle, Eliza C.	293C
Dunn, Columbia A.	100B	Gipson, Annie Laura	44C

Index of Brides

Going, Nancy	186C		Haynes, Mary A.	276B
Goin, Rexanna	111A		Healy, Lucy G.	209C
Goldman, Molly	67B		Healy, Nannie E.	145C
Good, Anne	26B		Henley, Emma	112B
Gordy, Nannie E.	33A		Henry, Ada	136B
Green, Bettie T.	259C		Henry, Ailsey	98C
Greenwood, Anna	73C		Henry, Cath.	86B
Greenwood, Mary	170C		Henry, Eliz.	63A
Greenwood, Virginia	150A		Henry, Emily	90A
Gresham, Louisa	78B		Henry, Martha	298A
Gresham, Mariah	284C		Hewett,	
Gresham, Mary E.	45C		Ella Florence	258A
Griffin, Harriet	162C		Hill, Betsey	88A
Griffin, Lucy	232C		Hill, Ella	139B
Griffin, Susan	138A		Hilliard, Lucelia C.	235A
Grinils, Betty	183B		Holliday, Ella	174C
Groom, Georgia A.	42C		Holliday, Isabella P.	30C
Gwyn, Adeline	23A		Holliway, Juna	289C
			Holmes, Charlott	70B
Hackney, Fannie M.	167C		Holmes, Mara E.	54A
Hale, Lucilla J.	97B		Holmes, Marg.	56C
Hale, M. A. V.	204A		Holmes, Martha	240B
Hale, Maria	101B		Holmes, Nancy	75C
Hall, Elizabeth	111B		Howard, Cilitan	282A
Hall, Emma J.	129A		Howe, Patsy	34A
Hall, Georgia S.	195A		Hudgins, Julia Lee	222C
Hall, Ida Sue	91A		Hudson, Sarah F.	281A
Hall, Letitia	103C		Hull, Missouri	300A
Hall, Lorelia B.	207C		Hundley, Cleopatra	61B
Hall, Mary Anna	74C		Hundley, Ella	300C
Hall, Nannie W.	130C		Hurley, Fannie	140C
Harris, Catharine	245B		Hurley, Gennia	100A
Harris, Cora	132A		Hurley, Hattie	222A
Harris, Eliz.	161B		Hurley, Rachel	24B
Harris, Lena	166A		Hurley, Sally L.	174A
Harris, Maggie	215C		Hush, Eliz. T.	252B
Harris, Margaret	173A		Husk, Eliz. T.	252B
Harris, Mary	51A			
Harris, Mary	64B		Ingram, Mary Alice	22C
Harris, Sarah Ann	82B			
Harris, Susan	185B		Jackson, Addie	128C
Harris, Virginia	230A		Jackson, Betty	101C
Harris, Virginia	221A		Jackson, Cath.	23C
Harris, Willintina	132C		Jackson, Edith P.	226C
Harrow, Irene	82C		Jackson, Emma V.	75A
Harrow, Lola M.	28A		Jackson, Fanny	52B
Hart, Emma J.	244C		Jackson, Frances	81C
Hart, Gertrude	65C		Jackson, Lessie F.	232B
Haynes, Henrietta	257B		Jackson, Lucy	211C

85

Index of Brides

Jackson,	Lucy	126B	Keiningham, Lelia		288C
Jackson,	Malvina V.	153A	Keinningham, Betty		25C
Jackson,	Mary Sue	169A	Kellum, Alice		156B
Jackson,	Mary	195C	Kellum, Eliza		58B
Jackson,	Mary	148B	Kellum, Mary Ann		38C
Jackson,	Sallie E.	188C	Kemp, Mary		113A
Jackson,	Savina	241B	Kennard, Margaret A.		163C
Jackson,	Susan	39B	Kenner, Virgin		265B
Jackson,	Tama	39C	Key, Eliza		152B
Jarvis,	Aida	298B	Key, Elmira		34B
Johnson,	Ada	141C	Key, Roberta		22B
Johnson,	Anna	41A	Kidd, Catharine		209B
Johnson,	Annah	184B	King, Josephine		43A
Johnson,	Buela	226B	King, Louisa		254B
Johnson,	Catharine	292C	King, Maria L.		239C
Johnson,	Easter	190A			
Johnson,	Hattie	168C	Lanning, Julia E.		222B
Johnson,	Ida B.	134C	Lanning, Lillie A.		122C
Johnson,	Jane	247C	Latanie, Mary Ellin		164B
Johnson,	Lizie	93B	Latine, Hester		138B
Johnson,	Lucy	246B	Laws, Coley		185A
Johnson,	Martha Ellen	253B	Laws, Fanny		33B
Johnson,	Mary	265C	Laws, Grace		274C
Johnson,	Mary	135A	Laws, Hester Ann		109A
Johnson,	Mattie Lee	293A	Laws, Julia A.		184A
Johnson,	Precilla	296B	Laws, Kitty A.		263B
Johnson,	Rebecca	267B	Laws, Levinia		219C
Johnson,	Rebecca	294A	Laws, Nancy		240A
Johnson,	Sallie	298C	Lee, Bettie		47C
Johnson,	Sally	123C	Lee, Caroline		296A
Johnston,	Esta	66A	Lee, Emeline		32B
Jones,	Alice	213B	Lee, Emeline		181A
Jones,	Bell	228A	Lee, Lucy		69A
Jones,	Belle	83B	Lee, Lulie W.		285B
Jones,	Cath.	279A	Lee, Trible		210C
Jones,	Elmira	26A	Lemon, Mary Cath.		202C
Jones,	Emma G.	249A	Lewis, Copie		258C
Jones,	Fanny	275C	Lewis, Elizabeth		24C
Jones,	Laura	288B	Lewis, Fannie C.		282B
Jones,	Louisa	105A	Lewis, Fanny		155B
Jones,	Mahaley	65B	Lewis, Maggie		227C
Jones,	Maria	200C	Lewis, Rosetta		81B
Jones,	Mariah	196A	Lewis, Tela Ann		137C
Jones,	Mary Ellen	260B	Lincoln, Emma L.		286A
Jones,	Mary E.	267A	Linkius, Sarah		29C
Jones,	Sarah	50B	Lipscomb, Willie A.		229C
Jones,	Susan	91B	Lockley, Alice V.		201C
			Lockley, Alice		235B
Kain,	Lucy G.	197A	Lockley, Fannie		114C

Index of Brides

Lockley, Geo. Anna	197B		Montague, Sallie E.	151C
Lockley, Jane	89C		Moody, Lizzie	161C
Lomax, Charlotte	213A		Moore, C. E.	261B
Lomax, Julia	177B		Morris, Acy	165B
Lyle, Mary F.	259B		Morris, Anna E.	300B
			Morris, Cath.	49B
Magedman, Lena	149C		Morris, Cath.	202B
Major, Beaula A.	225A		Morris, Ellen	257C
Major, Edda J.	61C		Morris, Hester Ann	158A
Major, Ellen M.	160C		Morris, Ida V.	299B
Major, Indianna	116B		Morris, Janetta	131C
Mann, Alice V.	234B		Morris, Laura	134A
Marchant, Annie M.	199C		Morris, Lucy	144A
Marchant, Hattie A.	263A		Morris, Maggie	299A
Marston, Roberta L.	256A		Morris, Malvina	28B
Martin, Emma A.	129B		Morris, Martha A.	118C
Martin, Ida	58A		Morris, Mary	193B
Mason, Corada	203A		Morris, Mary E.	159B
Mason, Maria S.	33C		Morris, Mary J.	179C
Mason, Rachel E.	136C		Morris, Nancy	143B
Mason, Sara M.	206C		Morris, Rosa	248A
Mason, Susan M.	177C		Morris, Sarah Ellen	35A
Massey, Mary S.	42B		Mosby, Fannie	70A
Massey, Mary S.	43B		Mosley, Alice	289A
Mathews, Lois	254A		Motley, Martha	48B
Mathews, Queen Vic.	269C		Motley, Rosa	37C
Matthews, Mary	176C		Muse, Blanche	185C
Maxwell, Willie L.	186A		Muse, Charlotte M.	105B
McCauley, Maria	23B		Muse, Margaret	266B
Mears, Grace L. C.	71A		Muse, Martha A.	250C
Mears, Saphronia A.	71B		Muse, Roberta	274B
Mears, Sarah A.	269B			
Mercer, Belle	254C		Nelson, Agnes	293B
Mercer, Ella N.	176B		Nelson, Mary	270C
Mercer, Macy	135B		Nest, Judy	133C
Mickelborough			Newbill, Josephine	115B
Bettie T.	87A		Nicolson, Polly Ann	166C
Mickleborough,			Norris, Viola	207A
Effie M.	141A		Norris, Vivian E.	225B
Miller, Fannie	106C		Northam, Bettie C.	41B
Miller, Sarah	167A		Northam, Fannie G.	252C
Miller, Susan	104C		Northam, Sarah B.	147C
Minnafield,			Norton, Louisa	124C
Willintina	217C			
Mitchell, Barbara A.	112A		Owen, Anna B.	289B
Mitchil, Caroline	166B		Owens, Lilly M.	277B
Monroe, Ellen	280B		Owens, Nellie	180C
Montague, Lucie E. B.	165A			
Montague, Rebecca	117A		Parker, Louise	297A

87

Index of Brides

Parks, Elvira I.	251B	Revere, Sarah V.	117C
Parrish, E. Florance	47A	Richeson, Mary	93C
Parrish, Vio. D.	84C	Roane, Grace	39A
Paul, Cathrine	68A	Roane, Mary A.	238A
Payne, Ada B.	231B	Roane, Mattie L.	271A
Payton, Blanche	146B	Robinson, Betty	214C
Payton, Eliza	151A	Robinson, Catharine	94A
Payton, Mira	58C	Robinson, Eliz.	177A
Payton, Sarah	142A	Robinson, Eliza	110B
Peade, Cleo.	245A	Robinson, Elizabeth	136A
Perry, Ginia	75B	Robinson, Fanny	125B
Perry, Vandelia	80B	Robinson, Louisa	97A
Peterson, Bettie	108B	Robinson, Louisa	128B
Peterson, Martha	36A	Robinson, Maggie	190C
Pittman, Sally	182A	Robinson, Margaret	137A
Pittman, Virginia F.	182B	Robinson, Marg't	275A
Pitt, Maryanna D.	25B	Robinson, Martha A.	262A
Pitts, Laura	216B	Robinson, Mary	150B
Pollard, Eugenia A.	189B	Robinson, Matty	72B
Pollard, Matilda	294B	Robinson, Mira	215A
Powell, Etta	277C	Robinson, Mry	202A
Powell, Jessie	299C	Robinson, Nancy	78A
Powell, Maria	48C	Robinson, Patsey	106A
Pratt, Jane	67C	Robinson, Percilla	121C
Prince, Ruth W.	85B	Robinson, Sally	280C
Prince, Susan Ann	242A	Robinson, Susan	122A
Prince, Susan A.	243C	Ross, Annice Stalia	96A
Purcell, Jennnie	94C	Ross, Mary	152A
Purcell, Mollie F.	79A	Rouzie, Lela A.	46B
Purkins, Eugenia A.	21B	Roy, Emily	191B
Purkins, Margaret	68C	Roy, Molley	36C
Purkins, Mary T.	268C	Royster, Sarah Eliza	103B
Purkins, Sallie J.	192A	Roy, Susan	297B
		Ruark, Maggie L.	210A
Rains, Adelade	249C	Ruffin, Lucy	218B
Rains, Liz. E.	162A	Ruffin, Matilda	217A
Reed, Alice	150C	Ruffin, Net.	104A
Reed, Alice	286C	Ruffin, Sarah	56A
Reed, Amanda	250A	Ruffin, Violet	83C
Reed, Anna	284B		
Reed, Fannie B.	250B	Saunders, Ada M.	107A
Reed, Mary	36B	Schools, Emma	158C
Reed, Mattie K.	287C	Schools, F. H.	94B
Reed, Rebecca	88B	Schools, Lucy B.	277A
Reeds, Agnes	291A	Schools, Luella	154B
Reed, Sarah	120A	Scott, Lucy	288A
Revere, Anndelusia	142A	Scott, Mildred Ann	228C
Revere, Fannie E.	47B	Scott, Susan	292A
Revere, Sarah E.	72A	Segar, Mary M.	236B

Index of Brides

Shackelford, Emma E.	176A		Street, Mary J.	253C
Shackleford, Lelia W.	206B		Street, Virginia	229A
Shrieves, Luly	232A		Stringer, Alice E.	236A
Shuman, Hattie A.	189C		Stringer, Mary C.	40A
Sibley, Cath. E.	129C		Strother, Eddie	168B
Sibley, Emma A.	238C		Stunt, Annie	203B
Sibley, Georgia	56B		Sutherlin, Mary	123B
Sibley, Mary	162B		Sutherlin, Rebecca	77B
Slaughter, Betty	213C		Swanson, Mary A.	237B
Slaughter, Elizabeth	34C			
Slaughter, Geo. Anna	63B		Tabb, Martha	27A
Slaughter, Hattie	71C		Taliaferro, Lavenia	115A
Slaughter, Maggie F.	52A		Taliaferro, Louisa	60A
Slaughter, Mary S.	24A		Taliaferro, Lucy	55A
Sleet, Mattie L.	190B		Taliaferro, Martha E.	217B
Smallwood, Martha	225C		Taliaferro, Nancy	223B
Smith, Alice	241A		Taliaferro, Rebecca	98A
Smith, Barbary A.	146A		Taliaferro, Rosa	105C
Smith, Charity A.	264B		Taliaferro, Susan	119B
Smith, Eliz.	223A		Taper, Dorothy	155C
Smither, Lucy A.	130B		Taylor, Irena J.	257A
Smither, Martha C.	199B		Taylor, Kate E.	269A
Smither, Mary A.	22A		Taylor, Lucy Ellen	173C
Smither, Sarah E.	237C		Taylor, Maggie A.	272A
Smith, Kitty	172B		Taylor, Mary L.	270B
Smith, Lucy Jane	76B		Taylor, Nellie G.	290A
Smith, Lucy	125A		Taylor, Peggy	234C
Smith, Marg.	171C		Thomas, Arametta	239A
Smith, Maria	291C		Thomas, Mary	236C
Smith, Mary J.	139C		Thomas, Mary E.	143A
Smith, Mary E.	92B		Thornton, Anna	170B
Smith, Percilla	20B		Thornton, Maggie	260C
Smith, Sally	99C		Thornton, Sarah	76A
Smith, Sarah	125C		Thurston, Christianna	200B
Smith, Sarah E.	234A		Thurston, Ella H.	201B
Smith, Sarah	235C		Thurston, Harriet	38B
Smith, Susan M.	290C		Thurston, Harriet	239B
Smith, Willie	301A		Thurston, Louisa J.	284A
Sorrell, Mary Ann	220A		Thurston, Lucie E.	154C
South, Elizabeth	74B		Thurston, Martha	278A
South, Lucy	67A		Towill, Fannie B.	249B
South, Martha	261C		Trader, Clarissa	134B
Staigal, Ella S.	139A		Trader, Louisa B.	37A
Stiff, Lelia V.	281B		Trader, Mary Liz	253A
Stiff, Mary E.	80C		Trader, Mary T.	140A
Stiff, Mary L.	264A		Trader, Susan	87B
Stiff, Sarah E.	199A		Trice, Mary L.	244B
Straughter, Eddie	168B		Tucker, Ella	215B
Street, Hannah	280A		Tucker, Henrietta	116C

Index of Brides

Tucker, Louisa	245C	West, Rebecca	44B
Tucker, Lucie	159C	Wheeler, Lucy C.	51C
Tunstall, Ellinora	156A	White, Mary	256B
		Whiting, Cordelia	194C
Upshaw, Lucinda	295C	Wicks, Mollie	48A
Upshaw, Nancy	118B	Wiese, Eugenie E.	211B
Upshaw, Sallie	275B	Williams, Hester	96C
Uptsier, Roberta	26C	Williams, Frances	219B
		Williams, Lavinia	25A
Vena, Sally	127C	Williams, Lucie	242C
		Williams, Margaret	242B
Wagner, Amanda	188A	Williams, Mary	208B
Wake, Felicia	53B	Williams, Mary C.	92C
Wake, Hellen	198A	Williams, Rebecca	264C
Wake, Mary	96B	Wilson, Ada Laws	55B
Walden, Julia May	38A	Wilson, Florence	153C
Walden, Mary J.	103A	Wilson, Hester	21C
Walker, Emma J.	66B	Wilson, Mary Jane	140B
Walker, Mary T.	181C	Winfield, Lea	160A
Waller, Grace	218A	Wingfield, Nancy	31C
Walton, Lucy	153B	Withers, Nancy	214A
Ward, Louisa	50A	Wood, Cora A.	169C
Ward, Mary	76C	Wood, Cordelia	45B
Ware, Mary E.	247A	Wood, Martha J.	196C
Washington, Emeline	50C	Wood, Mary	208A
Washington, Emma	110C	Wood, Milley	278C
Washington, Ida	220B	Woodward,	
Washington, Jane	90C	Caroline F.	255C
Washington, Juliet	231C	Woodward, Liz. T.	127A
Washington, Lucy Ann	144B	Woollard, Mary	113C
Washington, Maria	194A	Wormley, Alice	285C
Washington, Nancy	138C	Wormley, Anna	104B
Washington, Polly	197C	Wormley, Harriet	86C
Webb, Eliza Ann	69C	Wormley, Julia	70C
Webb, Harriet E.	201A	Wormley, Julia	114A
Webb, Ida	107B	Wormley, Mary	133B
Weeks, Maria	292B	Wormley, Mary E.	283C
Weeks, Sarah J.	212A	Wormley, Sarah	83A
Weems, Eliz.	62B		
Wells, Lydia D.	57B	Yates, Rebecca	287A
West, Josephine	157A	Young, Frances	37B
West, Maria Lou.	79C	Young, Mary Jane	207B
Weston, Georgia	112C	Young, Sarah	240C

Marriage Register 3, 1890-1904
Transcribed by
Carolyn H. Jett

As with Marriage Register 2, this Register contains three marriages per page. The letters A, B and C have been appended to the page number to indicate the location of the record on the page. Many of these records do not contain the names of the parents. In many cases where the parents names are not given, the words "not known" are entered on the line in the Register. However, in spot checking a number of these, the transcriber discovered that the marriage license had no such notation, but merely a blank line where the parents' names would have been entered. Therefore, in this transcription, the notations "not known" have not been included.

As with the previous registers, the race of the parties is transcribed just as it was entered in the original record.
    (B) - black
    (C) - colored
    (W) - white
For interpretation of other abbreviations used, see the introduction to Register of Marriages, 1853-1876.

   1A - 26 Oct. 1890 - **James Washington**, 22, single, oysterman, b. Goochland, residing Mid., son of Lewis & Judy Washington, married **Lulie Henry**, 21, single, b. & residing Mid., dau. of Lina Mathews. (C)
   1B - 30 Oct. 1890 - **Sam'l Lockley**, 58, widower, farmer, b. Gloucester, residing Mid., son of Daniel & Milley Lockley, married **Emily Jane Wormley**, 25, single, b. Gloucester, residing Mid., dau. of Wormley. (C)
   1C - 6 Nov. 1890 - **Carter Ailworth**, 20, single, oysterman, b. & residing Mid., son of Josiah & Sallie Ailworth, married **Carrie E. Shrieves**, 16, single, b. & residing Mid., dau. of George T. & Catherine Shrieves. (W) [Listed in Register as "colored," but marriage license says "white."]
   2A - 20 Nov. 1890 - **Nathan T. Bristow**, 39, widower, merchant, b. & residing Mid., son of Thos. S. & Eudora Bristow, married **Magie E. Creswill**, 23, single, b. King & Queen, residing Mid., dau. of Sarah Creswill. (W)
   2B - 27 Nov. 1890 - **Joseph Moton**, 22, single, oysterman, b. & residing Mid., son of John & Maria Moton, married **Peachy E. Braxton**, 19, single, b. & residing Mid., dau. of Ro. Henry & Lizzie Braxton. (C)

2C - 29 Nov. 1890 - **John W. Hart,** 53, widower, blacksmith, b. & residing Mid., son of Wm. & Virginia F. Hart, married **Mattie Thomas,** 21, single, b. & residing Mid., dau. of George W. Thomas. (W)

3A - 4 Dec. 1890 - **Jno. H. Trader,** 22, single, sailor, b. & residing Mid., son of Richard & Elizabeth Trader, married **Lydia Greenwood,** 17, single, b. & residing Mid., dau. of Ransom & Elizabeth Greenwood. (W)

3B - 3 Dec. 1890 - **Charles Lawson,** single, oysterman, b. & residing Mid., son of Thomas Y. & Sarah A. Lawson, married **Annie M. Segar,** 30, single, b. & residing Mid., dau. of Wm. R. & Lucie M. Segar. (W)

3C - 3 Dec. 1890 - **Jeremiah Ashborn,** 21, single, oysterman, b. Lancaster, residing Mid., son of Zackariah & Elizabeth Ashborn, married **Mary E. Sadler,** 18, single, b. & residing Mid., dau. of Absolom & Matilda Sadler. (W)

4A - 6 Dec. 1890 - **John W. Wood,** 36, widower, merchant, b. & residing Mid., son of John W. & Dorothy E. Wood, married **J. L. Blackburn,** 34, single, b. & residing Mid., dau. of Wm. & Anna Blackburn. (W)

4B - Dec. 1890 - **Charles H. Blake,** 25, single, farmer, b. Gloucester, residing Mid., son of John & Mary Blake, married **Louisa Owen,** 32, widow, b. Maryland, residing Mid., dau. of John & Louise [surname not given]. (W)

4C - 11 Dec. 1890 - **Frank Terry,** 21, single, oysterman, b. & residing Mid., son of Johnson & Susan Terry, married **Lucy Dennis,** 21, single, b. Gloucester, residing Mid., dau. of Letty Dennis. (C)

5A - 18 Dec. 1890 - **James Henry Ruffin,** 41, widower, laborer, b. & residing Mid., son of Jesse & Adeline Ruffin, married **Emma Wilson,** 18, single, b. & residing Mid., dau. of James & Betsy Wilson. (C)

5B - 21 Dec. 1890 - **Wm. Smith,** 24, single, oysterman, b. King & Queen, residing Mid., son of Wm. & Maria Smith, married **Betty Bagby,** 25, single, b. Hampton, residing Mid., dau. of Washington & Polly Bagby. (C)

5C - 21 Dec. 1890 - **Baylor Prosser,** 24, single, farmer, b. Gloucester, residing Mid., son of Cath. Bird, married **Harriet Tabb,** 22, single, b. & residing Mid., dau. of Phil. & Betsy Tabb. (C)

6A - 23 Dec. 1890 - **George E. Fitchett,** 26, single, oysterman, b. & residing Mid., son of S. P. & Salie Fitchett, married **Mason Hundley,** 16, single, b. & residing Mid., dau. of James & Mary Hundley. (W)

6B - 24 Dec. 1890 - **Walker Bagby,** 60, widower, farmer, b. & residing Mid., son of Armstead & Judy Bagby, married **Anna Morris,** 23, single, b. & residing

Mid., dau. of George Morris. (C)

6C - 30 Dec. 1890 - **Wm. Alonzo Moran**, 29, single, farmer, b. Mathews, residing Mid., son of Patrick & Louisianna Moran, married **Emma M. Frank**, 25, single, b. Milwaukee, Wisc., residing Mid., dau. of Henry J. & Lina Frank. (W)

7A - Dec. 1890 - **Geo. T. West**, 21, single, oysterman, b. & residing Mid., son of Caroline West, married **Clara Henry**, 21, single, b. & residing Mid., dau. of Charlotte Henry. (C)

7B - 25 Dec. 1890 - **John Bagby**, 24, single, farmer, b. & residing Mid., son of Walker & Phillis Bagby, married **Saphronia Holmes**, 23, single, b. & residing Mid., dau. of Wiley & Precilla Holmes. (C)

7C - 25 Dec. 1890 - **Edward S. Blake**, 20, single, farmer, b. & residing Mid., son of Alpheus & Ann Blake, married **Virginia Alice Robinson**, 16, single, b. & residing Mid., dau. of John & Margaret Robinson. (W)

8A - 25 Dec. 1890 - **Thornton F. Crow**, 29, single, farmer, b. Essex, residing Mid., son of Thornton & Susan Crow, married **Cath. New**, 16, single, b. & residing Mid., dau. of Wm. New. (W)

8B - 28 Dec. 1890 - **Geo. W. Harrow**, 23, single, oysterman, b. & residing Mid., son of Jeremiah J. & Catharine C. Harrow, married **Addie E. Yates**, 21, single, b. & residing Mid., dau. of Robert & Mary A. Yates. (W)

8C - 30 Dec. 1890 - **Thomas Lomax**, 24, single, oysterman, b. Essex, residing Mid., son of Cath. Lomax, married **Elizabeth Webb**, 17, single, b. & residing Mid., dau. of Claiborn & Polly Webb.

9A - 30 Dec. 1890 - **Joseph Wilson**, 21, single, farmer, b. & residing Mid., son of James & Mary Wilson, married **Bettie Kidd**, 20, single, b. & residing Mid., dau. of Carpenter & Winny Kidd. (C)

9B - 31 Dec. 1890 - **Thos. H. Braxton**, 24, single, farmer, b. & residing Mid., son of Carter & Eliza Braxon, married **Mary Susan Payton**, 20, single, b. & residing Mid., dau. of Solomon & Fanny Payton. (C)

9C - 8 Jan. 1891 - **Frederick Robinson**, 26, single, farmer, b. North Carolina, residing Mid., son of Andrew & Cath. Robinson, married **Janey Washington**, 21, single, b. & residing Mid., dau. of George & Susan Washington. (C)

10A - 10 Jan. 1891 - **Wm. J. Kellum**, 23, single, oysterman, b. & residing Mid., son of Wm. & Alice Kellum, married **Lillian B. Moffitt**, 18, single, b. & residing Mid., dau. of Ed. W. & Eva Moffitt. (W)

10B - 13 Jan. 1891 - **Edward H. Whitehurst**, , widower, merchant, b. Princess Ann, residing Norfolk, son of E. C. & Sarah Whitehurst, married **Susan P. Lawson**, 26, single, b. & residing Mid., dau. of Thomas Y. & Sarah A. Lawson. (W)

10C - 14 Jan. 1891 - **Robert B. Harris**, 32, single, merchant, b. & residing Mid., son of Rober & Fanny Harris, married **Sarah E. Robinson**, 21, single, b. & residing Mid., dau. of Henry & Mary Robinson. (C)

11A - 15 Jan. 1891 - **Robert Braxton**, 32, single, oysterman, b. & residing Mid., son of Carter & Mary Braxton, married **Susan Hoskins**, 17, single, b. & residing Mid., dau. of Booker Waring & Margaret Hoskins. (C)

11B - 26 Feb. 1891 - **James R. Cox, Jr.**, 23, single, farmer, b. & residing Essex, son of J. R. & Penelope Cox, married **Lulie B. Birch**, 16, single, b. Essex, residing Mid., dau. of Payne & Eliz. Burch. (W)

11C - 10 Mar. 1891 - **Samuel H. Mallory**, 25, single, clerk, son of S. S. & Ella H. Mallory, married **Mamie H. Shackelford**, 21, single, b. Richmond, residing Mid., dau. of H. H. & Mary J. Shackelford. (W)

12A - 22 Mar. 1891 - **Jackson Bundy**, 27, single, farmer, b. & residing Mid., son of Benjamin & Judy Bundy, married **Susan Lewis**, 18, single, b. & residing Mid., dau. of Moses & Margaret Lewis. (C)

12B - 12 Apr. 1891 - **John T. Padget**, 25, single, farmer, b. King & Queen, residing Mid., son of Mary Padget, married **Magie E. Blake**, 17, single, b. & residing Mid., dau. of Geo. S. & Susan E. Blake. (W)

12C - 26 Mar. 1891 - **W. H. Butler**, 27, single, oysterman, b. Gloucester, residing Mid., son of Thomas H. & Grace, married **Dora E. Snead**, 22, single, b. Northumberland, residing Mid., dau. of John M. & Mary E. [Tabitha entered and crossed out, and Mary E. penned in.] Snead. (W)

13A - 26 Mar. 1891 - **Richard Page**, 26, single, oysterman, b. Gloucester, residing Mid., son of Richard & Eliza Page, married **Catharine Roy**, 25, single, b. Essex, residing Mid., dau. of Thos. & Alcey Roy. (C)

13B - 5 Apr. 1891 - **John P. Prince**, 19, single, oysterman, b. & residing Mid., son of Jas. Ro. & Elizabeth Prince, married **Amanda P. Revere**, 20, single, b. & residing Mid., dau. of Joel & Mary Revere. (W)

13C - 9 Apr. 1891 - **Elijah Clarke**, single, oysterman, b. King George, residing Mid., son of Wm. Clarke, married **Mary Williams**, single, b. & residing Mid., dau. of Amanda Williams. (C)

14A - 18 Apr. 1891 - **John Borum**, 22, single, oysterman, b. Mathews, residing Mid., son of Borum, married **Mary E. Booker**, 19, single, b. & residing Mid., dau. of Rich'd T. & Frances Booker. (C)

14B - 19 Apr. 1891 - **George Johnson**, 60, widower,

farmer, b. & residing Mid., son of George & Jennie Johnson, married **Jennie Curtis**, 24, single, b. Gloucester, residing Mid., dau. of Wm. & Mary Curtis. (C)

14C - 28 Apr. 1891 - **John P. Bristow**, 41, single, physician, b. & residing Mid., son of Larkin S. & Catharine S. Bristow, married **Nettie A. Brown**, 35, single, b. Chesterfield, residing Mid., dau. of T. L. & M. W. Brown. (W)

15A - 31 Apr. 1891 - **Michael Braxton**, 23, single, oysterman, b. & residing Mid., son of Elijah Braxton, married **Christian Wake**, 17, single, b. & residing Mid., dau. of Christianna Wake. (C)

15B - 30 Apr. 1891 - **Edward T. Walden**, 21, single, oysterman, b. & residing Mid., son of Henry & Martha Walden, married **Florence L. Daniel**, 16, single, b. & residing Mid., dau. of Geo. W. & Mary Daniel. (W)

15C - 14 May 1891 - **George Yates**, 30, single, oysterman & farmer, b. Gloucester, residing Mid., son of Ro. & Mary Yates, married **Fanny Fisher**, 17, single, b. & residing Mid., dau. of Rhoda Robinson. (C)

No records entered on pages 16 & 17.

18A - 7 May 1891 - **Wm. Conway**, 22, single, oysterman, b. & residing Mid., son of Wm. & Emeline Conway, married **Peachy Reed**, 19, single, b. & residing Mid., dau. of Isaac Read. (C)

18B - 6 May 1891 - **Geo W. Hammons**, 22, single, oysterman, b. Gloucester, residing Mid., son of Abram & Rosetta Hammons, married **Patsy Harris**, 27, single, b. & residing Mid., dau. of Sam'l & Virginia Harris. (C)

18C - 11 May 1891 - **Robert Cheseman**, 24, single, farmer, b. & residing York Co., Virginia, son of Levi & Caroline Cheseman, married **Ida Cauthorn**, 21, single, b. & residing Mid., dau. of Jane Cauthorn. (C)

19A - 12 May 1891 - **Stewart Kellam**, widower, druggist, b. Accomack, residing Richmond, son of Thos. Hall Kellum & Susan P. Kellam, married **Kate Overlock**, widow, b. Thomaston, Maine, residing Mid., dau. of Thos. R. & Eliz. Hewett. (W)

19B - 19 May 1891 - **James Robinson**, 23, single, oysterman, b. York, residing Mid., son of Charles & Caroline Robinson, married **Henrietta Nickelson**, 19, single, b. & residing Mid., dau. of Richard & Henrietta Nicholson. (C)

19C - 17 Jun. 1891 - **Daniel F. Parker**, 38, single, farmer & oysterman, b. & residing Mid., son of John & Emily Parker, married **Inez Hodges**, 22, single, b. & residing Mid., dau. of Andrew N. & Laura Hodges. (W)

20A - 26 Jul. 1891 - **Littleton Clayville**, 20, single, sailor, b. & residing Mid., son of Elisha Clayville,

married **Mary F. Hudgins**, 28, single, b. Mathews, residing Mid., dau. of Isaac T. & Julia F. Hudgins. (W)
    20B - 30 Aug. 1891 - **John Baker**, 25, single, oysterman, b. Patchogue, New York, residing Mid., son of John & Mary Baker, married **Georgia K. Revere**, 22, single, b. & residing Mid., dau. of Joel & Mary Revere. (W)
    20C - 16 Sep. 1891 - **Christopher C. Carlton**, 23, single, oysterman, b. & residing Mid., son of John & Virginia Carlton, married **Grace C. Revere**, 18, single, b. & residing Mid., dau. of Joel & Mary Revere. (W)
    21A - 1 Oct. 1891 - **Thomas H. Levering**, widower, merchant, b. Baltimore, Maryland, residing Toledo, Ohio, son of Thos. W. & Martha B. Levering, married **Lucy C. Kerr**, single, b. Clarksville, Tennessee, residing Mid., dau. of Morris M. & Edmonia W. Kerr. (W)
    21B - 4 Oct. 1891 - **Spotswood Robinson**, 37, widower, farmer, b. & residing Mid., son of Polada & Racheal Robinson, married **Mattie Ward**, 24, single, b. & residing Mid., dau. of Zack & Martha Ward. (W)
    21C - 7 Oct. 1891 - **James M. Dickenson**, 32, single, oysterman, b. & residing Richmond Co., son of James & Sarah Dickenson, married **Lucy M. Jeffries**, 25, single, b. & residing Mid., dau. of James M. & Lucy B. Jeffries.
    22A - 8 Oct. 1891 - **Thomas H. Jackson**, 23, single, oysterman, b. & residing Mid., son of Dorah Jackson, married **Georgia E. Johnson**, 18, single, b. & residing Mid., dau. of Nelson & Eliz. Johnson. (C)
    22B - 22 Oct. 1891 - **Cornelius H. Brown**, 21, single, farmer, b. & residing King & Queen, son of Wm. & Mary Brown, married **Lucie Kate Saunders**, 21, single, b. & residing Mid., dau. of Thos. J. J. & Betty Saunders. (W)
    22C - 22 Oct. 1891 - **Joseph F. Jones**, 24, single, oysterman, b. & residing Mid., son of Mary Jones, married **Julia Burnett**, 21, single, b. Essex, residing Mid., dau. of Kiah & Sarah Burnett. (C)
    23A - 28 Oct. 1891 - **Jas. L. Davenport**, 26, widower, carpenter, b. Gloucester, residing Mid., son of George & Mira Davenport, married **Florence Harris**, 17, single, b. & residing Mid., dau. of Isaiah & Julia Harris. (C)
    23B - 28 Oct. 1891 - **George Foster**, 30, single, farmer, b. & residing Mid., son of George & Hannah Foster, married **Alice Minor**, 24, single, b. & residing Mid., dau. of Jefferson & Sarah Minor. (C)
    23C - 4 Nov. 1891 - **J. D. Pannell**, 30, single, farmer, b. Accomack, residing Mid., son of Wm. M. & Annie E. Pannell, married **Paulina A. Carter**, 30, single, b. & residing Mid., dau. of Adison & Sarah Carter. (W)
    24A - 8 Nov. 1891 - **Henry Scott**, 26, single,

oysterman, b. & residing Mid., son of Reubin & Nancy Scott, married **Nancy Robinson**, 26, single, b. & residing Mid., dau. of Walter & Louisa Robinson. (C)
24B - 25 Nov. 1891 - **Harvey E. Topping**, 28, single, merchant, b. & residing Mid., son of Edward & Kesiah Topping, married **Annie C. Blake**, 23, single, b. & residing Mid., dau. of Reubin L. & Margaret Blake. (W)
24C - 25 Nov. 1891 - **Ro. Reed**, 23, single, oysterman, b. & residing Mid., son of Wm. & Martha Reed, married **Ada Green**, 19, single, b. & residing Mid., dau. of Albert & Emma Green. (C)
25A - 26 Nov. 1891 - **Henry Tapscott**, 32, single, mechanic, b. Lancaster, residing Baltimore, Maryland, son of Tapscott, married **Nanie M. Eubank**, 29, single, b. & residing Mid., dau. of Jas. A. & Cordelia Eubank. (W)
25B - 26 Nov. 1891 - **Moses Taliaferro**, 22, single, oysterman, b. & residing Mid., son of Robert & Patsy Taliaferro, married **Frances Braxton**, 17, single, b. & residing Mid., dau. of Carter & Eliza Braxton. (C)
25C - 6 Dec. 1891 - **Doctor Johnson**, 48, widower, farmer, b. & residing Mid., son of Doctor & Jane Johnson, married **Hester Thomas**, 34, single, b. & residing Mid., dau. of Edwin & Sena Thomas. (C)
26A - 10 Dec. 1891 - **James H. Thomas**, 53, widower, farmer, b. Kent Co., Maryland, residing Mid., son of John & Mary D. Thomas, married **Louisa F. Williams**, 50, widow, b. & residing Mid., dau. of Zack W. Bristow. (W)
26B - 10 Dec. 1891 - **Charley Daughtry**, 22, single, oysterman, b. Portsmouth, Virginia, residing Mid., son of Charles & Hester Daughtry, married **Sally Goldman**, 18, single, b. & residing Mid., dau. of John Goldman. (C)
26C - 22 Dec. 1891 - **Thos. H. Miller**, 58, single, farmer, b. & residing Mid., son of James & Nancy Miller, married **Emma Sue Moody**, 28, single, b. & residing Mid., dau. of Woodson C. & Lucy F. Moody. (W)
27A - 1 Feb. 1892 - **Lee Walden**, 22, single, oysterman, b. & residing Mid., son of Henry & Martha Walden, married **S. Alice Hodges**, 21, single, b. & residing Mid., dau. of Jos. R. & Martha Hodges. (W)
27B - 30 Dec. 1891 - **George Peyton**, 21, single, farmer, b. & residing Mid., son of Robert & Catherine Payton, married **Georgeanna Wormley**, 19, single, b. & residing Mid., dau. of Richard & Louisa Wormley. (C)
27C - 31 Jan. 1892 - **Joshua Scott**, 24, single, farmer & oysterman, b. & residing Mid., son of Henry & Eliza Scott, married **Sarah Gouldman**, 24, single, b. & residing Mid., dau. of Elijah & Jane Gouldman. (B)
28A - 21 Jan. 1892 - **Charles W. Jenkins**, 27, single, merchant, b. King George, residing Mid., son of B. W. & Lucy Jenkins, married **Colista Beazley**, 21, single, b. &

residing Mid., dau. of Ed. W. & Catherine Beazley. (W)
28B - 4 Feb. 1892 - **Wm. H. Brooks**, 22, single, oysterman, b. & residing Gloucester, son of Gilbert & Carrie Brooks, married **Rina Dunaway**, 16, single, b. & residing Mid., dau. of James & Lizzie Dunaway. (C)
28C - 10 Feb. 1892 - **Charles Wilson**, 22, single, farmer, b. Gloucester, residing Mid., son of James & Betty Wilson, married **Francis Nelson**, 17, single, b. & residing Mid., dau. of Henry & Mary Francis Nelson. (B)
29A - 17 Feb. 1892 - **George W. Jones**, 22, single, oysterman, b. & residing Mid., son of John & Laura Jones, married **Elisia Ellis**, 23, single, b. & residing Mid., dau. of Carter & Martha Ellis. (B)
29B - 21 Feb. 1892 - **Samuel Jones**, 22, single, farmer, b. King & Queen, residing Mid., married **Amanda Williams**, , widow, b. & residing Mid. [parents names not given]. (B)
29C - 17 Feb. 1892 - **Wm. B. Dunlavy**, 33, widower, oysterman, b. & residing Mid., son of Wm. B., Sr. & Mary Dunlavy, married **Alice Garland**, 21, single, b. & residing Mid., dau. of R. C. & Amanda Garland. (W)
30A - 21 Feb. 1892 - **Lewis Holmes**, 25, single, oysterman, b. King & Queen, residing Mid., son of John & Emily Holmes, married **Millie A. Griffin**, 22, single, b. & residing Mid., dau. of Taylor & Mollie Griffin. (B)
30B - 1 Mar. 1892 - **Richard Burrell**, 23, single, oysterman, b. & residing Mid., son of Jessie & Hester Burrell, married **Ella Carter**, 21, single, b. & residing Mid., dau. of William & Mary Carter. (C)
30C - 15 Mar. 1892 - **John E. Blakey**, 20, single, farmer, b. & residing Mid., son of James A. & Lucy E. Blakey, married **Lena R. Ward**, 20, single, b. & residing Mid., dau. of A. H. & Eudora C. Ward. (W)
31A - 17 Mar. 1892 - **J. W. Foxwell**, 23, single, oysterman, b. Gloucester, residing Mid., son of Solomon & Sarah Foxwell, married **Mary E. Seawell**, 18, single, b. Gloucester, residing Mid., dau. of William & Mary Seawell. (W)
31B - 20 Mary. 1892 - **Andrew Johnson**, 26, single, oysterman, b. & residing Mid., son of Nelson & Bettie Johnson, married **Sophronia Wood**, 18, single, b. & residing Mid. (C)
31C - 15 Mar. 1892 - **Isaac Reed**, 45, widower, farmer, b. James City Co., residing Mid., son of Jacob & Lizzie Reed, married **Sallie Kimble**, 37, widow, b. & residing Mid., dau. of Lewis & Jane King. (C)
32A - 20 Mar. 1892 - **Carter Brown**, 22, single, oysterman, b. King & Queen, residing Mid., son of Alex & Maria Ann Brown, married **Mary M. Lincoln**, 21, single, b. & residing Mid., dau. of Silas & Violet Lincoln. (C)

32B - 31 Mar. 1892 - **Perrin Dickenson**, 21, single, oysterman, b. & residing Mid., son of Frederick & Ann Dickenson, married **Nannie Kidd**, 17, single, b. & residing Mid., dau. of Carpenter & Winnie Kidd. (C)

32C - 30 Mar. 1892 - **George Roy**, 25, single, oysterman, b. King & Queen, residing Mid., son of Braxton & Mahealy Roy, married **Eliza Banks**, 18, single, b. & residing Mid., dau. of Mingo Banks. (C)

33A - 30 Mar. 1892 - **Abison Waller**, 24, single, oysterman, b. & residing Mid., son of Clay & Catherine Waller, married **Maria Brown**, 20, single, b. & residing Mid., dau. of Alex & Maria Brown. (C)

33B - 30 Mar. 1892 - **Charles H. Gresham**, 24, single, oysterman, b. Essex, residing Mid., son of Samuel & Anna Gresham, married **Pacie Brown**, 21, single, b. & residing Mid., dau. of Alex & Maria Brown. (C)

33C - 8 May 1892 - **Armstead Williams**, 29, divorced, oysterman & farmer, b. Lancaster, residing Mid., son of Armstead & Sarah Williams, married **Lucy Griffin**, 20, single, b. & residing Mid., dau. of Richard & Anna Griffin. (C)

34A - 10 May 1892 - **Samuel Churchill**, 31, widower, plasterer, b. Richmond Co., residing Essex, son of Samuel & Jane Churchill, married **Lucinda Robinson**, 23, single, b. & residing Mid., dau. of Henry & Mary Robinson. (C)

34B - 25 May 1892 - **Ro. Nelson**, 24, single, oysterman, b. & residing Mid., son of Robert & Mary Ann Nelson, married **Lizzie Reed**, 26, widow, b. North Carolina, residing Mid., dau. of [not given]. (C)

34C - 14 Apr. 1892 - **T. J. Butler**, 25, single, b. Gloucester, residing Mid., son of T. H. & Gracie Butler, married **Mary T. Snead**, 21, single, b. Northumberland, residing Mid., dau. of John M. & Mary E. Snead. (W)

35A - 1 Jun. 1892 - **Edward Smith**, 24, single, farmer, b. & residing Gloucester, son of Henry & Hester Smith, married **Florence Bristow**, 16, single, b. & residing Mid., dau. of Wash. & Amanda Bristow. (W)

35B - 1 Jun. 1892 - **Jeremiah Carter**, 22, single, b. & residing Mid., son of David & Mollie Carter, married **Ida White**, 21, single, b. King & Queen, residing Mid., dau. of Rasmous & Martha White. (W)

35C - 31 Dec. 1891 - **Jacob Ward**, 26, single, farmer, b. & residing Mid., son of Zack & Martha Ward, married **Ollie L. Wood**, 21, single, b. & residing Mid., dau. of Geo. & Anna Wood. (C)

36A - 18 Jun. 1892 - **Jefferson Minor**, 35, single, farmer & oysterman, b. & residing Mid., son of Henry & Nellie Minor, married **Luly Lewis**, 38, widow, b. Gloucester, residing Mid., dau. of Charles & Betsy

Lewis. (C)

36B - 22 Jun. 1892 - **James Yarrington**, 24, single, farmer, b. King & Queen, residing Mid., son of R. T. & S. E. Yarrington, married **L. M. Gayle**, 24, single, b. & residing Mid., dau. of W. A. & E. C. Gayle. (W)

36C - 22 Jun. 1892 - **Syriese Conway**, 27, widower, laborer, b. & residing Mid., son of William & Emeline Conway, married **Mattie Lomax**, 21, single, b. & residing Mid., dau. of Ralph & Rachel Lomax. (C)

37A - 23 Jun. 1892 - **Chas. H. Banks**, 22, widower, oysterman, b. & residing Mid., son of Mingo & Emily Banks, married **Lettie Lee Morris**, 21, single, b. Maryland, residing Mid. (C)

37B - 29 Jun. 1892 - **J. Randolph Segar**, 32, single, farmer, b. & residing Mid., son of John E. & Mary Segar, married **Ada Brushwood**, 31, single, b. Gloucester, residing Baltimore, dau. of Eli C. & Elizb. E. Brushwood.

37C - 6 Ju. 1892 - **Randal Ward**, 35, single, farmer, b. & residing Mid., son of Zack & Martha Ward, married **Mary E. Hewlett**, 21, single, b. Richmond City, residing Mid., dau. of Robert & Margaret Hewlett. (C)

38A - 14 Jul. 1892 - **John Thurston**, 22, single, oysterman, b. & residing Mid., son of George & Frances Thurston, married **Julia Baaytop**, 24, single, b. & residing Mid., dau. of William & Betsy Baytop. (C)

38B - 17 Jul. 1892 - **Robt. Henry Myers**, 22, single, oysterman, b. Baltimore, Maryland, residing Mid., son of Charles & Mary Myers, married **Annie Sparrow**, 22, widow, b. Essex, residing Mid., dau. of James & Catherine Burch. (W)

38C - 27 Ju. 1892 - **Wm. Watson**, 38, widower, oysterman, b. Mathews, residing Mid., son of John & Frankie Watson, married **Maggie Trader**, 22, single, b. & residing Mid., dau. of Charles & Matilda Trader. (W)

39A - 7 Aug. 1892 - **G. A. Smith**, 25, single, oysterman, b. & residing Mid., son of J. L. & Maria Smith, married **Jeanette Davis**, 19, single, b. & residing Mid., dau. of Jessie & Fannie Davis. (C)

39B - 2 Aug. 1892 - **R. B. Taylor**, 23, single, farmer, b. & residing Mid., son of Ro. M. & L. A. Taylor, married **Maggie J. Humphries**, 23, single, b. & residing Mid., dau. of R. T. & Lucy A. Humphries. (W)

39C - 18 Aug. 1892 - **Eugene Folliard**, 34, single, plasterer, b. King & Queen, residing Atlantic City, Virginia, son of John P. & Susan Folliard, married **Mary McKan**, 23, single, b. & residing Mid., dau. of Robert & Ann McKan. (W)

40A - 18 Aug. 1892 - **Robert Wiatt**, 25, single, oysterman & farmer, b. Gloucester, residing Mid., son of

Richard & Judith Wiatt, married **Bettie Fields**, 16, single, b. & residing Mid., dau. of Peter & Jennie Fields. (B)

40B - 21 Aug. 1892 - **J. B. Harrow**, 33, widower, farmer, b. & residing Mid., son of Will & Almedia Harrow, married **Amelia B. Dunlavey**, 23, single, b. Mathews, residing Mid., dau. of James & Lucy Dunlavey. (W)

40C - 24 Aug. 1892 - **Wm. Goin**, 50, widower, farmer, b. & residing Mid., son of Essex & Katie Goin, married **Eliza Miller**, 25, single, b. & residing Mid., dau. of Adam & Betsy Miller. (B)

41A - 27 Sep. 1892 - **Cyrus W. Harris**, 36, single, farmer & oysterman, b. & residing Mid., son of George & Lucy Harris, married **Lucy Hill**, 31, divorced, b. & residing Mid., dau. of William & Martha Jackson. (C)

41B - 9 Oct. 1892 - **Geo. W. Reed**, 24, single, oysterman, b. & residing Mid., son of George & Purlina Reed, married **Mary A. Summons**, 24, single, b. Pennsylvania, residing Mid., dau. of Conrad & Jemenia Summons. (C)

41C - 17 Oct. 1892 - **Godfrey Robinson**, 28, single, farmer, b. King & Queen, residing Mid., son of General & Maria Robinson, married **June Scott**, 27, single, b. & residing Mid. (C)

42A - 13 Oct. 1892 - **George Jackson**, 26, single, farmer, b. & residing Mid., son of Judge & Betsy Jackson, married **Leah Banks**, 24, widow, b. York Co., residing Mid., dau. of Ralph & Millie Wicks. (C)

42B - 20 Oct. 1892 - **Robert Johnson**, 21, single, oysterman, b. & residing Mid., son of George & Cornelia Johnson, married **Mary Thornton**, 21, single, b. & residing Mid., dau. of Riden & Margaret Thornton. (C)

42C - 3 Nov. 1892 - **Chas. H. Deagle**, 30, single, oysterman, b. & residing Mid., son of Wm. H. & Nancy Deagle, married **Ida E. A. Kellam**, 21, single, b. & residing Mid., dau. of Wm. & Alice Kellam. (W)

43A - 2 Nov. 1892 - **Jno. B. Seward**, 24, single, farmer, b. & residing King & Queen, son of James T. & Francis E. Seward, married **Julia D. Thrift**, 17, single, b. & residing Mid., dau. of Wm. T. & Mary E. Thrift. (W)

43B - 13 Nov. 1892 - **Jno. T. Grymes**, 51, single, oysterman, b. Gloucester, residing Mid., son of Chas. H. & Dauphrey Grymes, married **Isabella Wormley**, 60, widow, b. & residing Mid. (C)

43C - 9 Nov. 1892 - **J. W. Mears**, 28, single, farmer & oysterman, b. & residing Mid., son of Jno. W. & Amanda Mears [The Register gives Jno. W. Macors & Amanda Mears, but the original license gives Jno. W. & Amanda Mears.], married **Sadie E. Wood,** 20, single, b. & residing Mid., dau. of James A. & Harriet C. Wood. (W)

44A - 1 Dec. 1892 - **Henry Walden,** 49, widower, oysterman, b. & residing Mid., son of Edward & Rebecca Walden, married **Ida Tabor,** 18, single, b. & residing Mid., dau. of Joseph & Nancy Tabor. (W)

44B - 1 Dec. 1892 - **Julius C. Blake,** 23, single, oysterman, b. & residing Mid., son of Wm. H. & Fannie Blake, married **Georgia B. Wilson,** 20, single, b. Gloucester, residing Mid., dau. of John & Cordelia Wilson. (W)

44C - 11 Dec. 1892 - **Lewis Griffin,** 37, widower, oysterman, b. & residing Mid., son of Richard & Anna Griffin, married **Eunice Cook,** 23, single, b. & residing Mid., dau. of James H. & Louisa Cook. (C)

45A - 22 Dec. 1892 - **Oscar Holliday,** 27, divorced, oysterman, b. Richmond City, residing Mid., son of Robert & Susan Holliday, married **Bettie A. Curtis,** 18, single, b. & residing Mid., dau. of Henry & Lucy Curtis. (C)

45B - 22 Dec. 1892 - **Henry Lewis,** 60, widower, farmer, b. Gloucester, residing Mid., son of Warner & Maria Lewis, married **Becky Johnson,** 30, single, b. & residing Mid., dau. of Washington & Hester Johnson. (C)

45C - 22 Dec. 1892 - **Thos. H. Carter,** , widower, merchant, b. & residing Mid., son of [not given], married **Ida E. Lyon,** 36, widow, b. Baltimore City, Maryland, residing Mid., dau. of Wm. H. Kelly. (W)

46A - 22 Dec. 1892 - **James Nelson,** 75, widower, farmer, b. & residing Mid., son of Henry & Maria Nelson, married **Mary Morris,** 35, single, b. King & Queen, residing Mid. (C)

46B - 25 Dec. 1892 - **J. A. Laws,** 27, single, oysterman, b. & residing Mid., son of [not given], married **Annie Taliaferro,** 21, single, b. & residing Mid., dau. of Lewis & Rebecca Taliaferro. (C)

46C - 25 Dec. 1892 - **George Dungee,** 24, single, farmer, b. & residing Mid., son of Elijah & Catharine Dungee, married **Fannie Easton,** 23, single, b. & residing Mid., dau. of Noah Easton. (C)

47A - 22 Dec. 1892 - **R. M. Trice,** 58, widower, farmer, b. & residing Mid., son of Thomas & Mary Trice, married **Bettie Carlton,** 42, single, b. & residing Mid., dau. of Frank & Ann Carlton. (W)

47B - 22 Dec. 1892 - **B. F. Smith,** 30, single, carpenter, b. Gloucester, residing Mid., son of J. W. & Alice A. Smith, married **Ida G. Bristow,** 24, single, b. & residing Mid., dau. of Zachary & Virginia Bristow. (W)

47C - 29 Dec. 1892 - **Joseph H. Thornton,** 21, single, farmer, b. Gloucester, residing Mid., son of Henry &

Caroline Thornton, married **Emma Pendleton**, 21, single, b. Gloucester, residing Mid., dau. of George & Peggy Pendleton. (C)

48A - 29 Dec. 1892 - **Thomas Lockley**, 22, single, farmer, b. Gloucester, residing Mid., son of Robert & Levinia Lockley, married **Francis Sutherland**, 22, single, b. & residing Mid., dau. of John & Eliza Sutherland. (C)

48B - 3 Jan. 1893 - **Louis C. Redd**, 25, single, farmer, b. King & Queen, residing Mid., son of James E. & Mary E. Redd, married **Luly B. Brim**, 21, single, b. & residing Mid., dau. of Wm. L. & R. B. Brim. (W)

48C - 15 Jan. 1893 - **Henry Brooks**, 37, widower, farmer, b. & residing Gloucester, son of Betsy Ruffin, married **Luly Washington**, 24, widow, b. & residing Mid., dau. of Harry & Lina Matthews. (C)

49A - 18 Jan. 1893 - **Maxwell Taliaferro**, 21, single, oysterman, b. & residing Mid., son of Rebecca Taliaferro, married **Belle Banks**, 18, single, b. & residing Mid., dau. of Lewis & Eudora Banks. (C)

49B - 20 Jan. 1893 - **Joseph Burrell**, 30, single, b. & residing Mid., son of Moses & Mary Burrell, married **Harriet Anderson**, 25, single, b. King & Queen, residing Mid., dau. of David & Rachel Anderson. (C)

49C - 25 Jan. 1893 - **Edmund Baytop**, 26, widower, farmer, b. Gloucester, residing Mid., son of Jacob & Basey Baytop, married **Georgiann Carter**, 18, single, b. & residing Mid. (C)

50A - 1 Feb. 1893 - **Walter Robinson**, 23, single, oysterman, b. King & Queen, residing Mid., son of Isaac & Lucy Robinson, married **Peachy Wingfield**, 21, single, b. & residing Mid., dau. of Scipio & Millie Wingfield. (C)

50B - 5 Feb. 1893 - **Geo. W. Crittenden**, 28, single, oysterman, b. York Co., residing Mid., son of Geo. W. & Ellen Crittenden, married **Ettie Miller**, 24, single, b. & residing Mid., dau. of Joseph & Belle Miller. (C)

50C - 16 Feb. 1893 - **Lewis Nelson**, 35, single, residing Mid., son of Wm. & Millie Nelson, married **Lavelia Lee**, 23, single, residing Mid., dau. of Moses & Nancy Lee. (C)

51A - 20 Feb. 1893 - **Jackson Ward**, 28, single, oysterman, b. & residing Mid., son of Wm. Gatewood & Millie Lomax, married **Kitty Smith**, 29, single, b. & residing Mid., dau. of Thomas & Margaret. (C)

51B - 2 Mar. 1893 - **Harrison Scott**, 18, single, oysterman, b. & residing Mid., son of Wm. & Levinia Scott, married **Martha Taylor**, 21, single, b. & residing Mid., dau. of Thornton & Amy Taylor. (C)

51C - 8 Mar. 1893 - **Jos. H. Broun**, 34, single,

13

farmer, b. Gloucester, residing Mid., son of Seymore & Sarah J. Broun, married **Lucy E. Creswell**, 22, single, b. King & Queen, residing Mid., dau. of John & Sarah E. Creswell. (W)

52A - 17 Apr. 1893 - **Z. R. Coates**, 58, widower, farmer, b. Gloucester, residing Mid., son of Belley & Nancy Coates, married **Mary F. Goode**, 26, single, b. King & Queen, residing Mid., dau. of John C. & Catherine N. Goode. (W)

52B - 27 Apr. 1893 - **Ralph Washington**, 23, single, oysterman, b. Gloucester, residing Mid., married **Lucy Lovings**, 21, single, residing Mid. (C)

52C - 26 Apr. 1893 - **Wm. C. Easton**, 24, single, farmer, b. & residing Mid., son of Henry & Lucy Ann Easton, married **Alice Lee**, 22, single, b. & residing Mid., dau. of Mary Lee. (C)

53A - 27 Apr. 1893 - **Andrew Jackson**, 24, single, farmer, b. & residing Mid., married **Mary Jones**, 43, widow, b. Mathews, residing Mid. (C)

53B - 10 May 1893 - **F. L. Fitchett**, 21, single, oysterman, b. & residing Mid., son of Piney & Sallie E. Fitchett, married **Minnie E. Thrift**, 18, single, b. & residing Mid., dau. of James H. & Emma J. Thrift. (W)

53C - 17 May 1893 - **John T. Wood**, 22, single, oysterman, b. & residing Mid., son of James A. & Harriet C. Wood, married **Hattie May Trader**, 18, single, b. & residing Mid., dau. of Alexander & Sarah Trader. (W)

54A - 11 May 1893 - **Franklin C. South**, 43, divorced, laborer, b. & residing Mid., son of Jos. C. & Melissa South, married **Plummie Newton**, 22, single, b. & residing Mid. (W)

54B - 22 May 1893 - **Andrew J. Blake**, 24, single, oysterman, b. & residing Mid., son of John A. & Mary Blake, married **Virginia B. Redd**, 21, single, b. King & Queen, residing Mid., dau. of William & Mary A. Redd. (W)

54C - 23 May 1893 - **Granville H. Walker**, 26, single, merchant, b. & residing Mid., son of Henry H. & Bettie J. Walker, married **Mamie C. Lumpkin**, 20, single, b. & residing Mid., dau. of Jno. R. & Lucy C. Lumpkin. (W)

55A - 1 Jun. 1893 - **W. J. Shrieves**, 24, single, farmer, b. & residing Mid., son of Geo. T. & Mary C. Shrieves, married **Luly D. Trymer**, 22, single, b. & residing Mid., dau. of W. S. & Sarah Trymer. (W)

55B - 7 Jun. 1893 - **Russell A. Davis**, 30, single, merchant, b. & residing Mid., son of Rich'd & Julia E. Davis, married **Mary Emma Evans**, 30, single, b. & residing Mid., dau. of Andrew B. & Alice Evans. (W)

55C - 14 Jun. 1893 - **Wm. A. Palmer**, 36, single, farmer, b. & residing Mid., son of Lewis & Martha J.

Palmer, married **Margaret J. Sibley**, 45, widow, b. & residing Mid., dau. of Jno. S. & Polly Green. (W)

56A - 21 Jun. 1893 - **Willoughby B. French**, 29, single, farmer, b. & residing Mid., son of Wm. T. & Edna E. French, married **Bettie M. Walker**, 23, single, b. & residing Mid., dau. of Francis M. & Elizabeth Walker. (W)

56B - 17 Jul. 1893 - **John H. Campbell**, 39, widower, merchant, b. & residing Mid., son of Warner & Easter Campbell, married **Louisiana Johnson**, 20, single, b. & residing Mid., dau. of Phillip & Jane Johnson. (C)

56C - 19 May 1893 - **James H. Thurston**, 22, single, farmer, b. & residing Mid., son of Cromwell & Chris Thurston, married **Hester Boyd**, 22, single, b. & residing Mid., dau. of Robert & Nancy Boyd. (C)

57A - 26 Jul. 1893 - **Henry Hill**, 22, single, oysterman, b. & residing Mid., son of James & Betsy Hill, married **Leah Hill**, 18, single, b. King & Queen, residing Mid., dau. of Daniel & Hannah Hill. (C)

57B - 6 Jul. 1893 - **Geo. W. Thomas**, 24, single, farmer, b. & residing Mid., son of Geo. W. & Carrie Thomas, married **Mary E. Foster**, 24, widow, b. Essex, residing Mid., dau. of Jas. W. & Martha Hodges. (W)

57C - 10 Aug. 1893 - **John H. Taliaferro**, 37, widower, oysterman, b. & residing Mid., son of William & Nancy Taliaferro, married **Lizzie E. Young**, 22, single, b. & residing Mid., dau. of Noah & Cena Young. (C)

58A - 19 Aug. 1893 - **Henry Miller**, 44, widower, merchant, b. Little York, Pennsylvania, residing Cape Charles, Virginia, married **Nannie Patyschke**, 27, widow, b. Germany, residing Mid., dau. of August & Annie Sutton. (W)

58B - 16 Aug. 1893 - **Abraham H. Bratton**, single, oysterman, b. & residing Mid., son of Thomas & Rosetta Bratton, married **Jennie L. Jackson**, single, b. & residing Mid., dau. of Noah F. & Anna E. Jackson. (W)

58C - 31 Aug. 1893 - **Walter S. Brooks**, 36, single, "gentleman of leisure," b. West Virginia, residing Mid., son of R. H. & J. C. Brooks, married **Lizzie P. Hill**, 22, single, b. Mathews, residing Mid., dau. of [not given]. (W)

59A - 29 Aug. 1893 - **Alfred H. Parker**, 50, widower, farmer, b. Essex, residing Mid., son of John & Emily Parker, married **Bettie L. Griffith**, 29, single, b. Essex, residing Mid., dau. of Joseph B. & Sarah Griffith. (W)

59B - 14 Sep. 1893 - **John C. Yates**, 26, single, oysterman, b. & residing Mid., son of Robert & Mary Yates, married **M. E. Harrow**, 22, single, b. & residing Mid., dau. of Jeremiah J. & Catherine Harrow. (W)

59C - 14 Sep. 1893 - **Jordun Morris**, 22, single, farmer, b. & residing Mid., son of Noah & Kitty Morris, married **Cornelia G. Lockley**, 21, single, b. & residing Mid., son of Samuel & Delpha Lockley. (C)
60A - 28 Sep. 1893 - **Wilbert Kandle**, 28, single, farmer, b. New Jersey, residing Mid., son of Samuel & Christianna Kandle, married **Mollie A. Daniel**, 15, single, b. Gloucester, residing Mid., dau. of Peter & Mary Daniel. (W)
60B - 5 Oct. 1893 - **Edward Fleming**, 28, single, oysterman, b. Gloucester, residing Mid., son of Edward & Rachel Fleming, married **Lucinda Thurston**, 26, single, b. & residing Mid., dau. of Daniel & June Thurston. (C)
60C - 19 Oct. 1893 - **Charles Carter**, 38, widower, oysterman, b. & residing Mid., married **Elizabeth Lee**, 36, widow, b. & residing Mid. (C)
61A - 2 Nov. 1893 - **Wm. Russ**, 64, widower, farmer, b. King & Queen, residing Mid., son of Robert & Jennie Russ, married **Francis Robinson**, 43, widow, b. King & Queen, residing Mid., dau. of of Morris & Annie Johnson. (C)
61B - 2 Nov. 1893 - **Robert Dungee**, 28, single, oysterman, b. & residing Mid., son of Elijah & Kate Dungee, married **Mary Davis**, 24, single, b. & residing Mid., dau. of Joseph & Emma Davis. (C)
61C - 9 Nov. 1893 - **Albert G. Cundiff**, 21, single, farmer, b. & residing Mid., son of G. & Annie Cundiff, married **Sarah L. Foster**, 17, single, b. & residing Mid., dau. of John W. & Arintha C. Foster. (W)
62A - 21 Nov.1893 - **Patrick C. Jones**, 34, single, merchant, b. & residing Mid., son of Ned & Eliza Jones, married **Mary A. Wormley**, 28, single, b. & residing Mid. (C)
62B - 28 Nov. 1893 - **Isaiah Wake**, 30, divorced, oysterman, b. & residing Mid., son of Minnie & Mollie Wake, married **Jennie Washington**, 28, single, b. & residing Mid. (C)
62C - 6 Dec. 1893 - **Ro. H. Farinholt**, 26, single, merchant, b. & residing Gloucester, son of John L. & Georgie Farinholt, married **B. B. Healy**, 19, single, b. & residing Mid., dau. of G. S. & Sue Healy. (W)
63A - 5 Dec. 1893 - **Ransom Roots**, 35, single, bridge keeper, b. & residing Mid., son of Manuel & Mary Roots, married **Lucy Webb**, 25, single, b. & residing Mid., dau. of John & Betsy Webb. (C)
63B - 29 Nov. 1893 - **Burgess Miller**, 25, single, oysterman, b. & residing Mid., son of Joseph & Belle Miller, married **Mary Nicholson**, 25, single, b. King & Queen, residing Mid., dau. of Major & Mary Nicholson. (C)

63C - 20 Dec. 1893 - **Richard A. Davis**, 59, widower, farmer, b. & residing Mid., son of Richard A. & E. B. Davis, married **Mary E. Moore**, 42, widow, b. Mathews, residing Mid., dau. of Wm. F. & Mary E. Pugh. (W)

64A - 19 Dec. 1893 - **Geo. W. Thurston**, 45, widower, oysterman, b. & residing Mid., son of Samuel & Harriet Thurston, married **Angelina Burrell**, 21, single, b. & residing Mid., dau. of Margaret Burrell. (C)

64B - 21 Dec. 1893 - **Grant Cook**, 25, single, sailor, b. & residing Dorchester Co., Maryland, son of Alfred & Catherine Cook, married **Indianna Nornelius**, 20, single, b. & residing Mid., dau. of Bezzilee & Sarah E. Cornelius. (W)

64C - 25 Dec. 1893 - **Thomas H. Robinson**, 28, single, oysterman, b. & residing Mid., son of Alex & Millie Robinson, married **Rebecca Wilson**, 36, widow, b. & residing Mid., dau. of Wm. & Lucy Taliaferro. (C)

65A - 25 Dec. 1893 - **Howard Chandler**, 24, single, oysterman, b. Essex, residing Mid., son of Archie & Margaret Chandler, married **Mary E. Lewis**, 22, single, b. & residing Mid., dau. of Moses & Margaret Lewis. (C)

65B - 27 Dec. 1893 - **C. H. Fletcher**, 25, single, blacksmith, b. Gloucester, residing Mid., son of Cyrus T. & Myra A. Fletcher, married **Mary Sue Hill**, 26, single, b. & residing Mid., dau. of Thos. S. & Paulina Hill. (W)

65C - 20 Dec. 1893 - **Richard Reed**, 39, widower, farmer, b. & residing Mid., son of Manuel & Francis Reed, married **Mary Smith**, 20, single, b. & residing Mid., dau. of Richard & Francis Smith. (C) [Only rarely in this Register was Frances spelled with an e.]

66A - 28 Dec. 1893 - **Albert Patterson**, 22, single, oysterman, b. & residing Mid., son of [not given], married **Lelia Bundy**, 18, single, b. & residing Mid., dau. of Betsy Bundy. (C)

66B - 28 Dec. 1893 - **Jessee Lockley**, 21, single, oysterman, b. & residing Mid., son of Daniel & Chris Lockley, married **Alice Scott**, 21, single, b. & residing Mid., dau. of [not given]. (C)

66C - 22 Jan. 1894 - **Henly Woodward**, 34, single, farmer, b. & residing Mid., son of Philemon T. & Mary E. Woodward, married **Fannie C. Purkins**, 30, single, b. & residing Mid., dau. of E. T. & Betty Purkins. (W)

67A - 11 Jan. 1894 - **Jake Jefferson**, 22, single, oysterman, b. & residing York Co., son of Jake & Margaret Jefferson, married **Eliza Curtis**, 21, single, b. & residing Mid., dau. of William & Lucy Curtis. (C)

67B - 18 Jan. 1894 - **Geo. D. Kellum**, 24, single, oysterman, b. & residing Mid., son of William & Alice Kellum, married **Etta Bratton**, 18, single, b. & residing

Mid., dau. of Thomas & Rosa Bratton. (W)
67C - 20 Jan. 1894 - **Thomas Jackson**, 22, single, laborer, b. Gloucester, residing Mid., son of Ned & Luncy Jackson, married **Alice King**, 17, single, b. King & Queen, residing Mid., dau. of Adam & Mary King. (C)
68A - 18 Jan. 1894 - **John G. Grinels**, 32, single, farmer, b. Accomack, residing Mid., son of Southey & Polly Grinels, married **Florence M. Hardy**, 22, single, b. & residing Mid., dau. of John & Louisa Hardy. (W)
68B - 26 Jan. 1894 - **Andrew Jackson**, 22, single, oysterman, b. & residing Mid., son of M. & Lizzie Jackson, married **Susie V. Owens**, 21, single, b. Mathews, residing Mid., dau. of Mary E. Owens. (W)
68C - 17 Jan. 1894 - **George Lincoln**, 29, single, farmer, b. & residing Mid., son of Cyrus & Violet Lincoln, married **Mary E. Burrel**, 21, single, b. & residing Mid., dau. of Lewis & Judy Burrill. (C)
69A - 31 Jan. 1894 - **Howard G. Shackelford**, 22, single, farmer, b. Augusta, residing Gloucester, son of H. H. & Mollie Shackelford, married **Minnie G. Chowning**, 19, single, b. & residing Mid., dau. of James & Ann Chowning. (W)
69B - 31 Jan. 1894 - **Henry Fields**, 21, single, oysterman, b. & residing Mid., son of Robert Haile & Eliza Fields, married **Millie Williams**, 17, single, b. & residing Mid., dau. of William & Margaret Williams. (C)
69C - 11 Feb. 1894 - **Joseph Taylor**, 21, single, waiter, b. & residing Gloucester, son of Samuel & Julia Taylor, married **Elizabeth Johnson**, 19, single, b. & residing Mid., dau. of Henry & Bettie Johnson. (C)
70A - 11 Feb. 1894 - **S. F. Foxwell**, 21, single, "steamboating", b. Gloucester, residing Norfolk City, married **Virginia F. Redd**, 20, single, b. King & Queen, residing Mid. (W)
70B - 24 Jan. 1894 - **Amond A. Ashburn**, 22, single, sailor, b. & residing Lancaster, son of Griffin & Olivia Ashburn, married **Abbie A. Sadler**, 16, single, b. & residing Mid., dau. of A. M. & Matilda Sadler. (W)
70C - 15 Feb. 1894 - **J. W. Deagle**, 43, widower, farmer, b. & residing Mid., son of Wm. H. & Nancy Deagle, married **Alfenetta Kellum**, 10, single, b. & residing Mid., dau. of Wm. & Alice Kellum. (W)
71A - 20 Feb. 1894 - **Walter W. Robinson**, 28, single, farmer, b. & residing Mid., son of Henry R. & Mary Robinson, married **Maggie Wood**, 29, widow, b. & residing Mid., dau. of Wellington & Betsy Purkins. (C)
71B - 22 Jan. 1894 - **Daniel Brown**, 30, single, oysterman, b. & residing Mid., son of Wm. & Julia Brown, married **Annie Hill**, 25, widow, b. King & Queen, residing Mid. (C)

71C - 22 Feb. 1894 - **Bruce Burrell**, 22, single, oysterman, b. Gloucester, residing Mid., son of Coleman & Eliza Burrell, married **Dora Morris**, 21, single, b. & residing Mid., dau. of Julius & Mary Morris. (C)
72A - 28 Feb. 1894 - **W. T. Robbins**, 29, single, farmer, b. Gloucester, residing Mid., son of Wm. & Lizzie Robbins, married **Fannie Revere**, 26, single, b. King & Queen, residing Mid., dau. of Lawson Revere. (W)
72B - 1 Mar. 1894 - **Jerry Braxton**, 24, single, oysterman, b. & residing Mid., son of Joshua & Jennie Braxton, married **Polly Hodges**, 21, single, b. & residing Mid., dau. of Isaac & Fannie Hodges. (C)
72C - 15 Mar. 1894 - **Edward B. Ginmell**, 25, single, merchant, b. Kent Co., Maryland, residing Mid., son of John H. & W. G. E. Ginmell, married **Lallah B. Blake**, 25, single, b. & residing Mid., dau. of John L. & Matilda Blake. (W)
73A - 21 Mar. 1894 - **John R. Callis**, 22, single, sailor, b. Mathews, residing Mid., son of Thomas C. & Elizabeth Callis, married **Minnie D. Wilson**, 19, single, b. & residing Mid., dau. of N. G. & S. E. Wilson. (W)
73B - 29 Mar. 1894 - **Moby Faulkner**, 22, single, farmer, b. & residing Mid., son of John & Esther Faulkner, married **Florence Padgett**, 17, single, b. & residing Mid. (W)
73C - 28 Mar. 1894 - **B. S. Blake**, 45, widower, farmer, b. & residing Mid., son of W. S. & Cordelia Blake, married **Addie Enos**, 35, single, b. & residing Mid., dau. of Wm. & Bittie Enos. (W)
74A - 29 Mar. 1894 - **Z. Clayville**, 45, widower, farmer, b. Accomack, residing Mid., son of Thomas & Comfort Clayville, married **Emmie Pannell**, 34, single, b. & residing Accomack. (W)
74B - 8 Apr. 1894 - **Jackson Morris**, 24, single, farmer, b. & residing Mid., son of Noah & Kitty Morris, married **M. S. Cook**, 19, single, b. & residing Mid., dau. of Ralph & Betsy Cook. (C)
74C - 12 Apr. 1894 - **John H. Banks**, 24, single, oysterman, b. & residing Mid., son of Lewis & Eudora Banks, married **Georgie Johnson**, 19, single, b. & residing Mid., dau. of John & Bettie Johnson. (C)
75A - 18 Apr. 1894 - **Edward W. Beazly**, 58, widower, farmer, b. & residing Mid., son of John H. & Laura Beazly, married **Henrietta Bristow**, 45, single, b. & residing Mid., dau. of Z. W. & Maria Bristow. (W)
75B - 24 Feb. 1894 - **Beverly Smith**, 28, widower, oysterman, b. Gloucester, residing Mid., son of John & Charlotte Smith, married **Lucy E. Morris**, 22, single, b. & residing Mid., dau. of James & Matilda Morris. (C)
75C - 25 Apr. 1894 - **C. S. Lawson**, 24, single,

carpenter, b. Gloucester, residing Mid., son of W. J. & Mary Lawson, married **L. B. Adams**, 24, widow, b. Essex, residing Mid., dau. of Leonard & Matilda Schools. (W)
    76A - 27 Apr. 1894 - **George E. Trice**, 30, single, clerk, b. King & Queen, residing Newport News, son of James C. & Louisa A. Trice, married **Lucy W. Bristow**, 23, single, b. & residing Mid., dau. of Calvin & Mary Bristow. (W)
    76B - 2 May 1894 - **Andrew J. Sable, Jr.**, 33, widower, oysterman, b. St. Marys, Maryland, residing Mid., son of Andrew J. & Sarah J. Sable, married **Sarah T. Shrives**, 27, single, b. & residing Mid., dau. of Thomas & Catherine Shrives. (W)
    76C - 6 May 1894 - **Geo. W. Brown**, 30, single, oysterman, b. Gloucester, residing Mid., son of Seymour & S. J. Brown, married **Mary Davis**, 22, single, b. & residing Mid., dau. of James Davis. (W)
    77A - 24 Jun. 1894 - **R. L. Didlake**, 21, single, blacksmith, b. Essex, residing Mid., son of Fisher & Mary E. Didlake, married **Blanche C. Garnett**, 17, single, b. & residing Mid., dau. of Lewis L. & Mary L. Garnett. (W)
    77B - 28 Jun. 1894 - **A. J. Wyatt**, 38, widower, farmer, b. & residing King & Queen, son of Andrew & Susan Wyatt, married **Rebecca Carter**, 19, single, b. King & Queen, residing Mid., dau. of John W. & Susan A. Carter. (W)
    77C - 1 Jul. 1894 - **Phillip Fairfax**, 26, single, farmer, b. Fluvanna, residing Gloucester, son of Lundy & Louisa Fairfax, married **Jane Jackson**, 27, single, b. & residing Mid., dau. of George & Adaline Jackson. (C)
    78A - 26 Jul. 1894 - **John W. Jones**, 22, single, clerk, b. & residing Mid., son of Edmund & Margaret Jones, married **Mattie Green**, 21, single, b. & residing Mid., dau. of Griffin & Judy Green. (C)
    78B - 7 Aug. 1894 - **T. E. Foster**, 27, single, mechanic, b. Mathews, residing Mid., son of John E. & M. L. Foster, married **Lauara Y. Clements**, 22, single, b. & residing Mid., dau. of Richard M. & O. V. Clements. (W)
    78C - 16 Aug. 1894 - **M. M. Bray**, 30, single, farmer, b. & residing Mid., son of Thomas M. & O. N. Bray, married **A. W. Armstrong**, 30, widow, b. King & Queen, residing Mid. (W)
    79A - 16 Aug. 1894 - **Thomas Jiles**, 22, single, oysterman, b. Nottaway, residing Mid., son of Henry & Fannie Jiles, married **Bettie Carter**, 21, single, b. & residing Mid., dau. of George & Lettie Carter. (C)
    79B - 7 Jul. 1894 - **Eddie Haynie**, 25, single, oysterman, b. Lancaster, residing Mid., son of Washington & Virginia Haynie, married **Annie Courtney**,

22, single, b. King & Queen, residing Mid., dau. of Wm. & Jane Courtney. (C)

79C - 4 Jul. 1894 - **Wm. H. Berry**, 46, divorced, shoemaker, b. Baltimore City, residing Mid., son of Wm. H. & Isabella Berry, married **Evelyn A. Riley**, 37, single, b. & residing Mid., dau. of G. D. & Eliza Riley. (W)

80A - 23 Aug. 1894 - **Gary T. Dobson**, 18, single, oysterman, b. Gloucester, residing Mid., son of B. F. & Georgeanna Dobson, married **Catherine Belvin**, 22, single, b. Gloucester, residing Mid., dau. of Ralph & Mary Belvin. (W)

80B - 30 Aug. 1894 - **Jacob Gaines**, 21, single, oysterman, b. & residing Mid., son of Aaron & Laura Gaines, married **Maggie Johnson**, 18, single, b. King & Queen, residing Mid., dau. of Ned & Rose Johnson. (C)

80C - 16 Sep. 1894 - **Henry Turner**, 51, widower, oysterman, b. King William, residing Mid., son of Reubin & Isabella Turner, married **Mollie Bet. Burke**, 23, single, b. & residing Mid., dau. of Moses & Lettie Ann Burke. (C)

81A - 9 Sep. 1894 - **Albert Taliaferro**, 21, single, oysterman, b. & residing Mid., son of Samuel & Mary J. Taliaferro, married **Emma Nelson**, 21, single, b. & residing Mid., dau. of Hannah Nelson. (C)

81B - 21 Nov. 1894 - **Ro. Burrell**, 25, single, oysterman, b. & residing Mid., son of Thomas & Margaret Burrell, married **Janie Lockley**, 18, single, b. & residing Mid., dau. of Henry & Lucy Lockley. (C)

81C - 27 Dec. 1894 - **Thomas Jackson**, 51, widower, farmer, b. & residing Mid., son of Phil & Mary Jackson, married **Anna Conway**, 28, widow, b. & residing Mid., dau. of Isaac & Fannie Reed. (C)

82A - 7 Oct. 1894 - **John T. Grymes**, 53, widower, farmer, b. Gloucester, residing Mid., son of Charles & Daufney Grymes, married **Deliah Harris**, 42, widow, b. & residing Mid., dau. of Wm. Wood. (C)

82B - 30 Oct. 1894 - **Wm. H. Lawson**, 32, single, farmer, b. & residing Mid., son of Thomas Y. & Sarah A. Lawson, married **Catharine B. Taliaferro**, 30, single, b. Gloucester, residing Mid., dau. of Thomas & Mary M. Taliaferro. (W)

82C - 15 Nov. 1894 - **M. B. Ashburn**, 22, single, sailor, b. & residing Lancaster, son of Griffin J. & Olivia Ashburn, married **Lucy D. Sadler**, 20, single, b. & residing Mid., dau. of A. M. & Matilda J. Sadler. (W)

83A - 1 Nov. 1894 - **John Merriwether**, 34 widower, "minister of gospel," b. Arkansas, residing Mid., son of John & Julia Merriwether, married **Coky Green**, 18, single, b. & residing Mid., dau. of Charles & Mary

Green. (C)
83B - 29 Nov. 1894 - **Isaiah Robinson**, 27, single, oysterman, b. King & Queen, residing Mid., son of General & Maria Robinson, married **Grace Boyd**, 22, single, b. & residing Mid., dau. of Joseph & Emily Boyd. (C)
83C - 6 Dec. 1894 - **Frank Gouldman**, 28, widower, farmer, b. & residing Mid., son of Elijah & June Gouldman, married **Mary Carter**, 26, single, b. Essex, residing Mid., dau. of Paul & Mary Carter. (C)
84A - 18Dec. 1894 - **Ro. Lee Muse**, 31, single, expressman, b. Mid., residing Baltimore City, son of Alfred A. & Bettie E. Muse, married **Leona Pearl Crittenden**, 24, single, b. & residing Mid., dau. of Geo. W. & Columbia F. Crittenden. (W)
84B - 19 Dec. 1894 - **C. R. Crow**, 36, single, farmer, b. Essex, residing Mid., son of Thornton & Ann Crow, married **Lucy J. Collier**, 18, single, b. Gloucester, residing Mid., dau. of Chas. H. & Catherine V. Collier. (W)
84C - 20 Dec. 1894 - **Mathew Carter**, 21, single, oysterman, b. & residing Mid., son of George & Lettie Carter, married **Pinkey Cooley**, 19, single, b. & residing Mid., dau. of Joshua & Martha Cooley. (C)
85A - 24 Dec. 1894 - **Edward Iverson**, 21, single, oysterman, b. & residing Mid., son of James & Venus Iverson, married **Josie Jarvis**, 18, single, b. Gloucester, residing Mid., dau. of Humphry & Lucy Jarvis. (C)
85B - 25 Dec. 1894 - **Geo. H. Robinson**, 24, single, farmer, b. & residing Mid., son of John H. & Margaret Robinson, married **Minnie J. Sibley**, 16, single, b. & residing Mid., dau. of R. H. & Mary S. Sibley. (W)
85C - 26 Dec. 1894 - **W. L. Griffin**, 32, single, oysterman, b. Southampton, residing Mid., son of George & Louisa Griffin, married **Mary J. Gayle**, 19, single, b. & residing Mid., dau. of Wm. A. & Eliza Gayle. (W)
86A - 27 Dec. 1894 - **Grant Ruffin**, 22, single, oysterman, b. & residing Mid., son of Louis & Caroline Ruffin, married **Bettie Burnett**, 22, single, b. & residing Mid., dau. of Kiah & Sarah Burnett. (C)
86B - 8 Jan. 1895 - **Wm. Washington**, 36, divorced, farmer, b. & residing Mid., son of George & Lucy Ann Washington, married **Macie Griffin**, 18, single, b. & residing Mid., dau. of Taylor & Mary Griffin. (C)
86C - 10 Jan. 1895 - **George Fields**, 23, single, b. & residing Mid., son of Landon & Roberta Fields, married **Lucy Johnson**, 21, single, b. & residing Mid., dau. of Andrew & Alberta Johnson. (C)
87A - 27 Dec. 1894 - **Richard Jackson**, 24, single, b.

Gloucester, residing Mid., son of Jinks & Tamer Jackson, married **Letta Ann Lymus**, 23, single, b. & residing Mid., dau. of Robert & Lucy Lymus. (C)

87B - 15 Jan. 1895 - **Henry Gibson**, 27, widower, farmer, b. & residing King & Queen, son of Edward & Bettie Gibson, married **Rachel Allen**, 16, single, b. Baltimore, Maryland, residing Mid., dau. of [parents not given, but consent signed by Mr. E. Woodward]. (W)

87C - 5 Dec. 1894 - **Addison Bagby**, 33, single, farmer, b. & residing Mid., son of Titus & Katie Bagby, married **Mary Boyd**, 37, widow, b. & residing Mid., dau. of Wm. & Mary Williams. (C)

88A - 22 Dec. 1894 - **Peyton Page**, 21, single, oysterman, b. & residing Mid., son of Manuel & Ellen Page, married **Annie Page**, 18, single, b. King & Queen, residing Mid., dau. of Stephen & Polly Page. (C)

88B - 25 Dec. 1894 - **John Taylor**, 21, single, oysterman, b. & residing Mid., son of Robert & Alice Taylor, married **Nancy Tucker**, 19, single, b. & residing Mid., dau. of Richard & Francis Tucker. (C)

88C - 23 Jan. 1895 - **Ro. H. Blackley**, 58, single, farmer, b. Essex, residing Mid., son of Ro. C. Blackley, married **Gay Ware**, 35, single, b. & residing Mid., dau. of Robert & Catharine Ware. (W)

89A - 28 Feb. 1895 - **Edward Eyre**, 30, single, sailor, b. England, residing Mid., son of Wm. & Lizzie Eyre, married **Jennie Pearson**, 23, single, b. Richmond Co., residing Mid., dau. of John & Sue Pearson. (W)

89B - 7 Mar. 1895 - **Eugene J. Miller**, 48, single, farmer, b. & residing Mid., son of Christopher & Elenora Miller, married **Mandy J. Miller**, 43, widow, b. & residing Mid., dau. of Norman Sibley. (W)

89C - 31 Mar. 1895 - **Henry Boyd**, 23, single, laborer, b. King & Queen, residing Mid., married **Hannah J. Jones**, 36, widow, b. & residing Mid. (C)

90A - 2 Mar. 1895 - **Elijah Gouldman**, 62, widower, farmer, b. & residing Mid., son of Robin Wilson & Sallie Gouldman, married **Maria Jones**, 42, divorced, b. King & Queen, residing Mid. (C)

90B - 4 Apr. 1895 - **John Ro. Brooks**, 27, single, farmer, b. & residing Mathews, son of William & Margaret Brooks, married **Columbia V. Harris**, 19, single, b. & residing Mid., dau. of David & Nancy Harris. (C)

90C - 2 May 1895 - **Thos. H. Harris**, 38, widower, oysterman, b. & residing Mid., son of Jack & Elizabeth Harris, married **Mary Alice Taylor**, 19, single, b. & residing Mid., dau. of Charles & Mary Taylor. (C)

91A - 16 Apr. 1895 - **Peter Hogg**, 36, widower, oysterman, b. & residing Gloucester, son of George & Rachel Hogg, married **Lottie L. Davis**, 17, single, b. &

residing Mid., dau. of James & Mildred Davis. (W)
91B - 11 May 1895 - **Samuel H. Jackson**, 20, single, farmer, b. & residing Mid., son of John & Bettie Jackson, married **Josephine Searborough**, 22, single, b. Accomack, residing Mid., dau. of Daniel & Sara Searborough. (C)
91C - 15 May 1895 - **Lester M. Riley**, 31, single, blacksmith, b. King & Queen, residing Mid., son of Geo. D. & Sarah A. Riley, married **Santie C. Gaines**, 18, single, b. & residing Mid., dau. of Wm. & Virginia Games. (W)
92A - 6 May 1895 - **James Bluford**, 23, single, b. King & Queen, residing Mid., son of James & Bettie Bluford, married **Maria A. Iverson**, 19, single, b. & residing Mid., dau. of James & Venus Iverson. (C)
92B - 25 May 1895 - **John Jackson**, 70, widower, farmer, b. Gloucester, residing Mid., son of Richard & Hettie Jackson, married **Lucy Ann Lymus**, 51, widower, b. King & Queen, residing Mid. (C)
92C - 26 May 1895 - **Wm. Brooks**, 25, single, b. Gloucester, residing Mid., married **Mary E. Johnson**, 19, single, b. & residing Mid. (C)
93A - 23 May 1895 - **Andrew Williams**, 25, single, farmer, b. & residing Mid., son of Albert & Bettie Williams, married **Sarah Robinson**, 27, single, b. King & Queen, residing Mid. (C)
93B - 21 May 1895 - **William T. Richardson**, 55, widower, farmer, b. King & Queen, residing Mid., son of Wm. H. & Sarah D. Richardson, married **Mary J. Hart**, 45, widow, b. King & Queen, residing Mid. (W)
93C - 5 Jun. 1895 - **Dahlgreen Cook**, 28, widower, sailor, b. King & Queen, residing Mid., son of Judy Cook, married **Ada Harris**, 17, single, b. & residing Mid., dau. of Eliza Wilson. (C)
94A - 26 Jun. 1895 - **R. K. Walden**, 32, single, farmer, b. King & Queen, residing Mid., son of William & Martha E. Walden, married **Hettie D. Franke**, 27, single, b. Milwaukee, Wisconsin, residing Mid., dau. of H. D. & Lena Franke. (W)
94B - 27 Jun. 1895 - **Beauaregard Hall**, 34, single, farmer, b. & residing Mid., son of Thomas S. & Pelina J. Hall, married **Emma L. Walker**, 26, single, b. & residing Mid., dau. of Monroe F. & E. A. Walker. (W)
94C - - 3 Jul. 1895 - **William Johnson**, 24, single, farmer, b. & residing Mid., son of Simon & Matilda Johnson, married **Mary Banks**, 19, single, b. & residing Mid., dau. of John & Laura Banks. (C)
95A - 18 Jul. 1895 - **Frank Stover**, 21, single, farmer, b. & residing Mid., son of George & Martha Stover, married **Sunie Smith**, 21, single, b. Gloucester,

residing Mid., dau. of Griffin & Lizzie Smith. (W)

95B - 22 Aug. 1895 - **J. E. Kain**, 24, single, farmer, b. & residing Mid., son of F. A. & L. A. Kain, married **Sallie S. Colly**, 18, single, b. King & Queen, residing Mid., dau. of Jas. H. & Sallie A. Colly. (W)

95C - 29 Aug. 1895 - **James Long**, 28, single, minister, b. Union Co., North Carolina, residing Rochester, New York, son of W. G. & Sarah E. Long, married **Mary E. Faulkner**, 22, single, b. Halifax Co., Virginia, residing Mid., dau. of John K. & V. C. Faulkner. (W)

96A - 29 Aug. 1895 - **James O. Powell**, 24, single, oysterman, b. Maryland, residing Mid., son of A. W. & A. Powell, married **Alice Pollard**, 29, single, b. King & Queen, residing Mid., dau. of Henry & Susan Pollard. (C)

96B - 12 Sep. 1895 - **William Shields**, 26, single, b. Norfolk, residing Mid., son of Isaac & Amanda Shields, married **Alice Pollard**, 29, single, b. King & Queen, residing Mid., dau. of Henry & Susan Pollard. (C)

96C - 29 Aug. 1895 - **Willie Smith**, 24, single, farmer, b. Gloucester, residing Mid., son of Jennie Smith, married **Blanche Ross**, 21, single, b. & residing Mid., dau. of Geo. & Ellen Ross. (C)

97A - 8 Oct. 1895 - **Thomas Hoskins**, 51, widower, oysterman, b. King & Queen, residing Mid., son of Washington & Rachel Hoskins, married **Mary Susan Carter**, 26, single, b. & residing Mid., dau. of Bettie Carter. (C)

97B - 13 Oct. 1895 - **Jas. A. Green**, 45, widower, residing Mid., married **Sarah A. Taber**, 65, single, residing Mid. (W)

97C - 16 Oct. 1895 - **Peter W. Gabor**, 35, single, oysterman, b. & residing Mid., son of John & Elizabeth Gabor, married **Phebe Pierson**, 22, single, b. Richmond Co., residing Mid., dau. of John & Fannie Pierson. (W)

98A - 18 Oct. 1895 - **Peter Jackson**, 38, widower, oysterman, b. Gloucester, residing Mid., son of John & DeLand Jackson, married **Mamie Thornton**, 23, widow, b. & residing Mid., dau. of James & Eliza Ann Nelson. (C)

98B - 29 Oct. 1895 - **E. M. Blake**, 25, single, merchant, b. Gloucester, residing Mid., son of C. L. & Kate Blake, married **Annie P. Bristow**, 19, single, b. & residing Mid., dau. of John P., Jr. & Sallie Bristow. (W)

98C - 14 Nov. 1895 - **James Muse**, 25, single, oysterman, b. & residing Mid., married **Mary Jackson**, 24, single, b. & residing Mid., dau. of Ellis & Mary Jackson. (C)

99A - 17 Nov. 1895 - **Samuel Edwards**, 27, single,

oysterman, b. & residing Essex, son of Erastus & Sallie Edwards, married **Cordelia Chamberlain**, 23, single, b. & residing Mid., dau. of George & Mollie Chamberlain. (C)

99B - 25 Nov. 1895 - **D. W. Washburn**, 25, single, traveling salesman, b. Cleveland Co., North Carolina, residing North Carolina, married **Francis C. Bristow**, 18, single, b. & residing Mid., dau. of Jos. A. & Bettie L. Bristow. (W)

99C - 28 Nov. 1895 - **Ransome Dudley**, 67, widower, farmer, b. Gloucester, residing Mid., son of John & Fannie Dudley, married **Emily Holmes**, 45, widow, b. King & Queen, residing Mid. (C)

100A - 10 Dec. 1895 - **George W. Ailworth**, 29, single, farmer, b. & residing Mid., son of Edmond W. & Martha A. Ailworth, married **Lillian E. Johnson**, 16, single, b. & residing Mid., dau. of J. W. & Lottie Johnson. (W)

100B - 11 Dec. 1895 - **Andrew J. Dunn**, 25, single, farmer, b. & residing Caroline, son of A. J. & Juliet Dunn, married **Floyd Armstrong**, 22, single, b. & residing Mid., dau. of Rich'd P. & Sarah Armstrong. (W)

100C - 12 Dec. 1895 - **Hesekiah Key**, 25, single, oysterman, b. & residing Mid., son of Carter & Catherine Key, married **Annie Green**, 21, single, b. & residing Mid., dau. of Manuel Green. (C)

101A - 15 Dec. 1895 - **W. E. Thompson**, 34, single, "minister of gospel,", b. Mecklinburg, residing Mid., son of John & Jane Thompson, married **Alice Muse**, 19, single, b. & residing Mid., dau. of Arthur & Nellie Muse. (C)

101B - 19 Dec. 1895 - **James C. Mercer**, 35, single, farmer, b. Gloucester, residing Mid., son of James C. & Elnora Mercer, married **Inez. G. Daniel**, 17, single, b. & residing Mid., dau. of Joseph & Eliza Daniel. (W)

101C - 25 Dec. 1895 - **Robert Lewis**, 27, single, oysterman, b. & residing Mid., son of Dinks & Eliza Lewis, married **Emma Thurston**, 21, single, b. Gloucester, residing Mid. (C)

102A - 26 Dec. 1895 - **Sonny Reed**, 23, single, oysterman, b. Richmond Co., residing Mid., son of Martha Reed, married **Nannie E. Johnson**, 22, single, b. & residing Mid., dau. of Simon & Matilda Johnson. (C)

102B - 25 Dec. 1895 - **Isaac Campbell**, 21, single, oysterman, b. Lancaster, residing Mid., son of Adam & Winnie Campbell, married **Bettie Curtis**, 22, single, b. King & Queen, residing Mid., dau. of Wm. & Mary Curtis. (C)

102C - 28 Dec. 1895 - **George Jones**, 48, divorced, farmer, b. & residing Mid., son of Killis & Lettie Jones, married **Rachel Anderson**, 38, widow, b. King & Queen, residing Mid. (C)

103A - 29 Dec. 1895 - **Thomas B. Smith**, 42, single, farmer, b. & residing Mid., son of Thos. B. & Margaret Smith, married **Amanda Lomax**, 25, single, b. & residing Mid., dau. of Frank & Millie Lomax. (C)

103B - 31 Dec. 1895 - **Frank Brooks**, 26, widower, oysterman, b. Gloucester, residing Mid., son of Ceaser & Mary Brooks, married **Maggie Holmes**, 24, single, b. & residing Mid., dau. of John & Mary Holmes. (C)

103C - 31 Dec. 1895 - **Samuel E. Walden**, 30, single, merchant, b. King & Queen, residing Mid., son of William & Martha E. Walden, married **Virgie M. Beazly**, 25, single, b. & residing Mid., dau. of George P. & Judy Beazly. (W)

104A - 8 Jan. 1896 - **Andrew Jackson**, 24, widower, oysterman, b. & residing Mid., son of Jeremiah & Elizabeth Jackson, married **Daisey D. Hart**, 21, single, b. & residing Mid., dau. of Jas. H. & Mary E. Hart. (W)

104B - 15 Dec. 1895 - **Josiah Campbell**, 28, single, oysterman, b. & residing Mid., son of Lee & Louisa Campbell, married **Sunie Johnson**, 23, single, b. & residing Mid., dau. of Simon & Matilda Johnson. (C)

104C - 25 Dec. 1895 - **James Eddie Robinson**, 24, single, oysterman, b. & residing Mid., son of Alex Robinson, married **Rosa Waller**, 20, single, b. & residing Mid., dau. of H. C. & Catherine Waller. (C)

105A - 29 Dec. 1895 - **Thos. H. Waller**, 34, single, oysterman, b. & residing Essex, son of Clay & Catherin Waller, married **Mattie Boyd**, 24, single, b. King & Queen, residing Mid., dau. of Wm. & Sarah Roane. (C)

105B - 29 Jan. 1896 - **E. S. Sydnor**, 23, single, fireman, b. Dinwiddie, residing Allegheny, son of Thos. J. & Amanda Sydnor, married **Carrie F. Whitmore**, 22, single, b. Dinwiddie, residing Mid., dau. of Geo. A. & Amanda Whitmore. (W)

105C - 29 Jan. 1896 - **John Carter**, 22, single, oysterman, b. York Co., residing Mid., son of Lewis & Sallie Carter, married **Sallie Young**, 21, single, b. & residing Mid., dau. of Sheadrick & Sallie Young. (C)

106A - 6 Feb. 1896 - **James Hy Colley**, 51, widower, farmer, b. King & Queen, residing Mid., son of William & Sallie Colley, married **Elanore Bartlett**, 28, widow, b. King & Queen, residing Mid., dau. of Peter & Martha Davis. (W)

106B - 12 Feb. 1896 - **J. Q. Collie**, 24, single, farmer, b. King & Queen, residing Mid., son of James P. & Mary J. Collie, married **Theodocia E. Blake**, 22, single, b. & residing Mid., dau. of B. S. & Cornelia Blake. (W)

106C - 13 Feb. 1896 - **Elijah Cary**, 27, single, oysterman, b. & residing Mid., son of Henry Cary, married **Sarah E. Harris**, 22, single, b. & residing Mid., dau. of David & Nancy Harris. (C)

107A - 28 Jan. 1896 - **Stanley J. Barnes**, 25, single, b. North Carolina, residing Mid., son of John & Sarah Barnes, married **Fannie W. Kemp**, 21, single, b. & residing Mid., dau. of Mathew & Sallie Kemp. (W)

107B - 12 Feb. 1896 - **Thomas J. Chowning**, 27, single, farmer, b. & residing Mid., son of James & Ann E. Chowning, married **Maggie R. Ward**, 20, single, b. & residing Mid., dau. of A. D. & C. C. Ward. (W)

107C - 13 Feb. 1896 - **Jas. H. Goode**, 55, single, farmer, b. Essex, residing Mid., son of John & Juliza Goode, married **Mary S. Ball**, 21, single, b. & residing Mid., dau. of Taswell & Polly Ball. (W)

108A - 25 Dec. 1896 [sic - should be 1895, as license was returned in Feb. 1896] - **G. T. Goode**, 28, single, farmer, b. Essex, residing Mid., son of James H. & Mary Goode, married **Lina Julia Groome**, 20, single, b. & residing Mid., dau. of William & Julia Groome. (W)

108B - 16 FEb. 1896 - **Edward Walden**, 25, widower, oysterman, b. & residing Mid., son of Henry & Martha Walden, married **Alice Tabor**, 21, single, b. Mathews, residing Mid., dau. of Thos. & Sarah Tabor. (W)

108C - 16 Feb. 1896 - **Geo. B. Koegel**, 29, single, merchant, b. New York state, residing Mid., son of Nicolas & Mary E. Koegel, married **Lucy E. Daniel**, 21, single, b. & residing Mid., dau. of Wm. H. & Isabella Daniel. (W)

109A - 25 Feb. 1896 - **J. L. Montgomery**, 35, widower, farmer, b. & residing Mid., son of James & Eliza Montgomery, married **Bertha Wilson**, 22, single, b. & residing Mid., dau. of George & Mary Wilson. (W)

109B - 8 Mar. 1896 - **John Norris**, 22, single, oysterman, b. & residing Mid., son of Jessie & Lucy Norris, married **Ada Johnson**, 15, single, b. Gloucester, residing Mid., dau. of Lucy Johnson. (C)

109C - 26 Mar. 1896 - **W. F. Garnett**, 25, single, oysterman, b. & residing Mid., son of John T. & Sallie Garnett, married **Maria Johnson**, 17, single, b. & residing Mid., dau. of Doctor & Mandy Johnson. (C)

110A - 12 Apr. 1896 - **Wm. Stuart**, 26, single, oysterman, b. Gloucester, residing Mid., son of George & Lizzie Stuart, married **Mattie Gundy**, 22, single, b. & residing Mid., dau. of Linday Gundy. (C)

110B - 30 Apr. 1896 - **Wm. Green**, 22, single, oysterman, b. King & Queen, residing Mid., son of Richard & Mary Green, married **Alice Boyd**, 22, single, b. & residing Mid., dau. of Washington & Chris Boyd. (C)

110C - 25 Mar. 1896 - **Ro. Logan Street**, 22, single, farmer, b. & residing Mid., son of R. H. & V. A. Street,

married **Ruby P. Carlton**, 21, single, b. & residing Mid., dau. of H. L. & Virginia Carlton. (W)
    111A - 3 May 1896 - **John Spillman**, 26, single, oysterman, b. Lancaster, residing Mid., son of Wm. & Mary Spillman, married **Dora McKenny**, 21, single, b. Essex, residing Mid., dau. of Thomas & Mary McKenny. (W)
    111B - 3 May 1896 - **John Key**, 42, single, b. & residing Mid., married **Bettie Williams**, 30, single, b. & residing Mid., dau. of Zachariah & Charity Williams. (C)
    111C - 20 May 1896 - **Charles Roy**, 24, single, oysterman, b. & residing Mid., son of Joseph & Dinah Roy, married **Judith Mathews**, 26, single, b. Accomack, residing Mid., dau. of Leah Mathews. (C)
    112A - 14 May 1896 - **Gustine Lewis**, 25, single, farmer, b. King & Queen, residing Mid., son of Albert & Agnes Lewis, married **Maggie King**, 22, single, b. King & Queen, residing Mid., dau. of Adam & Mary King. (C)
    112B - 20 May 1896 - **John Gouldman**, 23, single, oysterman, b. & residing Mid., son of John & Francis Gouldman, married **Maria Bush**, 22, single, b. & residing Mid., dau. of Hannah Bush. (C)
    112C - 8 Jun. 1896 - **L. M. Carlton**, 24, single, sailor, b. King & Queen, residing Mid., son of Richard & Lettie A. Carlton, married **Lee H. Major**, 24, single, b. & residing Mid., dau. of L. O. B. & Mary Major. (W)
    113A - 18 Dec. 1895 - **Wm. H. Carter**, 26, single, merchant, b. Mid., residing Spotsylvania, son of Ro. R. & Mary A. Carter, married **Sallie D. Hancock**, 21, single, b. & residing Spotsylvania, dau. of F. J. & Mary E. Hancock. (W)
    113B - 14 May 1896 - **Rolly Banks**, 29, divorced, farmer, b. King & Queen, residing Mid., son of Latane & Sarah Banks, married **Martha Foster**, 22, single, b. & residing Mid., dau. of George & Hannah Foster. (C)
    113C - 4 Jun. 1896 - **Roderick H. Bland**, 31, single, merchant, b. King & Queen, residing Mid., son of Roderick & A. B. Bland, married **Blanche Carlton**, 30, single, b. & residing Mid., dau. of John A. & Eliza Carlton. (W)
    114A - 7 Jul. 1896 - **Thomas Ritchie Bland**, 36, single, merchant, b. King & Queen, residing Essex, son of Roderick & A. B. Bland, married **Lucille Florence Carlton**, 25, single, b. & residing Mid., dau. of Jno. A. & Eliza Carlton. (W)
    114B - 13 Aug. 1896 - **Moses J. Johnson**, 38, widower, carpenter, b. King & Queen, residing Mid., son of Maurice & Annie Johnson, married **Susie A. Moody**, 22, single, b. & residing Mid., dau. of Gustavus & Rebecca

Moody. (C)

114C - 1 Sep. 1896 - **Wm. H. Roane**, 26, widower, oysterman, b. King & Queen, residing Mid., son of Wm. F. & Sarah Roane, married **Millie Ann Kemp**, 22, single, b. & residing Mid., dau. of Mary Kemp. (C)

115A - 1 Sep. 1896 - **Sam'l L. Brown**, 24, single, merchant, b. King & Queen, residing Mid., son of James & Maria Brown, married **Louie P. Trader**, 19, single, b. & residing Mid., dau. of Alexander & Sarah Trader. (W)

115B - Sep. 1896 - **John Lewis**, 25, single, farmer, b. & residing Mid., son of Albert & Bella Lewis, married **Sarah Davis**, 19, single, b. Essex, residing Mid., dau. of Listem & Sarah Davis. (C)

115C - 7 Oct. 1896 - **George Major**, 22, single, oysterman, b. Gloucester, residing Mid., son of Alfred & Maria Major, married **Mary Griffin**, 21, single, b. & residing Mid., dau. of Green & Judy Griffin. (C)

116A - 20 Oct. 1896 - **John J. Bennett**, , widower, farmer, b. & residing Mid., son of William & Adeline Bennett, married **Fannie L. Bristow**, 32, single, b. & residing Mid., dau. of Lewis S. & Octavius Bristow. (W)

116B - 1 Nov. 1896 - **Willie Walker**, 22, single, oysterman, b. Gloucester, residing Mid., son of Thornton & Julia Walker, married **Mary Gundy**, 28, single, b. Essex, residing Mid., dau. of James & Malinda Gundy. (C)

116C - 5 Nov. 1896 - **James Davis**, 28, single, oysterman, b. & residing Mid., son of Robert & Mary Davis, married **Maggie Foster**, 22, single, b. & residing Mid., dau. of John & Reuthie Foster. (W)

117A - 4 Nov. 1896 - **Melville W. Revere**, 35, single, sailor, b. & residing Mid., son of Jas. B. & Farly P. Revere, married **L. C. Hall**, 26, single, b. & residing Mid., dau. of John A. & Lucy H. Hall. (W)

117B - 22 Oct. 1896 - **Napoleon B. Taylor**, 21, single, oysterman, b. & residing Mid., son of Thomas & Annie Taylor, married **Hester Taylor**, 17, single, b. & residing Mid. (C)

117C - 12 Nov. 1896 - **Robert S. Bristow**, 44, widower, merchant, b. & residing Mid., son of Larkin S. & Catherine Bristow, married **Nellie G. Christian**, 35, single, b. & residing Mid., dau. of William S. & Hellen E. Christian. (W)

118A - 4 Nov. 1896 - **George R. West**, 24, single, farmer, b. King & Queen, residing Mid., son of Alex & Ann Eliza West, married **Pinkie Kidd**, 19, single, b. & residing Mid., dau. of James & Parke Kidd. (C)

118B - 21 Nov. 1896 - **Amos Johnson**, 21, single, oysterman, b. Mathews, residing Mid., son of Amos & Eliza Johnson, married **Emma Jackson**, 17, single, b. &

residing Mid., dau. of Samuel & Fannie Jackson. (C)

118C - 25 Nov. 1896 - **John Mason Dew**, 35, single, farmer, b. & residing King & Queen, son of Roderick & Julia Dew, married **Lillian S. Segar**, 25, single, b. & residing Mid., dau. of Jn. R., Sr. & Sallie Segar. (W)

119A - 16 Dec. 1896 - **Lester Clyde Crittenden**, 25, single, oysterman, b. & residing Mid., son of George W. & Columbia F. Crittenden, married **Maud Olive Pace**, 22, single, b. & residing Mid., dau. of Harley E. & Fannie E. Pace. (W)

119B - 24 Dec. 1896 - **Cuffy Washington, Jr.**, 28, single, farmer, b. Washington, D. C., residing Mid., son of Moses & Frances Washington, married **Belle Fossett**, 20, single, b. & residing Mid., dau. of Wallace & Fannie Fossett. (C) [For more information on the family of Moses Washington see Jett, *Howland School, 1867* and the journal and letters of Miss Emily Howland, founder of Howland School in Northumberland County, Virginia. See also, Breault, Judith Colucci, *The World of Emily Howland*, (Millbrae, CA: Les Femmes, 1976).]

119C - 23 Dec. 1896 - **Willie Smith**, 30, single, farmer, b. King & Queen, residing Mid., son of William & Maria Smith, married **Malisie Bagby**, 21, single, b. & residing Mid., dau. of Washington & Polly Bagby. (C)

120A - 24 Dec. 1896 - **Charles Stewart**, 24, single, oysterman, b. Gloucester, residing Mid., son of Parker & Lizzie Stewart, married **Ida Gundy**, 21, single, b. & residing Mid., dau. of James & Lindy Gundy. (C)

120B - 23 Dec. 1896 - **Elgie D. Moor**, 24, single, oysterman, b. & residing Mid., son of Wm. P. & Mary E. Moore, married **Almedia S. Moffett**, 19, single, b. & residing Mid., dau. of E. W. & Eva Moffett. (W)

120C - 30 Dec. 1896 - **Robinson Bristow**, 23, single, farmer, b. Gloucester, residing Mid., son of Edward & Eliza Bristow, married **Mary S. Lawson**, 16, single, b. King & Queen, residing Mid., dau. of Wm. C. & Mary S. Lawson. (W)

121A - 30 Dec. 1896 - **Japeth Redd**, 27, single, farmer, b. King & Queen, residing Mid., son of J. E. & Mary E. Redd, married **Virginia V. Seawell**, 21, single, b. Gloucester, residing Mid., dau. of W. O. & Dora Seawell. (W)

121B - 23 Dec. 1896 - **Zack Braxton**, 33, single, farmer, b. & residing Mid., son of Henry & Betsey Braxton, married **Celia Burrell**, 23, single, b. & residing Mid., dau. of Jessie & Hester Burrell. (C)

121C - 30 Dec. 1896 - **Joseph Goldman**, 22, single, oysterman, b. & residing Mid., son of Elijah & Jane Goldman, married **Mollie Scott**, 21, single, b. & residing Mid., dau. of Henry & Eliza Scott. (C)

122A - 24 Dec. 1896 - **Thornton Monroe**, 21, single, b. Maryland, residing Mid., son of Beckey Monroe, married **Jannie Burrell**, 18, single, b. & residing Mid., dau. of Robert & Josephine Bird.
122B - 30 Dec. 1896 - **Granville Nelson**, 21, single, oysterman, b. & residing Mid., son of Henry Helson, married **Kizzie Key**, 22, single, b. & residing Mid., dau. of Carter & Catherine Key. (C)
122C - 30 Dec. 1896 - **Jas. H. Kimbell**, 24, single, oysterman, b. & residing Mid., son of James & Sallie Kimball, married **Rosa Redd**, 19, single, b. & residing Mid., dau. of Isaac & Fannie Reed. (C) [See Marriage Register 2, 1876-1890, document 33B.]
123A - 24 Dec. 1896 - **John Davenport**, 24, single, oysterman, b. King & Queen, residing Mid., son of Joshua & Mary Davenport, married **Lizzie Campbell**, 21, single, b. & residing Mid., dau. of James & Esperilla Campbell. (C)
123B - 30 Dec. 1896 - **Thomas Davis**, 26, single, oysterman, b. & residing Mid., son of Reubin & Jennie Davis, married **Bettie Boyd**, 25, single, b. & residing Mid., dau. of John & Julia Boyd. (C)
123C - No record.
124A - 6 Jan. 1898 - **Daniel Dixon**, 25, single, farmer, b. Chambersburg, Pennsylvania, residing Mid., son of J. J. & Lidia Dixon, married **Mary Ellen Carter**, 18, single, b. King & Queen, residing Mid., dau. of John W. & Susannah Carter. (W)
124B - 29 Dec. 1896 - **Willie Payne**, 22, single, farmer, b. & residing Mid., son of Wm. Payne & Martha Foster, married **Rosa Davis**, 22, single, b. & residing Mid., dau. of George & Anna Davis. (C)
124C - 30 Dec. 1896 - **Anderson Harris**, 59, widower, farmer, b. & residing Mid., son of Henry & Margaret Harris, married **Anna Jackson**, 60, widow, b. King & Queen, residing Mid. (C)
125A - 30 Dec. 1896 - **Nathaniel Norris**, 26, single, farmer, b. & residing Mid., son of Julius & Mary Norris, married **Elizabeth Robinson**, 17, single, b. & residing Mid., dau. of Benjamin & C. A. Robinson. (C)
125B - 29 Dec. 1896 - **John Harris**, 23, single, oysterman, b. King & Queen, residing Mid., son of Wm. & Juliann Harris, married **Dora Reed**, 24, single, b. & residing Mid., dau. of Jessee & Laura Reed. (C)
125C - 3 Dec. 1896 - **E. G. Street**, 26, single, farmer, b. & residing Mid., son of R. H. & Virginia H. Street, married **Maggie V. Carlton**, 21, single, b. & residing Mid., dau. of H. L. & Virginia Carlton. (W)
126A - 25 Jan. 1897 - **Jas. W. Hoge**, 42, widower, farmer, b. & residing King & Queen, son of Wm. & Julia

Hoge, married **Mary E. South**, 32, single, b. Mid., residing King & Queen, dau. of Ann E. South. (W)

126B - 4 Jan. 1897 - **Iverson Brown**, 26, single, oysterman, b. Essex, residing Mid., son of Eligah & Judy Brown, married **Lucy J. Moody**, 24, single, b. & residing Mid., dau. of R. Augustin & Rebecca Moody. (C)

126C- 1 Feb. 1897 - **James Richardson**, 23, single, b. Washington, D. C., residing Mid., married **Emma J. Jackson**, 20, single, b. & residing Mid., dau. of Ellis & Grace Jackson.

127A - 31 Jan. 1897 - **Henry Stokes**, 39, widower, farmer, b. Gloucester, residing Mid., son of Christopher & Ann Stokes, married **Betty Bundy**, 39, widow, b. & residing Mid., dau. of Martha Ann Stokes. (C)

127B - 20 Jan. 1897 - **Jas. H. Webb**, 28, single, farmer, b. & residing Mid., son of John & Betsy Webb, married **Mary E. Williams**, 22, single, b. & residing Mid., dau. of Henderson & Cath. Williams. (C)

127C - 4 Feb. 1897 - **James E. Harris**, 28, single, oysterman, b. & residing Mid., son of Robt. & Fannie Harris, married **Elizabeth J. Webb**, 24, single, b. & residing Mid., dau. of John & Betsy Webb. (C)

128A - 4 Mar. 1897 - **Albert Williams**, 43, widower, well digger, married **Susan Johnson**, 19, single, b. & residing Mid., dau. of Henry Garnett & Mary Johnson. (C)

128B - 16 Feb. 1897 - **Thos W. Wright**, 22, single, oysterman, b. & residing Mid., son of Wm. W. & Elizabeth Wright, married **Carrie V. Snead**, 19, single, b. & residing Mid., dau. of Jno. M. & Mary E. Snead. (W)

128C - 2 Mar. 1897 - **John Mason**, 25, single, oysterman, b. & residing Mid., son of Jas. Thornton & Mary Taylor, married **Hattie Smith**, 16, single, b. & residing Mid., dau. of Benj. & Lucy Smith. (C)

129A - 16 Mar. 1897 - **Wm. Bush**, 26, single, oysterman, b. & residing Mid., son of Chas. & Hannah Bush, married **Pelle Norris**, 22, single, b. & residing Mid., dau. of Noah & Kitty Norris. (C)

129B - 18 Mar. 1897 - **Chas Towles**, 34, single, minister, b. Lancaster, residing West Point [Virginia], son of Mary J. Lee, married **L. A. V. Harris**, 29, single, b. Mid., residing West Point, dau. of Geo. & Lucy Harris. (C)

129C - 28 Mar. 1897 - **Willie Burrell**, 26, single, oysterman, b. Gloucester, residing Mid., son of Wm. & Mary Burrell, married **Rosa Temple**, 24, single, b. & residing Mid. (C)

130A - 31 Mar. 1897 - **Richard Laws**, 26, single, oysterman, b. & residing Mid., son of Miles C. & Francis Laws, married **Pinkie Carter**, 18, single, b. & residing

Mid., dau. of Paul & Mary Carter. (C)

130B - 18 Mar. 1897 - **Augustus Travis**, 22, single, farmer, b. Gloucester, residing Mid., son of Carl & Judy Travis, married **Dolly Holliday**, 18, single, b. Essex, residing Mid., dau. of R. H. & Addie Holliday. (C)

130C - 14 Apr. 1897 - **Nelson Johnson**, 22, single, oysterman, b. & residing Mid., son of Nelson & Betty Johnson, married **Ella Taliaferro**, 19, single, b. & residing Mid., dau. of Rebecca Robinson. (C)

131A - 27 Apr. 1897 - **Sam'l Vanburen Hurley**, 23, single, oysterman & farmer, b. & residing Mid., son of Sam'l & Leavey Hellen Hurley, married **Nannie Ware Hardy**, 22, single, b. Tennessee, residing Mid., dau. of John & Louisa Hardy. (W)

131B - 20 May 1897 - **Bernard Boyd Dunston**, 26, single, farmer, b. Isle of Wight, residing Gloucester, son of Powathan & Rebecca A. Dunston, married **Nannie B. Gunn**, 26, single, b. King & Queen, residing Mid., dau. of Wm. T. & Mary E. Gunn. (W)

131C - 27 Apr. 1897 - **Thomas Clayton Hurly**, 32, single, mechanic, b. Kent Co., Maryland, residing Mid., son of David & Jane Hurly, married **Bessie Crittenden**, 23, single, b. & residing Mid., dau. of Geo. W. & C. F. Crittenden. (W)

132A - 1 May 1897 - **Charles Robinson**, 24, single, farmer, b. & residing Mid., son of Spottsy. & Francis Robinson, married **Elsie Page**, 18, single, b. & residing Mid., dau. of Manuel & Ellen Page. (C)

132B - 9 Jun. 1897 - **Geo. Richard Northam**, 34, single, merchant, b. & residing Mid., son of H. C. & Susan H. Northam, married **Sallie Richardson**, 22, single, b. King & Queen, residing Mid., dau. of W. T. & Sarah Richardson. (W)

132C - 16 Jun. 1897 - **Julius C. Sale**, 44, widower, farmer, b. & residing Caroline, son of Thomas & Elizabeth Sale, married **Sue B. Evans**, 33, single, b. & residing Mid., dau. of J. M. & E. B. Evans. (W)

133A - 2 Jun. 1897 - **Henry C. Farinholt**, 23, single, oyster dealer, b. Essex, residing Mid., dau. of B. L. & Lelia M. Farinholt, married **Clare M. Carlton**, 23, single, b. & residing Mid., dau. of John A. & Eliza Carlton. (W)

133B - 23 Jun. 1897 - **Jos. W. Revere**, 33, single, oysterman, b. & residing Mid., son of James & Folly Revere, married **Maud L. Keilingham**, 22, single, b. & residing Mid., dau. of Julius & Mollie Keilingham. (W)

133C - 23 Jun. 1897 - **Kerney Yates**, 22, single, oysterman, b. & residing Mid., son of Robert & Mary Yates, married **Ida May Ailsworth**, 21, single, b. & residing Mid., dau. of Robert & Mary Ailsworth. (W)

134A - 26 Jul. 1897 - **James Little**, 25, single, oysterman, b. Tarboro, North Carolina, residing Mid., son of Wright Little, married **Delia Carter**, 24, single, b. & residing Mid., dau. of Robert A. Carter. (C)
134B - 5 Aug. 1897 - **Willie H. Banks**, 25, single, oysterman, b. & residing Mid., son of Lewis & Nancy Banks, married **Belle Roy**, 21, single, b. & residing Mid., dau. of Chas. & Bettie Roy. (B)
134C - 19 Aug. 1897 - **Richard Holmes**, 33, widower, oysterman, b. & residing Mid., son of John & Rachel Holmes, married **Louisa Monroe**, 27, single, b. Maryland, residing Mid., dau. of Alfred & Annie Monroe. (B)
135A - 21 Aug. 1897 - **Sandy Bottom**, 22, single, oysterman, b. & residing Mid., son of Ro. & Annie Howlett, married **Sallie Chrisanger**, 24, b. & residing Mid. (W)
135B - 21 Aug. 1897 - **Ben Smith**, 65, widower, oysterman, b. Goucester, residing Mid., son of Elijah & Fannie Smith, married **Hannah Sales**, 55, widow, b. Goucester, residing Mid., dau. of Harry & Isabella Sales. (B)
135C - 19 Aug. 1897 - **Johnson Ackers**, 22, single, farmer, b. & residing Mid., son of Johnson & Lucy Ackers, married **Sarah Burnett**, 21, single, b. & residing Mid., dau. of Hezekiah & Lucy Burnett. (B)
136A - 9 Sep. 1897 - **Thos. H. Wormley**, 42, widower, farmer, b. & residing Mid., son of Thos. & Isabella Wormley, married **Virginia Laws**, 20, single, b. & residing Mid., dau. of Miles & Fannie Laws. (B)
136B - 16 Sep. 1897 - **Chas. Henry Banks**, 23, single, oysterman, b. & residing Mid., son of Lewis & Vaney Banks, married **Mamie Boyd**, 21, single, b. & residing Mid., dau. of Allen & Judy Boyd. (C)
136C - 15 Sep. 1897 - **Charles Jackson**, 27, single, oysterman, b. & residing Mid., son of John & Cordelia Jackson, married **Elizabeth Richardson**, 21, single, b. & residing Mid., dau. of Lewis & Ann Richardson. (C)
137A - 22 Sep. 1897 - **Chas. D. Moody**, 26, single, oysterman, b. & residing Mid., son of Carter & Priscilla Moody, married **Cora Byrd**, 25, single, b. & residing Mid., dau. of Emory & Catherine Byrd. (C)
137B - 25 Sep. 1897 - **Richard A. Oliver**, 23, single, oysterman, b. Essex, residing Mid., son of Allen & Nellie Oliver, married **Margaret Holmes**, 17, single, b. King & Queen, residing Mid., dau. of Sampson & Martha Holmes. (C)
137C - 30 Sep. 1897 - **Rob't G. Banks**, 25, single, farmer, b. King & Queen, residing Mid., son of Geo. & Winnie Banks, married **Ella T. Peyton**, 23, single, b. & residing Mid., dau. of Solomon & Fannie Peyton. (C)

138A - 30 Sep. 1897 - **Geo. W. Morris**, 22, single, oysterman, b. & residing Mid., son of John & Rose Morris, married **Lizzie Robinson**, 21, single, b. & residing Mid., dau. of Joe & Cely Robinson. (C)
138B - 3 Oct. 1897 - **Robert Crump**, 23, single, oysterman, b. & residing Mid., son of Chas. H. & Mary E. Crump, married **Ida Garnett**, 17, single, b. King & Queen, residing Mid., dau. of Henry & Fannie E. Garnett. (C)
138C - 6 Oct. 1897 - **W. F. Kennard**, 24, single, farmer, b. & residing Mid., son of W. J. & M. J. Kennard, married **Mattie Johnson**, 23, single, b. Goucester, residing Mid., dau. of Thomas & J. Johnson. (W)
139A - 14 Oct. 1897 - **Walter H. Ashberry**, 32, single, shoe & bootmaker, b. Mathews, residing Mid., son of Wm. H. & Ann E. Ashberry, married **Mamie C. Archibald**, 18, single, b. & residing Mid., dau. of J. H. & Mary Archibald. (W)
139B - 14 Oct. 1897 - **Rob't G. Chowning**, 32, single, carpenter, b. & residing Mid., son of James & Ann E. Chowning, married **Mattie Archibald**, 19, single, b. & residing Mid., dau. of J. H. & Mary Archibald. (W)
139C - 17 Oct. 1897 - **James E. Ransom**, 45, widower, farmer, b. Goucester, residing Mid., son of J. W. & Mary A. Ransom, married **Mary Lillie Hibble**, 18, single, b. Goucester, residing Mid., dau. of Geo. W. & Martha E. Hibble. (W)
140A - 26 Oct. 1897 - **David K. Garnett**, 32, single, teacher, b. & residing Mid., son of Booker & Bettie Garnett, married **Lelia W. Bland**, 36, widow, b. & residing Mid., dau. of Wm. & Alice Shackelford. (W)
140B - 2 Nov. 1897 - **W. W. Haynes**, 27, single, merchant, b. King & Queen, residing Richmond, son of W. T. & Celia Haynes, married **Lillie M. Evans**, 25, single, b. & residing Mid., dau. of J. M. & Ellen B. Evans. (W)
140C - 28 Oct. 1897 - **Chas. A. Ashburn**, 26, single, mariner, b. & residing Lancaster, son of Lewis E. & Mary E. Ashburn, married **Annie M. Sadler**, 16, single, b. & residing Mid., dau. of A. M. & Matilda Sadler. (W)
141A - 10 Nov. 1897 - **Emmett S. Christopher**, 36, widower, oysterman, b. & residing Mid., son of Riley & Fannie Ann Christopher, married **Victoria L. Green**, 20, single, b. Portsmouth, residing Mid., dau. of James & Virginia L. V. Green. (W)
141B - 11 Nov. 1897 - **Washington Reed**, 34, widower, oysterman, b. & residing Mid., son of Kendal & Hannah Reed, married **Mary Cook**, 21, single, b. & residing Mid., dau. of James & Louisa Cook. (C)
141C - 23 Nov. 1897 - **Daniel Abbott**, 21, single, oysterman, b. Northampton, residing Lancaster, son of J.

Tom & Jane T. Abbott, married **Ida A. Hibble**, 15, single, b. Goucester, residing Mid., dau. of Geo. W. & Martha Hibble. (W)

142A - 28 Nov. 1897 - **Columbus Hearn**, 26, single, oysterman, b. & residing Mid., son of William & Sallie Hearn, married **Cora Montgomery**, 19, single, b. & residing Mid., dau. of J. L. & Mary Montgomery. (W)

142B - 11 Dec. 1897 - **John A. Daniel**, 25, single, farmer, b. & residing Mid., son of George & Mary Daniel, married **Jennie Dutton**, 23, single, b. Goucester, residing Mid., parents "dead." (W)

142C - 8 Dec. 1897 - **Wm. G. New**, 50, widower, carpenter, b. & residing Mid., son of J. C. & Louisa M. New, married **Sallie B. Greenwood**, 24, single, b. Essex, residing Mid., dau. of Wm. & Sarah Greenwood. (W)

143A - 9 Dec. 1897 - **Thos. Lewis**, 21, single, oysterman, b. & residing Mid., son of Sam & Lucy Ann Lewis, married **Lizzie Mason**, 23, single, b. Mathews, residing Mid., parents "both dead, don't know names." (C)

143B - 17 Dec. 1897 - **Vespasian Walden**, 24, single, farmer, b. & residing Mid., son of Henry Walden, married **Jane Kellum**, 21, single, b. & residing Mid., parents "dead." (W)

143C - 5 Dec. 1897 - **John N. Rowe**, 40, single, oysterman, b. King & Queen, residing Mid., son of Nelson & Eliza Banks, married **Mary Julia Smith Dangerfield**, 32, widow, b. & residing Mid., dau. of John & Jane Smith. (C)

144A - 11 Dec. 1897 - **Robert Baylor**, 35, single, oysterman, b. & residing Mid., son of John & Circe Baylor, married **Eliza Fields**, 45, single, b. & residing Mid., dau. of Fielding & Catherine Fields. (C)

144B - 23 Dec. 1897 - **James Morris, Jr.**, 39, widower, oysterman, b. & residing Mid., son of Frank & Martha Morris, married **Bettie Alice Smith**, 24, single, b. & residing Mid., dau. of John & Emma Jane Smith. (C)

144C - 23 Dec. 1897 - **Samuel J. Lewis**, 40, widower, oysterman, b. & residing Mid., son of Frank & Amy Lewis, married **Millie Lomax**, 39, widow, b. & residing Mid., dau. of Zishery & Martha Ward. (C)

145A - 29 Dec. 1897 - **Henry Taliaferro**, 21, single, oysterman, b. King & Queen, residing Mid., son of John & Euphemia Taliaferro, married **Georgianna Lymus**, 24, single, b. & residing Mid., dau. of Jno. & Lucy Lymus. (C)

145B - 28 Dec. 1897 - **Clarence W. Mercer**, 29, single, wheelright, son of John L. & Louisa Mercer, married **Daisy Vivian Garland**, 19, single, b. & residing Mid., dau. of Rob't & Amanda Garland. (W)

145C - Repeat of 145B.
146A - 30 Dec. 1897 - **Junius A. Byrd**, 21, single, oysterman, b. King & Queen, residing Mid., son of Augustus & Mary Byrd, married **Mary Johnson**, 20, single, b. & residing Mid., dau. of Washington & Hester Johnson. (C)
146B - 23 Dec. 1897 - **Thos. J. Revere**, 26, single, wheelright, b. & residing Mid., son of McKay & Sarah Revere, married **Maud C. Walker**, 25, single, b. & residing Mid., dau. of Monroe & Lizzie Walker. (W)
146C - 29 Dec. 1897 - **Richard Tucker**, 24, single, oysterman, b. & residing Mid., son of Dick & Fannie Tucker, married **Alice Richardson**, 20, single, b. & residing Mid., grandaughter of Millie Washington. (C)
147A - 17 Jan. 1898 - **William King**, 30, widower, oysterman, b. King & Queen, residing Mid., married **Sarah Burrell**, 18, single, b. & residing Mid., dau. of Thomas & Mary Ann Burrell. (C)
147B - 13 Jan. 1898 - **William Roane**, 26, single, oysterman, b. & residing Mid., son of Bettie Roane, married **Frances Fields**, 25, single, b. & residing Mid., dau. of Nancy Fields. (C)
147C - 23 Dec. 1897 - **Harry E. Robinson**, 23, single, oysterman, b. & residing Mid., son of Spottswood & Fannie Robinson, married **Jennie A. Morris**, 22, single, b. & residing Mid., dau. of James & Bell Morris. (C)
148A - 26 Dec. 1897 - **James H. Moody**, 28, single, oysterman, b. & residing Mid., son of Augustus & Rebecca Moody, married **Mary E. Holmes**, 23, single, b. & residing Mid., dau. of Geo. & Anna Holmes. (C)
148B - 27 Jan. 1898 - **John Laws**, 22, single, farmer, b. & residing Mid., son of Frank & Fannie Laws, married **Alice Bumpass**, 21, single, b. North Carolina, residing Mid. (C)
148C - 1 Feb. 1898 - **Samuel Thornton**, 23, single, oysterman, b. & residing Mid., son of Anthony & Eliza Thornton, married **Ada Gregory**, 21, single, b. & residing Mid., dau. of Peter & Eliza Gregory. (C)
149A - 2 Feb. 1898 - **Morris A. Kellum**, 22, single, oysterman, b. & residing Mid., son of Wm. & Alice Kellum, married **Amelia Wilson**, 21, single, b. & residing Mid., dau. of N. G. & Vir. W. G. Wilson. (W)
149B - 2 Feb. 1898 - **Fillmore Henry**, 40, widower, farmer, b. & residing Mid., son of Patrick & Louisa Henry, married **Jane Johnson**, dau. of Samuel Johnson & Lucy Patterson. (C)
149C - 12 Feb. 1898 - **Chas. R. Grinels**, 23, single, merchant, b. & residing Mid., son of S. & Sallie Grinels, married **Mildred A. Cundiff**, 23, single, b. & residing Mid., dau. of J. T. & Neale Cundiff. (W)

150A - 17 Feb. 1898 - **James Taliaferro**, 27, single, oysterman, b. & residing Mid., son of Martha Taliaferro, married **Maggie Harris**, 26, single, b. & residing Mid., dau. of Nancy & David Harris. (C)

150B - 16 Feb. 1898 - **Thos C. Garrett**, 27, single, farmer, b. King & Queen, residing Mid., son of Thos. C. & Polly A. Garrett, married **Ella Johnson**, 22, single, b. Essex, residing Mid., dau. of John Lewis & Johnson. (W)

150C - 2 Feb. 1898 - **James Gressum**, 28, single, oysterman, b. & residing Mid., son of Sam & Anna Gressum, married **Linda Ann Miller**, 28, single, b. & residing Mid., dau. of John & Susan Miller. (C)

151A - 24 Feb. 1898 - **James Johnson**, 23, single, oysterman, son of Davy & Mary Johnson, married **Addie Woods**, 17, "consent by S. Grenels," single, b. & residing Mid., dau. of Chrissie Wilson. (C)

151B - This marriage was "returned not executed." [However, the couple, James R. Davis and Lucy Blake, married later. See 153A.]

151C - 1 Mar. 1898 - **John Jackson**, 21, single, oysterman, b. & residing Mid., son of Ellis & Grace Jackson, married **Lena Jones**, 25, single, b. & residing Mid., dau. of Mary & Pompei Jones. (C)

152A - 1 Mar. 1898 - **Robert Wake**, 30, single, oysterman, b. & residing Mid., son of Edmund & Elisa Wake, married **Susie Revvell**, 18, single, b. & residing Mid., dau. of Mariah & Gen'l Revvell. (C)

152B - 3 Mar. 1898 - **John W. Robinson**, 30, single, oysterman, b. & residing Mid., son of Walter & Louisa Robinson, married **Emma Smith**, 20, single, dau. of Kittie Smith, b. & residing Mid. (C)

152C - 10 Mar. 1898 - **Willie Garnett**, 21, single, oysterman, b. & residing Mid., son of T. Garnett, married **Mary W. Anderson**, 16, single, b. & residing Mid., dau. of Harriet Burrell. (C)

153A - 17 Mar. 1898 - **James R. Davis**, 52, widower, oysterman, b. & residing Mid., son of Bartlett & Nancy Davis, married **Lucy Blake**, 31, widow, b. & residing Mid. (W)

153B - 20 Mar. 1898 - **Rev. D. Fields**, 43, widower, "minister of the gospel," b. & residing Lancaster, son of Cupid & Sallie Fields, married **Rosetta A. Billups**, 17, single, b. & residing Mid., dau. of Gibson & Minerva Billups. (C)

153C - 24 Feb. 1898 - **Obie Jackson**, 36, widower, oysterman, b. Caroline, residing Mid., son of John & Eliza Jackson, married **Emma Carey**, 37, widow, b. & residing Mid., dau. of Geo. & Lucy Carter. (C)

154A - 8 Mar. 1898 - **Jeff Anderson**, 21, single, oysterman, b. King & Queen, residing Mid., son of David

& Rachel Anderson, married **Eva Davis**, 21, single, b. & residing Mid., dau. of Geo. & Emma Davis. (C)

154B - 22 Mar. 1898 - **Samuel Hodges**, 22, single, oysterman, b. & residing Mid., married **Clara Nelson**, 18, single, b. & residing Mid., dau. of Lewis Nelson. (C)

154C - 29 Mar. 1898 - **Walter Young Shackelford**, 28, single, carriage maker, b. Gloucester, residing Mid., son of Wm. & Mary Shackelford, married **Helen Eugenia Watts**, 27, single, b. Albemarle, residing Mid., dau. of M. S. & S. A. Watts. (W)

155A - 29 Mar. 1898 - **Henry A. Moran**, 39, single, farmer, b. Mathews, residing Mid., dau. of Patrick & Louisiana Moran, married **Mariah Louisa Collins**, 19, single, b. King & Queen, residing Mid., dau. of Geo. A. & Marian F. Collins. (W)

155B - 6 Apr. 1898 - **Arthur Foster Nicholson**, 29, widower, architect & builder, b. & residing Prince Georges Co., Maryland, married **Eva Hart**, 22, single, b. & residing Mid., dau. of B. F. & Sarah C. Hart. (W)

155C - 1 Apr. 1898 - **Samuel Conway**, 22, single, oysterman, b. & residing Mid., son of Wm. & Emmeline Conway, married **Martha Terry**, 21, single, b. & residing Mid., dau. of Johnson & Susan Terry. (C)

156A - 14 Apr. 1898 - **Henry Graham**, 24, single, farmer, b. & residing Mid., son of J. K. & C. F. Graham, married **Loty Jackson**, 21, single, b. & residing Mid., dau. of R. & Bell Jackson. (W)

156B - 16 Apr. 1898 - **Anthony Robinson**, 23, single, oysterman, b. & residing Mid., son of Mamie Robinson, married **Lizzie Whiting**, 20, single, b. & residing Mid., dau. of Geo. & Mattie Whiting. (C)

156C - 31 Mar. 1898 - **Rob't West**, 23, single, oysterman, b. Essex, residing Mid., son of Tom & Rebecca West, married **Willie Ann Morris**, 17, single, b. & residing Mid., dau. of James & Belle Morris. (C)

157A - 14 May 1898 - **Geo. Washington Whiting**, 42, widower, farmer, b. & residing Mid., son of Samuel & Patsy Whiting, married **Lucy Miles**, 23, single, b. & residing Mid., dau. of Jerry & Lucy Miles. (C)

157B - 22 May 1898 - **Israel Williams**, 45, divorced, farmer, b. Baltimore, Maryland, residing Mid., son of Henry & Mary Williams, married **Mattie Griffin**, 28, single, b. & residing Mid., dau. of Edmund & Anna Griffin. (C)

157C - 24 May 1898 - **Columbus Lorrimore**, 21, single, oysterman, b. King & Queen, residing Mid., son of Walker & Catharine Lorrimore, married **Josephine Willis**, 22, single, b. & residing Mid., dau. of Rob't & Georgiana Willis. (C)

158A - 2 Jun. 1898 - **Harvey Henry**, 27, single,

oysterman, b. & residing Mid., son of Nathan & Charlotte Henry, married **Martha Burke**, 21, single, b. & residing Mid., dau. of Alberta Trusil. (C)

158B - 29 May 1898 - **Earnest Wormley**, 23, single, oysterman, b. King & Queen, residing Mid., son of James & Mary Wormley, married **Lulie Bagby**, 19, single, b. & residing Mid., dau. of Washington & Polly Bagby. (C)

158C - 7 Jun. 1898 - **Thos. H. Gemmill**, 29, single, merchant, b. Kent Co., Maryland, residing Mid., son of John H. & Annie E. Gemmill, married **Nina E. Ailsworth**, 22, single, b. & residing Mid., dau. of Joseph C. & Fannie B. Ailsworth. (W)

159A - 16 Jun. 1898 - **William R. Jackson**, 83, widower, farmer, b. & residing Mid., son of Edmund & Sallie Jackson, married **Elizabeth Burlin**, 35, widow, b. King & Queen, residing Mid. (C)

159B - 17 Jul. 1898 - **John R. Ramey**, 33, single, insurance agent, b. Prince George, Virginia, residing Baltimore, son of R. R. & Lucy A. Ramey, married **Mary A. Bland**, 28, single, b. & residing Mid., dau. of R. T. & J. C. Bland. (W)

159C - 12 Jul. 1898 - **A. J. Blake**, 28, widower, oysterman, b. & residing Mid., son of John Allen & Mary Blake, married **Rachel E. Allin**, 21, divorced, b. Maryland, residing Mid., dau. of Wm. & Lizzie Allin. (W)

160A - 11 Jul. 1898 - **George G. Thomas**, 35, widower, farmer, b. Mathews, residing Mid., son of Rev. George E. & Lucy V. Thomas, married **Mildred South**, 32, single, b. & residing Mid., dau. of Joseph V. & Mildred South. (W)

160B - 24 Aug. 1898 - **Liston D. Lyon**, 17, single, sailor, b. & residing Mid., son of A. C. & Ida E. Lyon, married **Margaret E. Wilson**, 20, single, b. New York, residing Brooklyn, New York, dau. of G. W. & M. J. Wilson. (W) Consent for groom, by mother, for bride, by brother.

160C - 24 Aug. 1898 - **John J. Fleet**, 23, single, oysterman, b. & residing Mid., son of John H. & Mary Fleet, married **Pauline Trader**, 18, single, b. & residing Mid., dau. of James & Elizabeth Trader. (W) Consent for bride by guardian.

161A - 25 Aug. 1898 - **Robert Carter Braxton**, 34, single, oysterman, b. & residing Mid., son of Robt. H. & Lizzie Braxton, married **Estelle Corr**, 19, single, b. & residing Mid., dau. of Millie Ann Corr. (C)

161B - 13 Sep. 1898 - **James Castor Lewis**, 23, single, oysterman, b. & residing Mid., son of Moses & Margaret Lewis, married **Sarah Johnson**, 22, single, b. & residing Mid., dau. of Simon & Matilda Johnson. (C)

161C - 21 Sep. 1898 - **Chas. H. Walker, Jr.**, 30,

divorced, oysterman, b. & residing Mid., son of Chas. H.
& Tiny Walker, married **Winnie F. Thurston**, 24, single,
b. & residing Mid., dau. of Geo. W. & Francis Thurston.
(C)

162A - 21 Sep. 1898 - **Schuyler E. Bland**, 20, single,
farmer, b. & residing Mid., son of R. T. & J. C. Bland,
married **Lee F. Hall**, 18, single, b. & residing Mid.,
dau. of P. B. & I. M. Hall. (W)

162B - 22 Sep. 1898 - **Richard Lee**, 22, single,
oysterman, b. & residing Mid., son of Bernard & Betty
Lee, married **Ora Reed**, 17, single, b. & residing Mid.,
dau. of Isaac & Fannie Reed. (C) Consent by Thomas
Jackson, brother-in-law.

162C - 25 Sep. 1898 - **Rob't Martin Smith**, 23, single,
fisherman, b. & residing Gloucester, son of Thos. &
Lucretia Smith, married **Maggie L. Bonniville**, 20,
single, b. Gloucester, residing Mid., dau. of Geo. W. &
Mary E. Bonniville. (W)

163A - 19 Oct. 1898 - **Ledford E. Wilson**, 20, single,
oysterman, b. & residing Mid., son of Wm. & Virginia
Wilson, married **Mary V. Guinn**, 20, single, b. & residing
Mid., dau. of Rob't & Nancy Guinn. (C)

163B - 26 Oct. 1898 - **H. J. H. Washington** [Hanamiah
James H. on license], 22, single, oysterman, b. King &
Queen, residing Mid., son of Beverly & Matilda
Washington, married **Elvey Dickison**, 24, single, b. &
residing Mid., dau. of Fayette & Martha Dickison. (C)

163C - 25 Oct. 1898 - **Dr. R. Lee Robinson**, 24,
single, dentist, b. Baltimore, Maryland, residing
Newport News, son of Logan & T. Robinson, married **Alice
T. Major**, 24, single, b. & residing Mid., dau. of John
M. & Fannie A. Major. (W)

164A - 3 Nov. 1898 - **Thomas Griffin**, 31, single,
oysterman, b. North Carolina, residing Mid., son of
Taylor & Mollie Griffin, married **Evalina Robinson**, 27,
single, b. & residing Mid., dau. of Walter Robinson.
(C)

164B - 3 Nov. 1898 - **Eli P. Carter**, 28, single,
oysterman, b. & residing Mid., son of Lewis & Ella
Carter, married **Rosa Bond**, 23, single, b. & residing
Mid., dau. of West & Louisa Bond. (C)

164C - 14 Nov. 1898 - **A. J. Jarvis**, 29, single,
merchant, b. Mathews, residing Mid., son of Peter W. &
Annie C. Jarvis, married **Lena Bedford Wood**, 22, single,
b. & residing Mid., dau. of James A. & Harriet Wood.
(W)

165A - 15 Nov. 1898 - **Henry Thos. Daniel**, 22, single,
oysterman, b. & residing Mid., married **Mary Catharine
Johnson**, 18, single, b. & residing Mid., dau. of Thos.
E. & Julia W. Johnson. (W)

165B - 16 Nov. 1898 - **Luther Hackett,** 24, single, oysterman, b. & residing Mid., son of Sam & Sindy Hackett, married **Lucinda Young,** 23, single, b. & residing Mid., dau. of Joshua & Mary Young. (C)

165C - 15 Nov. 1898 - **Beverly Lewis,** 27, single, oysterman, b. & residing Mid., son of Allie & Willie Lewis, married **Lizzie Jones,** 21, single, b. & residing Mid., dau. of Stephen & Belle Jones. (C)

166A - 30 Nov. 1898 - **William Burke,** 28, single, oysterman, b. & residing Mid., son of Harry & Letty Burke, married **Eliza Burke,** 28, widow, b. & residing Mid., dau. of Tilly Taliaferro. (C)

166B - 8 Dec. 1898 - **John Brown,** 27, single, oysterman, b. & residing Mid., son of Maratha Ellen Brown & Walter Key, married **Maggie Reed,** 23, divorced, b. & residing Mid., dau. of Ella Reed. (C)

166C - 8 Dec. 1898 - **Julius H. Cook,** 24, single, oysterman, b. & residing Mid., son of James H. & Louisa Cook, married **Emma J. Johnson,** 28, single, b. & residing Mid., dau. of Lizzie Johnson. (C)

167A - 21 Dec. 1898 - **R. Ernest Fox,** 21, single, blacksmith, b. Culpeper, residing Mid., son of Walker T. & Mary Eugenia Fox, married **Sadie C. Evans,** 17, single, b. & residing Mid., dau. of W. R. & Sarah Evans. (W)

167B - 21 Dec. 1898 - **Oliver George Paul,** 30, single, farmer, b. New Jersey, residing Mid., son of Wm. & Kate Paul, married **Exie Healy,** 22, single, b. & residing Mid., dau. of James & Vashti [Healy]. (W)

167C - 21 Dec. 1898 - **Clinton E. Thurston,** 23, single, marine engineer, b. King William, residing Norfolk, married **Eula E. Brown,** 21, single, b. King & Queen, residing Mid., dau. of J. M. & Emmah Brown. (W)

168A - 22 Dec. 1898 - **W. L. Trimyer,** 24, single, blacksmith, b. & residing Mid., son of W. L. & Sarah Trimyer, married **Ada B. Hundley,** 18, single, b. & residing Mid., dau. of W. W. & Emma Hundley. (W)

168B - 21 Dec. 1898 - **Martin Pace,** 20, single, oysterman, b. & residing Mid., son of Harley & Fannie Pace, married **Emma Eilsworth,** 17, single, b. & residing Mid., dau. of Rob't & M. E. Ailsworth. (W)

168C - 24 Dec. 1898 - **Richard Roane,** 26, single, oysterman, b. & residing Mid., son of Henry & Louisa Roane, married **Lucy Townsend,** 24, single, b. & residing Mid., dau. of Isaiah & Harriet Townsend. (C)

169A - 25 Dec. 1898 - **Moses Carr,** 34, divorced, oysterman, b. & residing Mid., son of Burrell & Mary Carr, married **Harriet Trivous,** 35, widow, b. & residing Mid., dau. of Wm. & Eliza Griffin. (C)

169B - 26 Dec. 1898 - **Edward Thomas Ingram,** 23, single, oysterman, b. & residing Mid., son of Lloyd &

Sallie N. Ingraham, married **Gertrude Price**, 22, single, b. & residing Mid., dau. of Joseph & Gertrude Blanche Price. (W)

169C - 22 Dec. 1898 - **Philip Beverly**, 25, single, oysterman, b. & residing Mid., son of Richard & Mary Beverly, married **Ellen Jane Lewis**, 19, single, b. & residing Mid., dau. of Alonzo & Mary E. Lewis. (C)

170A - 28 Dec. 1898 - **Rob't Henry Robinson**, 25, single, oysterman, b. & residing Mid., son of Harry & Martha Robinson, married **Cora Jones**, 23, single, b. & residing Mid., dau. of Edmund Jones. (C)

170B - 27 Dec. 1898 - **Armstead Ruffin**, 19, single, farmer, b. & residing Mid., son of Lewis & Caroline Ruffin, married **Annie Taylor**, 16, single, b. & residing Mid., dau. of Thornton & Amy Taylor. (C)

170C - 28 Dec. 1898 - **Absolom T. Gibson**, 40, widower, carpenter, b. King & Queen, residing Mid., son of James & Antoinette Gibson, married **Blanche F. Gresham**, 20, single, b. King & Queen, residing Mid., dau. of Wm. & Elizabeth Gresham. (W)

171A - 29 Dec. 1898 - **Moses Boyd**, 27, single, oysterman, b. & residing Mid., son of Henry & Henrietta Boyd, married **Gertrude Goldman**, 22, single, b. & residing Mid., dau. of John Goldman. (C)

171B - 3 Jan. 1899 - **William Weston**, 23, single, oysterman, b. & residing Mid., son of Geo. & Columbia Weston, married **Oshia C. Jackson**, 19, single, b. & residing Mid., dau. of Noah & Anna Jackson. (W)

171C - 4 Jan. 1899 - **John Fields**, 32, single, oysterman, b. & residing Mid., son of Solomon & Jane Fields, married **Alice Thurston**, 32, single, b. & residing Mid., dau. of Edward & Sylvia Thurston. (C)

172A - 5 Jan. 1899 - **Archibald Russ**, 29, single, oyster shucker, b. & residing Mid., son of James & Peggy Russ, married **Louisa Green**, 36, widow, b. & residing Mid., dau. of Polly & James Robinson. (C)

172B - 18 Jan. 1899 - **Laurence F. Parker**, 23, single, oysterman, b. & residing Mid., son of Sandy & Emily Parker, married **Sarah E. French**, 25, single, b. & residing Mid., dau. of Thomas & Edna French. (W)

172C - 2 Feb. 1899 - **James Henry Cook**, 63, widower, farmer, b. & residing Mid., son of James & Frankie Cook, married **Betty Johnson**, 60, widow, b. Gloucester, residing Mid.. (C)

173A - 5 Feb. 1899 - **William P. Moore**, 48, widower, farmer, b. & residing Mid., son of John & Nancy Moore, married **Columbus F. Crittenden**, 47, widow, b. & residing Mid., dau. of Samuel R. & Maria R. Cole. (W)

173B - 8 Feb. 1899 - **John Thomas Robinson**, 27, single, farmer, b. & residing Mid., son of Henry & Mary

Robinson, married **Addie Leigh Banks**, 22, single, b. & residing Mid., dau. of Lucius & Julia Banks. (C)

173C - 23 Feb. 1899 - **Granville Harvey Ball**, 30, single, tinner, b. & residing Mid., son of John & Mollie Ball, married **Emma Lee Ward**, 18, single, b. & residing Mid., dau. of A. H. & E. C. Ward. (W)

174A - 21 Feb. 1899 - **Stephen Paul**, 24, single, oysterman, b. North Carolina, residing Mid., son of Fred. S. & Mary Paul, married **Musette Grafton Fears**, 24, single, b. Maryland, residing Mid., dau. of Joseph & Amanda Fears. (W)

174B - 21 Feb. 1899 - **Clarence E. Parks**, 20, single, carpenter, b. & residing Mid., son of "father dead, mother Mrs. E. J. Hanson, nee Parks," married **Nellie Vandergrift Eaton**, 27, widow, b. Maryland, residing Mid., dau. of Joseph & Amanda Fears. (W)

174C - 2 Mar. 1899 - **Jack Hogg**, 63, widower, oysterman, b. Gloucester, residing Mid., son of Wm. & Martha Hogg, married **Nannie Davis**, 22, single, b. & residing Mid., dau. of James & Mary Davis. (W)

175A - 8 Jan. 1899 - **Paul Bagby**, 25, single, farmer, b. & residing Mid., son of Washington & Polly Bagby, married **Harriet Dangerfield**, 18, single, b. & residing Mid., dau. of stepfather Thos. Mitchell & Rose Mitchell. (C)

175B - 9 Mar. 1899 - **James Foster**, 24, single, oysterman, b. & residing Mid., son of Marcus F. & Mary J. Foster, married **Mary Williams**, 25, widow, b. & residing Mid., dau. of Zackary & Charity Williams. (C)

175C - 12 Mar. 1899 - **John R. Lumpkin**, 63, widower, farmer, b. Mathews, residing Mid., son of John R. & Catharine W. Lumpkin, married **Ida E. Carter**, 41, widow, b. Baltimore, Maryland, residing Mid., dau. of W. H. & Nancy Kelly. (W)

176A - 11 Mar. 1899 - **Randal Taylor**, 22, single, oysterman, b. & residing Mid., son of Rob't & Mary Taylor, married **Jennie Jackson**, 18, single, b. & residing Mid., dau. of J. H. M. & Frances Jackson. (C)

176B - 15 Mar. 1899 - **Joseph B. Dixon**, 36, single, merchant, b. Mathews, residing Mid., son of W. B. & Mary E. Dixon, married **Effie L. Greene**, 21, single, b. Gloucester, residing Mid., dau. of Geo. & Jennie Greene. (W)

176C - 15 Mar. 1899 - **James Taylor**, 21, single, sailor, b. & residing Mid., son of D. A. & A. E. Taylor, married **Nannie Moore**, 19, single, b. & residing Mid., dau. of W. P. & M. A. Moore. (W)

177A - 16 Mar. 1899 - **Rob't Greene**, 22, single, oysterman, b. & residing Mid., son of Manuel & Cora Greene, married **Victoria Holmes**, 30, single, b. &

residing Mid., dau. of May Beverly. (C)
177B - 16 Mar. 1899 - **Nelson Hill**, 27, single, oysterman, b. & residing Mid., son of Geo. & Polly Hill, married **Mollie Braxton**, 25, single, b. & residing Mid., dau. of Carter & Eliza Braxton. (C)
177C - 17 Mar. 1899 - **Joseph Lee**, 21, single, oysterman, b. & residing Mid., son of Washington & Mary Ellen Lee, married **Nellie Virginia Johnson**, 19, single, b. & residing Mid., dau. of Curtis C. & Cordelia Johnson. (C)
178A - 23 Mar. 1899 - **John M. Coleman**, 47, single, farmer, b. Portsmouth, residing Mid., son of James & Emily Coleman, married **Eliza Jane Belvin**, 23, single, b. Gloucester, residing Mid., dau. of Ralph & Nancy Belvin. (W)
178B - 21 Mar. 1899 - **Isaiah Holmes**, 24, single, oysterman, b. & residing Mid., son of John & Rachel Holmes, married **Sarah Greene**, 21, single, b. & residing Mid., dau. of Rich'd & Mary Greene. (C)
178C - 23 Mar. 1899 - **Henry Charles Blake**, 31, single, farmer, b. & residing Mid., son of R. L. & Margaret Blake, married **Sallie Mercer**, 26, single, b. & residing Mid., dau. of J. C. & Bettie Mercer. (W)
179A - 30 Mar. 1899 - **John H. Banks**, 27, widower, oysterman, b. & residing Mid., son of Lewis & Dora Banks, married **Martha Jane Thurston**, 16, single, b. & residing Mid., dau. of Lucy Fleming. (C)
179B - 2 Apr. 1899 - **Samuel Wiatt**, 22, single, oysterman, b. King & Queen, residing Mid., son of Rob't & Laura Wiatt, married **Eudora Carr**, 18, single, b. & residing Mid., dau. of J. Allin & Tama Ann Carr. (C)
179C - 16 Apr. 1899 - **Eugene Greenstreet**, 24, single, farmer, b. Essex, residing Mid., son of Wm. T. & Mary E. Greenstreet, married **Maggie Slaughter**, 17, single, b. Essex, residing Mid., dau. of Hamilton & Lizzie Slaughter. (W)
180A - 19 Apr. 1899 - **R. L. Towill**, 38, single, farmer, b. & residing Mid., son of M. W. & Amanda Towill, married **Lorina Grenils**, 35, widow, b. & residing Mid., dau. of Thos. & Pauline Hall. (W)
180B - 9 Apr. 1899 - **Alex Gaines**, 26, single, oysterman, b. & residing Essex, son of Carter A. & Sarah Gaines, married **Maggie Cauthorn**, 18, single, b. Baltimore, Maryland, residing Mid., dau. of Wm. & Caroline Cauthorn. (C)
180C - 26 Apr. 1899 - **V. Muse Vaughan**, 24, single, farmer, b. & residing Mid., son of Vespasian & Julia M. Vaughan, married **Sallie D. Taylor**, 20, single, b. & residing Mid., dau. of David A. & Nannie E. Taylor. (W)
181A - 27 Apr. 1899 - **Alex West**, 33, single,

oysterman, b. & residing Mid., son of Alex & Caroline West, married **Virginia Adelaide Blackburn**, 22, single, b. & residing Mid., dau. of Lucy Harris. (C)

181B - 30 Apr. 1899 - **Chas. Roy**, 30, divorced, farmer, b. & residing Mid., son of Henry & Chris Roy, married **Lizzie Jackson**, 24, single, b. & residing Mid., dau. of Alex & Grace Jackson. (C)

181C - 3 May 1899 - **Samuel Woolridge**, 39, single, farmer, b. & residing Mid., son of John & Sarah Woolridge, married **Edna M. Glenn**, 22, single, b. & residing Mid., dau. of R. M. & Ann M. Glenn. (W)

182A - 3 May 1899 - **J. W. Foxwell**, 30, widower, oysterman, b. Gloucester, residing Mid., son of Solomon & Sarah Foxwell, married **Rassie Redd**, 24, single, b. King & Queen, residing Mid., dau. of J. E. & Edna Redd. (W)

182B - 3 May 1899 - **W. A. Redd**, 21, single, farmer, b. King & Queen, residing Mid., son of J. E. & Edna Redd, married **Sallie Jewell**, 19, single, b. Gloucester, residing Mid., dau. of W. O. & Dora Jewell. (W)

182C - 25 Apr. 1899 - **Clinton Lee**, 29, single, clerk, b. & residing Mid., son of Obadiah & E. N. Lee, married **Bertha Bristow**, 17, single, b. & residing Mid., dau. of W. & Adda Bristow. (W)

183A - 26 Apr. 1899 - **J. A. Moody**, 26, single, oysterman, b. & residing Mid., son of Dennis C. & Priscilla Moody, married **Mary E. Cook**, 25, single, b. & residing Mid., dau. of Ralph & Elizabeth Cook. (C)

183B - 30 Apr. 1899 - **Wrighter Garnett**, 23, single, oysterman, b. & residing Mid., son of Henry & Lucy Garnett, married **Rilla Davis**, 21, single, b. & residing Mid., dau. of Rhoda Robinson. (C)

183C - 1 Jun. 1899 - **John Laws**, 37, single, farmer, b. & residing Mid., son of Frank & Fannie Laws, married **Virgie Jefferson**, 21, single, b. & residing Mid., dau. of Thos. Jefferson. (C)

184A - 8 Jun. 1899 - **William R. Robinson**, 21, single, farmer, b. Essex, residing Mid., son of Pat & Rebecca Robinson, married **Mollie Robinson**, 21, single, b. & residing Mid., dau. of Wm. & Matilda Taliaferro. (C)

184B - 14 Jun. 1899 - **Percy N. Fells**, 25, single, blacksmith, b. New York, residing Mid., son of P. W. & May Fells, married **Maggie B. Mayo**, 21, single, b. & residing Mid., dau. of James W. & Ellen Mayo. (W)

184C - 20 Jun. 1899 - **Walter M. Hurley**, 27, single, carpenter, b. & residing Mid., son of David & Jane Hurley, married **Julia Clayville**, 23, single, b. & residing Mid., dau. of Elisha & Mary Clayville. (W)

185A - 20 Jun. 1899 - **Lloyd Roane**, 21, single, b. & residing Mid., son of Geo. R. Finch, married **Lizzie**

Wormley, 22, single, b. & residing Mid., dau. of Solomon & Eliza Wormley. (C)

185B - 17 Jul. 1899 - **James Foster**, 24, single, oysterman, b. & residing Mid., son of Lewis & Fanny Foster, married **Lucy Jane Minor**, 17, single, b. & residing Mid., dau. of George & Susan Minor. (C)

185C - 18 Jul. 1899 - **Philip Banks**, 55, widower, farmer, b. & residing Mid., son of Henry & Beckie Banks, married **Lizzie Lewis**, 28, widow, b. Mathews, residing Mid., parents "both dead, names not known." (C)

186A - 30 Jul. 1899 - **Julius Carey**, 22, single, oysterman, b. King & Queen, residing Mid., son of Julius & Misie Carey, married **Bessie Fleet** or **Lee**, 19, single, b. & residing Mid., dau. of Mary Lee. (C)

186B - 2 Aug. 1899 - **James R. Cannon**, 23, single, mariner, b. Maryland, residing Westmoreland, son of John H. & Addie F. Cannon, married **Eulah H. Burch**, 25, single, b. King & Queen, residing Mid., dau. of John R. & T. Burch. (W)

186C - 2 Aug. 1899 - **R. H. Griffith**, 28, single, farmer, b. Essex, residing Mid., son of Joseph B. & Sarah A. Griffith, married **Mary H. Walker**, 26, single, b. & residing Mid., dau. of Robinson & Lucy H. Walker. (W)

187A - 31 Aug. 1899 - **John Roane**, 38, widower, oysterman, b. & residing Mid., son of John Henry & Jane Braxton, married **Eddie Foster**, 32, widow, b. & residing Mid., dau. of David & Betsey Slaughter. (C)

187B - 28 Sep. 1899 - **R. H. Evans**, 43, widower, oysterman, b. & residing Mid., son of Mortimer Evans & May Foster, married **Ellen Jane Roane**, 33, single, b. King & Queen, residing Mid., dau. of Wm. H. & Sallie Roane. (C)

187C - 3 Oct. 1899 - **Francis H. Wilshin**, 25, single, mechanic, b. Norfolk Co., residing Atlantic City, Virginia, son of Francis & Jane Wilshin, married **Gay Montague Folliard**, 22, single, b. & residing Mid., dau. of John P. & Susan Folliard. (W)

188A - 23 Sep. 1899 - **Clifton Johnson**, 34, single, oysterman, b. & residing Mid., son of Billy & Clara Johnson, married **Mary Roy**, 34, single, b. & residing Mid., dau. of Harry & Patty Young. (C)

188B - 5 Oct. 1899 - **Daniel Cook**, 26, single, farmer, b. Gloucester, residing Mid., son of Indiana Cook & Allen Brooking, married **Mary Lewis**, 27, single, b. & residing Mid., dau. of Rob't Evans & Isabella Lewis. (C)

188C - 4 Oct. 1899 - **Nathan Henry**, 30, widower, oysterman, b. & residing Mid., son of Nathan & Charlotte Henry, married **Lucy Lewis**, 23, single, b. & residing

Mid., dau. of Allie & Minnie Lewis. (C)

189A - 1 Nov. 1899 - **James R. Prince**, 26, single, oysterman, b. & residing Mid., son of James R. & Elizabeth Prince, married **Eva Alice Dunlevy**, 18, single, b. & residing Mid., dau. of J. J. & Sarah Dunlevy. (W)

189B - 9 Nov. 1899 - **Merton Emery Clarke**, 30, single, merchant, b. & residing Mid., son of John C. & Elizabeth Clarke, married **Ida Waverly Lawson**, 27, single, b. & residing Mid., dau. of Thos. James & Sarah A. Lawson. (W)

189C - 10 Nov. 1899 - **George Russ**, 22, single, oysterman, b. & residing Mid., son of Luellen & Winnie Russ, married **Jennie Lewis**, 19, single, b. & residing Mid., dau. of Lucy Ann Lewis. (B)

190A - 30 Nov. 1899 - **Vester Muse**, 21, single, oysterman, b. & residing Mid., son of Anthony & Milly Muse, married **Mariah Scarber**, 21, single, b. & residing Mid., dau. of Betty Scarber. (B)

190B - 6 Dec. 1899 - **John A. Payne**, 46, widower, farmer, b. Lancaster, residing Mid., son of Thos. B. & Catharine E. Payne, married **Alice Elden Hurley**, 18, single, b. New Jersey, residing Mid., dau. of Obadiah Hurley. (W)

190C - 5 Dec. 1899 - **James A. Fones**, 23, single, farmer, b. Richmond Co., residing Mid., son of Richard & Mary Fones, married **Maud G. Keiningham**, 22, single, b. & residing Mid., dau. of Geo. & Ida Keiningham. (W)

191A - 14 Dec. 1899 - **John H. Hogg**, 28, single, oysterman, b. Gloucester, residing Mid., son of Geo. W. & Sarah E. Hogg, married **Lucy J. Ransom**, 22, single, b. Gloucester, residing Mid., dau. of James T. & Pinkie Ransom. |

191B - 21 Dec. 1899 - **Samuel Wingfield**, 22, single, farmer, b. & residing Mid., son of Scipio & Mildred Wingfield, married **Etta Banks**, 23, single, b. & residing Mid., dau. of Alex & Nancy Banks, now Beverly. (B)

191C - 25 Dec. 1899 - **Wm. Lewis Johnson**, 24, single, oysterman, b. Essex, residing Mid., son of John S. & Louisianna Johnson, married **Lolla May Dunlevy**, 19, single, b. & residing Mid., dau. of J. J. & Sarah Dunlevy. (W)

192A - 27 Dec. 1899 - **Ernest Johnson**, 21, single, oysterman, b. & residing Mid., son of Gus & Emmeline Johnson, married **Maggie Beckett**, 20, single, b. & residing Mid., dau. of Allen & Mona Beckett. (B)

192B - 28 Dec. 1899 - **James Baker, Jr.**, 25, single, farmer, b. & residing Mid., son of James & Betsy Baker, married **Lena Robinson**, 21, single, b. & residing Mid., dau. of Susan Dudly. (B)

192C - 29 Dec. 1899 - **James Laws**, 21, single, farmer,

b. & residing Mid., son of Frank & Fanny Laws, married **Jane Holmes**, 21, single, b. & residing Mid., dau. of Braxton Holmes & Nancy Young. (B)

193A - 3 Jan. 1900 - **Lucius F. Harper**, 28, single, merchant, b. & residing King & Queen, son of Claybrook & Fannie L. Harper, married **Louisa M. Chowning**, 27, single, b. & residing Mid., dau. of James & Ann E. Chowning. (W)

193B - 3 Jan. 1900 - **Ralph T. Wormley**, 24, single, oysterman, b. & residing Mid., son of Rich'd & Louisa Wormley, married **Maggie Goldman**, 18, single, b. & residing Mid., dau. of Elijah Goldman. (B)

193C - 4 Jan. 1900 - **Willie Jones**, 26, single, oysterman, b. & residing Mid., son of Wallace & Martha Ellen Jones, married **Maggie Davis**, 23, single, b. & residing Mid., dau. of Uriah & Tillie Davis. (B)

194A - 4 Jan. 1900 - **James Monroe**, 28, single, sailor, b. & residing Mid., son of Washington & Maria Bagby, married **Mary Brooks**, 24, single, b. Essex, residing Mid., dau. of Solomon Brooks. (B)

194B - 27 Dec. 1899 - **Henry Clay Morris**, 29, widower, oysterman, b. & residing Mid., son of Bruce Robinson, married **Lizzie Reed**, 24, single, b. & residing Mid., dau. of Jesse & Laura Reed. (B)

194C - 27 Dec. 1899 - **Allen Reede**, 40, widower, oysterman, b. & residing Mid., son of Austin & Fanny Reed, married **Emmeline Chamberlain**, 25, widow, b. & residing Mid. (B)

195A - 31 Dec. 1899 - **Earney Chamberlain**, 23, single, oysterman, b. & residing Mid., son of Thomas & Emmeline Chamberline, married **Welthy Reed**, 22, single, b. & residing Mid., dau. of Frank & Hester Reed. (B)

195B - 16 Jan. 1900 - **George Lomax**, 26, single, oysterman, b. King & Queen, residing Mid., son of James & Eudora Lomax, married **Bettie Reed**, 21, single, b. & residing Mid., dau. of Jesse & Laura Reed. (B)

195C - 16 Jan. 1900 - **Joe Yarbrough**, 24, single, pickle manufacturer, b. North Carolina, residing Mid., son of Jobe & Anna Yarbrough, married **Ella Holiday**, 16, single, b. & residing Mid., dau. of Oscar & Fanny Holiday. (B)

196A - 25 Jan. 1900 - **Thos. White**, 24, single, laborer, b. Tennessee, residing Mid., son of Ike & Martha White, married **Betty Ann Carr**, 20, single, b. & residing Mid., dau. of Allen & Tama Ann Carr. (B)

196B - 1 Feb. 1900 - **John Smith**, 24, single, oysterman, b. Gloucester, residing Mid., son of Robert & Sallie Smith, married **Fannie Belvin**, 19, single, b. Gloucester, residing Mid., dau. of Ralph & Nannie Belvin. (W)

196C - 1 Feb. 1900 - **Rob't B. Covington**, 26, single, farmer, b. & residing Mid., son of Jas. E. & Sarah E. Covington, married **Lucy Carter Trice**, 22, single, b. & residing Mid., dau. of Rob't M. & Ann C. Trice. (W)

197A - 1 Feb. 1900 - **Isaiah Townsley**, 41, widower, oysterman, b. & residing Mid., son of Geo. & Sarah Ann Townsley, married **Mamie Jackson**, 23, single, b. Gloucester, residing Mid., dau. of John & Cordelia Jackson. (B)

197B - 7 Feb. 1900 - **Jefferson D. Pannell**, 38, widower, oysterman, b. Accomack, residing Mid., married **Carrie E. Taylor**, 25, single, b. & residing Mid., dau. of D. A. & H. E. Taylor. (W)

197C - 7 Feb. 1900 - **Wm. E. Finkle**, 32, single, fireman engineer, b. Maryland, residing Mid., married **Carrie E. Warrington**, 18, single, b. Delaware, residing Mid., dau. of Geo. E. & Mary Warrington. (W)

198A - 20 Feb. 1900 - **Edward Fields**, 29, single, oysterman, b. Gloucester, residing Mid., son of Geo. & Matilda Fields, married **W. T. Kerr**, 35, widow, b. & residing Mid., dau. of Landon & Roberta Manfield. (B)

198B - 5 Mar. 1900 - **Samuel Ranson**, 50, single, oysterman, b. Gloucester, residing Mid., son of Sam & Delphy Ranson, married **Ellen Ruffin**, 28, single, b. & residing Mid. (B)

198C - 8 Mar. 1900 - **R. H. Carter**, 22, single, farmer, b. & residing King & Queen, son of James & Sarah Carter, married **Nollie Brown**, 20, single, b. King & Queen, residing Mid., dau. of James & Mona L. Brown. (W)

199A - 14 Mar. 1900 - **William A. Thomas**, 24, single, oysterman, b. & residing York, son of Wise & Nettie Thomas, married **Charlotte Deagle**, 20, single, b. & residing Mid., dau. of J. W. & Susan Deagle. (W)

199B - 15 Mar. 1900 - **Geo. Wm. Daniel**, 21, single, oysterman, b. & residing Mid., son of George & Annie Daniel, married **Addie Trader**, 18, single, b. & residing Mid., dau. of D. & A. Trader. (W)

199C - 22 Apr. 1900 - **Robert Stewart**, 24, single, oysterman, b. & residing Gloucester, son of Geo. & Lizzie Stewart, married **Lucy Minor**, 30, single, b. & residing Mid., dau. of Frank. (B)

200A - 3 May 1900 - **Alex Cook**, 35, widower, oysterman, b. Mathews, residing Mid., son of Frank & Mary Cook, married **Mattie Lewis**, 23, single, b. & residing Mid., dau. of John & Lucy Lewis. (B)

200B - 4 Apr. 1900 - **Thos. R. French**, 40, single, sailor, b. & residing Mid., son of W. T. & Amanda French, married **Mattie E. Prince**, 36, single, b. King & Queen, residing Mid., dau. of H. D. & Sallie Prince.

(W)
200C - 29 Mar. 1900 - **Christ Green**, 24, single, oysterman, b. King & Queen, residing Mid., son of Richard & Mary Green, married **Lelia Holmes**, 22, single, b. & residing Mid., dau. of John & Rachel Holmes. (B)
201A - 9 May 1900 - **Thos. Jackson Mayo**, 28, single, carpenter, b. King & Queen, residing Mid., son of Thos. & Lucy Jane Mayo, married **Carrie May Miller**, 19, single, b. & residing Mid., dau. of J. C. & Hetty Miller. (W)
201B 26 Apr. 1900 - **General Washington Smith**, 22, single, oysterman, b. & residing Mid., son of John & Emma J. Smith, married **Lelia Johnson**, 21, single, b. & residing Mid., dau. of George Johnson. (B)
201C - 24 May 1900 - **Cornelius H. Brown**, 30, widower, farmer, b. King & Queen, residing Mid., son of Wm. & Mary Brown, married **Evelina Bristow**, 22, single, b. & residing Mid., dau. of Washington & Amanda Bristow. (W)
202A - 7 Jun. 1900 - **Edward W. Hart**, 23, single, clerk, b. & residing Mid., son of J. W. & Mary Hart, married **Helen G. Fleet**, 20, single, b. & residing Mid., dau. of Jno. H. & Mary E. Fleet. (W)
202B - 6 Jun. 1900 - **Edward Billups**, 25, single, oysterman, b. & residing Mid., son of Gip & Minerva Billups, married **Eliza Baytop**, 27, single, b. & residing Mid., dau. of Wm. & Betsey Baytop. (B)
202C - 24 Apr. 1900 - **Dan Munroe**, 22, single, oysterman, b. & residing Mid., son of James & Rebecca Monroe, married **Mary Eliza Holmes**, 20, single, b. & residing Mid., dau. of John & Martha Holmes. (B)
203A - 20 Jun. & - **H. Harry Vail**, 24, single, salesman, b. & residing New Jersey, son of David & Emma Vail, married **Lula A. Gaines**, 24, single, b. & residing Mid., dau. of Thos. & Sallie J. Gaines. (W)
203B - 6 Jun. 1900 - **John C. Major**, 23, single, farmer, b. & residing Mid., son of John M. & Fannie A. Major, married **Lottie C. Miller**, 23, single, b. & residing Mid., dau. of H. I. & Mary Miller. (W)
203C - 27 Jun. 1900 - **John Smith Richardson**, 26, single, merchant, b. King & Queen, residing Mid., son of Wm. T. & Sarah Richardson, married **A. Maude McKann**, 21, single, b. & residing Mid., dau. of R. H. & Ann McKann. (W)
204A - 28 Jun. 1900 - **C. Read Moses**, 30, single, minister, b. Montgomery, residing Mid., son of Archie & Nancy Moses, married **Anna R. Jackson**, 30, single, b. & residing Mid., dau. of James H. & Anna B. Jackson. (W)
204B - 10 Jul. 1900 - **Wm. S. Christian**, 69, widower, physician & surgeon, b. & residing Mid., son of R. H. & E. A. Christian, married **Alice F. Woodward**, 46, single, b. & residing Mid., dau. of Philemon & Mary E. Woodward.

(W)
204C - 7 Aug. 1900 - **Chas. Henry Burrell**, 32, single, oysterman, b. & residing Mid., son of Moses & Mary Ann Burrell, married **Virginia Chatman**, 22, single, b. Gloucester, residing Mid., dau. of Wesley & Margaret Chatman. (B)
205A - 12 Aug. 1900 - **James Garner**, 24, single, oysterman, b. St. Marys Co., Maryland, residing Mid., son of Louisa & Henry Garner, married **Ella Townsley**, 19, single, b. & residing Mid., dau. of Harriet & Isaiah Townsley. (B)
205B - 22 Aug. 1900 - **John Key**, 22, single, oysterman, b. & residing Mid., son of Walker & Delia Key, married **Mattie Easton**, 21, single, b. & residing Mid., dau. of Henry & Lucia Ann Easton. (B)
205C - 22 Aug. 1900 - **Thos. M. Eastman**, 28, single, oysterman, b. Butler, Pennsylvania, residing Mid., son of F. W. & Margaret Eastman, married **Lulu M. Wilson**, 18, single, b. Gloucester, residing Mid., dau. of John W. & Cordelia Wilson. (W)
206A - 6 Sep. 1900 - **Moses Robinson**, 47, widower, oysterman, b. Mathews, residing Mid., son of Kit & Maria Robinson, married **Lucinda Fountain**, 30, single, b. & residing Mid., dau. of Geo. & Maria Fountain. (B)
206B - 5 Sep. 1900 - **Doctor Linken**, 24, single, oysterman, b. & residing Mid., son of Cyrus & Violet Linken, married **Caroline Harris**, 20, single, b. & residing Mid., dau. of Polly Harris. (B)
206C - 9 Sep. 1900 - **Albert Taliaferro**, 25, widower, oysterman, b. & residing Mid., son of Sam & Mary Jane Taliaferro, married **Florence Jones**, 23, single, b. & residing Mid., dau. of Prophet & Mary Jones. (B)
207A - 23 Sep. 1900 - **William Gwynn**, 24, single, oysterman, b. & residing Mid., son of Wm. & Margaret Gwynn, married **Georgia A. Iverson**, 22, single, b. & residing Mid., dau. of James & Venus Iverson. (B)
207B - 19 Sep. 1900 - **Cary Lattimore**, 27, single, oysterman, b. & residing Mid., son of Emily Bank, married **Lenora Scott**, 22, single, b. & residing Mid., dau. of Sallie Ann Scott. (C)
207C - 26 Sep. 1900 - **Chas. E. Taylor**, 37, widower, farmer, b. King & Queen, residing Mid., son of Thos. J. & Sarah J. Taylor, married **Mary E. Wood**, 27, widow, b. & residing Essex, dau. of Philip & Bettie Taylor. (W)
208A - 27 Sep. 1900 - **Julius F. Hughes**, 26, single, merchant, b. Mathews, residing Mid., son of J. T. & Sarah E. Hughes, married **Blanche Armstrong**, 23, single, b. & residing Mid., dau. of R. P. & Eliza Armstrong. (W)
208B - 13 Oct. 1900 - **Dan Laws**, 23, single,

oysterman, son of John & Martha Laws, married **Frances Jackson**, 22, single, b. & residing Mid., dau. of Scipio & Frances Jackson. (B)

208C - 11 Oct. 1900 - **Joseph Roy**, 24, single, oysterman, b. & residing Mid., son of Joe & Dinah Roy, married **Lizzie Reed**, 22, single, b. & residing Mid., dau. of John Reed. (B)

209A - 23 Oct. 1900 - **Edward H. Sibley**, 40, widower, lighthouse keeper, b. & residing Mid., son of James & Susan Sibley, married **Carrie A. Major**, 30, single, b. & residing Mid., dau. of Walter & Betty Major. (W)

209B - 1 Nov. 1900 - **James Key**, 28, divorced, oysterman, b. & residing Mid., son of Carter & Fanny Key, married **Ellen Green**, 20, single, b. & residing Mid., dau. of Chas. & Mary Green. (B)

209C - 1 Nov. 1900 - **George Bagby**, 32, single, oysterman, b. & residing Mid., son of Washington & Polly Bagby, married **Catharine Holmes**, 23, single, b. Essex, residing Mid., dau. of John & Rachel Holmes. (B)

210A - 4 Nov. 1900 - **John Smith**, 21, single, oysterman, b. & residing Gloucester, son of John & Emma Smith, married **Lucy Francis Blake**, 15, single, b. & residing Mid., dau. of Wm. Henry & Susan Elizabeth Blake. (W)

210B - 8 Nov. 1900 - **Ashby L. Jones**, 32, single, Commissioner of Revenue, son of Lewis & Maria Jones, married **Mary B. Lawson**, 23, single, b. & residing Mid., dau. of Ty & Sarah A. Lawson. (W)

210C - 29 Nov. 1900 - **W. L. Waller**, 24, single, oysterman, b. & residing Mid., son of H. C. & Jane Waller, married **Maude Esther Ruffin**, 21, single, b. & residing Mid., dau. of Griffin & Susan Ruffin. (B)

211A - 29 Nov. 1900 - **John Lightford**, 35, divorced, oysterman, b. & residing Mid., son of William & Maria Lightford, married **Maria Morris**, 26, single, b. & residing Mid., dau. of Bettie Morris. (B)

211B - 29 Nov. 1900 - **E. D. Rock**, 27, single, lumber dealer, b. Lancaster, residing Mid., son of W. W. & Frances Rock, married **E. Waller Richardson**, 31, single, b. King William, residing Mid., dau. of W. T. & Sarah Richardson. (W)

211C - 15 Nov. 1900 - **Adolphus Beadles**, 35, widower, oysterman, b. Lancaster, residing Mid., married **Elizabeth Ruffin**, 18, single, b. & residing Mid. (B)

212A - 6 Dec. 1900 - **P. J. Warren**, 61, widower, farmer, b. Delaware, residing Mid., son of Burton & Nancy Warren, married **Lidie Sue Sibley**, 21, single, b. & residing Mid., dau. of Thos. H. & Lulie Sibley. (W)

212B - 5 Dec. 1900 - **Geo. T. Daniel**, 40, single, farmer, b. Mathews, residing Mid., son of Geo. B. & Mary

Daniel, married **Eudora Walton**, 21, single, b. & residing Mid., dau. of Wm. & Sarah Walton. (W)

212C - 12 Dec. 1900 - **Wm. Taliaferro**, 35, single, oysterman, b. & residing Mid., son of Samuel & Susan Taliaferro, married **Kate Graffin**, 35, divorced, b. & residing Mid., dau. of Thos. & Martha E. Henry. (C)

213A - 1 Dec. 1900 - **James Gundy**, 23, single, oysterman, b. & residing Mid., son of James & Ann L. Gundy, married **Lulu Wormley**, 22, widow, b. & residing Mid., dau. of Washington & Polly Bagby. (B)

213B - 19 Dec. 1900 - **D. S. Soles**, 30, single, blacksmith, b. & residing Mathews, son of J. H. & Mary S. Soles, married **Lucy Lumpkin**, 21, single, b. & residing Mid., dau. of J. R. & Lucy C. Lumpkin. (W)

213C - 19 Dec. 1900 - **Ernest Smoot**, 22, single, "government service," b. Caroline, residing Washington, D. C., son of Benj. & P. A. Smoot, married **Eva Nelson**, 22, single, b. Somerset Co., Maryland, residing Mid., dau. of D. M. & Elizabeth Nelson. (W)

214A - 16 Dec. 1900 - **J. T. Figg**, 22, single, oysterman, b. Gloucester, residing Mid., son of John H. & Chestina Figg, married **Cammie Netine Prince**, 17, single, b. Gloucester, residing Mid., dau. of A. P. & Mary C. Prince. (W)

214B - 24 Dec. 1900 - **John Philips**, 23, single, oysterman, b. & residing Gloucester, son of Washington & Mary Philips, married **Julia Reed**, 18, single, b. & residing Mid., dau. of Willie & Fannie Reed. (B)

214C - 25 Dec. 1900 - **John W. New**, 22, single, oysterman, b. & residing Mid., son of W. G. & Nannie New, married **Susie Greenwood**, 22, single, b. & residing Essex, dau. of Wm. & Sarah Greenwood. (W)

215A - 26 Dec. 1900 - **Dinkey L. Fary**, 26, single, farmer, b. & residing Gloucester, son of Edward & Josie Fary, married **Shellie Robinson**, 19, single, b. & residing Mid., dau. of A. C. & Rosie Ann Robinson. (W)

215B - 19 Dec. 1900 - **Daniel Lockley, Sr.**, 64, widower, farmer, b. Gloucester, residing Mid., son of Daniel & Millie Lockley, married **Lee Scott**, 28, single, b. & residing Mid., dau. of Coley Scott. (B)

215C - 27 Dec. 1900 - **Harry Robinson**, 25, single, oysterman, b. & residing Mid., son of Harry & Martha Robinson, married **Katie Lockley**, 21, single, b. & residing Mid., dau. of Henry & Lucy Lockley. (B)

216A - 29 Dec. 1900 - **Beverly Smith**, 38, widower, oysterman, b. Gloucester, residing Mid., son of John & Charlotte Smith, married **Mary Ellen Latne**, 35, divorced, b. & residing Mid., dau. of Adam & Fannie Latne. (B)

216B - 1 Jan. 1901 - **Addison W. Cornelius**, 23, single, oysterman, b. & residing Mid., son of B. J. &

Sarah E. Cornelius, married **Fannie B. Yates**, single, b. & residing Mid., dau. of Rob't W. & Mary C. Yates. (W)
216C - 1 Jan. 1901 - **William Fitchett**, 23, single, farmer, b. & residing Mid., son of Piney & Sallie Fitchett, married **Lillian Bristow**, 25, widow, b. & residing Mid., dau. of Walter & Caroline Bristow. (W)
217A - 2 Jan. 1901 - **James Johnson**, 30, single, farmer, b. & residing Mid., son of Moses & Etta Johnson, married **Maria Page**, 20, single, b. & residing Mid., dau. of Manuel Page. (B)
217B - 15 Jan. 1901 - **John R. Callis**, 22, single, oysterman, b. & residing Mathews, son of Geo. W. & Julia Callis, married **Daisy V. Payne**, 20, single, b. & residing Mid., dau. of Wm. E. & Lolla B. Payne. (W)
217C - 20 Dec. 1901 - **Henry Gaines**, 28, single, oysterman, b. & residing Essex, son of Thos. Lewis & Bell Gaines, married **Bell Brown**, 24, single, b. & residing Mid., dau. of Wm. Morris & Martha Ellen Brown. (B)
218A - 22 Jan. 1901 - **John N. Apperson**, 25, single, sailor, b. & residing Mathews, married **Mary E. Nuttall**, 22, single, b. Gloucester, residing Mid., dau. of Rich'd & Bettie Nuttall. (W)
218B - 31 Jan. 1901 - **James Boyd, Jr.**, 23, single, oysterman, b. & residing Mid., son of James & Sylvia Boyd, married **Mattie Bundy**, 20, single, b. & residing Mid., dau. of Ben & Bettie Bundy. (B)
218C - 18 Dec. 1901 - **Thomas Peterson**, 25, single, oysterman, b. & residing Mid., son of Rob't & Mary Peterson, married **Emma Davis**, 20, single, b. & residing Mid., dau. of Joseph & Emma Davis. (B)
219A - 7 Feb. 1901 - **J. P. Bristow**, 28, single, oysterman, b. & residing Mid., son of W. C. & Mona Bristow, married **Mary S. Lindsey**, 23, single, b. & residing Mid., dau. of David & May S. Lindsey. (W)
219B - 27 Dec. 1900 - **T. T. Jackson**, 23, single, oysterman, b. & residing Mid., son of John & Mal Jackson, married **Edgie Wilson**, 21, single, b. & residing Mid., dau. of Mar. & Bet Wilson. (W)
219C - 14 Jan. 1901 - **Philip Henry Burrell**, 21, single, farmer, b. Gloucester, residing Mid., son of Philip & Sarah Burrell, married **Hatty Ross**, 21, single, b. Gloucester, residing Mid., dau. of Washington & Jno. Ross. (C)
220A - 1 Jan. 1901 - **Beverly Taliaferro**, 36, widower, oysterman, b. & residing Mid., son of Simon & Manurva Taliaferro, married **Harriett Holmes**, 29, widow, b. & residing Mid., dau. of Mack & Dorcus Travers. (C)
220B - 17 Feb. 1901 - **Walker Miller**, 21, single, oysterman, b. & residing Mid., son of John & Susan

Miller, married **Nannie Braxton**, 16, single, b. & residing Mid., dau. of Isaac & Sarah Braxton. (B)

220C - 10 Mar. 1901 - **Washington Bagby**, 62, widower, farmer, b. King & Queen, residing Mid., son of Titus & Katey Bagby, married **Catharine Banks**, 27, widow, b. King & Queen, residing Mid., dau. of Lewis & Catharine Tuppenel. (B)

221A - 13 Mar. 1901 - **John R. Brooke**, 32, widower, farmer, b. & residing Mathews, son of Wm. & Margaret Brooks, married **Mary E. Powell**, 23, single, b. & residing Mid., dau. of Joseph & Louisa Powell. (B)

221B - 21 Mar. 1901 - **T. L. Shreeves**, 22, single, oysterman, b. & residing Mid., son of Geo. T. & Mary C. Shreeves, married **Mannie Graham**, 21, single, b. & residing Mid., dau. of James & Deal Graham. (W)

221C - 6 Mar. 1901 - **Peter Thomas Cosby**, 22, single, minister, b. & residing Mathews, son of Daniel & Louisa Cosby, married **Emily Keziah Robinson**, 25, single, b. & residing Mid., dau. of C. A. & M. E. Robinson. (B)

222A - 20 Mar. 1901 - **Lloyd C. Apsley**, 21, single, farmer, b. & residing Mid., son of W. R. & M. F. Apsley, married **Ellsie Mayo**, 19, single, b. & residing Mid., dau. of J. W. & Nellie A. Mayo. (W)

222B - 7 Apr. 1901 - **George W. Eastman**, 27, single, merchant, b. Butler, Pennsylvania, residing Mid., son of F. M. & Margaret M. Eastman, married **Sallie G. Ailsworth**, 23, single, b. & residing Mid., dau. of Rob't N. & Mary E. Ailsworth. (W)

222C - 12 Mar. 1901 - **Eugene A. Taylor**, 26, single, marine engineer, b. Accomack, residing Mid., son of Rob't S. & Vernetta S. Taylor, married **Ida L. Harrow**, 18, single, b. & residing Mid., dau. of Alonzo W. & Hattie E. Harrow. (W)

223A - 28 Mar. 1901 - **Geo. W. Jackson**, 23, single, oysterman, b. & residing Mid., son of Noah & Annie Jackson, married **Sallie Sable**, 20, single, b. & residing Mid., dau. of Duck & Catharine Sable. (W)

223B - 24 Apr. 1901 - **Silas Bilups**, 34, widower, oysterman, b. & residing Mid., son of Isaac & Fanny Billups, married **Victoria Jackson**, 26, single, b. & residing Mid., dau. of James & Dolly Jackson. (B)

223C - 24 Apr. 1901 - **James Bundy**, 25, single, oysterman, b. & residing Mid., married **Mattie Kate Minor**, 16, single, b. & residing Mid., dau. of Ellen Ransom. (B)

224A - 25 Apr. 1901 - **Isaac Claude Mercer**, 27, single, oysterman, b. & residing Mid., son of James C. & Bettie E. Mercer, married **Lillian Virginia Barrick**, 24, single, b. & residing Mid., dau. of John W. & Fannie Barrick. (W)

224B - 5 May 1901 - **G. M. Collins**, 26, single, oysterman, b. King & Queen, residing Mid., son of Wm. & Irene Collins, married **Ida Laws**, 20, single, b. & residing Mid., dau. of John & Martha Laws. (B)
224C - 6 May 1901 - **Wm. Thos. Reed**, 38, widower, oysterman, b. North Carolina, residing Mid., son of Phoebe Whitley, married **Mary Bilups**, 27, single, b. Mathews, residing Mid. (B)
225A - 15 May 1901 - **Carroll Lee Clements**, 27, single, ship fitter, b. Mid., residing Newport News, son of Rich'd M. & Virginia O. Clements, married **Annie E. George**, 20, single, b. Stafford, residing Mid., dau. of J. M. & E. J. George. (W)
225B - 26 May 1901 - **Atwill Burch**, 23, single, oysterman, b. King & Queen, residing Mid., son of J. R. & Mrs. J. R. Burch, married **Blanche Hazelwood**, 21, single, b. & residing Mid., dau. of J. R. & Mary Lee Hazelwood. (W)
225C - 27 Jun. 1901 - **H. Jeter Haydon**, 28, single, editor, b. Lancaster, residing Mid., son of Thos. J. & Sarah C. Haydon, married **Sue H. Burton**, 24, single, b. & residing Mid., dau. of C. S. & Lucy Burton. (W)
226A - 27 Jun. 1901 - **Newton W. French**, 27, single, oysterman, b. & residing Mid., son of John & Edna E. French, married **Lillie Virginia Fleet**, 26, single, b. & residing Mid., dau. of John H. & Mary E. Fleet. (W)
226B - 19 Jun. 1901 - **Edward S. Lamberth**, 26, single, blacksmith, b. Gloucester, residing Mid., son of R. T. & Susan E. Lambert, married **Lillian Gardner**, 25, single, b. & residing Mid., dau. of Lewis & Elizabeth Gardner. (W)
226C - 17 Jun. 1901 - **William Corbin**, 38, divorced, oysterman, b. & residing Mid., son of Mille Corbin & Wm. Holmes, married **Cordelia Gwathmey**, 25, single, b. King & Queen, residing Mid., dau. of John Gwathmey. (B)
227A - 24 Jul. 1901 - **Holland Sibley**, 24, single, oysterman, b. & residing Mid., son of R. B. & Mona E. Sibley, married **Mamie F. Thrift**, 19, single, b. & residing Mid., dau. of L. K. & Ellen J. Thrift. (W)
227B - 24 Jul. 1901 - **Herman E. Graves**, 22, single, oysterman, b. & residing Mid., son of M. & Mary Graves, married **Maude V. Blake**, 19, single, b. & residing Mid., dau. of J. H. & Sue Blake. (W)
227C - 15 Aug. 1901 - **Jas. R. Byrd**, 39, widower, farmer, b. King & Queen, residing Mid., son of Rob't & Frances Byrd, married **Elnora Kidd**, 24, single, b. & residing Mid., dau. of James & P. A. Kidd. (C)
228A - 15 Aug. 1901 - **Benjamin Jones**, 32, widower, oysterman, b. King & Queen, residing Mid., son of John & Julia Jones, married **Lucy Waller**, 28, widow, b. &

residing Mid., dau. of Anne Ruffin. (B)
    228B - 27 Aug. 1901 - **Shelbon Dunn**, 22, single, farmer, b. & residing Mid., son of C. L. & Ada A. Dunn, married **Bertha B. Marchant**, 20, single, b. & residing Mid., dau. of J. S. & Maria L. Marchant. (W)
    228C - 28 Aug. 1901 - **Howard C. Erdman**, 24, single, gardener, b. & residing Baltimore, Maryland, married **Effie M. Bulle**, 23, single, b. & residing Mid., dau. of Geo. T. & Sarah Bull. (W)
    229A - 29 Aug. 1901 - **Sidney L. Johnson**, 29, single, "doctor of medicine," b. Washington, D. C., residing Ohio, son of D. & L. H. Johnson, married **Maria L. Saunders**, 21, single, b. Essex, residing Mid., dau. of O. H. & L. A. R. Saunders. (W)
    229B - 29 Aug. 1901 - **Albert Sidney Spencer**, 23, single, oyster dealer, b. & residing Mid., son of R. B. & Judia Spencer, married **Louise Powell**, 21, single, b. York Co., residing Mid., dau. of A. W. & Angeline Powell (W)
    229C - 29 Aug. 1901 - **Daniel Wormley**, 42, widower, oysterman, b. & residing Mid., son of Thos. & Isabella Wormley, married **Rebecca Wormley**, 19, single, b. & residing Mid., dau. of Wm. & Elsie Wormley. **(C)**
    230A - 12 Sep. 1901 - **James H. Bayton**, 27, single, merchant, b. & residing Mid., son of Rich'd & Hannah Bayton, married **Mary E. Jackson**, 27, single, b. & residing Mid., dau. of Samuel & Fannie Jackson. (C)
    230B - 22 Aug. 1901 - **John Henry Banks**, 28, single, oysterman, b. & residing Mid., son of John & Laura Banks, married **Ella Page**, 23, single, b. & residing Mid., dau. of Alex & Frankie Page. (B)
    230C - 5 Sep. 1901 - **Monroe Furgeson**, 23, single, oysterman, b. Mathews, residing Mid., son of John & Rebecca Furgeson, married **Addie M. Minor**, 20, single, b. & residing Mid., dau. of W. B. & Lucy A. Minor. (B)
    231A - 26 Sep. 1901 - **Chas. Ruffin**, 24, single, oysterman, b. & residing Mid., son of Lewis & Caroline Ruffin, married **Sarah Taylor**, 21, single, b. & residing Mid., dau. of Fountain & Amy Taylor. (B)
    231B - 2 Oct. 1901 - **Walter F. Rowe**, 23, single, oysterman, b. Gloucester, residing Mid., son of Washington & Matilda J. Rowe, married **Peachie Hibble**, 17, single, b. Gloucester, residing Mid., dau. of Geo. W. & Martha A. Hibble. (W)
    231C - 2 Oct. 1901 - **Henry Roy**, 64, widower, oysterman, b. & residing Mid., son of Mary Roy, married **Mary Young**, 50, widow, b. & residing Mid., dau. of Beverly Thurston & Fannie Simms. (B)
    232A - 9 Oct. 1901 - **Thos. Davis**, 30, widower, oysterman, b. & residing Mid., son of Reubin & Jennie

Davis, married **Emma Jane Reed**, 35, widower, b. & residing Mid., dau. of Geo. & Lina Reed. (B)

232B - 9 Oct. 1901 - **Corbin Robinson**, 70, widower, farmer, b. & residing Mid., son of Fannie Lee, married **Harriet Wake**, 57, widow, b. Gloucester, residing Mid., dau. of King Solomon. (B)

232C - 16 Oct. 1901 - **Daniel Lockley, Jr.**, 27, single, oysterman, b. & residing Mid., son of Daniel Lockley, Sr., married **Celestine Dudley**, 20, single, b. & residing Mid., dau. of Joshu Dudley. (B)

233A - 16 Oct. 1901 - **Cornelius Scott**, 25, single, oysterman, b. & residing Mid., son of James & Barbara Scott, married **Elizabeth Purkins**, 21, single, b. & residing Mid., dau. of Pharoah & Sarah Purkins. (B)

233B - 12 Nov. 1901 - **Ches. A. Setton**, 37, single, farmer, b. Germany, residing Mid., son of August & Annie Setton, married **Nealie F. Condiff**, 31, single, b. & residing Mid., dau. of Griffin & Anna Condiff. (W) [See 58A.]

233C - 14 Nov. 1901 - **Harry A. Gaskins**, 27, single, fisherman, b. & residing Lancaster, son of R. & J. T. Gaskins, married **M. J. Crittenden**, 19, single, b. & residing Mid., dau. of Thos. & Lucy Crittenden. (W)

234A - 19 Nov. 1901 - **Percy L. Richardson**, 28, single, merchant, b. Northampton, residing Lancaster, son of W. T. & Sarah Richardson, married **Emma R. Northam**, 22, single, b. & residing Mid., dau. of Henry C. & Susan H. Northam. (W)

234B - 20 Nov. 1901 - **Jesse Eubank**, 25, single, farmer, b. King & Queen, residing Mid., son of B. F. & Martha E. Eubank, married **Bessie Collie**, 22, single, b. King & Queen, residing Mid., dau. of James & Sallie Collie. (W)

234C - 21 Nov. 1901 - **Chas. Smith**, 21, single, oysterman, b. Gloucester, residing Mid., son of Arthur & Harriett Smith, married **Tamie Curtis**, 19, single, b. Gloucester, residing Mid., dau. of Joseph Curtis & Jenny Johnson. (B)

235A - 11 Dec. 1901 - **Virginius L. Clayvell**, 30, single, oysterman, b. & residing Mid., son of Zadoc & Sarah Clayvell, married **Sarah H. Hall**, 28, single, b. & residing Mid., dau. of John & Tiny Hall. (W) [See Claybill.]

235B - 12 Dec. 1901 - **Lewis Banks**, 52, widower, oysterman, b. & residing Mid., son of York & Lucinda Banks, married **Malissa Wake**, 45, widow, b. & residing Mid., dau. of Edmond Diggs. (B)

235C - 13 Dec. 1901 - **Wilbur J. Brooks**, 21, single, farmer, b. & residing Richmond Co., son of D. J. & Sarah J. Brooks, married **Annie Morris**, 21, single, b. &

residing Mid., dau. of J. B. & Ella Morris. (W)
236A - 12 Dec. 1901 - **S. C. Regensburg**, 27, widower, farmer, b. King & Queen, residing Gloucester, son of S. A. & Rosa Regensburg, married **Louisa Davis**, 24, single, b. King & Queen, residing Mid., dau. of Joseph & Essa Davis. (W)
236B - 18 Dec. 1901 - **Dave B. Ailsworth**, 25, single, oysterman, b. & residing Mid., son of Joseph & Sallie Ailsworth, married **Amy C. Crittenden**, 21, single, b. & residing Mid., dau. of Geo. W. & Columbia Crittenden. (W)
236C - 19 Dec. 1901 - **John Dawson**, 41, widower, oysterman, b. Norfolk Co., residing Mid., son of Everett & Harriett Dawson, married **Catharine Griffin**, 23, single, b. & residing Mid., dau. of Edmund & Maria Griffin. (B)
237A - 20 Dec. 1901 - **Thomas Tilden Tresler**, 23, single, oysterman, b. & residing Mid., son of Jacob B. & Susan Ann Tresler, married **Leatha Gyneth Hurd**, 20, single, b. & residing Mid., dau. of Jesse & Ida Hurd. (W)
237B - 25 Dec. 1901 - **Edward S. Vaughan**, 55, single, farmer, b. & residing Mid., son of Wm. P. & Harriett Vaughan, married **Vessie B. Blake**, 25, single, b. & residing Mid., dau. of R. L. & Margaret Blake. (W)
237C - 22 Dec. 1901 - **Silas Bagby**, 27, single, farmer, b. & residing Mid., son of Washington & Polly Bagby, married **Feanie Miller**, 26, single, b. & residing Mid., dau. of Jeff & Mollie Miller. (B)
238A - 23 Dec. 1901 - **Chas. Roy**, 30, divorced widower, oysterman, b. & residing Mid., son of Henry & Chris Roy, married **Catharine Jackson**, 19, single, b. & residing Mid., dau. of Ellis & Grace Jackson. (B)
238B - 24 Dec. 1901 - **Henry Rowe**, 25, single, millright, b. Gloucester, residing Mid., son of J. H. & A. M. Rowe, married **Bessie E. Kennard**, 18, single, b. & residing Mid., dau. of W. J. & M. J. Kennard. (W)
238C - 25 Dec. 1901 - **Chas. Lewis**, 22, single, oysterman, b. & residing Mid., son of Henry & Mollie Lewis, married **Lottie Fields**, 21, single, b. & residing Mid., dau. of Peter & Jennie Fields. (B)
239A - 24 Dec. 1901 - **John Collier**, 23, single, oysterman, b. King & Queen, residing Mid., son of Chas. & Catherine Collier, married **Mildred Janie Lecompt**, 17, single, b. & residing Mid., dau. of Samuel & Courtney Lecompt. (W)
239B - 26 Dec. 1901 - **James L. Lambert**, 28, single, blacksmith, b. Gloucester, residing Mid., son of R. T. & Susan E. Lamberth, married **Mattie B. Walton**, 17, single, b. King & Queen, residing Mid., dau. of E. & Fannie E.

Walton. (W)

239C - 31 Dec. 1901 - **William G. Hart**, 41, single, carpenter, b. & residing Mid., son of Columbus & Mary E. Hart, married **Mary W. Chowning**, 24, single, b. & residing Mid., dau. of John & Fannie Chowning. (W)

240A - 1 Jan. 1902 - **Claude Neale**, 22, single, merchant, b. Essex, residing Mid., son of K. M. & Kate N. Neale, married **Bernice E. Smither**, 21, single, b. & residing Mid., dau. of H. L. & Fannie Smither. (W)

240B - 9 Jan. 1902 - **Chas. H. Robinson**, 26, single, oysterman, b. Baltimore, residing Mid., married **Lucinda Robinson**, 30, widow, b. & residing Mid., dau. of Geo. & Maria Fountain. (C)

240C - 15 Jan. 1902 - **Harry Fountain**, 37, single, farmer, b. & residing Mid., son of Harrison & Rachel Fountain, married **Octavia Roots**, 23, single, b. King & Queen, residing Mid., dau. of Ralph Roots. (B)

241A - 19 Jan. 1902 - **W. H. Randolph**, 49, widower, steamboat pilot, b. Baltimore, residing Mid., son of Harris & Ellen Randolph, married **Emma J. Lockly**, 36, widow, b. Gloucester, residing Mid. (B)

241B - 21 Jan. 1902 - **Berkley S. Richardson**, 35, widower, farmer, b. King & Queen, residing Mid., son of W. T. & Sarah Richardson, married **Fannie E. Hilliard**, 24, single, b. & residing Mid., dau. of R. D. & Fannie Hilliard. (W)

241C - 20 Jan. 1902 - **Chas. H. Ruperti**, 25, single, receiving clerk, b. & residing Baltimore, son of John H. & Martha H. Ruperti, married **Effie L. Kellum**, 23, single, b. Mid., dau. of John T. & Nettie Kellum. (W)

242A - 21 Jan. 1902 - **John Valentine Richardson**, 29, single, real estate dealer, b. & residing Baltimore, son of Chas. J. & Sarah F. Richardson, married **Bessie Epler**, 25, single, b. Reynoldsville, Pennsylvania, residing Baltimore, dau. of Wm. & Susan Epler. (W)

242B - 27 Jan. 1902 - **F. H. Newell**, 46, single, salesman, b. & residing Baltimore, son of Peter & Sarah Newell, married **Mary M. Swinney**, 30, divorced, b. Baltimore, residing Mid., dau. of Epaphroditus & Elizabeth Swinney. (W)

242C - 25 Jan. 1902 - **Joseph H. Brooks**, 57, widower, farmer, b. & residing Mid., son of Jessie & Bettie Brooks, married **Miranda White**, 30, widow, b. King & Queen, residing Mid., dau. of James Brockenbrough. (B)

243A - 29 Jan. 1902 - **David Braxton**, 23, single, oysterman, b. & residing Mid., son of Peter & Sallie Braxton, married **Elizabeth Redd**, 20, single, b. & residing Mid., dau. of James & Park Kidd. (B)

243B - 6 Feb. 1902 - **Joseph E. Smither**, 32, single, farmer, b. & residing Mid., son of Revan & Catherine

Smither, married **Bertha Estelle Townsend**, 22, single, b. & residing Mid., dau. of J. D. & Suley Townsend. (W)
243C - 6 Feb. 1902 - **John Fields**, 25, single, oysterman, b. & residing Mid., son of Rob't & Miranda Fields, married **Mamie Courtney**, 20, single, b. & residing Mid. (B)
244A - 12 Feb. 1902 - **James H. Jefferson**, 26, single, oysterman, b. & residing Mid., son of Thos. & Viola Jefferson, married **Gena Griffin**, 20, single, b. & residing Mid., dau. of Taylor & Mollie Griffin. (B)
244B - 13 Feb. 1902 - **Simon Gregory**, 24, single, oysterman, b. Gloucester, residing Mid., son of Nat & Lucy Gregory, married **Pearl Clayton**, 18, single, b. King & Queen, residing Mid., dau. of Jack & Lelia Clayton. (B)
244C - 16 Feb. 1902 - **Grant Williams**, 21, single, oysterman, b. & residing Mid., son of Zacky & Bettie Williams, married **Maggie Johnson**, 22, single, b. & residing Mid., dau. of Simon & Matilda Johnson. (B)
245A - 20 Feb. 1902 - **John E. Regan**, 42, widower, miller, b. Wicomico Co., Maryland, residing Mid., son of Elijah & Hattie Regan, married **Estella E. Tingle**, 22, single, b. Chincoteague Island, Accomack, residing Mid., dau. of Samuel & Vesta Tingle. (W)
245B - 2 Mar. 1902 - **James Wormley**, 23, single, farmer, b. & residing Mid., son of James & Mary Wormley, married **Ida Minor**, 23, single, b. & residing Mid., dau. of Jeff & Mallie Minor. (B)
245C - 30 Mar. 1902 - **W. L. Haydon**, 23, single, oysterman, b. & residing Mid., son of M. & Leda B. Haydon, married **Virginia Groome**, 16, single, b. Gloucester, residing Mid., son of A. C. & Susie Groome. (W)
246A - 27 Mar. 1902 - **Lorenzo Taylor**, 22, single, sailor, b. & residing Mid., son of Robert Boyd & Lucy Ellen Braxton, married **Alice Banks**, 25, single, b. & residing Mid., dau. of Rich & Mary Banks. (B)
246B - 1 Apr. 1902 - **Austin Wilson**, 38, widower, oysterman, b. King & Queen, residing Mid., son of James & Mary Wilson, married **Susan Braxton**, 32, widow, b. & residing Mid., dau. of Margaret Hoskins. (B)
246C - 3 Apr. 1902 - **Peter Buckner**, 53, single, farmer, b. Virginia, residing Mid., married **Hannah Wake**, 50, single, b. & residing Mid., dau. of Addison Wake. (B)
247A - 6 Apr. 1902 - **James H. Goode**, 59, widower, farmer, b. Essex, residing Mid., son of John & Juliza Good, married **Anne E. Smith**, 40, single, b. Gloucester, residing Mid. (W)
247B - 9 Apr. 1902 - **John C. Revere**, 20, single,

farmer, b. & residing Mid., son of Isaac P. & Deberah C. Revere, married **Bertie M. Johnson**, 17, single, b. Essex, residing Mid., dau. of John L. & Louisiana Johnson. (W)
247C - 16 Apr. 1902 - **Willie Weeks**, 22, single, oysterman, b. & residing Mid., son of Lucy Weeks & Walter Russ, married **Maggie Berry**, 21, single, b. & residing Mid., dau. of Daniel Berry. (B)
248A - 14 Apr. 1902 - **Braxton Muse**, 26, single, oysterman, b. & residing Mid., married **Lena Johnson**, 27, single, b. & residing Mid., dau. of John & Bettie Johnson. (B)
248B - 6 May 1902 - **Thomas Baytop**, 26, single, oysterman, b. King & Queen, residing Mid., son of Tollie Baytop, married **Sadie Ruffin**, 23, single, b. & residing Mid., dau. of Lida Ruffin. (B)
248C - 6 May 1902 - **Simon Taliaferro**, 22, single, oysterman, b. & residing Mid., son of Rebecca Taliaferro, married **Lena Goldman**, 19, single, b. & residing Mid., dau. of Elijah & Jane Goldman. (B)
249A - 21 May 1902 - **Henry E. Thrift**, 21, single, farmer, b. & residing Mid., son of Henry & Emma Thrift, married **Lizzie Redd**, 23, single, b. King & Queen, residing Mid., dau. of Wm. L. & Adeline Redd. (W)
249B - 4 Jun. 1902 - **Jno. R. Lumpkin**, 66, widower, farmer, b. Mathews, residing Mid., son of J. N. & C. W. Lumpkin, married **L. M. Walker**, 48, widow, b. & residing Mid., dau. of Wm. H. & Francis Burrell. (W)
249C - 5 Jun. 1902 - **James R. Jackson**, 21, single, oysterman, b. & residing Mid., son of Noah & Annie Jackson, married **Ira Anna Mason**, 21, single, b. & residing Mid., dau. of Sam & Sue Mason. (W)
250A - 4 Jun. 1902 - **Ernest Albert Gaines**, 28, single, sailor, b. & residing Mid., son of Thomas & Sallie Gaines, married **Nellie M. Marchant**, 21, single, b. & residing Mid., dau. of John & Kate Marchant. (W)
250B - 18 Jun. 1902 - **John Cornelius Clarke**, 65, widower, farmer, b. Essex, residing Mid., son of James & Emily Clarke, married **Margaret F. Apsley**, 44, widow, b. & residing Mid., dau. of Richeson & Nancy Slaughter. (W)
250C - 17 Jun. 1902 - **Rich'd Henry Taliaferro**, 25, single, b. & residing Mid., married **Ida Thurston**, 21, single, b. & residing Mid. (B)
251A - 24 Jun. 1902 - **Rob't W. Webb**, 45, widower, oysterman, b. & residing Mid., son of John & Betsy Webb, married **Margaret Roots**, 33, widow, b. King & Queen, residing Mid., dau. of Alfred Major. (B)
251B - 25 Jun. 1902 - **Nathaniel Robinson**, 26, single, farmer, b. & residing King & Queen, son of Archie & Maria Robinson, married **Mary E. W. Fields**, 27, single,

b. & residing Mid., dau. of Rob't & Malinda Fields. (B)
  251C - 2 Jul. 1902 - **Henry Wise Thomas**, 24, single, merchant, b. & residing York Co., son of Wise & Mary Thomas, married **Mary Katherine Deagle**, 22, single, b. & residing Mid., dau. of J. W. & Susie Deagle. (W)
  252A - 2 Jul. 1902 - **Chas. Harmon**, 24, single, farmer, b. Maryland, residing Mid., son of Joseph & Sarah Harmon, married **Nellie C. Davis**, 17, single, b. & residing Mid., dau. of Jane Davis. (W)
  252B - 5 Jul. 1902 - **Geo. C. Wood**, 23, single, oysterman, b. & residing Mid., married **Emma Alice Blake**, 17, single, b. & residing Mid., dau. of Samuel R. & Mary E. Blake. (W)
  252C - 20 Jul. 1902 - **Geo. T. Faucett**, 31, single, farmer, b. Mid., residing New Jersey, son of John R. & Sarah C. Faucett, married **Blanche Street**, 24, single, b. & residing Mid., dau. of Rich'd & Virginia Street. (W)
  253A - 22 Jul. 1902 - **David A. Flippin**, 50, widower, oysterman, b. & residing Lancaster, son of Armstead & Elizabeth Flippin, married **Annie Davis**, 34, widow, b. & residing Mid., dau. of Wm. C. & Mina Bristow. (W)
  253B - 7 Aug. 1902 - **John H. Smith**, 23, single, oysterman, b. & residing Mid., son of Beverly Smith & Adaline Harris, married **Alice Robinson**, 27, single, b. & residing Mid., dau. of Joseph & Celie Robinson. (B)
  253C - 13 Aug. 1902 - **Henry Jones**, 40, widower, oysterman, b. & residing Mid., son of Ned & Eliza Jones, married **Maude Perkins**, 19, single, b. & residing Mid., dau. of Lewis H. & Martha Perkins. (B)
  254A - 20 Aug. 1902 - **Beauregard Hall**, 41, widower, farmer, b. & residing Mid., son of Thos. & Pauline G. Hall, married **Anna Bell Hudgins**, 36, single, b. & residing Mid., dau. of Wm. H. & Mildred H. Hudgins. (W)
  254B - 24 Aug. 1902 - **Squire Morris**, 28, single, oysterman, b. & residing Mid., son of Silas & Sarah Morris, married **Lucelle Williams**, 22, single, b. & residing Mid., dau. of James & Chaney Williams. (B)
  254C - 5 Sep. 1902 - **Cornelius Keyser**, 21, single, oysterman, b. & residing Mid., son of Joseph Keyser, married **Elizabeth Jones**, 22, single, b. & residing Mid., dau. of Hannah Jones. (B)
  255A - 9 Sep. 1902 - **Wilton H. Bristow**, 24, single, farmer, b. & residing Mid., son of Walter & Adeline Bristow, married **Alice Johnson**, 17, single, b. & residing Mid., dau. of J. W. & Charlotte Johnson. (W)
  255B - 8 Sep. 1902 - **Ezra Reed**, 26, single, oysterman, b. & residing Mid., son of Silas & Mary Reed, married **Susan B. Ruffin**, 17, single, b. & residing Mid., dau. of Griffin & Susan A. Ruffin. (B)
  255C - 16 Sep. 1902 - **Chas West**, 40, widower,

oysterman, b. & residing Mid., son of Caroline West, married **Lottie F. Jones**, 26, single, b. Mathews, residing Mid., dau. of Mary E. Jones. (B)

256A - 16 Sep. 1902 - **Rob't S. Ellis**, 35, single, farmer, b. & residing Orange, son of J. H. & Mary E. Ellis, married **Bessie M. Watts**, 25, single, b. Tennessee, residing Albemarle, dau. of M. S. & Susan Watts. (W)

256B - 4 Sep. 1902 - **William D. Rucker**, 38, single, farmer, b. Amherst, residing Fauquier, son of W. A. & Ann C. Rucker, married **Beulah Parrish**, 29, single, b. & residing Mid., dau. of Wm. F. & Cordelia F. Parrish. (W)

256C - 18 Sep. 1902 - **Rich'd H. Banks**, 60, widower, farmer, b. & residing Mid., son of Solomon & Lucy Banks, married **Virginia Davis**, 40, widow, b. Portsmouth, residing Mid., dau. of Bristow Foreman. (B)

257A - 24 Sep. 1902 - **Morris Thurston**, 23, single, oysterman, b. & residing Mid., son of Daniel & Jane Thurston, married **Cora Banks**, 21, single, b. & residing Mid., dau. of Lewis & Dora Banks. (B)

257B - 25 Sep. 1902 - **Cornelius Johnson**, 28, single, farmer, b. King & Queen, residing Mid., son of Rosa & Ned Johnson, married **Lena Banks**, 25, single, b. & residing Mid., dau. of Emily & Alex Banks. (B)

257C - 18 Sep. 1902 - **E. W. Mears**, 24, single, oysterman, b. & residing Mid., son of R. T. & Matilda Mears, married **Sadie Tabor**, 21, single, b. & residing Mid., dau. of Joseph & Nancy Tabor. (W)

258A - 7 Oct. 1902 - **William E. Walker**, 26, single, sailor, b. & residing Mid., son of Wm. & Virginia Walker, married **Florence Hall**, 25, single, b. & residing Mid., dau. of John & Tiny Hall. (W)

258B - 9 Oct. 1902 - **Daniel Cook**, 29, widower, farmer, b. & residing Mid., son of Indiana Cook, married **Retha Burrell**, 21, single, b. & residing Mid., dau. of Tom & Mattie Burrell. (B)

258C - 14 Sep. 1902 - **James W. Jordan**, 21, single, oysterman, b. & residing Mid., son of Geo. & Anna Jordan, married **Mary Eliza Page**, 21, single, b. & residing Mid., dau. of Richard Page. (B)

259A - 16 Oct. 1902 - **James Lockley**, 27, single, oysterman, b. King & Queen, residing Mid., son of Wiley & Phillis Ann Lockley, married **Emmeline Key**, 15, single, b. & residing Mid., dau. of James & Phoebe Key. (B)

259B - 16 Oct. 1902 - **Andrew Wiatt**, 22, single, oysterman, b. & residing Mid., son of Rob't & Columbus Wiatt, married **Mona L. Burke**, 27, single, b. & residing Mid., dau. of Moses & Lidie Ann Burke. (B)

259C - 14 Oct. 1902 - **Thaddeus Burrell**, 22, single,

laborer, b. & residing Mid., son of Tom & Mary Burrell, married **India Holliday**, 23, single, b. & residing Mid., dau. of Pat & Mary Holliday. (B)

260A - 1902 - **Ransom Davis**, 26, single, oysterman, b. & residing Mid., son of Rob't & Mary Davis, married **Anna Elizabeth Walden**, 18, single, b. & residing Mid., dau. of Henry & Nellie Walden. (W)

260B - 22 Oct. 1902 - **Emanuel Dudly**, 27, single, oysterman, b. & residing Mid., son of Ransom & Anna Dudley, married **Prue Taylor**, 21, single, b. & residing Mid., dau. of Churchill & Martha Taylor. (B)

260C - 10 Nov. 1902 - **Ed Thomas Russ**, 23, single, oysterman, b. & residing Mid., son of Lewellen & Winnie Russ, married **Vina Holmes**, 24, single, b. & residing Mid., dau. of John Holmes. (C)

261A - 13 Nov. 1902 - **Ardell Smith**, 24, single, oysterman, b. Gloucester, residing Mid., son of Ray & Bettie Smith, married **Emma Booker**, 23, single, b. Gloucester, residing Baltimore, Maryland, dau. of Tyler & Booker. (B)

261B - 30 Nov. 1902 - **N. G. Wilson**, 19, single, oysterman, b. & residing Mid., son of N. G., Sr. & Bettie Wilson, married **Alice Jackson**, 18, single, b. & residing Mid., dau. of Hermas & Alice Jackson. (W)

261C - 23 Nov. 1902 - **Rob't Curtis**, 22, single, oysterman, b. & residing Mid., son of Henry & Lucy Curtis, married **Margaret Randel**, 23, single, b. King & Queen, residing Mid., dau. of Fleming & Alice Randel. (B)

262A - 28 Nov. 1902 - **J. C. Fears**, 25, single, oysterman, b. Cecil Co., Maryland, residing Mid., son of Joseph & Amanda Fears, married **Roberta Sibley**, 18, single, b. & residing Mid., dau. of R. B. & Minah Sibley. (W)

262B - 7 Dec. 1902 - **Sam Jones**, 32, widower, oysterman, b. & residing Mid., son of Cornelius & Saphronia Jones, married **Lizzie Key**, 21, single, b. & residing Mid., dau. of John & Bettie Key. (B)

262C - 10 Dec. 1902 - **John R. Moore**, 26, single, oysterman, b. King & Queen, residing Mid., son of Wm. R. & Margaret Moore, married **Estelle B. Carter**, 18, single, b. Essex, residing Mid., dau. of Jas. H. & Edna R. Dunn. (W)

263A - 17 Dec. 1902 - **Tyler Payne**, 22, single, oysterman, b. & residing Mid., son of Wm. & Judy Payne, married **Maggie Lewis**, 23, single, b. & residing Mid., dau. of Moses & Margaret Lewis. (C)

263B - 17 Dec. 1902 - **Ben Wormley**, 22, single, oysterman, b. & residing Mid., son of Ben Wormley & Bettie Mitchell, married **Eliza Greenwood**, 21, single, b.

& residing Mid., dau. of Billy & Henrietta Greenwood. (C)

263C - 17 Dec. 1902 - **Cernus James Duster**, 22, single, oysterman, b. & residing Mid., son of Chas. & Mary Duster, married **Lillian Virginia Johnson**, 19, single, b. & residing Mid., dau. of Warner & Esther Johnson. (B)

264A - 21 Dec. 1902 - **Johnnie Reed**, 24, single, farmer, b. & residing Mid., son of Frank & Maggie Reed, married **Louisa Bird**, 17, single, b. & residing Mid., dau. of George & Caroline Bird. (B)

264B - 20 Dec. 1902 - **John Lambert Norris**, 21, single, oysterman, b. & residing Mid., son of John W. & Sallie E. Norris, married **Mary Virginia Ruark**, 18, single, b. & residing Mid., dau. of M. F. & Florence Ruark. (W)

264C - 25 Dec. 1902 - **Edmund Johnson**, 24, single, oysterman, b. & residing Mid., son of Doctor & Amanda Johnson, married **Lucy R. Minor**, 18, single, b. & residing Mid., dau. of Wm. & Lucy Minor. (B)

265A - 23 Dec. 1902 - **Elijah Lomax**, 25, single, lumberman, b. & residing Mid., son of Jacob & Mary Lomax, married **Maggie Gatewood**, 25, single, b. & residing Mid., dau. of R. B. & Sarah Gatewood. (B)

265B - 23 Dec. 1902 - **Chas. W. Morris**, 22, single, oysterman, b. & residing Mid., son of John & Rose Morris, married **Mary Smith**, 15, single, b. & residing Mid., dau. of Chas. & Lelia Smith. (B)

265C - 25 Dec. 1902 - **E. J. Brooks**, 28, single, farmer, b. King & Queen, residing Mid., son of Wm. R. & Lucy Brooks, married **Nettie Boughton**, 22, single, b. King & Queen, residing Mid., dau. of Henry & Mirah A. Boughton. (W)

266A - 23 Dec. 1902 - **James Cook**, 21, single, oysterman, b. Gloucester, residing Mid., son of Chas. & Emily Cook, married **Sarah Gwynn**, 19, single, b. & residing Mid., dau. of Tom & Mat. Gwynn. (B)

266B - 25 Dec. 1902 - **Philip H. Jackson**, 25, single, oysterman, b. Gloucester, residing Mid., son of Philip W. & Eliza Jackson, married **Virgia A. Kemble**, 22, single, b. & residing Mid. (B)

266C - 24 Dec. 1902 - **Lewis Wilson**, 40, widower, farmer, b. King & Queen, residing Mid., son of James & Mary Wilson, married **Bettie Garnett**, 29, widow, b. Essex, residing Mid. (B)

267A - 25 Dec. 1902 - **Walter Braxton**, 22, single, oysterman, b. & residing Mid., son of Peter & Sallie Braxton, married **Alice Sirus** [or **Sims**], 19, single, b. & residing Mid., dau. of Josiah & Mollie Sirus [or Sims]. (B)

267B - 25 Dec. 1902 - **Geo. L. Yates**, 22, single, oysterman, b. Gloucester, residing Mid., son of Geo. & Fannie Yates, married **Addie Burrell**, 18, single, b. & residing Mid., dau. of Wm. & Fannie Burrell. (B)
267C - 25 Dec. 1902 - **Rich'd Key**, 22, single, farmer, b. & residing Mid., son of Walker & Cordelia Key, married **Emma Keyser**, 18, single, b. & residing Mid., dau. of Joe & Fannie Keyser. (B)
268A - 20 Dec. 1902 - **Leuellen Abbott**, 23, single, oysterman, b. & residing Lancaster, son of J. T. & J. V. Abbott, married **Florence V. Blake**, 13, single, b. Gloucester, residing Mid., dau. of W. H. & E. S. Blake. (W)
268B - 30 Dec. 1902 - **Joseph Goldman**, 28, widower, oysterman, b. & residing Mid., son of Elijah & Jane Goldman, married **Emma J. Jones**, 19, single, b. & residing Mid., dau. of Mina Goldman. (B)
268C - 30 Dec. 1902 - **Allen Burrell**, 30, single, farmer, b. & residing Mid., son of Henry & Nettie Burrell, married **Elmira Jones**, 30, single, b. & residing Mid., dau. of Geo. & Maria Jones. (B)
269A - 30 Dec. 1902 - **Frank Banks**, 28, single, oysterman, b. & residing Mid., son of Lewis & Nancy Banks, married **Laura Peyton**, 24, single, b. & residing Mid., dau. of Solomon & Fanny Peyton. (B)
269B - 31 Dec. 1902 - **J. R. Smith**, 40, single, sawyer, b. & residing King & Queen, son of Thomas & Millie A. Smith, married **Lucinda Corbin**, 18, single, b. & residing Mid., dau. of Thomas & Millie A. Corbin. (B)
269C - 13 Jan. 1903 - **Geo. W. Snead**, 45, single, oysterman, b. Accomack, residing Mid., son of John L. & Tabitha Snead, married **Maggie M. Lewis**, 25, single, b. & residing Mid., dau. of James T. & Louisa Lewis. (W)
270A - No record.
270B - 20 Jan. 1903 - **Sam Boyd**, 40, single, oysterman, b. & residing Mid., son of Allen & Nancy Boyd, married **Fannie Harris**, 17, single, b. & residing Mid., dau. of Henry & Winnie Harris. (C)
270C - 18 Jan. 1903 - **John R. Mears**, 21, single, oysterman, b. & residing Mid., son of R. T. & Matilda Mears, married **Ruby Perry**, 19, single, b. & residing Mid., dau. of A. T. & C. G. Perry. (W)
271A - 21 Jan. 1903 - **Henry N. Lockley**, 28, single, brick mason, b. Louisiana, residing Mid., son of Louis & Catharin Lockley, married **Fannie B. Carter**, 23, single, b. & residing Mid., dau. of Chas. & Bettie Carter. (B)
271B - 25 Jan. 1903 - **Thos. L. Gaines**, 21, single, oysterman, b. & residing Mid., son of Aaron & Laura Gaines, married **Rose Lee**, 19, single, b. & residing Mid., dau. of Catharin Lee. (B)

271C - 8 Feb. 1903 - **Lewis Thurston**, 36, widower, oysterman, b. & residing Mid., son of Daniel & Jane Thurston, married **Tama Carr**, 51, widow, b. Gloucester, residing Mid., dau. of John & Delia Ann Jackson. (B)

272A - 28 Jan. 1903 - **V. W. Philips**, 28, single, oysterman, b. King & Queen, residing Gloucester, son of Wm. & Susan Philips, married **Mary Alice Fauntleroy**, 21, single, b. & residing Mid., dau. of John & Mollie Fauntleroy. (B)

272B - 5 Feb. 1903 - **Zachariah Holmes**, 27, single, oysterman, b. & residing Mid., son of John & Martha Holmes, married **Lelie Latane**, 22, single, b. & residing Mid., dau. of Hester Latane. (B)

272C - 9 Feb. 1903 - **Thomas O. Foster**, 22, single, oysterman, b. & residing Mathews, son of James W. & Julia G. Foster, married **Gertie Davis**, 21, single, b. King & Queen, residing Mid., dau. of James & Ethel Davis. (W)

273A - 17 Feb. 1903 - **Joseph Gundy**, 22, single, oysterman, b. & residing Mid., son of James & Malinda Gundy, married **Martha Ellen Tucker**, 21, single, b. & residing Mid., dau. of Richard & Francis Tucker. (B)

273B - 18 Feb. 1903 - **Benjamin Stanley Wright**, 30, single, traveling salesman, b. King & Queen, residing Mid., son of Wm. G. & Mary Ellen Wright, married **Gabrielle Roane Ward**, 28, single, b. & residing Mid., dau. of A. H. & Eudora Ward. (W)

273C - 26 Feb. 1903 - **William Gardner**, 32, single, sailor, b. & residing Mid., son of Lewis & Lizzie Gardner, married **Maude Redd**, 20, single, b. King & Queen, residing Mid., dau. of Wm. & Addie Redd. (W)

274A - 26 Feb. 1903 - **Samuel Brown**, 22, single, oysterman, b. & residing Mid., son of Martha Reed [license says Dorathea Reed], married **Annie Carey**, 23, single, b. & residing Mid., dau. of Amanda Bray. (C)

274B - 1 Mar. 1903 - **Eddie Stockes**, 20, single, oysterman, b. & residing Mid., son of Henry & Lettie Stockes, married **Blanche Bundy**, 17, single, b. & residing Mid., dau. of Ben & Bettie Bundy. (C)

274C - 19 Mar. 1903 - **J. H. Trader**, 36, widower, oysterman, b. & residing Mid., son of Rich'd & Elizabeth Trader, married **Emma Groome**, 18, single, b. & residing Mid., dau. of Joe & Liza Groom. (W)

275A - 16 Mar. 1903 - **J. W. Jerman** [**German** on license], 23, single, farmer, b. & residing Gloucester, son of A. & N. Jerman, married **Eva D. Deagle**, 19, single, b. & residing Mid., dau. of I. W. & T. Deagle. (W)

275B - 31 Mar. 1903 - **O. G. Paul**, 35, widower, farmer, b. New Jersey, residing Mid., son of Katie Paul, married **Mary V. Sibley**, 22, single, b. & residing Mid., dau. of R. H. & Mary Sibley. (W)

275C - 2 Apr. 1903 - **C. A. Miller**, 27, single, oysterman, b. & residing Mid., son of W. M. & Amanda Miller, married **B. L. Sibley**, 19, single, b. Gloucester, residing Mid., son of A. A. [or S. A.] & Belinda Sibley. (W)

276A - 16 Apr. 1903 - **James Brown**, 27, single, oysterman, b. & residing Mid., son of Martha Ellen Brown, married **Florence Hill**, 21, single, b. & residing Mid., dau. of John & Nannie Hill. (C)

276B - 16 Apr. 1903 - **Clifford Henslee**, 33, single, physician, b. Ohio, residing Dillon, South Carolina, son of Samuel H. & Mary Henslee, married **Sadie L. Towill**, 31, single, b. & residing Mid., dau. of R. & M. F. Towill. (W)

276C - 16 Apr. 1903 - **Enerst Linwood Keiningham**, 23, single, oyster dealer, b. & residing Mid., son of J. G. & M. H. Keiningham, married **Clyde Georgie Payne**, 22, single, b. & residing Mid., dau. of John A. & M. E. Payne. (W)

277A - 22 Apr. 1903 - **Jerry Lively**, 29, single, oysterman, b. & residing Mid., son of Lucy & Chas. Lively, married **Julia Taliaferro**, 25, single, b. & residing Mid., dau. of Wm. & Matilda Taliaferro. (C)

277B - 30 Apr. 1903 - **Edward B. Revere**, 27, single, carpenter, b. & residing Mid., son of John M. & Sarah F. Revere, married **Lulu Catherine Revere**, 23, single, b. & residing Mid., dau. of Rob't Revere. (W)

277C - 26 Apr. 1903 - **John E. Wright**, 26, single, sailor, b. & residing Mid., son of Wm. & Betty Wright, married **Blanche Harrow**, 19, single, b. & residing Mid., dau. of A. W. & Hattie Harrow. (W)

278A - 29 Apr. 1903 - **Joshua Wicks**, 28, single, oysterman, b. & residing Mid., son of John & Annie Wicks, married **Mary Florence Smith**, 21, single, b. & residing Mid., dau. of Peter & Nancy Smith. (B)

278B - 29 Apr. 1903 - **Bennie Frank Hart**, 23, single, farmer, b. & residing Mid., son of B. F. & Sarah C. Hart, married **Mattie Lee Major**, 22, single, b. & residing Mid., dau. of Jno. M. & Fannie Major. (W)

278C - 29 Apr. 1903 - **Chas. Boyd Holmes**, 23, single, oysterman, b. & residing Mid., son of John & Martha Holmes, married **Ida Bell Perrin**, 21, single, b. & residing Mid., dau. of Alex & Rena Perrin. (B)

279A - 14 May 1903 - **Geo. Fountain, Jr.**, 31, single, farmer, b. & residing Mid., son of Geo. & Maria Fountain, married **Susan Davis**, 39, widow, b. & residing Mid., dau. of Wm. & Lucy Taliaferro. (B)

279B - 28 May 1903 - **William H. Boyd**, 28, widower,

oysterman, b. King & Queen, residing Mid., son of Chas.
H. & Adaline Boyd, married **Alberta Taliaferro**, 32,
widow, b. & residing Mid., dau. of Upshur. (C)
 279C - 3 Jun. 1903 - **Rob't Gabriel Brooks**, 28,
single, street car conductor, b. Person Co., North
Carolina, residing Pittsburg, Pennsylvania, son of
Robert & Virginia Brooks, married **Hattie L. Rhodes**, 26,
single, b. Rankin Co., Mississippi, residing Saluda
[Mid.], dau. of Lee F. & Clemmie B. Rhodes. (W)
 280A - 7 Jun. 1903 - **John Thomas Figg**, 24, widower,
mechanic, b. Gloucester, residing Mid., son of John H. &
Justina Figg, married **Salome Fletcher**, 21, single, b. &
residing Gloucester, dau. of Lewis W. & Lucy Fletcher.
(W)
 280B - 17 Jun. 1903 - **Andrew Jett Edwards**, 29,
single, b. Northumberland, residing Reedville, Virginia
[Northumberland], son of Thos. A. & Elizabeth Edwards,
married **Gertrude Viola Coombs**, b. New Bedford,
Massachusetts, residing Mid., dau. of Othniel R. &
Violima Coombs. (W)
 280C - 28 Jun. 1903 - **Richard C. Washington**, 31,
single, farmer, b. & residing Mid., son of Cuffy &
Elizabeth Washington, married **Roberta H. Harris**, 23,
divorced, b. & residing Mid., dau. of Joseph & Addie
Harris. (C)
 281A - 30 Jun. 1903 - **Ashby Jones**, 22, single,
oysterman, b. & residing Mid., son of Ellen & Stephen
Jones, married **Mitchie Green**, 22, single, b. & residing
Mid., dau. of Louisa & Manuel Green. (C)
 281B - 8 Jul. 1903 - **Chas. H. Hart**, 17, single,
oysterman, b. & residing Mid., son of James H. & Mary E.
Hart, married **Bessie O. Trader**, 18, single, b. &
residing Mid., dau. of Alex & Sarah G. Trader. (W)
 281C - 9 Jul. 1903 - **Philip Boyd**, 25, single, farmer,
b. & residing Mid., son of Albert & Judy Boyd, married
Sarah Coor, 18, single, b. & residing Mid., dau. of W.
E. & Lilly A. Corr. (C)
 282A - Error made; marriage re-recorded at 282B.
 282B - 16 Jul. 1903 - **Thos. H. Frazier**, 22, single,
oysterman, b. & residing Mid., son of Thos. & Eliza
Frazier, married **Lizzie Scott**, 20, single, b. & residing
Mid., dau. of Sallie Ann Scott. (B)
 282C - 16 Jul. 1903 - **Willie Payne**, 18, single,
oysterman, b. & residing Mid., son of Wm. & Tute Payne,
married **Kate Lewis**, 20, single, b. & residing Mid., dau.
of Mase & Margaret Lewis. (B)
 283A - 17 Jul. 1903 - **Rob't Boyd**, 27, single,
oysterman, b. & residing Mid., son of Nancy Gwynn,
married **Mary Williams**, 19, single, b. & residing Mid.,
dau. of Elijah & Sallie Williams. (B)

283B - 27 Jul. 1903 - **Wm. A. George**, 35, single, life insurance agent, b. & residing Lancaster, son of Joseph & May C. George, married **Emily A. Walters**, 32, widow, b. & residing Brooklyn, New York, dau. of Samuel Magee. (W)

283C - 6 Aug. 1903 - **Geo. W. Taliaferro**, 43, single, oysterman, b. & residing Mid., son of Simon & W. Taliaferro, married **Ada White**, 38, widow, b. & residing Mid., dau. of Geo. M. Johnson. (C)

284A - License issued to **C. W. Ridgell** & **Susan Tapor** "was not used but destroyed."

284B - 10 Aug. 1903 - **Walter Campbell**, 22, single, oysterman, b. & residing Mid., son of Eli & Lulu Campbell, married **Sue Ward**, 21, single, b. & residing Mid., dau. of Zack & Bettie Ward. (C)

284C - 2 Sep. 1903 - **Scipio Wingfield**, 28, single, oysterman, b. & residing Mid., son of Scipio & Millie Wingfield, married **Mary B. Fitchett**, 19, single, b. & residing Mid., dau. of Washington & Lizzie Fitchett. (C)

285A - 3 Sep. 1903 - **Leslie T. Wood**, 60, widower, farmer, b. Mid., residing Gloucester, son of Levi & Mary Ann Wood, married **Ann Eliza Norman**, 49, widow, b. King & Queen, residing Mid., dau. of Rob't & Ann Carter. (W)

285B - 9 Sep. 1903 - **William H. Trevillian**, 22, single, merchant, b. & residing Gloucester, son of Wm. C. & Mary E. Trevillian, married **Edna E. Hart**, 23, single, b. & residing Mid., dau. of John W. & Mary Hart. (W)

285C - 13 Sep. 1903 - **Henry Jackson**, 18, single, oysterman, b. & residing Mid., son of N. F. & Annie Jackson, married **Mollie Mason**, 17, single, b. & residing Mid., dau. of Sam & Sue Mason. (W)

286A - 16 Sep. 1903 - **Willie Fields**, 29, single, oysterman, b. & residing Mid., son of Rob't & Malinda Fields, married **Elizabeth Robinson**, 24, single, b. & residing Mid., dau. of Joseph & Elton Robinson. (C)

286B - 15 Sep. 1903 - **John T. Jones**, 32, single, oysterman, b. King & Queen, residing Mid., son of John & Maria Jones, married **Mary F. Thornton**, 32, widow, b. & residing Mid., dau. of Ransom & Harriet Dudley. (B)

286C - 16 Sep. 1903 - **James Edgar Smith**, 55, divorced, farmer, b. & residing Mid., son of Francis & Caroline Smith, married **H. E. Keiningham**, 37, single, b. & residing Mid., dau. of Gideon & M. M. Keiningham. (W)

287A - 6 Oct. 1903 - **Gordon F. Taylor**, 27, single, merchant, b. Westmoreland, residing Mid., son of Thos. N. & Kate B. Taylor, married **Blanche Davis**, 28, single, b. & residing Mid., dau. of Rich'd A. & E. J. Davis. (W)

287B - 8 Oct. 1903 - **A. J. Jarvis**, 23, single, oysterman, b. Gloucester, residing Mid., son of George Johnson, married **Nellie Sutherlin**, 20, single, b. & residing Mid., dau. of Rich'd W. & Eliza Sutherlin. (C)
287C - 8 Oct. 1903 - **Rich'd Green**, 22, single, oysterman, b. & residing Mid., son of Manuel & Louise Green, married **Roxie Braxton**, 21, single, b. & residing Mid., dau. of Carter & Eliza Braxton [License says Carter & Louiza Braxton.] (C)
288A - 13 Oct. 1903 - **Johnny Johnson**, 36, single, oysterman, b. & residing Mid., son of J. J. & Betty Johnson, married **Lavina Thurston**, 34, single, b. & residing Mid., dau. of Edward & Sylvia Thurston. (B)
288B - 15 Oct. 1903 - **Harry Mathews**, 58, widower, farmer, b. & residing Mid., son of Lawson & Martha Mathews, married **L. B. Harris**, 49, widow, b. & residing Mid., dau. of Rich'd O. & Anna Griffin. (C)
288C - License for **Walter Heile** & **Pauline Whitteker** "not issued."
289A - 20 Oct. 1903 - **Welford W. Burruss**, 25, single, painter, b. & residing Richmond, son of Wm. P. & Sarah C. Burruss, married **Annie L. Robinson**, 19, single, b. Gloucester, residing Mid., dau. of Jas. & Alice Robinson. (W)
289B - 25 Oct. 1903 - **James H. Corbin**, 35, single, oysterman, b. & residing Mid., son of Geo. & Sarah Corbin, married **Emma Blanch Williams**, 20, single, b. Essex, residing Mid., dau. of John R. & Anna Williams. (B) "This license was not returned until Mar. 23, 1904."
289C - 1 Nov. 1903 - **Edward Maxwell New**, 23, single, carpenter, b. & residing Mid., son of Wm. G. & Nannie New, married **Mary Gertrude Wilson**, 25, single, b. Gloucester, residing Mid., dau. of John W. & Cordelia Wilson. (W)
290A - 4 Nov. 1903 - **Chas. H. Revere**, 30, single, merchant, b. & residing Mid., son of John M. & Sarah F. Revere, married **Nannie Lee Blake**, 23, single, b. & residing Mid., dau. of Rob't M. & Georgie Blake. (W)
290B - 12 Nov. 1903 - **G. R. Cottingham**, 26, single, physician, b. Lancaster, residing Rennington, Fauquier, son of Geo. & Virginia Cottingham, married **Nannie F. Segar**, 29, single, b. & residing Mid., dau. of John R. & Sallie Segar. (W)
290C - 18 Nov. 1903 - **J. Raymond Wallace**, 27, single, "mercantile," b. Richmond Co., residing Mid., son of Wm. G. & Lucille A. Wallace, married **Lillian B. Bristow**, 22, single, b. & residing Mid., dau. of Weston & Ida Bristow. (W)
291A - 26 Nov. 1903 - **Henry Harris**, 22, single,

oysterman, b. & residing Mid., son of Isaiah & Julia Harris, married **Martha Anne Rebecca Jordan**, 18, single, b. & residing Mid., dau. of George & Anna Jordan. (C)

291B - 17 Dec. 1903 - **Henry Turner**, 62, widower, farmer, b. King William, residing Mid., son of Reuben & Isabella Turner, married **Elizabeth Washington**, 54, widow, b. & residing Mid., dau. of Millie Henry. (C)

291C - 17 Dec. 1903 - **Geo. P. Taylor**, 26, single, oysterman, b. & residing Mid., son of Churchill & Martha Taylor, married **Cora Ann Williams**, 23, single, b. & residing Mid., dau. of Henderson & Catherine Williams. (C)

292A - 18 Dec. 1903 - **Isaac Reddick**, 25, single, oysterman, b. & residing Mid., married **Harriet Minor**, 21, single, b. & residing Mid., dau. of Henry & Mary Minor. (B)

292B - 28 Dec. 1903 - **George Thomas Goode**, 36, widower, farmer, b. & residing Mid., son of James H. & Mary E. Goode, married **Lucy Fleet Groome**, 32, single, b. & residing Mid., dau. of Wm. H. & Juliet Groome. (W)

292C - 23 Dec. 1903 - **Saywood M. Tomlinson**, 25, single, pilot, b. & residing Mid., son of E. S. & L. E. Tomlinson, married **Nora E. Warren**, 23, single, b. England, residing Ashville, North Carolina, dau. of Wm. W. & Emily C. Warren. (W)

293A - 23 Dec. 1903 - **W. C. Johnson**, 21, single, farmer, b. & residing Mid., son of J. W. & Charlotte Johnson, married **Annie V. Shelton**, 21, single, b. Lancaster, residing Mid., dau. of Oscar & Georgie Shelton. (W)

293B - 22 Dec. 1903 - **Wm. W. Sherman**, 27, single, oysterman, b. & residing Mid., son of Eli & Mary Jane Sherman, married **Mary Ann Beany**, 23, single, b. & residing Mid., dau. of Sam & Susan Beany. (C)

293C - 29 Dec. 1903 - **Walter Banks**, 25, single, farmer, b. & residing Mid., son of Lewis & Nancy Banks, married **Maggie Frazier**, 20, single, b. & residing Mid., dau. of Chas. & Eliza Frazier. (C)

294A - 30 Dec. 1903 - **Eddie New**, 28, single, oysterman, b. & residing Essex, son of Rob't & Mary Ann New, married **Mary Louise Garrett**, 24, single, b. & residing Mid., dau. of Lewis & Mary E. Garrett. (W)

294B - 13 Jan. 1904 - **W. T. Healy**, 20, single, farmer, b. & residing Mid., son of W. H. & Mary E. Healy, married **Mary L. Hinman**, 17, single, b. & residing Mid., dau. of O. F. & Ellen Hinman. (W)

294C - 14 Jan. 1904 - **James C. Braxton**, 31, single, farmer, b. & residing Mid., son of Carter & Eliza Braxton, married **Martha Lewis**, 20, single, b. & residing Mid., dau. of Allie & Winnie Lewis. (C)

295A - 17 Jan. 1904 - **Chas. R. Davis**, 22, single, oysterman, b. & residing Mid., son of A. W. Davis, married **Nettie May Kellum**, 18, single, b. & residing Mid., dau. of J. T. Kellum. (W)
295B - 20 Jan. 1904 - **Harold Thomas**, 21, single, "clerk in store," b. Essex, residing Mid., son of M. S. & Archibal Thomas, married **Grace Homer**, 24, single, b. Westmoreland, residing Mid., dau. of Henry J. & Susan B. Homer. (W)
295C - 20 Jan. 1904 - **Rob't Minor**, 27, single, farmer, b. & residing Mid., son of Wm. & Lucy A. Minor, married **Hattie Key**, 20, single, b. & residing Mid., dau. of Walker & Cordelia Key. (C)
296A - 20 Jan. 1904 - **Bennie Easton**, 25, single, oysterman, b. & residing Mid., son of Noah & Julia Easton, married **Ruth Washington**, 19, single, b. & residing Mid., dau. of Christian & Susan Washington. (C)
296B - 2 Feb. 1904 - **Willie Robinson**, 28, single, laborer farmer, b. & residing Essex, son of James H. & Martha Ellen Robinson, married **Annie Harris**, 23, single, b. & residing Mid., dau. of Tunstall & Cath. Harris. (C)
296B2 - 28 Jan. 1904 - **Rich'd Grissum**, 30, single, farmer, b. & residing Mid., married **Roberta Corr**, 30, divorced, b. & residing Mid., dau. of Wm. & Mary Corr. (C) [This marriage is not indexed in Middlesex County records.]
296C - 7 Feb. 1904 - **Samuel Mason**, 19, single, oysterman, b. & residing Mid., son of Samuel P. & Susan Mason, married **Mamie Jackson**, 18, single, b. & residing Mid., dau. of C. R. & Bell Jackson. (W)
297A - 10 Feb. 1904 - **G. W. Rowe**, 52, widower, farmer, b. York Co., residing Mid., son of Washington & Betsy Rowe, married **Kate Dobbson**, 30, widow, b. Gloucester, residing Mid., dau. of Ralph & Nancy Belvin. (W)
297B - 18 Feb. 1904 - **Elijah Robinson**, 22, single, oysterman, b. King & Queen, residing Mid., son of Willie & Rachel Robinson, married **Adda Johnson**, 22, single, b. & residing Mid., dau. of Coleman & Bettie Johnson. (C)
297C - 21 Feb. 1904 - **James Rob't Jones**, 24, single, oysterman, b. & residing Mid., son of Geo. & Maria Jones, married **Otalia Kidd**, 20, single, b. & residing Mid., dau. of Wm. & Amanda Kidd. (C)
298A - 18 Feb. 1904 - **Rich'd H. Page**, 27, single, oysterman, b. & residing Mid., son of Dennis & Jennie Page, married **Kizzie Nelson**, 30, widow, b. & residing Mid., dau. of Carter & Catherine Nelson. (C)
298B - 2 Mar. 1904 - **J. P. Jackson**, 34, single,

oysterman, b. & residing Mid., son of John & M. Jackson, married **Sallie Wilson**, 20, single, b. & residing Mid., dau. of N. G. & I. B. Wilson. (W)

298C - 9 Mar. 1904 - **James A. Collins**, 30, single, farmer, b. King & Queen, residing Mid., son of Priscilla Banks, married **Ella Banks**, 21, single, b. & residing Mid., dau. of Lewis & Nancy Banks. (C)

299A - 20 Mar. 1904 - **Willie H. Jackson**, 21, single, oysterman, b. & residing Mid., son of C. R. & Belle Jackson, married **Mamie Montgomery**, 20, single, b. & residing Mid., dau. of J. L. & Mary A. Montgomery. (W)

299B - 22 Mar. 1904 - **Geo. T. Duvall**, 32, single, sailor, b. & residing Mathews, son of Frank & Maggie A. Duvall, married **Nannie H. Dyke**, 29, single, b. King & Queen, residing Mid., dau. of W. T. & Jenette C. Dyke. (W)

299C - 23 Mar. 1904 - **G. T. Hogg**, 34, widower, farmer, b. Gloucester, residing Mid., son of Anderson & Sue Hogg, married **Sadie Vandergrift**, 21, single, b. & residing Mid., dau. of James & Latitia Vandergrift. (W)

300A - 4 Apr. 1904 - **Geo. H. Fields**, 32, widower, oysterman, b. & residing Mid., son of Roberta H. Fields, married **Saphronia West**, 20, single, b. & residing Mid., dau. of Edwin & Hetty West. (C)

300B - 1 Apr. 1904 - **Stephen H. Cephas**, 37, widower, laborer, b. Maryland, residing Baltimore, Maryland, son of Stephen & Mary Cephas, married **Hannah Jones**, 32, single, b. & residing Mid., dau. of John & Laura Jones. (C)

300C - 6 Apr. 1904 - **Rich'd H. Humphries**, 32, single, carpenter, b. & residing Mid., son of R. T. & Lucy A. Humphries, married **Lottie P. Clare**, 28, single, b. & residing Mid., dau. of Hamilton & Almedia Clare. (W)

Index of Grooms

Abbott, Daniel	141C	Bilups, Silas	223B
Abbott, Leuellen	268A	Blackley, Ro. H.	88C
Ackers, Johnson	135C	Blake, A. J.	159C
Ailsworth, Dave B.	236B	Blake, Andrew	54B
Ailworth, Carter	1C	Blake, B. S.	73C
Ailworth, George W.	100A	Blake, Charles H.	4B
Anderson, Jeff	154A	Blake, E. M.	98B
Apperson, John N.	218A	Blake, Edward S.	7C
Apsley, Lloyd	222A	Blake, Henry Charles	178C
Ashberry, Walter H.	139A	Blake, Julius C.	44B
Ashborn, Jeremiah	3C	Blakey, John E.	30C
Ashburn, Amond A.	70B	Bland, Roderick H.	113C
Ashburn, Chas. A.	140C	Bland, Schuyler E.	162A
Ashburn, M. B.	82C	Bland, Thomas Ritchie	114A
		Bluford, James	92A
Bagby, Addison	87C	Borum, John	14A
Bagby, George	209C	Bottom, Sandy	135A
Bagby, John	7B	Boyd, Henry	89C
Bagby, Paul	175A	Boyd, James, Jr.	218B
Bagby, Silas	237C	Boyd, Moses	171A
Bagby, Walker	6B	Boyd, Philip	281C
Bagby, Washington	220C	Boyd, Rob't	283A
Baker, James, Jr.	192B	Boyd, Sam	270B
Baker, John	20B	Boyd, William H.	279B
Ball, Granville Harvey	173C	Bratton, Abraham H.	58B
Banks, Chas. Henry	136B	Braxton, David	243A
Banks, Chas. H.	37A	Braxton, James C.	294C
Banks, Frank	269A	Braxton, Jerry	72B
Banks, John Henry	230B	Braxton, Michael	15A
Banks, John H.	74C	Braxton, Robert	11A
Banks, John H.	179A	Braxton, Robert Carter	161A
Banks, Lewis	235B	Braxton, Thos. H.	9B
Banks, Philip	185C	Braxton, Walter	267A
Banks, Rich'd H.	256C	Braxton, Zack	121B
Banks, Rob't G.	137C	Bray, M. M.	78C
Banks, Rolly	113B	Bristow, J. P.	219A
Banks, Walter	293C	Bristow, John P.	14C
Banks, Willie H.	134B	Bristow, Nathan T.	2A
Barnes, Stanley J.	107A	Bristow, Robert S.	117C
Baylor, Rob't	144A	Bristow, Robinson	120C
Bayton, James H.	230A	Bristow, Wilton H.	255A
Baytop, Edmune	49C	Brooke, John R.	221A
Baytop, Thomas	248B	Brooks, E. J.	265C
Beadles, Adolphus	211C	Brooks, Frank	103B
Beazly, Edward W.	75A	Brooks, Henry	48C
Bennett, John J.	116A	Brooks, John Ro.	90B
Berry, Wm. H.	79C	Brooks, Joseph H.	242C
Beverly, Philip	169C	Brooks, Rob't Gabriel	279C
Billups, Edward	202B	Brooks, Walter S.	58C

Index of Grooms

Brooks, Wilbur J.	235C	Carter, John	105C
Brooks, Wm. H.	28B	Carter, Mathew	84C
Brooks, Wm.	92C	Carter, R. H.	198C
Broun, Jos. H.	51C	Carter, Thos. H.	45C
Brown, Carter	32A	Carter, Wm. H.	113A
Brown, Cornelius H.	201C	Cary, Elijah	106C
Brown, Cornelius H.	22B	Cephas, Stephen H.	300B
Brown, Daniel	71B	Chamberlain, Earney	195A
Brown, Geo. W.	76C	Chandler, Howard	65A
Brown, Iverson	126B	Cheseman, Robert	18C
Brown, James	276A	Chowning, Rob't G.	139B
Brown, John	166B	Chowning, Thomas J.	107B
Brown, Samuel	274A	Christian, Wm. S.	204B
Brown, Sam'l L.	115A	Christopher, Emmett S.	141A
Buckner, Peter	246C	Churchill, Samuel	34A
Bundy, Jackson	12A	Clarke, Elijah	13C
Bundy, James	223C	Clarke, John Cornelius	250B
Burch, Atwill	225B	Clarke, Merton Emery	189B
Burke, William	166A	Clayvell, see Clavel,	
Burrell, Allen	268C	Claybill, Clayville	
Burrell, Bruce	71C	Clayvell, Virginius L.	235A
Burrell, Chas. Henry	204C	Clayville, Littleton	20A
Burrell, Joseph	49B	Clayville, Z.	74A
Burrell, Philip Henry	219C	Clements, Carroll Lee	225A
Burrell, Richard	30B	Coates, Z. R.	52A
Burrell, Ro.	81B	Coleman, John M.	178A
Burrell, Thaddeus	259C	Colley, James Hy	106A
Burrell, Willie	129C	Collie, J. Q.	106B
Burruss, Welford W.	289A	Collier, John	239A
Bush, Wm.	129A	Collins, G. M.	224B
Butler, T. J.	34C	Collins, James A.	298C
Butler, W. H.	12C	Conway, Samuel	155C
Byrd, Jas. R.	227C	Conway, Syriese	36C
Byrd, Junius	146A	Conway, Wm.	18A
		Cook, Alex	200A
Callis, John R.	217B	Cook, Dahlgreen	93C
Callis, John R.	73A	Cook, Daniel	188B
Campbell, Isaac	102B	Cook, Daniel	258B
Campbell, John H.	56B	Cook, Grant	64B
Campbell, Josiah	104B	Cook, James Henry	172C
Campbell, Walter	284B	Cook, James	266A
Cannon, James R.	186B	Cook, Julius H.	166C
Carey, Julius	186A	Corbin, James H.	289B
Carlton, Christopher C.	20C	Corbin, William	226C
Carlton, L. M.	112C	Cornelius, Addison W.	216B
Carr, Moses	169A	Cosby, Peter Thomas	221C
Carter, Charles	60C	Cottingham, G. R.	290B
Carter, Eli P.	164B	Covington, Rob't B.	196C
Carter, Jeremiah	35B	Cox, James R., Jr.	11B

Index of Grooms

Crittenden, Geo. W.	50B	Easton, Wm. C.	52C
Crittenden, Lester Clyde	119A	Edwards, Andrew Jett	280B
		Edwards, Samuel	99A
Crow, C. R.	84B	Ellis, Rob't S.	256A
Crow, Thornton F.	8A	Erdman, Howard C.	228C
Crump, Robert	138B	Eubank, Jesse	234B
Cundiff, Albert G.	61C	Evans, R. H.	187B
Curtis, Rob't	261C	Eyre, Edward	89A
Daniel, Geo. Wm.	199B	Fairfax, Phillip	77C
Daniel, Geo. T.	212B	Farinholt, Henry C.	133A
Daniel, Henry Thos.	165A	Farinholt, Ro. H.	62C
Daniel, John A.	142B	Fary, Dinkey L.	215A
Daughtry, Charley	26B	Faucett, Geo. T.	252C
Davenport, Jas. L.	23A	Faulkner, Moby	73B
Davenport, John	123A	Fears, J. C.	262A
Davis, Chas. R.	295A	Fells, Percy N.	184B
Davis, James R.	153A	Fields, Edward	198A
Davis, James	116C	Fields, Geo. H.	300A
Davis, James R.	151B	Fields, George	86C
Davis, Ransom	260A	Fields, Henry	69B
Davis, Richard A.	63C	Fields, John	171C
Davis, Russell A.	55B	Fields, John	243C
Davis, Thomas	123B	Fields, Rev. D.	153B
Davis, Thos.	232A	Fields, Willie	286A
Dawson, John	236C	Figg, J. T.	214A
Deagle, Chas. H.	42C	Figg, John Thomas	280A
Deagle, J. W.	70C	Finkle, Wm. E.	197C
Dew, John Mason	118C	Fitchett, F. L.	53B
Dickenson, James M.	21C	Fitchett, George E.	6A
Dickenson, Perrin	32B	Fitchett, Han. William	216C
Didlake, R. L.	77A	Fleet, John J.	160C
Dixon, Daniel	124A	Fleming, Edward	60B
Dixon, Joseph B.	176B	Fletcher, C. H.	65B
Dobson, Gary	80A	Flippin, David A.	253A
Dudley, Ransome	99C	Folliard, Eugene	39C
Dudly, Emanuel	260B	Fones, James A.	190C
Dungee, George	46C	Foster, George	23B
Dungee, Robert	61B	Foster, James	175B
Dunlavy, Wm. B.	29C	Foster, James	185B
Dunn, Andrew J.	100B	Foster, T. E.	78B
Dunn, Shelbon	228B	Foster, Thomas O.	272C
Dunston, Bernard Boyd	131B	Fountain, Geo. Jr.	279A
Duster, Cernus James	263C	Fountain, Harry	240C
Duvall, Geo. T.	299B	Fox, R. Ernest	167A
		Foxwell, J. W.	31A
Eastman, George W.	222B	Foxwell, J. W.	182A
Eastman, Thos. M.	205C	Foxwell, S. F.	70A
Easton, Bennie	296A	Frazier, Thos. H.	282B

Index of Grooms

French, Newton W.	226A		Griffith, R. H.	186C
French, Thos. R.	200B		Grinels, Chas. R.	149C
French, Willoughby B.	56A		Grinels, John G.	68A
Furgeson, Monroe	230C		Grymes, Jno. T.	43B
			Grymes, John T.	82A
Gabor, Peter W.	97C		Gundy, James	213A
Gaines, Alex	180B		Gundy, Joseph	273A
Gaines, Ernest Albert	250A		Gwynn, William	207A
Gaines, Henry	217C			
Gaines, Jacob	80B		Hackett, Luther	165B
Gaines, Thos. L.	271B		Hall, Beauregard	94B
Gardner, William	273C		Hall, Beauregard	254A
Garner, James	205A		Hammons, Geo. W.	18B
Garnett, David K.	140A		Harmon, Chas.	252A
Garnett, W. F.	109C		Harper, Lucius F.	193A
Garnett, Willie	152C		Harris, Anderson	124C
Garnett, Wrighter	183B		Harris, Cyrus W.	41A
Garrett, Thos. C.	150B		Harris, Henry	291A
Gaskins, Harry A.	233C		Harris, James E.	127C
Geman, J. W.	275W		Harris, John	125B
Gemmill, Thos. H.	158C		Harris, Robert B.	10C
George, Wm. A.	283B		Harris, Thos. H.	90C
Gibson, Absolom T.	170C		Harrow, Geo. W.	8B
Gibson, Henry	87B		Harrow, J. B.	40B
Ginmell, Edward B.	72C		Hart, Bennie Frank	278B
Goin, Wm.	40C		Hart, Chas. H.	281B
Goldman, Joseph	268B		Hart, Edward W.	202A
Goode, G. T.	108A		Hart, John W.	2C
Goode, James H.	247A		Hart, William G.	239C
Goode, Jas. H.	107C		Haydon, H. Jeter	225C
Good, George Thomas	292B		Haydon, W. L.	245C
Gouldman, Elijah	90A		Haynes, W. W.	140B
Gouldman, Frank	83C		Haynie, Eddie	79B
Gouldman, John	112B		Healy, W. T.	294B
Gouldman, Joseph	121C		Hearn, Columbus	142A
Graham, Henry	156A		Heile, Walter	288C
Graves, Herman E.	227B		Henry, Fillmore	149B
Green, Christ	200C		Henry, Harvey	158A
Greene, Rob't	177A		Henry, Nathan	188C
Green, Jas. A.	97B		Henslee, Clifford	276B
Green, Rich'd	287C		Hill, Henry	57A
Greenstreet, Eugene	179C		Hill, Nelson	177B
Green, Wm.	110C		Hodges, Samuel	154B
Gregory, Simon	244B		Hoge, Jas. W.	126A
Gresham, Chas. H.	33B		Hogg, G. T.	299C
Gressum, James	150C		Hogg, Jack	174C
Griffin, Lewis	44C		Hogg, John H.	191A
Griffin, Thomas	164A		Hogg, Peter	91A
Griffin, W. L.	85C		Holliday, Oscar	45A

Index of Grooms

Holmes, Boyd	278C	
Holmes, Isaiah	178B	
Holmes, Lewis	30A	
Holmes, Richard	134C	
Holmes, Zachariah	272B	
Hoskins, Thomas	97A	
Hughes, Julius F.	208A	
Humphries, Rich'd H.	300C	
Hurley, Sam'l Vanburen	131A	
Hurley, Walter, M.	184C	
Hurly, Thomas Clayton	131C	
Ingram, Edward Thomas	169B	
Iverson, Edward	85A	
Jackson, Andrew	68B	
Jackson, Andrew	104A	
Jackson, Andrew	53A	
Jackson, Charles	136C	
Jackson, Geo. W.	223A	
Jackson, George	42A	
Jackson, Henry	285C	
Jackson, J. P.	298B	
Jackson, James R.	249C	
Jackson, John	151C	
Jackson, John	92B	
Jackson, Obie	153C	
Jackson, Peter	98A	
Jackson, Philip H.	266B	
Jackson, Richard	87A	
Jackson, Samuel H.	91B	
Jackson, T. T.	219B	
Jackson, Thomas	81C	
Jackson, Thomas	67C	
Jackson, Thos. H.	22A	
Jackson, William R.	159A	
Jackson, Willie H.	299A	
Jarvis, A. J.	164C	
Jarvis, A. J.	287B	
Jefferson, Jake	67A	
Jefferson, James H.	244A	
Jenkins, Charles W.	28A	
Jerman, J. W.	275A	
Jiles, Thomas	79A	
Johnson, Amos	118B	
Johnson, Andrew	31B	
Johnson, Clifton	188A	
Johnson, Cornelius	257B	
Johnson, Doctor	25C	
Johnson, Edmund	264C	
Johnson, Ernest	192A	
Johnson, George	14B	
Johnson, James	151A	
Johnson, James	217A	
Johnson, Johnny	288A	
Johnson, Moses J.	114B	
Johnson, Nelson	130C	
Johnson, Robert	42B	
Johnson, Sidney L.	229A	
Johnson, W. C.	293A	
Johnson, William	94C	
Johnson, Wm. Lewis	191C	
Jones, Ashby L.	210B	
Jones, Ashby	281A	
Jones, Benjamin	228A	
Jones, Geo. W.	29A	
Jones, George	102C	
Jones, Henry	253C	
Jones, James Rob't	297C	
Jones, John W.	78A	
Jones, John T.	286B	
Jones, Joseph F.	22C	
Jones, Patrick C.	62A	
Jones, Sam	262B	
Jones, Samuel	29B	
Jones, Willie	193C	
Jordan, James W.	258C	
Kain, J. E.	95B	
Kandle, Wilbert	60A	
Keiningham, Enerst Linwood	276C	
Kellam, Stewart	19A	
Kellum, Geo. D.	67B	
Kellum, Morris A.	149A	
Kellum, Wm. J.	10A	
Kennard, W. F.	138C	
Key, Hesekiah	100C	
Key, James	209B	
Key, John	205B	
Key, John	111B	
Key, Rich'd	267C	
Keyser, Cornelius	254C	
Kimbell, Jas. H.	122C	
King, William	147A	
Koegel, Geo. B.	108C	
Lamberth, Edward S.	226B	

Index of Grooms

Lambert, James L.	239B		Mason, Samuel	296C
Lattimore, Cary	207B		Mathews, Harry	288B
Laws, Dan	208B		Mayo, Thos. Jackson	201A
Laws, J. A.	46B		Mears, E. W.	257C
Laws, James	192C		Mears, J. W.	43C
Laws, John	183C		Mears, John R.	270C
Laws, John	148B		Mercer, Clarence W.	145B
Lawson, C. S.	75C		Mercer, Isaac Claude	224A
Lawson, Charles	3B		Mercer, James C.	101B
Lawson, Wm. H.	82B		Merriwether, John	83A
Laws, Richard	130A		Miller, Burgess	63B
Lee, Clinton	182C		Miller, C. A.	275C
Lee, Joseph	177C		Miller, Eugene J.	89B
Lee, Richard	162B		Miller, Henry	58A
Levering, Thomas H.	21A		Miller, Thos. H.	26C
Lewis, Beverly	165C		Miller, Walker	220B
Lewis, Chas.	238C		Minor, Jefferson	36A
Lewis, Gustine	112A		Minor, Rob't	295C
Lewis, Henry	45B		Monroe, James	194A
Lewis, James Castor	161B		Monroe, Thornton	122A
Lewis, John	115B		Montgomery, J. L.	109A
Lewis, Robert	101C		Moody, Chas. D.	137A
Lewis, Samuel J.	144C		Moody, J. A.	183A
Lewis, Thos.	143A		Moody, James H.	148A
Lightford, John	211A		Moore, John R.	262C
Lincoln, George	68C		Moor, Elgie D.	120B
Linken, Doctor	206B		Moore, William P.	173A
Little, James	134A		Moran, Henry A.	155A
Lively, Jerry	277A		Moran, Wm. Alonzo	6C
Lockley, Daniel, Jr.	232C		Morris, Chas. W.	265B
Lockley, Daniel, Sr.	215B		Morris, Geo. W.	138A
Lockley, Henry N.	271A		Morris, Henry Clay	194B
Lockley, James	259A		Morris, Jackson	74B
Lockley, Jessee	66B		Morris, James, Jr.	144B
Lockley, Sam'l	1B		Morris, Jordun	59C
Lockley, Thomas	48A		Morris, Squire	254B
Lomax, Elijah	265A		Moses, C. Read	204A
Lomax, George	195B		Moton, Joseph	2B
Lomax, Thomas	8C		Munroe, Dan	202C
Long, James	95C		Muse, Braxton	248A
Lorrimore, Columbus	157C		Muse, James	98C
Lumpkin, Jno. R.	249B		Muse, Ro. Lee	84A
Lumpkin, John R.	175C		Muse, Vester	190A
Lyon, Liston D.	160B		Myers, Robt. Henry	38B
Major, George	115C		Neale, Claude	240A
Major, John C.	203B		Nelson, Granville	122B
Mallory, Samuel H.	11C		Nelson, James	46A
Mason, John	128C		Nelson, Lewis	50C

Index of Grooms

Nelson, Ro.	34B	Redd, Japeth	121A
New, Eddie	294A	Redd, Louis C.	48B
New, Edward Maxwell	289C	Redd, W. A.	182B
Newell, F. H.	242B	Reede, Allen	194C
New, John W.	214C	Reed, Ezra	255B
New, Wm. G.	142C	Reed, Geo. W.	41B
Nicholson,		Reed, Isaac	31C
Arthur Foster	155B	Reed, Johnnie	264A
Norris, John	109B	Reed, Richard	65C
Norris, John Lambert	264B	Reed, Ro.	24C
Norris, Nathaniel	125A	Reed, Sonny	102A
Northam, Geo. Richard	132B	Reed, Washington	141B
		Reed, Wm. Thos.	224C
Oliver, Richard A.	137B	Regan, John E.	245A
		Regensburg, S. C.	236A
Pace, Martin	168B	Revere, Chas. H.	290A
Padget, John T.	12B	Revere, Edward B.	277B
Page, Peyton	88A	Revere, John C.	247B
Page, Richard	13A	Revere, Jos. W.	133B
Page, Rich'd H.	298A	Revere, Melville W.	117A
Palmer, Wm. A.	55C	Revere, Thos. J.	146B
Pannell, J. D.	23C	Richardson, Berkley S.	241B
Pannell, Jefferson D.	197B	Richardson, James	126C
Parker, Alfred	59A	Richardson, John Smith	203C
Parker, Daniel F.	19C	Richardson,	
Parker, Laurence F.	172B	John Valentine	242A
Parks, Clarence E.	174B	Richardson, Percy L.	234A
Patterson, Albert	66A	Richardson, William T.	93B
Paul, O. G.	275B	Ridgell, C. W.	284A
Paul, Oliver George	167B	Riley, Lester	91C
Paul, Stephen	174A	Roane, John	187A
Payne, John A.	190B	Roane, Lloyd	185A
Payne, Tyler	263A	Roane, Richard	168C
Payne, Willie	124B	Roane, William	147B
Payne, Willie	282C	Roane, Wm. H.	114C
Peterson, Thomas	218C	Robbins, W. T.	72A
Peyton, George	27B	Robinson, Anthony	156B
Philips, John	214B	Robinson, Charles	132A
Philips, V. W.	272A	Robinson, Chas. H.	240B
Powell, James O.	96A	Robinson, Corbin	232B
Prince, James R.	189A	Robinson, Dr. R. Lee	163C
Prince, John P.	13B	Robinson, Elijah	297B
Prosser, Baylor	5C	Robinson, Frederick	9C
		Robinson, Geo. H.	85B
Ramey, John R.	159B	Robinson, Godfrey	41C
Randolph, W. H.	241A	Robinson, Harry E.	147C
Ransom, James E.	139C	Robinson, Harry	215C
Ranson, Samuel	198B	Robinson, Isaiah	83B
Reddick, Isaac	292A	Robinson, James Eddie	104C

Index of Grooms

Robinson, James	19B		Shreeves, T. L.	221B
Robinson, John Thomas	173B		Shrieves, W. J.	55A
Robinson, John W.	152B		Sibley, Edward H.	209A
Robinson, Moses	206A		Sibley, Holland	227A
Robinson, Nathaniel	251B		Smith, Ardell	261A
Robinson, Rob't Henry	170A		Smith, B. F.	47B
Robinson, Spotswood	21B		Smith, Ben	135B
Robinson, Thomas H.	64C		Smith, Beverly	216A
Robinson, Walter W.	71A		Smith, Beverly	75B
Robinson, Walter	50A		Smith, Chas.	234C
Robinson, William R.	184A		Smith, Edward	35A
Robinson, Willie	296B		Smither, Joseph E.	243B
Rock, E. D.	211B		Smith, G. A.	39A
Roots, Ransom	63A		Smith,	
Rowe, G. W.	297A		General Washington	201B
Rowe, Henry	238B		Smith, J. R.	269B
Rowe, John N.	143C		Smith, James Edgar	286C
Rowe, Walter F.	231B		Smith, John	196B
Roy, Charles	111C		Smith, John	210A
Roy, Chas.	238A		Smith, John H.	253B
Roy, Chas.	181B		Smith, Rob't Martin	162C
Roy, George	32C		Smith, Thomas B.	103A
Roy, Henry	231C		Smith, Willie	96C
Roy, Joseph	208C		Smith, Willie	119C
Rucker, William D.	256B		Smith, Wm.	5B
Ruffin, Armstead	170B		Smoot, Ernest	213C
Ruffin, Chas.	231A		Snead, Geo. W.	269C
Ruffin, Grant	86A		Soles, D. S.	213B
Ruffin, James Henry	5A		South, Franklin C.	54A
Ruperti, Chas. H.	241C		Spencer, Albert Sidney	229B
Russ, Archibald	172A		Spillman, John	111A
Russ, Ed Thomas	260C		Stewart, Charles	120A
Russ, George	189C		Stewart, Robert	199C
Russ, Wm.	61A		Stockes, Eddie	274B
			Stokes, Henry	127A
Sable, Andrew J., Jr.	76B		Stover, Frank	95A
Sale, Julius C.	132C		Street, E. G.	125C
Scott, Cornelius	233A		Street, Ro. Logan	110B
Scott, Harrison	51B		Stuart, Wm.	110A
Scott, Henry	24A		Sydnor, E. S.	105B
Scott, Joshua	27C			
Segar, J. Randolph	37B		Taliaferro, Albert	81A
Setton, Chas. A.	233B		Taliaferro, Albert	206C
Seward, Jno. B.	43A		Taliaferro, Beverly	220A
Shackelford, Howard G.	69A		Taliaferro, Geo. W.	283C
Shackelford,			Taliaferro, Henry	145A
Walter Young	154C		Taliaferro, James	150A
Sherman, Wm. W.	293B		Taliaferro, John H.	57C
Shields, William	96B		Taliaferro, Maxwell	49A

Index of Grooms

Taliaferro, Moses	25B		Turner, Henry	291B
Taliaferro, Rich'd Henry	250C		Vail, H. Harry	203A
Taliaferro, Simon	248C		Vaughan, Edward S.	237B
Taliaferro, Wm.	212C		Vaughan, V. Muse	180C
Tapscott, Henry	25A			
Taylor, Chas. E.	207C		Wake, Isaiah	62B
Taylor, Eugene A.	222C		Wake, Robert	152A
Taylor, Geo. P.	291C		Walden, Edward	108B
Taylor, Gordon F.	287A		Walden, Edward T.	15B
Taylor, James	176C		Walden, Henry	44A
Taylor, John	88B		Walden, Lee	27A
Taylor, Joseph	69C		Walden, R. K.	94A
Taylor, Lorenzo	246A		Walden, Samuel E.	103C
Taylor, Napoleon B.	117B		Walden, Vespasian	143B
Taylor, R. B.	39B		Walker, Chas. H., Jr.	161C
Taylor, Randal	176A		Walker, Granville H.	54C
Terry, Frank	4C		Walker, William E.	258A
Thomas, Geo. W.	57B		Walker, Willie	116B
Thomas, George G.	160A		Wallace, J. Raymond	290C
Thomas, Harold	295B		Waller, Abison	33A
Thomas, Henry Wise	251C		Waller, Thos. H.	105A
Thomas, James H.	26A		Waller, W. L.	210C
Thomas, William A.	199A		Ward, Jackson	51A
Thompson, W. E.	101A		Ward, Jacob	35C
Thornton, Joseph H.	47C		Ward, Randal	37C
Thornton, Samuel	148C		Warren, P. J.	212A
Thrift, Henry E.	249A		Washburn, D. W.	99B
Thurston, Clinton E.	167C		Washington, Cuffy, Jr.	119B
Thurston, Geo. W.	64A		Washington, H. J. H.	163B
Thurston, James H.	56C		Washington, James	1A
Thurston, John	38A		Washington, Ralph	52B
Thurston, Lewis	271C		Washington, Richard C.	280C
Thurston, Morris	257A		Washington, Wm.	86B
Tomlinson, Saywood, M.	292C		Watson, Wm.	38C
Topping, Harvey E.	24B		Webb, Jas. H.	127B
Towill, R. L.	180A		Webb, Rob't W.	251A
Towles, Chas.	129B		Weeks, Willie	247C
Townsley, Isaiah	197A		West, Alex	181A
Trader, J. H.	274C		West, Chas.	255C
Trader, Jno. H.	3A		West, Geo. T.	7A
Travis, Augustus	130B		West, George R.	118A
Tresler, Thomas Tilden	237A		Weston, William	171B
Trevilian, William H.	285B		West, Rob't	156C
Trice, George E.	76A		Whitehurst, Edward H.	10B
Trice, R. M.	47A		White, Thos.	196A
Trimyer, W. L.	168A		Whiting, Geo. Washington	157A
Tucker, Richard	146C			
Turner, Henry	80C		Wiatt, Andrew	259B

86

Index of Grooms

Wiatt, Robert	40A	Woodward, R. Henly	66C
Wiatt, Samuel	179B	Woolridge, Samuel	181C
Wicks, Joshua	278A	Wormley, Ben	263B
William Andrew	93A	Wormley, Daniel	229C
Williams, Albert	128A	Wormley, Earnest	158B
Williams, Armstead	33C	Wormley, James	245B
Williams, Grant	244C	Wormley, Ralph T.	193B
Williams, Israel	157B	Wormley, Thos. N.	136A
Wilshin, Frances H.	187C	Wright,	
Wilson, Austin	246B	Benjamin Stanley	273B
Wilson, Charles	28C	Wright, John E.	277C
Wilson, Joseph	9A	Wright, Thos. W.	128B
Wilson, Ledford E.	163A	Wyatt, A. J.	77B
Wilson, Lewis	266C		
Wilson, N. G.	261B	Yarbrough, Joe	195C
Wingfield, Samuel	191B	Yarrington, James	36B
Wingfield, Scipio	284C	Yates, Geo. L.	267B
Wood, Geo. C.	252B	Yates, George	15C
Wood, John W.	4A	Yates, John C.	59B
Wood, John T.	53C	Yates, Kenny	133C
Wood, Leslie T.	285A		

Index of Brides

Adams, L. B.	75C	Blackburn, J. L.	4A
Ailsworth, Emma	168B	Blackburn,	
Ailsworth, Ida May	133C	Virginia Adelaide	181A
Ailsworth, Nina E.	158C	Blake, Annie C.	24B
Ailsworth, Sallie G.	222B	Blake, Emma Alice	252B
Allen, Rachel	87B	Blake, Florence V.	268A
Allin, Rachel E.	159C	Blake, Lallah B.	72C
Anderson, Harriet	49B	Blake, Lucy Francis	210A
Anderson, Mary W.	152C	Blake, Lucy	151B
Anderson, Rachel	102C	Blake, Lucy	153A
Apsley, Margaret F.	250B	Blake, Magie E.	12B
Archibald, Mamie C.	139A	Blake, Maude V.	227B
Archibald, Mattie	139B	Blake, Nannie Lee	290A
Armstrong, A. W.	78C	Blake, Theodocia E.	106B
Armstrong, Blanche	208A	Blake, Vessie B.	237B
Armstrong, Floyd	100B	Bland, Lelia W.	140A
		Bland, Mary A.	159B
Bagby, Betty	5B	Bond, Rosa	164B
Bagby, Lulie	158B	Bonniville, Maggie L.	162C
Bagby, Malisie	119C	Booker, Emma	261A
Ball, Mary S.	107C	Booker, Mary E.	14A
Banks, Addie Leigh	173B	Boughton, Nettie	265C
Banks, Alice	246A	Boyd, Alice	110B
Banks, Belle	49A	Boyd, Bettie	123B
Banks, Catharine	220C	Boyd, Grace	83B
Banks, Cora	257A	Boyd, Hester	56C
Banks, Eliza	32C	Boyd, Mamie	136B
Banks, Ella	298C	Boyd, Mary	87C
Banks, Etta	191B	Boyd, Mattie	105A
Banks, Leah	42A	Bratton, Etta	67B
Banks, Lena	257B	Braxton, Frances	25B
Banks, Mary	94C	Braxton, Mollie	177B
Barrick,		Braxton, Nannie	220B
Lillian Virginia	224A	Braxton, Peachy E.	2B
Bartlett, Elanora	106A	Braxton, Roxie	287C
Baytop, Eliza	202B	Braxton, Susan	246B
Baytop, Julia	38A	Brim, Luly B.	48B
Beany, Mary Ann	293B	Bristow, Annie P.	98B
Beazley, Colista	28A	Bristow, Bertha	182C
Beazly, Virgie M.	103C	Bristow, Evelina	201C
Beckett, Maggie	192A	Bristow, Fannie L.	116A
Belvin, Catherine	80A	Bristow, Florence	35A
Belvin, Eliza Jane	178A	Bristow, Francis C.	99B
Belvin, Fannie	196B	Bristow, Henrietta	75A
Berry, Maggie	247C	Bristow, Ida G.	47B
Billups, Rosetta A.	153B	Bristow, Lillian	216C
Bilups, Mary	224C	Bristow, Lillian	290C
Birch, Lulie B.	11B	Bristow, Lucy W.	76A
Bird, Louisa	264A	Brooks, Mary	194A

Index of Brides

Brown, Bell	217C		Carter, Ella	30B
Brown, Eula E.	167C		Carter, Estelle B.	262C
Brown, Maria	33A		Carter, Fannie B.	271A
Brown, Nettie A.	14C		Carter, Georgiann	49C
Brown, Nollie	198C		Carter, Ida E.	175C
Brown, Pacie	33B		Carter, Mary Ellen	124A
Brushwood, Ada	37B		Carter, Mary	83C
Bulle, Effie M.	228C		Carter, Mary Susan	97A
Bumpass, Alice	148B		Carter, Paulina A.	23C
Bundy, Betty	127A		Carter, Pinkie	130A
Bundy, Blanche	274B		Carter, Rebecca	77B
Bundy, Lelia	66A		Cauthorn, Ida	18C
Bundy, Mattie	218B		Cauthorn, Maggie	180B
Burch, Eulah H.	186B		Chaamberlain, Cordelia	99A
Burke, Eliza	166A		Chamberlain, Emmeline	194C
Burke, Martha	158A		Chatman, Virginia	204C
Burke, Mollie Bet.	80C		Chowning, Louisa M.	193A
Burke, Mona L.	259B		Chowning, Mary W.	239C
Burlin, Elizabeth	159A		Chowning, Minnie G.	69A
Burnett, Bettie	86A		Chrissager, Sallie	135A
Burnett, Julia	22C		Christian, Nellie G.	117C
Burnett, Sarah	135C		Clare, Lottie P.	300C
Burrell, Mary E.	68C		Clayton, Pearl	244C
Burrell, Addie	267B		Clayville, Julia	184C
Burrell, Angelina	64A		Clements, Laura Y.	78B
Burrell, Celia	121B		Collie, Bessie	234B
Burrell, Jannie	122A		Collier, Lucy J.	84B
Burrell, Retha	258B		Collins, Mariah Louisa	155A
Burrell, Sarah	147A		Colly, Sallie S.	95B
Burton, Sue H.	225C		Condiff, Nealie F.	233B
Bush, Maria	112B		Conway, Anna	81C
Byrd, Cora	137A		Cook, Eunice	44C
			Cook, M. S.	74B
Campbell, Lizzie	123A		Cook, Mary	141B
Carey, Annie	274A		Cook, Mary E.	183A
Carey, Emma	153C		Cooley, Pinkey	84C
Carlton, Bettie	47A		Coombs, Gertrude Viola	280B
Carlton, Blanche	113C		Coor, Sarah	281C
Carlton, Clare M.	133A		Corbin, Lucinda	269B
Carlton, Lucille Florence	114A		Cornelius, Indianna	64B
Carlton, Maggie V.	125C		Corr, see Carr & Coor	
Carlton, Ruby P.	110C		Corr, Est.	161A
Carr, see Corr & Coor			Corr, Roberta	292B-2
Carr, Betty Ann	196A		Courtney, Annie	79B
Carr, Eudora	179B		Courtney, Mamie	243C
Carr, Tama	271C		Creswell, Lucy E.	51C
Carter, Bettie	79A		Creswill, Magie E.	2A
Carter, Delia	134A		Crittenden, Amy C.	236B
			Crittenden, Bessie	131C

89

Index of Brides

Crittenden, Columbus	173A	Dyke, Nannie H.	299B
Crittenden, Leona Pearl	84A	Easton, Fannie	46C
Crittenden, M. J.	233C	Easton, Mattie	205B
Cundiff, Mildred A.	149C	Eaton, Nellie Vandergrift	174B
Curtis, Bettie	102B	Ellis, Elisia	29A
Curtis, Bettie A.	45A	Enos, Addie	73C
Curtis, Eliza	67A	Epler, Bessie	242A
Curtis, Jennie	14B	Eubank, Nanie M.	25A
Curtis, Tamie	234C	Evans, Lillie M.	140B
Dangerfield, Harriet	175A	Evans, Mary Emma	55B
Dangerfield, Mary Julia Smith	143C	Evans, Sadie C.	167A
Daniel, Florence L.	15B	Evans, Sue. B.	132C
Daniel, Inez G.	101B	Faulkner, Mary E.	95C
Daniel, Lucy E.	108C	Fauntleroy, Mary Alice	272A
Daniel, Mollie A.	60A		
Davis, A. Blanche	287A	Fears, Musette Grafton	174A
Davis, Annie	253A	Field, Bettie	40A
Davis, Emma	218C	Fields, Eliza	144A
Davis, Eva	154A	Fields, Frances	147B
Davis, Gertie	272C	Fields, Lottie	238C
Davis, Jeanette	39A	Fields, Mary E. W.	251B
Davis, Lottie L.	91A	Fisher, Fanny	15C
Davis, Louisa	236A	Fitchett, Mary B.	284C
Davis, Maggie	193C	Fleet, Bessie	186A
Davis, Mary	76C	Fleet, Helen G.	202A
Davis, Mary	61B	Fleet, Lillie Virginia	226A
Davis, Nannie	174C	Fletcher, Salome	280A
Davis, Nellie C.	252A	Folliard, Gay Montague	187C
Davis, Rilla	183B	Fossett, Belle	119B
Davis, Rosa	124B	Foster, Eddie	187A
Davis, Sarah	115B	Foster, Maggie	116C
Davis, Susan	279A	Foster, Martha	113B
Davis, Virginia	256C	Foster, Mary E.	57B
Deagle, Charlotte	199A	Foster, Sarah L.	61C
Deagle, Eva D.	275A	Fountain, Lucinda	206A
Deagle, Mary Katherine	251C	Franke, Hettie D.	94A
Dennis, Lucy	4C	Frank, Emma M.	6C
Dickison, Elvey	163B	Frazier, Maggie	293C
Dobbson, Kate	297A	French, Sarah E.	172B
Dudley, Celestine	232C		
Dunaway, Rina	28B	Gaines, Lula A.	203A
Dunlavey, Amelia	40B	Gaines, Santie C.	91C
Dunlevy, Eva Alice	189A	Gardner, Lillian	226B
Dunlevy, Lolla May	191C		
Dutton, Jennie	142B		

Index of Brides

Garland, Alice	29C		Gundy, Mary	116B
Garland, Daisy Vivian	145B		Gundy, Mattie	110A
Garnett, Bettie	266C		Gunn, Nannie B.	131B
Garnett, Blanche C.	77A		Gwathmey, Cordelia	226C
Garnett, Ida	138B		Gwynn, Sarah	266A
Garrett, Mary Louise	294A			
Gatewood, Maggie	265A		Hall, Florence	258A
Gayle, L. M.	36B		Hall, L. C.	117A
Gayle, Mary J.	85C		Hall, Lee F.	162A
George, Annie E.	225A		Hall, Mary Sue	65B
Glenn, Edna M.	181C		Hall, Sarah H.	235A
Goldman, Gertrude	171A		Hancock, Sallie D.	113A
Goldman, Lena	248C		Hardy, Florence M.	68A
Goldman, Maggie	193B		Hardy, Nannie Ware	131A
Goldman, Sally	26B		Harris, Ada	93C
Goode, Mary F.	52A		Harris, Annie	296B
Gouldman, Sarah	27C		Harris, Caroline	206B
Graffin, Kate	212C		Harris, Columbia V.	90B
Graham, Mannie	221B		Harris, Deliah	82A
Green, Ada	24C		Harris, Fannie	270B
Green, Annie	100C		Harris, Florence	23A
Green, Coky	83A		Harris, L. A. V.	129B
Greene, Effie L.	176B		Harris, L. B.	288B
Green, Ellen	209B		Harris, Maggie	150A
Greene, Sarah	178B		Harris, Patsy	18B
Green, Louisa	172A		Harris, Roberta H.	280C
Green, Mattie	78A		Harris, Sarah E.	106C
Green, Mitchie	281A		Harrow, Blanche	277C
Green, Victoria L.	141A		Harrow, Ida L.	222C
Greenwood, Eliza	263B		Harrow, M. E.	59B
Greenwood, Lyda	3A		Hart, Daisey, D.	104A
Greenwood, Sallie B.	142C		Hart, Edna E.	285B
Greenwood, Susie	214C		Hart, Eva	155B
Gregory, Ada	148C		Hart, Mary J.	93B
Gresham, Blanche F.	170C		Hazelwood, Blanche	225B
Griffin, Catharine	236C		Healy, B. B.	62C
Griffin, Gena	244A		Healy, Exie	167B
Griffin, Lucy	33C		Henry, Clara	7A
Griffin, Macie	86B		Henry, Lulie	1A
Griffin, Mary	115C		Hewlett, Mary E.	37C
Griffin, Mattie	157B		Hibble, Ida A.	141C
Griffin, Mattie A.	30A		Hibble, Mary Lillie	139C
Griffith, Bettie L.	59A		Hibble, Peachie	231B
Groome, Emma	274C		Hill, Annie	71B
Groome, Lina Julia	108A		Hill, Florence	276A
Groome, Lucy Fleet	292B		Hilliard, Fannie E.	241B
Groome, Virginia	245C		Hill, Leah	57A
Guinn, Mary V.	163A		Hill, Lizzie P.	58C
Gundy, Ida	120A		Hill, Lucy	41A

Index of Brides

Hinman, Mary L.	294B	Jackson, Victoria	223B
Hodges, Inez	19C	Jarvis, Josie	85A
Hodges, Polly	72B	Jefferson, Virgie	183C
Hodges, S. Alice	27A	Jeffries, Lucy M.	21C
Holiday, Ella	195C	Jewell, Sallie	182B
Holliday, Dolly	130B	Johnson, Ada	109B
Holliday, India	259C	Johnson, Adda	297B
Holmes, Catharine	209C	Johnson, Alice	255A
Holmes, Emily	99C	Johnson, Becky	45B
Holmes, Harriett	220A	Johnson, Bertie M.	247B
Holmes, Jane	192C	Johnson, Betty	172C
Holmes, Lelia	200C	Johnson, Elizabeth	69C
Holmes, Maggie	103B	Johnson, Ella	150B
Holmes, Margaret	137B	Johnson, Emma J.	166C
Holmes, Mary E.	148A	Johnson, Georgia E.	22A
Holmes, Mary Eliza	202C	Johnson, Georgie	74C
Holmes, Saphronia	7B	Johnson, Jane	149B
Holmes, Victoria	177A	Johnson, Lelia	201B
Holmes, Vina	260C	Johnson, Lena	248A
Homer, Grace	295B	Johnson, Lillian E.	100A
Hoskins, Susan	11A	Johnson,	
Hudgins, Anna Bell	254A	Lillian Virginia	263C
Hudgins, Mary E.	20A	Johnson, Louisiana	56B
Humphries, Maggie J.	39B	Johnson, Lucy	86C
Hundley, Ada B.	168A	Johnson, Maggie	244C
Hundley, Mason	6A	Johnson, Maggie	80B
Hurd, Leatha Gyneth	237A	Johnson, Maria	109C
Hurley, Alice Elden	190B	Johnson, Mary E.	92C
		Johnson, Mary	146A
Iverson, Georgia A.	207A	Johnson,	
Iverson, Maria A.	92A	Mary Catharine	165A
		Johnson, Mattie	138C
Jackson, Alice	261B	Johnson, Nannie E.	102A
Jackson, Anna R.	204A	Johnson,	
Jackson, Anna	124C	Nellie Virginia	177C
Jackson, Catharine	238A	Johnson, Sarah	161B
Jackson, Emma	118B	Johnson, Sunie	104B
Jackson, Emma J.	126C	Johnson, Susan	128A
Jackson, Frances	208B	Jones, Cora	170A
Jackson, Jane	77C	Jones, Elizabeth	254C
Jackson, Jennie	176A	Jones, Elmira	268C
Jackson, Jennie L.	58B	Jones, Emma J.	268B
Jackson, Lizzie	181B	Jones, Florence	206C
Jackson, Loty	156A	Jones, Hannah J.	89C
Jackson, Mamie	197A	Jones, Hannah	300C
Jackson, Mamie	296C	Jones, Lena	151C
Jackson, Mary	98C	Jones, Lizzie	165C
Jackson, Mary E.	230A	Jones, Lottie F.	255C
Jackson, Oshia C.	171B	Jones, Maria	90A

Index of Brides

Jones, Mary	53A		Lewis, Kate	282C
Jordan,			Lewis, Lizzie	185C
Martha Anne Rebecca	291A		Lewis, Lucy	188C
			Lewis, Luly	36A
Keilingham, Maud L.	133B		Lewis, Maggie M.	269C
Keiningham, H. E.	286C		Lewis, Maggie	263A
Keiningham, Maud G.	190C		Lewis, Martha	294C
Kellam, Ida E. A.	42C		Lewis, Mary E.	65A
Kellum, Alfenetta	70C		Lewis, Mary	188B
Kellum, Effie L.	241C		Lewis, Mattie	200A
Kellum, Jane	143B		Lewis, Susan	12A
Kellum, Nettie May	295A		Lincoln, Mary M.	32A
Kemble, Virgia A.	266B		Lindsey, Mary S.	219A
Kemp, Fannie W.	107A		Lockley, Cornelia G.	59C
Kemp, Millie Ann	114C		Lockley, Janie	81B
Kennard, Bessie E.	238B		Lockley, Katie	215C
Kerr, Lucy C.	21A		Lockly, Emma J.	241A
Kerr, W. T.	198A		Lomax, Amanda	103A
Key, Emmeline	259A		Lomax, Mattie	36C
Key, Hattie	295C		Lomax, Millie	144C
Key, Kizzie	122B		Lorina Grenils	180A
Key, Lizzie	262B		Lovings, Lucy	52B
Keyser, Emma	267C		Lumpkin, Lucy	213B
Kidd, Bettie	9A		Lumpkin, Mamie C.	54C
Kidd, Elnora	227C		Lymus, Georgiana	145A
Kidd, Nannie	32B		Lymus, Letta Ann	87A
Kidd, Otalia	297C		Lymus, Lucy Ann	92B
Kidd, Pinkie	118A		Lyon, Ida E.	45C
Kimble, Sallie	31C			
King, Alice	67C		Major, Alice T.	163C
King, Maggie	112A		Major, Carrie A.	209A
			Major, Lee H.	112C
Latane, Lelie	272B		Major, Mattie Lee	278B
Latne, Mary Ellen	216A		Marchant, Bertha B.	228B
Laws, Ida	224B		Marchant, Nellie M.	250A
Lawson, Ida Waverly	189B		Mason, Ira Anna	249C
Lawson, Mary S.	120C		Mason, Lizzie	143A
Lawson, Mary B.	210B		Mason, Mollie	285C
Lawson, Susan P.	10B		Mathews, Judith	111C
Laws, Virginia	136A		Mayo, Ellsie	222A
Lecompt,			Mayo, Maggie B.	184B
Mildred Janie	239A		McKan, Mary	39C
Lee, Alice	52C		McKann, A. Maude	203C
Lee, Bessie	186A		McKenny, Dora	111A
Lee, Elizabeth	60C		Mercer, Sallie	178C
Lee, Lavelia	50C		Miles, Lucy	157A
Lee, Rose	271B		Miller, Carrie May	201A
Lewis, Ellen Jane	169C		Miller, Eliza	40C
Lewis, Jennie	189C		Miller, Ettie	50B

Index of Brides

Miller, Feenie	237C	Owens, Susie V.	68B
Miller, Linda Ann	150C		
Miller, Lottie C.	203B	Pace, Maud Olive	119A
Miller, Mandy J.	89B	Padgett, Florence	73B
Minor, Addie M.	230C	Page, Annie	88A
Minor, Alice	23B	Page, Ella	230B
Minor, Harriet	292A	Page, Elsie	132A
Minor, Ida	245B	Page, Maria	217A
Minor, Lucy	199C	Page, Mary Eliza	258C
Minor, Lucy Jane	185B	Pannell, Emmie	74A
Minor, Lucy R.	264C	Parker, Evelyne	96A
Minor, Mattie Kate	223C	Parrish, Beulah	256B
Moffett, Almedia S.	120B	Patyschke, Nannie	58A
Moffitt, Lillian B.	10A	Payne, Clyde Georgie	276C
Monroe, Louisa	134C	Payne, Daisy V.	217B
Montgomery, Cora	142A	Payton, Mary Susan	9B
Montgomery, Mamie	299A	Pearson, Jennie	89A
Moody, Emma Sue	26C	Pendleton, Emma	47C
Moody, Lucy J.	126B	Perkins, Maude	253C
Moody, Susie A.	114B	Perrin, Ida Bell	278C
Moore, Mary E.	63C	Perry, Ruby	270C
Moore, Nannie	176C	Peyton, Ella T.	137C
Morris, Anna	6B	Peyton, Laura	269A
Morris, Annie	235C	Pierson, Phebe	97C
Morris, Dora	71C	Pollard, Alice	96B
Morris, Jennie A.	147C	Powell, Louise	229B
Morris, Lettie Lee	37A	Powell, Mary E.	221A
Morris, Lucy E.	75B	Price, Gertrude	169B
Morris, Maria	211A	Prince, Cammie Netine	214A
Morris, Mary	46A	Prince, Mattie E.	200B
Morris, Willie Ann	156C	Purkins, Elizabeth	233A
Muse, Alice	101A	Purkins, Fannie C.	66C
Nelson, Clara	154B	Randel, Margaret	261C
Nelson, Emma	81A	Ransom, Lucy J.	191A
Nelson, Eva	213C	Redd, Elizabeth	243A
Nelson, Francis	28C	Redd, Lizzie	249A
Nelson, Kizzie	298A	Redd, Maude	273C
New, Cath.	8A	Redd, Rassie	182A
Newton, Plummie	54A	Redd, Rosa	122C
Nicholson, Mary	63B	Redd, Virginia B.	54B
Nickelson, Henrietta	19B	Redd, Virginia	70A
Norman, Ann Eliza	285A	Reed, Bettie	195B
Norris, Pelle	129A	Reed, Dora	125B
Northam, Emma R.	234A	Reed, Emma Jane	232A
Nuttall, Mary E.	218A	Reed, Julia	214B
		Reed, Lizzie	208C
Overlock, Kate	19A	Reed, Lizzie	34B
Owen, Louise	4B	Reed, Lizzie	194B

Index of Brides

Reed, Maggie	166B		Ruffin, Elizabeth	211C
Reed, Ora	162B		Ruffin, Ellen	198B
Reed, Peachy	18A		Ruffin, Maude Esther	210C
Reed, Rosa	122C		Ruffin, Sadie	248B
Reed, Welthy	195A		Ruffin, Susan B.	255B
Revere, Amanda P.	13B			
Revere, Fannie	72A		Sable, Sallie	223A
Revere, Georgia K.	20B		Sadler, Abbie A.	70B
Revere, Grace C.	20C		Sadler, Annie M.	140C
Revere,			Sadler, Lucy D.	82C
Lulu Catherine	277B		Sadler, Mary E.	3C
Revvell, Susie	152A		Sales, Hannah	135B
Rhodes, Hattie L.	279C		Saunders, Lucie Kate	22B
Richardson, Alice	146C		Saunders, Maria L.	229A
Richardson,			Scarber, Mariah	190A
E. Waller	211B		Scott, Alice	66B
Richardson,			Scott, June	41C
Elizabeth	136C		Scott, Lee	215B
Richardson, Sallie	132B		Scott, Lenora	207B
Riley, Evelyn	79C		Scott, Lizzie	282B
Roane, Ellen Jane	187B		Scott, Mollie	121C
Robinson, Alice	253B		Searborough,	
Robinson, Annie L.	289A		Josephine	91B
Robinson, Elizabeth	125A		Seawell, Mary E.	31A
Robinson, Elizabeth	286A		Seawell, Virginia V.	121A
Robinson,			Segar, Annie M.	3B
Emily Keziah	221C		Segar, Lillian S.	118C
Robinson, Evalina	164A		Segar, Nannie F.	290B
Robinson, Francis	61A		Shackelford,	
Robinson, Lena	192B		Mamie H.	11C
Robinson, Lizzie	138A		Shelton, Annie V.	293A
Robinson, Lucinda	34A		Shrieves, Carrie E.	1C
Robinson, Lucinda	240B		Shrives, Sarah T.	76B
Robinson, Mollie	184A		Sibley, B. L.	275C
Robinson, Nancy	24A		Sibley, Lidie Sue	212A
Robinson, Sarah	93A		Sibley, Margaret J.	55C
Robinson, Sarah E.	10C		Sibley, Mary V.	275B
Robinson, Shellie	215A		Sibley, Minnie J.	85B
Robinson,			Sibley, Roberta	262A
Virginia Alice	7C		Sims, Alice	267A
Roots, Margaret	251A		Sirus, Alice	267A
Roots, Octavia	240C		Slaughter, Maggie	179C
Ross, Blanche	96C		Smith, Anne E.	247A
Ross, Hatty	219C		Smith, Bettie Alice	144B
Roy, Belle	134B		Smith, Emma	152B
Roy, Catharine	13A		Smither, Bernice E.	240A
Roy, Mary	188A		Smith, Hattie	128C
Ruark,			Smith, Kitty	51A
Mary Virginia	264B		Smith, Mary	65C

Index of Brides

Smith, Mary Florence	278A		Thurston, Lucinda	60B
Smith, Mary	265B		Thurston, Martha Jane	179A
Smith, Sunie	95A		Thurston, Winnie F.	161C
Snead, Carie V.	128B		Tingle, Estella E.	245A
Snead, Dora E.	12C		Towill, Sadie L.	276B
Snead, Mary T.	34C		Townsend,	
South, Mary E.	126A		Bertha Estelle	243B
South, Mildred	160A		Townsend, Lucy	168C
Sparrow, Annie	38B		Townsley, Ella	205A
Street, Blanch	252C		Trader, Addie	199B
Summons, Mary A.	41B		Trader, Bessie O.	281B
Sutherland, Francis	48A		Trader, Hattie May	53C
Sutherlin, Nellie	287B		Trader, Louie P.	115A
Swinney, Mary M.	242B		Trader, Maggie	38C
			Trader, Pauline	160C
Tabb, Harriet	5C		Trice, Lucy Carter	196C
Taber, Sarah A.	97B		Trivous, Harriet	169A
Tabor, Alice	108B		Trymer, Luly D.	55A
Tabor, Ida	44A		Tucker,	
Tabor, Sadie	257C		Martha Ellen	273A
Taliaferro, Alberta	279B		Tucker, Nancy	88B
Taliaferro, Annie	46B			
Taliaferro,			Vandergrift, Sadie	299C
Catherine B.	82B			
Taliaferro, Ella	130C		Wake, Christian	15A
Taliaferro, Julia	277A		Wake, Hannah	246C
Tapor, Susan	284A		Wake, Harriet	232B
Taylor, Annie	170B		Wake, Malissa	235B
Taylor, Carrie E.	197B		Walden,	
Taylor, Hester	117B		Anna Elizabeth	260A
Taylor, Martha	51B		Walker, Bettie M.	56A
Taylor, Mary Alice	90C		Walker, Emma L.	94B
Taylor, Prue	260B		Walker, L. M.	249B
Taylor, Sallie D.	180C		Walker, Mary H.	186C
Taylor, Sarah	231A		Walker, Maud C.	146B
Temple, Rosa	129C		Waller, Lucy	228A
Terry, Martha	155C		Waller, Rosa	104C
Thomas, Hester	25C		Walters, Emily A.	283B
Thomas, Mattie	2C		Walton, Eudora	212B
Thornton, Mamie	98A		Walton, Mattie B.	239B
Thornton, Mary	42B		Ward, Emma Lee	173C
Thornton, Mary F.	286B		Ward,	
Thrift, Julia D.	43A		Gabrielle Roane	273B
Thrift, Mamie F.	227A		Ward, Lena R.	30C
Thrift, Minnie E.	53B		Ward, Maggie R.	107B
Thurston, Alice	171C		Ward, Mattie	21B
Thurston, Emma	101C		Ward, Sue	284B
Thurston, Ida	250C		Ware, Gay	88C
Thurston, Lavina	288A		Warren, Nora E.	292C

Index of Brides

Warrington, Carrie E.	197C	Wilson, Bertha	109A
Washington, Elizabeth	291B	Wilson, Edgie	219B
Washington, Janey	9C	Wilson, Emma	5A
Washington, Jennie	62B	Wilson, Georgia B.	44B
Washington, Luly	48C	Wilson, Lulu M.	205C
Washington, Ruth	296A	Wilson, Margaret E.	160B
Watts, Bessie M.	256A	Wilson, Mary Gertrude	289C
Watts, Helen Eugenia	154C	Wilson, Minnie D.	73A
Webb, Elizabeth J.	127C	Wilson, Rebecca	64C
Webb, Elizabeth	8C	Wilson, Sallie	298B
Webb, Lucy	63A	Wingfield, Peachy	50A
West, Saphronia	300A	Wood, Lena Bedford	164C
White, Ada	283C	Wood, Maggie	71A
White, Ida	35B	Wood, Mary E.	207C
White, Miranda	242C	Wood, Ollie L.	35C
Whiting, Lizzie	156B	Woods, Addie	151A
Whitmore, Carrie F.	105B	Wood, Sadie E.	43C
Whitteker, Pauline	288C	Wood, Sophronia	31B
Williams, Amanda	29B	Woodward, Alice F.	204B
Williams, Bettie	111B	Wormley, Emily Jane	1B
Williams, Cora Ann	291C	Wormley, Georgeanna	27B
Williams, Emma Blanch	289B	Wormley, Isabella	43B
Williams, Louisa F.	26A	Wormley, Lizzie	185A
Williams, Lucelle	254B	Wormley, Lulu	213A
Williams, Mary	175B	Wormley, Mary A.	62A
Williams, Mary E.	127B	Wormley, Rebecca	229C
Williams, Mary	13C	Yates, Addie E.	8B
Williams, Mary	283A	Yates, Fannie B.	216B
Williams, Millie	69B	Young, Lizzie E.	57C
Willis, Josephine	157C	Young, Lucinda	165B
Wilson, Amelia	149A	Young, Mary	231C
		Young, Sallie	105C

Middlesex County, Virginia
Marriage Records
1853-1904

ERRATA

Book 1   Page 6   2:05
Mother of the bride is Jane Burns; not Jane Benns

Book 1   Page 17   6:03
Groom is Robert South; not Robert Smith

Book 1   Page 30   13:19
Bride is A. E. Ball; not A. E. Bull

Book 1   Page 56   26:42
Groom is George S. Blake; not Leo S. Blake

Book 2   Page 64   270A
Groom is R. Y. [Yancy] Blake; not R. G. Blake

Book 3   Page 71   275C
B. L. Sibley should be daughter of...; not son of...

www.ingramcontent.com/pod-product-compliance
Lightning Source LLC
Chambersburg PA
CBHW062002220426
43662CB00010B/1206